SEVEN AGAINST CHRIST

A STUDY OF 'ESSAYS AND REVIEWS'

STUDIES IN THE HISTORY
OF
CHRISTIAN THOUGHT

EDITED BY

HEIKO A. OBERMAN, Tübingen

IN COOPERATION WITH

HENRY CHADWICK, Cambridge
EDWARD A. DOWEY, Princeton, N.J.
JAROSLAV PELIKAN, New Haven, Conn.
BRIAN TIERNEY, Ithaca, N.Y.
E. DAVID WILLIS, Princeton, N.J.

VOLUME XXIII

IEUAN ELLIS

SEVEN AGAINST CHRIST

A STUDY OF 'ESSAYS AND REVIEWS'

LEIDEN
E. J. BRILL
1980

SEVEN AGAINST CHRIST

A STUDY OF 'ESSAYS AND REVIEWS'

BY

IEUAN ELLIS

LEIDEN
E. J. BRILL
1980

ISBN 90 04 06200 9

To my mother

אֵם בְּיִשְׂרָאֵל

CONTENTS

CONTENTS

INTRODUCTION

" '*The Septem Contra Christum*' ... the title which unhappily its
blasphemous levity and its wicked uncharitableness has not excluded from journals professing to write in the name of religion".
A. P. Stanley, *Edinburgh Review*, April 1861, p. 465

The story of *Essays and Reviews* is the story of the greatest religious
crisis of the Victorian age. The Archbishop of Canterbury said in 1864
that no graver matter since the Reformation or in the next 200 or 300
years could be imagined. The Privy Council judgment on the book
established the right of Anglican clergymen to preach biblical criticism
and also to deny the eternity of hell-fire for which, as recently as 1853,
F. D. Maurice had lost his chair at King's College. Along with the
Gorham case in 1850 the judgment suggested how Christian denominations must adjust themselves to the new scientific and historical
outlook of the nineteenth century. But *Essays and Reviews* is also the
story of the failure of a radical attempt within the Church to accept these
changes without pressure from the state. From the point of view of the
authors the Church of England became not more liberal but less, and a
decisive shift in favour of the High Church party occurred. This had
various repercussions: it delayed the general acceptance of biblical
criticism for thirty years, it ensured the collapse of the Broad Church
movement which had challenged the older parties for leadership in the
1850's, and it destroyed the theological promise of Benjamin Jowett who,
otherwise, might have become one of the most important religious
thinkers of his time. A renaissance led by Jowett would have had
far-reaching effects on English theology, even into the twentieth century.

It was possible to claim that the events had a greater significance.
Mark Pattison argued that the controversy over *Essays and Reviews*
was the touchstone for a larger conflict, between a new liberal vision of
society, scholarly in approach and European in sympathy, and an
opposing conservative movement which drew on the most reactionary
and anti-intellectual elements in the nation. So the issue was only
disguised as a theological squabble, and the essayists themselves were
genuine examples, with their European culture and social and political
ideals, of the new liberalism, while it was not accidental that High
Churchmen led the opposition to them.

This claim would certainly explain the sheer hysteria generated by the book. The most puzzling aspect of *Essays and Reviews* is that such a badly-written work was not left alone or relegated to mere academic discussion. But the writers were denounced as heretics and regarded, not as the distinct individuals that they were, but as an organised movement pledged to subvert Christianity. The pathology of Victorian religion, so astonishingly revealed in the controversy, thus had deep and ominous causes. Pattison deplored the fact that *Essays and Reviews* was never seen for itself, particularly when in 1860 there was a better prospect than at any time since 1688 of the "final reconciliation between Christianity and science, between the Church and the philosophers"*.

Whatever the reason, the essayists' opponents felt that only one course was possible : the Church must assert its distinctive authority and divine origin. The battle over the religious liberalism of *Essays and Reviews* sharpened its understanding of both. It opposed the state by synodically condemning the book after the Privy Council judgment and by trying to discipline several of the authors. The essayists themselves were also justified in their attitude. Pattison's argument may have gone beyond the facts, but a great opportunity for theological advance undoubtedly existed in 1860 which, on the face of it, seems to have been deliberately, if not perversely, thrown away. Readers will come to their own conclusions; but it seemed best in the following account of the controversy to adopt as wide a treatment as possible, to place the book in its setting which, historically, stretched from at least 1845 to 1889, but also detailed enough to warrant the aspects suggested in this introduction.

The limitations and faults in this treatment are mine, but I would like to thank those who helped me in the work of research in many ways, Professor Walter Houghton, Peter Carlsson, Malcolm Chapman, Jean Howson, Alistair Kee and Edmund Little, and the Librarians of Balliol and Keble Colleges and Pusey House, Oxford, Trinity College, Cambridge, and Lambeth Palace. I am grateful to the Master and Fellows of Balliol College for permission to quote from Jowett's correspondence, and to the other institutions and authorities who have made available manuscript material in their possession. I honour the memory of Ethel Hatch who answered my questions patiently and generously allowed me to see her father's papers.

The University of Hull   IEUAN ELLIS

---

* *National Review*, January, 1863, p. 197.

ABBREVIATIONS

Abbott:	Abbott, E and Campbell, L. *Life and Letters of Benjamin Jowett.*
Church:	Church, M. C. *Life and Letters of Dean Church.*
Davidson:	Davidson, R.T. and Benham, W. *Life of Archibald Campbell Tait, Archbishop of Canterbury.*
Epistles:	Jowett, B. *The Epistles of St. Paul to the Thessalonians, Galatians, and Romans.*
ER:	*Essays and Reviews.*
G:	*The Guardian*
Hort:	Hort, A. F. *Life and Letters of Fenton John Anthony Hort.*
Liddon:	Liddon, H. P. *Life of Edward Bouverie Pusey.*
Maurice:	Maurice, J. F. *The Life of Frederick Denison Maurice.*
Prothero:	Prothero, R. E. *The Life and Correspondence of Arthur Penrhyn Stanley.*
Temple Appreciation:	Sandford, E. G., ed. *Frederick Temple. An Appreciation.*
Temple Memoirs:	Sandford, E. G., ed. *Memoirs of Archbishop Temple, by seven friends.*
WR:	*Westminster Review.*
Williams:	*The Life and Letters of Rowland Williams, edited by his wife.*

CHAPTER ONE

A TIME OF PREPARATION 1845-1859

Samuel Davidson, the Congregationalist scholar, had assembled a collection of German portraits in his home by the 1850's. These included Luther, Ewald, Gesenius, Neander, Schleiermacher, Tholuck and (as a pioneer like the Germans) Bishop Colenso. Hengstenberg, scourge of all radicals, also glowered down from the walls as well as de Wette.[1]

No eighteenth-century Englishman would have paid tribute to German divinity in this manner, but Davidson was typical of a certain kind of new liberal thinker. Carlyle had similar portraits in Cheyne Row. Benjamin Jowett hung a likeness of Niebuhr in his study, and Julius Charles Hare decorated his library with busts of Niebuhr, Schleiermacher and Bunsen; and these three were only part of the "regeneration coming from Germany" that Connop Thirlwall spoke about.[2]

By the 'fifties an exchange of views was taking place : the movement of new religious ideas was like a second Reformation, beginning in Germany, but (as Mark Pattison said), like the Reformation it leapt over national boundaries. Indeed, a book which prophesied the final stage of the movement — a new form of Christianity corresponding to the new form of Europe after 1789 — Baron Bunsen's *Constitution of the Church of the Future*, believed than an Englishman, Thomas Arnold, was the true inspirer of the age to come. He was to be ranked with Kant, Fichte, Schelling and Schleiermacher among those who had recovered for humanity the truths of the eternal religion which it had lost. After eighteenth-century darkness, Arnold had appeared as the preacher of the universal priesthood of Christians, by which the Baron meant the freedom of the laity to aspire to all knowledge and not merely the narrow doctrinal theology of the "clergy Church". Arnold was the "revered apostle of the Church of the future"[3].

How ready was the average English churchman to participate in this new theological endeavour? If the Scottish situation described by John

---

[1] *The Autobiography and Diary of Samuel Davidson*, p. 299.

[2] J.C. Hare, *The Victory of Faith*, p. xlv. Abbott, I, p. 216. *Letters Literary and Theological of Connop Thirlwall*, p. 66.

[3] C.C.J. Bunsen, *The Constitution of the Church of the Future*, pp. 221-2.

Tulloch in an inaugural lecture in 1854 was any indication, he was ill-prepared. Tulloch held that a crisis existed in the Church: "the very rudimentary idea of theology as the ever-fresh product of scripture and criticism, in short as a living science and not a dead system, is unknown", he declared.[4]

Nearer home was a celebrated article, "Church Parties, Past and Present", by W. J. Conybeare, which appeared in the *Edinburgh Review* in 1853. Conybeare wrote the liberal answer to the Catholic and agnostic conversion novels of Newman and Froude, *Loss and Gain* and *The Nemesis of Faith*. His undergraduate hero in *Perversion* ("a tale for the times") passed from Low Churchmanship, through doubt, to a liberal faith, and the influence of positive German theology played an important part in the development.[5] Perhaps that was why the conservative *Christian Remembrancer* said that it was the "worst novel that a man of any ability ever wrote, the most ill-contrived, clumsy and outrageously improbable in its plot, the most deficient in all graces of taste, feeling and temper" (and yet the reviewer had to admit that this "strange and unprofitable" book had found many readers).[6] Conybeare meant that Anglican liberal churchmanship was an alternative to reaction on the one hand and a collapse into unbelief on the other. The article, subsequently amended and enlarged in *Essays Ecclesiastical and Social* in 1855, spelled out in detail what the novel merely suggested. Conybeare examined the state of the parties in turn: the Evangelicals were numerous and active, and the High Church party, though in temporary eclipse in Oxford, contained some of the best minds in the Church; but the newly-emerging Broad Church party, neither High nor Low, nor yet the same as the old Latitudinarian party of the eighteenth century, seemed most potent of all. It showed that the Church was responding to the new age; as well as representing the "balancing and compromising character" of the Church of England, it affirmed a growing belief in toleration and held to the great truth that what united Christians in every age and denomination was far greater than that which divided them.[7]

Conybeare's identification was useful. The name "Broad Church" was used by A. P. Stanley in a sermon in 1847 and A. H. Clough had

---

[4] J. Tulloch, *Theological Tendencies of the Age*, p. 10.

[5] *Perversion, or, The Causes and Consequences of Infidelity*, II, p. 82, III, p. 120.

[6] *Christian Remembrancer*, January, 1857, p. 133; cf. complimentary notice by Baden Powell in *Oxford Essays*, *1857*, p. 199.

[7] *Edinburgh Review*, October, 1853, pp. 272-342. W.J. Conybeare, *Essays Ecclesiastical and Social*, pp. 57-164.

spoken of it even before that.[8] However, Conybeare thrust the title before the public and envisaged an actual movement with leaders and a recognisable theology. F. D. Maurice, significantly, felt that he was wrong to do this. "I always took it [the Broad Church] to be a fiction of Conybeare". "I never had and never will have anything to do with it".[9] Nevertheless, there was a large group of churchmen who belonged to neither of the two main parties, who believed in the "broad" principles of Anglicanism and who found themselves anticipated in the Latitudinarians. The *Remembrancer*, which disparaged the article, acknowledged that the theme won a large circle of sympathisers and a wide reputation "amongst general, we should rather say thoughtless, readers", and Caroline Fox thought it "clever".[10]

Conybeare's argument, however, took a darker turn. Like Tulloch he found the Church distracted, while elements in the new theology compromised its effectiveness. Maurice's point was conceded: the Broad Church party was so wide in its sympathies that "it can hardly be called a party at all". And there were serious deficiencies in the other parties: the Evangelicals were narrow and rigid, the High Churchmen lacked leadership and discipline. A sinister feature now asserted itself. Each party contained a group or extreme wing who wished to take the lead, the "Recordites" (Sabbatarians and literalists) among the Evangelicals, the "wild young men" (liturgical innovators) among the High Churchmen, and a group of radicals in the Broad Church. The views of the latter tended to an "indifference in dogma which, when pushed to extremes, becomes an indifference to truth", while their leaders (twenty "prominent churchmen" out of the ten bishops and 2,800 clergy who composed the party) were, in reality, concealed infidels. Conybeare was worried about all three groups but particularly about the third, for his hopes for theology depended on the success of a reasonable and responsible Broad Churchmanship.

In their aims and activities the three groups threw light on the situation in the Victorian Church by the 'fifties and its receptivity to new thought. First, the "Recordites" (so called from their notorious and hysterical weekly newspaper) proposed the obvious answer which the Evangelical must give in the face of biblical criticism and "honest doubt" — the scriptures must be restored to priority, and, coupled with this, the penal

---

[8] *Edinburgh Review*, July, 1850, p. 266.

[9] C.R. Sanders, *Coleridge and the Broad Church Movement*, p. 8.

[10] C. Fox, *Memories of old Friends*, p. 295. *Christian Remembrancer*, January, 1857, p. 125.

substitutionary view of the Atonement and the doctrine of the everlasting punishment of sinners must be reasserted. Of course, the solution was too simple and too reactionary. Conybeare said that it drove people into atheism. But the temptation to be a literalist was a real one. Nor were Evangelicals alone in feeling this. The most famous statement of complete literalism in these years was trumpeted by the High Churchman J. W., later Dean, Burgon in the university pulpit in Oxford in 1862, to the effect that the books, sentences, words, syllables — "aye, and the very letters" — of the bible were absolutely infallible.[11] Maurice held that the Quakers began to question their "doctrine of the divine Word as the light which lightens every man", because it "interfered with reverence for the written word and with the doctrine of human depravity".[12] Cardinal Wiseman said in 1864 that inspiration of the scriptures and the eternal duration of hell-fire were for Catholics "vital doctrines of the sacred deposit".[13]

The need which linked these otherwise diverse figures was consistency in argument. Evangelical difficulties over the Atonement were equalled by High Church qualms about Christology, and both seemed to demand a conservative approach to the bible. When R. W. Church reviewed Darwin's *The Origin of Species* in *The Guardian*, he spoke for intelligent churchmen who had taken the trouble to study the new biology and geology, and books like Renan's *De l'Origine du Langage* in 1848, which threw doubt on the possibility of the human race having come from only two parents. He did not condemn Darwin, but he was worried about the implications for the first chapter of Genesis.[14] Another reviewer, later in the year, was more forthright. Genesis must be defended: if man originated not from one but many sources, "what becomes of the headship of our race in Adam and again in the antitype, the second Adam? What becomes of the Incarnation in all its deeper bearings and significances? What of the Atonement?... What of our Justification? What of the general resurrection, if we be in no real sense members of a risen Head?".[15]

Consistency was a mirage. The inroads of the new theories were plain in the standard commentary used by students and clergymen, Horne's three-volume *Introduction to the Holy Scriptures*. In volume one of the

[11]   J.W. Burgon, *Inspiration and Interpretation*, p. 76.
[12]   Maurice, I, p. 237.
[13]   *Pastoral Letter of H.E. Cardinal Wiseman on Trinity Sunday 1864*, pp. 14-15.
[14]   G, 8 February, 1860, p. 134.
[15]   *Ibid.*, 23 May, 1860, p. 473.

1856 edition Horne affirmed the complete historicity of both Old and New Testaments; Moses wrote the Pentateuch, the sun stood still in Joshua 10, Balaam's ass spoke, Elijah was fed by ravens and Jonah was swallowed by a large *shark* (in answer to objections that a whale's gullet would have been too small). But Samuel Davidson, in volume two, pointed out chronological errors, transpositions and other imperfections in the sacred books. Inspiration was of "religious and moral truth" and did not convey infallibility on matters in which the writers were limited by the knowledge of their own times. Two levels existed in the bible which he illustrated on the analogy of Kant's demarcation between physical and moral worlds. As a pupil of Lücke and Gieseler he suggested that German scholars were the best guides.[16] Volume three by Samuel P. Tregelles was rather less startling.

The *Westminster Review* unsparingly pointed out the contradictions; how could Horne's own volume, unchanged since the first edition 38 years before, be reconciled with modern research?[17] Davidson was denounced in Evangelical papers and forced to resign his professorship in Lancashire Independent College. The *Morning Advertiser* said that he denied the inspiration of scripture; *The Record* called him a "German Rationalist" and ran a campaign which the *Journal of Sacred Literature* described as disgraceful.[18] Horne hurriedly withdrew the volume and John Ayre rewrote it entirely. The lesson was plain: only the most modest advances in biblical criticism would be tolerated, and the Evangelicals were in a dangerous mood.

The protest group among the High Churchmen suggested other strains. Conybeare noticed their liturgical excesses; he might also have mentioned other hot-heads who talked openly about freeing the Church. Fear of the state and its machinations had haunted High Churchmen ever since the first Reform Act, recalling the Tory sentiments of an earlier age when E. B. Pusey's father spoke of the evils of a government compounded of "Whigs and atheists".[19] Of course, this was flamboyant. But many churchmen half assented to the extremists and pointed to the evidence of the political agitation of the 1850's when a series of

---

[16] T.H. Horne, ed., *An Introduction to the Critical Study and Knowledge of the Holy Scriptures*, I, p. 596, II, p. 207.

[17] *WR*, January, 1857, p. 170.

[18] *The Autobiography and Diary of Samuel Davidson*, p. 41 f., and cf. S. Davidson, *Facts, Statements and Explanations connected with the publication of the 10th Edition of Horne's Introduction*, pp. 4-5, also Anon., *Dr Davidson: his heresies, contradictions and plagiarisms*, and *The Record*, 5 November, 1856.

[19] Liddon, I, p. 2.

parliamentary bills was mounted with the aim of altering the establishment in some way or other and depriving the Church of certain
privileges. The tenor of most episcopal charges in 1860 was not *Essays
and Reviews* (that came later) but the Church Rates measure debated in
1857, 8, 9 (when it was only narrowly defeated), and 1860 successively.
Bishop Samuel Wilberforce said that the bill was only the first step in an
attempt to disestablish the Church.[20] Though warning against over-
reaction, Bishop Thirlwall held that the supporters of the bill condemned
the Church of England as unhallowed and pernicious: if they were
victorious they would go on until not one stone of it remained.[21] (This
was the later Thirlwall: his appointment to St. David's in 1840 had
gradually modified his earlier enthusiasm for radical theology).
Archdeacon Utterton saw the agitation as a "great scheme for doing
away with the Established Church altogether and applying its endowments to secular objects", while Bishop Ollivant of Llandaff said that it
was the precursor of other invasions on the Church's rights and
property.[22] *The Times* noticed how "that solemn old impostor, the
Church rate", figured largely at the Oxford Church Congress in 1862
when churchmen were in fighting mood to defend their privileges.[23]
While such a spirit persisted, there was little hope of fresh thinking about
the relations of Church and Society. There was certainly a great deal of
suspicion about any movement springing from Arnold: his *Principles of
Church Reform* was not forgotten.[24] The pressure group among the High
Churchmen was probably more significant than Conybeare allowed.

It is not difficult to see what the extremists among the Broad
Churchmen took as their platform. For they would be the first to suffer
in any situation where free thought was lacking and where reaction got
the upper hand. The volume of evidence about repression, particularly of
"Germanism", in these years is too large to be ignored. Thirlwall said in
1841 that English theological journals studiously kept their readers in the
dark about German theology.[25] Examples of this were the *North British
Review*, which condemned German infidelity by way of de Wette's
Introduction to the Old Testament in 1847, William Palmer's article,

---

[20] S. Wilberforce, *Charge to the Diocese of Oxford, November, 1860*, p. 48.

[21] C. Thirlwall, *Charge delivered to the Diocese of St. David's, 1860*, p. 24.

[22] J. Utterton, *Charge to the Archdeaconry of Surrey, 1860*, p. 27. A. Ollivant, *Charge
delivered to the Clergy of the Diocese of Llandaff, 1860*, p. 60.

[23] *The Times*, 15 July, 1862, p. 10.

[24] Cf. Maurice, I, pp. 545-7.

[25] *Letters Literary and Theological of Connop Thirlwall*, p. 175; cf. G. Pearson, *The
Dangers of Abrogating the Religious Tests and Subscriptions*, pp. 11-15.

"On Tendencies towards the Subversion of Faith" in the *English Review* in 1848, and notorious articles in *The Record* and the *Christian Observer* in March and July, 1849. Dean Church said that "strong dislike and condemnation" had been taught to him as the only correct attitude to foreign divinity.[26] Bishop Blomfield was said to have asked a candidate for holy orders, "I trust, sir, that you don't understand German?"[27]

Understandably, the liberals protested. A French visitor, de Pressensé, reported sarcastically that "an eminent representative of strict English orthodoxy" had to admit to the gentle Tholuck that he had read none of the modern theology which he had just condemned *in toto* and spoke only from hearsay.[28] Hare added his testimony: "I love the Germans ... Some of these writers are among the greatest that the world has ever seen; and yet all my life I have seen them reviled in a mass by those who evidently know next to nothing about them".[29] Hare was accused of "Schleiermachery" when he published his memoir of John Sterling in 1848. His Germanism (said *The Record* and the *Christian Observer*) led to the archdeacon's "whispering away the plenary inspiration of scripture".[30]

The class under pressure in this situation was, naturally, the clergy, and the *crux* of the matter was their binding subscription to the XXXIX Articles. Traditional views were thus safeguarded by the moral obligation of the clergy to obey authority. "Free inquiry only for free inquirers" said Disraeli, and any attempts to relax subscription were opposed. But the dangers of sloth and formalism were obvious, and the intellectual standing of the clergy suffered. Negroes, Catholics, university graduates had been freed, "the clergyman, it is to be feared, must wait for emancipation".[31] The grave effects on ministerial training were pointed out by the German writer J. A. Voigt in 1857 in a heavily critical study of theological education in England and Scotland. A man emerging after four years at Oxford was no better equipped in theology than a philological student in Germany. Voigt spoke of incompetent professors and superficial courses. "English theologians have nothing more in common with Prussian theologians than the name". The knowledge

---

[26] Church, p. 177.

[27] *The Rambler*, March, 1861, p. 288.

[28] E. de Pressensé, *Contemporary Portraits*, p. 324.

[29] MS. Eng. Lett., e 86, f. 104.

[30] A.K. Tuell, *John Sterling, a Representative Victorian*, p. 287. *The Record*, 19 March, 1849.

[31] R.W. MacKay, *The Tübingen School and its Antecedents*, p. 12.

required for the Oxford D.D. by accumulation was "spiegelfechterei", "a pretence and humbug".[32] Pusey also held, according to Thirlwall, that under the present university regime the Church of England obtained the worst trained clergy in Europe.[33] Bishop Sumner of Winchester complained in 1862 of the decline in the quality of ordinands. Oxford candidates for ordination between 1841 and 1862 had fallen by 34%, those from Cambridge by 19%, while non-graduates, increased by a huge 193%, failed to fill the gaps.[34]

The failure of nerve was also a response to a new climate outside the Church — the growth of "honest doubt". Conybeare said that the higher classes and professions were "influenced by sceptical opinions to an extent which twenty years ago would have seemed incredible".[35] Churchmen were unsure of their ground in facing this because they were, naturally if unconsciously, affected by the same currents of thought. The age was, as *The Rambler* said, one of lyric poetry and subjective creed, and of sorrowful, unhopeful and almost reluctant doubt which gave a tinge of romance to its literature and even to its art and of which Tennyson was the representative poet.[36] Jowett said that for liberal men *In Memoriam* "opened our minds in the best manner to the new ideas of the nineteenth century",[37] and F. W. Robertson ended an analysis of the same poem correctly when he wrote that "there are truths which are only to be proved by faith and feeling".[38] But feeling, like history, was ambivalent; in the hands of doubters it became a weapon against Christianity. H. L. Mansell, in his Bampton lectures of 1858 on *The Limits of Religious Thought*, warned of subjective tendencies in modern theology and too easy an acceptance of the idea of progress.[39] Sara Hennell in *Thoughts in aid of Faith* in 1860 held that "feeling was as real

---

[32] J.A. Voigt, *Mittheilungen über das Unterrichtswesen Englands und Schottlands*, p. 64 and *passim*. Voigt's contention is borne out by the fact that the copies of his book in the Bodleian Library and Cambridge University Library remain uncut to this day.

[33] W.R. Ward, *Victorian Oxford*, p. 88; cf. E.B. Pusey, *Remarks on the Prospective and Past Benefits of Cathedral Institutions in the Promotion of Sound Religious Knowledge and of Clerical Education*, pp. 51, 70.

[34] C. Sumner, *A Charge delivered to the Diocese of Winchester, 1862*, pp. 22-3; cf. E. Phillips, *The Church and the Ecclesiastical Commissioners*, p. 4.

[35] *Edinburgh Review*, October, 1853, p. 342.

[36] *The Rambler*, March, 1861, p. 296.

[37] Abbott, II, p. 419. Jowett quotes Tennyson's "the heir of all the ages" in Epistles, II (2 ed.), p. 624.

[38] F.W. Robertson, *Analysis of Mr Tennyson's* "In Memoriam", no. 130.

[39] H.L. Mansel, *The Limits of Religious Thought*, p. 258.

as logic" (Christianity being too logical), but she denied miracle and prophecy and the need for dogmatic faith.[40]

The point of this for liberal churchmen was clear. In the present mood of suspicion and uncertainty, their cause would succeed only if subscription were removed. If conservatives persisted in their policy, the emancipation movement would die through sheer frustration.

This analysis of the situation in the Church, as reflected in the Church parties and their tendencies, may now be referred to *Essays and Reviews* itself. No more need be said about Conybeare's actual identification of the groups; he was certainly wrong in seeing Dawes, Dean of Hereford, Maurice and Hare as leaders of the theological Left. Maurice, however, though he denied Conybeare's argument, suggested where theological radicalism might find a home. Cambridge, being Platonist, did not run to extremes but Oxford, being Aristotelian, did.[41]

Oxford in the 'fifties was in a ferment. There were agnostics, positivists, followers of John Stuart Mill, all busily propagating their views on religion. There were Arnoldites — F. J. A. Hort spoke of a "knot of Rugby men" in Oxford, Keble thought that rationalism in the university was mainly traceable to "our poor dear friend at Rugby".[42] There were Germanists — when Pusey met Friedrich Max-Müller in the High Street he used to sigh piteously, "I know you are a German".[43] But Maurice's real "Aristotelians" were not found in groups but comprised individuals like Stanley, Jowett, Baden Powell, Pattison, Goldwin Smith and their friends. Some were prominent, and this lent an edge to their heterodoxy. Powell had held a chair (the Savilian Professorship of Geometry) for longer than almost anyone else in the university, since 1827. Pattison, an ardent Germanist,[44] became head of his college in 1860. Jowett and Stanley owed their professorships (Greek 1855, and Ecclesiastical History 1857) to Palmerston, and High Church writers complained, "that the Whig ministry, while flattering Evangelicals on one side, steadily pushes the neological interest on the other, has long been apparent".[45] Was there even greater support? Disraeli held that the

---

[40] S. Hennell, *Essay on the Sceptical Tendency of Butler's Theology*, p. 12, and cf. her *Thoughts in aid of Faith*, p. 174.

[41] J.C. Hare, *op. cit.*, pp. xix, xii-iii.

[42] Hort, I, p. 85. G. Battiscombe, *John Keble, A Study in Limitations*, p. 326. Cf. A. Peel, *These Hundred Years*, p. 221.

[43] F. Max-Müller, *My Autobiography*, p. 288.

[44] Cf. M.J. Shaen, *Memorials of Two Sisters*, p. 194.

[45] W. Brock, *Infidelity in High Places*, p. 55. Cf. Abbott, I, p. 345.

hopes of the Broad Church were "very high" in regard to the Prince Consort who naturally favoured German-speaking theologians and who had appointed Stanley and Frederick Temple as his chaplains.[46] When the question arose of religious instruction for the Prince of Wales while an undergraduate, Albert had replied, "I cannot endure to see him placed under any of those extreme influences [Positivists at one end or High Churchmen at the other]. There is only one man in Oxford to whom I could intrust him for this — that is Dr Stanley".[47]

These writers and thinkers remained as individuals; Powell was separated from the others by his age and seniority, Pattison by his shyness, Goldwin Smith by his increasing religious apathy. But one group — Stanley, Jowett and Temple — emerged clearly, for they were united in a bond of friendship which survived Temple's departure from Oxford in 1848 and Stanley's temporary absence while a residentiary canon of Canterbury between 1852 and 1857. The nucleus was Stanley, who united all the progressive tendencies in the university in himself, as secretary of the Reform Commission, as the biographer of Arnold, and leader of the Germanists. Of the three, Jowett owed the most to friendship. By nature he was reserved, even withdrawn, nor would he be lionised: Hort, who recognised Jowett's importance by 1851, could not stir him out when visiting Oxford to see for himself the new forces there.[48] Nor had Jowett been taught by Arnold, and he disliked systematizing his views (in fact, "I hate the expression", he told Florence Nightingale when people claimed that he was a Broad Churchman)[49]. "I have no reason to suppose that the Liberals in Oxford regard me as their head", he wrote in 1861, "and have no wish to be thought so. I want to work with others, not to lead them".[50] But Stanley and Temple drew out Jowett's capacity for affection and love, and this became an intellectual release as well. He shared with Stanley the translation of Kant and with Temple worked on an edition of Hegel. And he no longer hesitated to make his ideas known, so that he soon outstripped his companions.

The larger importance of this friendship can be measured by the effect of the Commentary on St. Paul's epistles issued by Stanley and Jowett in 1855. It suggested to scattered liberals that they might all be saying the same thing. "I cannot but think that Jowett's plan was a good one, of

[46] G.E. Buckle and W.F. Monypenny, *The Life of Benjamin Disraeli*, IV, pp. 369-70.
[47] Prothero, II, p. 64.
[48] Hort, I, p. 348.
[49] Jowett MSS, f. 35, letter to Florence Nightingale, July, 1862.
[50] E. Abbott and L. Campbell, eds., *Letters of Benjamin Jowett*, p. 15.

exemplifying his principles *at once* in an actual Commentary", as Hort said.[51] Perhaps there was no direct influence upon the others, but Powell in five short years between 1855 and 1860, when he died, produced a spate of books and articles which made him the most notorious of all. Pattison and Henry Bristow Wilson, two others who shared a friendship, were comparable figures who felt encouraged by the trend of events. It was not easy to find precise analogies in Cambridge. But one teacher was active who claimed a kinship with the Oxford men, Rowland Williams, of King's College.

Do the single, isolated radicals of the 'fifties evolve naturally into the essayists of 1860? Dr Pusey and his supporters said, "of course"; they pointed to the obvious fact that most of the advanced authors of the previous decade had found their way into the book. The essays must have been planned, and that suggested that a neological group had been in existence for some time. Pusey thought that the date was 1851 when he first noticed Stanley's "Germanizing school" — Stanley "in common reputation is the leader of a Rationalizing School"[52] — and some years later he told Keble that "that party is trying to make themselves a position in the Church", by which he meant Stanley, Jowett and their friends.[53] Bishops, divines and religious newspapers all made similar claims about the essayists' association before 1860. But the essayists protested, and they were right to do so. The book was a chance production. There was no conspiracy; many differences existed between them — Jowett told Stanley on one occasion that Powell was "odious", Temple was disappointed with Stanley's *Corinthians*[54] — and prior to 1860 they were no more united than the Broad Church itself. If they had any association it was a fellowship in adversity, since they had some bitter experiences at the hands of religious zealots.

The difficulty in the following account, which deals with the period 1845-59, is to give them a name. J. B. Mozley described them as the "go-aheads" at Oxford, which is attractive but not very useful. To call them the essayists or the "Broad Church radicals" is too definite. They were not Arnoldites either; but Pusey's complaint about "Mr Stanley's school" suggests an identification that can be adapted. All this activity before 1860 was "Stanleyite"; even Rowland Williams, ploughing his lonely furrow at Cambridge, was a Stanleyite, and Stanley made early

---

[51] Hort, I, p. 436.
[52] Liddon, III, p. 334.
[53] Pusey MSS, letter to Keble, 10 November, 1862.
[54] W.R. Ward, op. cit., pp. 132, 153. Temple Appreciation, p. 107.

gestures of friendship towards him. The term also puts *Essays and Reviews* in the right relation to prior events in Oxford; Stanley would have nothing to do with *Essays and Reviews* when it was projected, precisely because it would be seen as the natural outcome of what had gone on before and as the manifesto of an extreme *cabal* out to capture the Broad Church. This was Hamlet without the prince, as many a puzzled commentator must have murmured when seeing the list of contributors and contents.

The rise of men with new theological views in Oxford can be dated exactly; it followed on the Tractarian defeat in 1845. Newman said that he was driven from the university by the liberals, Church bewailed Oxford left open to the enemy: "the 13th February, 1845... was the birthday of the modern Liberalism of Oxford".[55] In Pattison's *Memoirs*, the change, coloured by the years in between, appears vast and overwhelming: light let in in an instant after thirteen years in which science and learning fell to their lowest ebb; a flood of reform, new principles on the march, and every Oxford man becoming a liberal.[56] Maurice anticipated this in 1834; Tractarianism could not dominate the university for ever, but there must arise from the reaction a "better seed, a nobler generation".[57]

The form taken by the reaction was obviously important; a religious vacuum must be filled, otherwise scepticism and mere frivolity would take control. The men of the hour emerged significantly as Stanley, Jowett and their friends. This meant that the religion which replaced Tractarianism would be serious and scholarly, but it was also bound to be more liberal than anything that Maurice expected. Jowett's humorous comment illustrated this: after the Tractarian impulse subsided, "while some of us took to German Philosophy, others turned to lobster suppers and champagne"[58] : those who had no taste for the latter must, therefore, accept a good deal of new religious thought. The evidence of these years is of the Stanleyites' heady optimism but also of the suspicion excited by their views. Stanley was suspected of "Latitudinarianism" by 1845, and by 1846, Pusey, or someone of his party, was already accusing Jowett of "atrocities".[59] A. C. Tait warned the new competitors to Tractarianism

---

[55] J.H. Newman, *Apologia Pro Vita Sua*, p. 184. R.W. Church, *The Oxford Movement*, p. 340.
[56] M. Pattison, *Memoirs*, p. 238.
[57] Maurice, I, p. 162.
[58] Abbott, I, p. 74.
[59] *Ibid.*, I, pp. 115, 211.

not to be too rash, in the preface to his Oxford sermons of 1846, and, as a sign of things to come, Northcote, Gladstone's lieutenant at the victorious "Liberal" election of 1847, listed Stanley, Jowett and Temple as the "greatest names in the Germanizing party".[60] There were dangers in this situation: leadership had, perhaps, come too easily, while High Churchmen still had great strength in the university. Max-Müller felt that liberalism was beleaguered when he arrived in Oxford in 1848; it battled with Voltairian scepticism on one hand and with conservatism on the other. Fifty years after he said that the mood at that time still filled him with wonder. "Stanley shrugged his shoulders and advised me to keep aloof and say nothing."[61]

The transition between the old and the new, between the old Oxford rent by religious dissension and the new university waiting for reform, was pictured in Stanley's sermons on the Apostolic Age, given in St. Mary's in 1846. Stanley showed the liberal direction of historical and biblical studies. His apostolical personages were less actual characters — "because their precise history is uncertain" — than representatives of vast classes of human thought. He spoke of his debt to Bunsen, Rothe, Schelling and others and of the indefatigable industry of German critics, to whose profound thought and love of knowledge English writers were inferior. Scripture, he said, must be examined by the "same tests by which all other writings of antiquity are tried". The character and scope of the evidences must be changed, for a new class of difficulties for belief had arisen which the standard authorities, Jackson, Stillingfleet, Butler and Paley, could not meet. As he wrote in another context, "the attempts of Paley to rest Christianity solely upon its external evidences have, in our time, been rejected by a higher and more comprehensive philosophy".[62]

Stanley's sermons were the first instalment in the liberal polemic against Bishop Butler which became marked ten years later. *The Analogy of Religion* was no longer the defence of the faith that it had once been. Nothing quite like the sermons had been heard in Oxford since R. D. Hampden's Bampton Lectures of 1832. Stanley was courageous but, having launched the new liberalism, he wondered by 1848 whether he had spoken too plainly. Jowett, now more determined, thought it far

---

[60] J. Morley, *The Life of William Ewart Gladstone*, I, pp. 334-5.

[61] F. Max-Müller, *op. cit.*, pp. 290, 294.

[62] A.P. Stanley, *Sermons on the Apostolic Age*, pp. vi, vii, 4, 69; cf. A.P. Stanley, *The Epistles of St. Paul to the Corinthians*, I, p. 310.

preferable to the "sort of ambiguous orthodoxy of Hare, Maurice, and Bunsen", which he considered a great evil.[63]

Undergraduates began to notice the trend: that was the evidence of H. B. Wilson's Bampton Lectures on *The Communion of Saints*, preached in 1851, which attracted an increasing audience as word got around about their modernity. Wilson, incumbent of Great Staughton in Huntingdonshire, was a former Tutor of St. John's. He had drunk deeply of Schleiermacher's ethics in *Die Christliche Sitte* and admitted the challenge which psychology presented to traditional theology. Why not, therefore, apply the Gospel to human nature "as it really is and not as it has been represented by Manichaean doctors"? "The words of Scripture [are] to receive their true interpretation from what shall turn out, on careful observation and analysis, to be the real phenomena which [human] nature presents, than is the account of these phenomena to be forced in accordance with a preconceived interpretation of the Scripture expressions". That either positive dogma or negation of dogma should be absolutely final and for ever fixed "is inconsistent with man's condition as a progressive being", Wilson declared. Scripture terms dealing with matters of ordinary observation or speculation, and capable of being verified by human experience, were not evidences of absolute objective truth but of the modes of thinking and limits of understanding of a certain age. This limitation applied not only to the material facts of scripture but also to the "moral and intellectual" world therein. Wilson's safeguard, that the process of observation and analysis itself established the authority of scripture, was weaker than he thought: "the mental faculties have been trained, and their methods perfected, by the discipline of *mathematical and physical* science". Such inductive reasoning showed that the phrase, the "Communion of *Saints*", as a description of the Church, was not generally received until the fifth century; but, in any case, it implied the potentiality of all human beings to be Christian. Wilson, like Stanley, referred to Richard Rothe, author of one of the most important nineteenth-century works on the Church, as well as Gieseler, Staüdlin and Auguste Comte, and ended with a lengthy quotation from August Ritter's *Christliche Philosophie*.[64]

Hort realised that Oxford must be watched; though they had made a "great stir" in the university, the lectures were "perfectly horrible", presenting a dreary Utilitarian gospel.[65] He did not realise that Wilson's

---

[63] Abbott, I, p. 143 n.
[64] H. B. Wilson, *The Communion of Saints*, pp. 5, 52, 75, 106 n., 114-5, 124, 281.
[65] Hort, I, p. 210.

purpose was to challenge the Tractarian doctrine of the Church; no programme of reform would succeed unless this was done.

In 1855 Stanley and Jowett entered the arena with their four large volumes on St. Paul's epistles. Stanley dealt with I and II Corinthians, Jowett provided over 900 pages on the letters to the Romans, Galatians and Thessalonians. These were a revolutionary departure for biblical criticism in England; Tulloch, thirty years later, held that a "new historical epoch" began in 1855,[66] and the liberals put themselves forward as serious scholars. But in addition to learned exegesis of the Greek text were the supplementary notes in which Jowett's famous clarity and Stanley's pictorial imagination brought out the supposed real meaning of St. Paul's words; when the commentary was first mooted Jowett had spoken of the need to discover the " 'subjective mind' of the Apostolic age, *historisch-psychologisch dargestellt*".[67] If that mind emerged surprisingly like the convictions of a nineteenth-century don, it was no worse than happened in other radical treatments of well-worn themes: Grote's history of Greece, declared one writer in 1860, was simply a political pamphlet in favour of universal suffrage, vote by ballot, and mob courts of law, while under the manipulations of Niebuhr, Arnold and Dean Liddell, Roman authors were made to teach democracy.[68] So St. Paul, held Professor Jowett, taught natural theology, a moral Atonement, and much else that orthodox writers were surprised to discover.

The method in the Commentary was simple: Jowett wrote as a classicist rather than a theologian and with absolute freedom from tradition lifted St. Paul bodily out of the world of formulae into one of literature where a psychological treatment could be applied. The treatment was secular: St. Paul and his books were part of the age in which he lived; "men did not know what to make of this Paul".[69] The conservative interpretations were criticised because they stood in no living relation to the original meaning of the passage expounded. But, of course, it was not the old bible which emerged from Jowett's interpretation; it was a piece of religious writing, instinct with life and movement, but it was not quite revelation. What would happen if commentaries followed on the rest of scripture, for this must only be the

---

[66] J.Tulloch, *Movements of Religious Thought in Britain during the Nineteenth Century*, p. 331.

[67] Abbott, I, pp. 100-101.

[68] *Christian Remembrancer*, October, 1860, pp. 322-3.

[69] *Contemporary Review*, March, 1897, p. 353.

first instalment in a total refurbishing of the bible? If the same techniques were applied to Jesus and the apostles, the whole face of religion might be altered. Bunsen saw the significance, "I am overjoyed", and Hort, though critical, afterwards found conservative commentaries arid in comparison; Lightfoot, for instance, failed to fathom St. Paul's mind and compare it with the facts of life as Jowett did.[70]

Jowett opposed penal substitutionary views of the Atonement; far better to see it as "the greatest moral act ever done in this world — the act, too, of one in our likeness", which assured us that God in Christ was reconciled to the world. The commentator drew some of his inspiration from modern writers, and in the second edition he referred to Kant, Fichte, Hegel and Schleiermacher. But Jowett had a mind of his own and, while agreeing with Schleiermacher that the subjective part of the work of redemption was the individual's consciousness of union with God, he criticised his emphasis on the Church as the objective part. The Church indeed derived its life from the Spirit of God and it was the depository of the truth of Christ, but Jowett preferred a more immediate personal relation of the believer to Christ.[71]

The most interesting essay, though it drew less hostile comment, proposed to do away with the distinction between natural and revealed knowledge. Jowett suggested that the glory of Christianity was not to be as unlike other religions as possible but to be their perfection and fulfilment. These religions were so many steps in the education of the human race. Who could tell where natural knowledge ended and revealed knowledge began? The old apologists stressed the limitations of the natural, Jowett held that it embraced "all conceptions of religion or morality which are not consciously derived from the Old or New Testament". Thus, "there is a truth independent of Christianity". Further, "Revealed religion is ever taking the form of the voice of nature within; experience is ever modifying our application of the truths of Scripture". The existence of many religions should not be seen as a consequence of the Fall. "New conceptions of human nature do not allow us to look at man from one aspect only... the original forms of all religions are seen to fall under the category of nature and less under that of mind, or free will". If religion was a natural product it allowed us to see Christianity in a new light. "The use of the study of the heathen religions is just this: it teaches us to separate the externals or accidents of

---

[70] F. Bunsen, *A Memoir of Baron Bunsen*, II, p. 380. Hort, II, p. 79.
[71] Epistles (1 ed.), II, p. 481. (2 ed.), II, p. 583.

Christianity from its essence; its local, temporary type from its true spirit and life".

Jowett had a new role for the missionary movement. There should be less conversions and martyr zeal and more concern for the amelioration of the social and physical condition of mankind. If in the process Christianity lost its distinctive marks, "let us not doubt that the increase of justice and mercy, the growing sense of truth, even the progress of industry, are in themselves so many steps towards the kingdom of heaven".

From this point of view, Jowett was not much interested in abstract arguments for the existence of God. He criticised the argument from first causes, and evidential theories should not be upheld as sacrosanct merely because they derived from Butler or Paley. Jowett, as always, was afraid of the constricting effects of language, of the attempts at definition by which religious men laid hold on their experience. "We speak in a figure only... names by which we describe the being or attributes of God need a correction in the silences of thought. Even logical categories may give as false a notion of the Divine nature in our own age, as graven images in the days of the patriarchs. However legitimate or perhaps necessary the employment of them may be, we must place ourselves not below, but above them".[72] Was that an echo of Fichte and his belief that mental no less than bodily images of God were false and idolatrous, and it would be better to speak of God as absolute and not conditioned by the limitations of human thought? Some critics held that it was, but the reference to the "silences of thought" was an early hint of a mystical strain which later became much more apparent in Jowett's thought and which was entirely his own. Yet he did not evaluate Paul's own mysticism.

Stanley was less daring, less tendentious than Jowett, but the Church which emerged from his study of the Corinthian epistles was as unlike the Tractarian model of the early Christian *ecclesia* as could be imagined. In Coleridgean mood he referred to the "idea" of the early Church, and he recommended study of Arnold's "fragment" on the subject. The first Christians, on Stanley's argument, formed a natural society, broad in outlook and practice, and lacking any definite form of government or constitution. This was the Christianisation, not of the Levitical hierarchy

---

[72] Epistles (1 ed.), II, pp. 385-6, 392, 404, 410. (2 ed.), II, pp. 434, 437, 438, 443, 448, 476.

but of the republic of Plato, and in its broadness it was a microcosm of the world at large.

The doctrinal latitude which prevailed in the Corinthian Church allowed that even those who denied the Resurrection could remain as members, said Stanley, "and their position was not deemed either by themselves or the Apostle, as necessarily incompatible with the outward profession of Christianity". "The Apostle's renunciation of any infallible claims, shows that large concessions were made in the apostolical age to the principle of freedom, in spite of some of the manifold disorders which it produced". Openness, absence of mystery and concealment, and a contrast between "letter" and "spirit", were the characteristics of primitive Christianity. "The expansiveness, the comprehensiveness, the free inquiry, the truth-seeking spirit of the modern, as distinguished from the ancient world, is not only sanctioned but originated by the most authentic documents of Christianity".

This "natural" approach showed that St. Paul vindicated for himself the position of a layman (i.e., one who spoke in a "spontaneous, disinterested and unprofessional way", unlike the clergy), instead of upholding the supernatural authority of an apostle. Accordingly, we must not lay too much stress on adherence to the "letter of even the most important institutions of the early Church". In particular, St. Paul's denunciations against unworthy partakers of the Eucharist could no longer apply to the ordinance itself: Stanley thought that a cheerful and innocent gaiety might be the best approach if we were to reproduce the attitude of the early Church. The apostle told us not to trust in external, supernatural signs but in acts of usefulness and instruction which made religion social (instead of a matter of "mere reverence and contemplation"), and the best analogies for charismatic possession were the gifts of "reasoning powers, thought, activity, the means of beneficence", which a proper national Church would evince. But, though Stanley allowed that there were discrepancies between gospels and epistles, and that the substance rather than the actual words of Christ was reproduced, he rejected F. C. Baur's utter contrast between Paul and Jesus.[73]

In the same year, Professor Baden Powell took up his pen as a theologian once more. He had written little of a controversial religious nature since his broadside against the Tractarians, entitled *Tradition Unveiled*, in 1839, but now became more active. As a populariser of

---

[73] A.P. Stanley, *The Epistles of St. Paul to the Corinthians*, I, pp. 149-150, 325, 342. II, pp. 43, 76, 183, 197, 251.

science, in books like the *History of Natural Philosophy* in 1834, the Savilian Professor wrote for an age increasingly convinced of the uniformity of nature. As a churchman he tried to harmonise science and religion on the same basis. He, too, criticised Butler and the evidentialists who found the reason for faith in an external world, but he went further than Jowett. For the Greek Professor miracles were unnecessary because (for one thing) man's religious instinct no longer depended on them. Powell simply said that, as popularly understood, they were scientifically impossible. He preferred a God of order whose rule excluded any arbitrary interruption of nature; but even this shadowy deity seemed to be too external, and Powell abandoned him. In his *Essays on the Spirit of the Inductive Philosophy* (the title was significant) in 1855 he held that, by use of analogy, men might postulate an intelligence behind the universe, but in *The Order of Nature* in 1859 he preferred to speak of an "invariable, universal system", intractable to the usual theistic arguments.[74]

Powell was a symbol: his large works, though not his pamphlets, were difficult to read, and their technical jargon and increasingly abstract tone, removed from the realities of current religious life, justified the average churchman's dread of science. But when Powell referred to the Church situation in his shorter works he was usually polemical and frequently extreme. As a result, his role as apologist was forgotten. The Savilian Professor was no Germanist (he seems not to have known the language), but he was under the same spell as the younger radicals.

In *Christianity without Judaism* (1857) Powell showed why he had become short-tempered with conventional churchmanship: he even criticised his relative and one-time colleague, the formidable Archbishop Richard Whately, for advocating Paley in the modern era, and he was obviously worried about the unscientific nature of conservative biblical scholarship. After pointing out the mistakes in Genesis — the Mosaic narrative could not be regarded as historical, he said — he proposed an evolutionary view of Christian doctrine. "The Bible professedly contains the account of *progressive disclosures* of Divine truth". This recalled an earlier assertion: the bible ought to be looked at "rather in the *spirit of doctrine*" than in "the *letter of history*" — a result elicited, of course, by historical study.[75] The book went into a second edition in 1866, so there

----

[74] B. Powell, *The Spirit of the Inductive Philosophy*, p. 166, and *The Order of Nature*, p. 247.

[75] B. Powell, *Christianity without Judaism*, pp. 74, 80, 98, 202, 212, and *The Order of Nature*, p. 376.

were readers. In the *Oxford Essays* of 1857, writing on the evidences, Powell quoted Feuerbach approvingly for exposing the "vapid and narrow" theology of the English natural philosophers, and maintained that the High Churchman W. J. Irons' recent restatement of the argument from final causes had (in fact) rejected the argument as affording any real proof of a deity from independent reasoning. But he would not accept Irons' conclusion which upheld the Church as the source of religious truth: the source must be interior.[76]

In the same volume of essays, H. B. Wilson showed how a startling clergyman like Powell could be accommodated. His *Schemes of Christian Comprehension* held that Church unity should not be attempted on a doctrinal basis because there were bound to be differences of opinion over the meaning of doctrine. However, his real objection was a Kantian one: all knowledge was relative, not only of the doctrines themselves but also of the scriptural facts on which they claimed to rest. "The question is not, whether we will believe on God's word, but, what is his word? how far has he spoken? what has he said? ... No creeds can be extracted from probable matter. Modality clings to them. They are founded on historical documents". Thus, a man could not be metaphysically certain that a person who differed from himself was fundamentally in error, absolutely or relatively. There was as much difference between Luke and John as between Xenophon and Plato; the gospels were not simple annals but traditions with a clothing, while the epistles showed "how largely probable evidence enters into the deduction of doctrine".[77]

Wilson's most productive area after 1851 was the *Westminster Review*. Pattison introduced him to the publisher, John Chapman, and he agreed to edit the theology and philosophy section. Conservative churchmen found it odd, not to say distasteful, that a Bampton lecturer should write for the organ of the honest doubters. But Wilson saw it as an apologetic necessity. So did Pattison. Wilson wrote 61 reviews and four articles between 1855 and 1870. Pattison contributed ten articles and shared some of the theology and philosophy notices. In April, 1855 Wilson criticised the sloth of traditional divines. "Every department of learned research, thought, philosophy, scholarship, in this country supplies itself from German sources, with one signal exception" — theology. "We not only repudiate results, but we ignore the whole discussion which produces them".[78]

---

[76] *Oxford Essays, 1857*, pp. 179, 186, 201-3.

[77] *Ibid.*, pp. 115, 117, 118, 120, 125.

[78] *WR*, April, 1855, p. 524.

On the other hand, Wilson thought that Jowett's Commentary was only a beginning. In a review in 1857 of J. H. Rigg's alarmist book *Modern Anglican Theology*, which had denounced Jowett as a heretic, Wilson thought that "neither a Lutheran nor an Alexandrian mysticism can establish a permanent school in this country". Jowett's exegetical method, as an example of the latter, neo-Platonist school, was an attempt to "throw oneself voluntarily into the mental condition of another man, in order to rest in it", but this was an abdication of the individual reason and inconsistent with precise thought. Wilson was not really critical of Jowett; he asked for sterner solutions to the theological crisis facing the Church. His real "Alexandrians" were Maurice, Kingsley and Hare. Jowett, evidently aware of the article, denied being associated with Maurice and "that modern Neo-Platonism ... it is so easy to substitute one mysticism for another".[79]

Jowett, Stanley, Wilson had broadened the Church and stressed the impact of new studies. Were they mistakenly applying the short-term perspectives of a critical age to Church and doctrine which were ageless and unchangeable? A sample of Pattison's work for the *Westminster Review*, an article in 1857 on the "Present State of Theology in Germany", faced this question. The article was sufficiently like Wilson's ideas for George Eliot to ascribe it to him,[80] and it presented an argument very different from Hugh James Rose's complaints of "violence, rashness, self-will and ignorance" in *The State of Protestantism in Germany Described*, thirty years earlier. Pattison saw the German churches as a paradigm for all others, particularly in their experience of the ebb and flow of rationalism since 1800. Hare had said, "in Germany the mighty intellectual war of Christendom has been waged for the last half-century", while Philip Schaff, like Bunsen, believed that the German church unions heralded the great Church to come.[81] Now Pattison presented an evolutionary theory of German thought which meant that its dominance *must* be acknowledged. He saw Christian history as divided up into three earlier periods of doctrinal development, Greek, Latin and the vernacular (the Reformation), and now a fourth, beginning with Kant, which was approaching its consummation: "the historical law of the progress of the human mind" had, therefore, produced it. The movement was not the arbitrary creation of hallucinating

---

[79] *Ibid.*, October, 1857, pp. 537-8. Abbott, I, p. 262.
[80] *The George Eliot Letters*, II, p. 319.
[81] P. Schaff, *Germany, Its Universities, Theology and Religion*, pp. 158, 199. C.C.J. Bunsen, *op. cit.*, p. 273 f.

professors, rather, the "capital of learning lies in the hands of Germans, and theirs has been the enterprise which has directed it into theological channels". English distrust was the more surprising, and Pattison put it down to incompetence. "If we have not been drawn into it, or contributed to it, it is not because we have found a better channel for thought but because we have dispensed with thought on such subjects altogether". The liberals as the exception to this rule assumed great importance.

The writer's perspective was significant. Of all the movements in Germany he placed first, not the constructive school of Schleiermacher, still less "German Puseyites" like Hengstenberg, but the strict, historical approach represented by Baur. That gave an insight into the convictions of the Stanleyites generally: adopting the critical method meant that the Church's institutions and beliefs could be examined as the historical subjects that they were. That also suggested the limitations of the approach; anything that Baur proposed beyond pure criticism was for Pattison mere speculation. In view of the conservative attitude the great need was to establish the rights of scholarship, but he was not much interested in what should follow it.

The forces which produced the doctrinal epochs were engendered (he wrote) outside Christianity. The Renaissance had determined the Reformation, and the same critical spirit had been re-admitted into the Church, after centuries of neglect, by the Tübingen School. As that spirit had once questioned the authority of the Church, now it questioned the authority of the bible. "Should it be found that the basis to which Christine doctrine was shifted by the Reformers was an insufficient one, we are under the same obligations to transfer it to what appears to the best of our knowledge to be a sounder position, as the Reformers were when they substituted Scripture for the Church". But Pattison did not describe the new basis, whether it was the sense of moral duty, or the feeling of absolute dependence, or something else : it was enough to point to a scholarly movement maturing into a "habit of careful research, governed by a conscientious spirit, and armed with all the resources of knowledge", but, as he admitted, lacking the "freedom and elasticity" of its earlier days. Little assurance seemed to emerge from these researches. "Probability is the essence of historical criticism; nor can that criticism divest its reasonings of their probable character, because the records to which it is applied are religious records. So far as divine facts have been suffered to be incorporated into the world's history, — so far as they have become *events*, — so far they must needs be described, recorded, interpreted, and arranged by the same means as any other events". A false principle of interpretation had vitiated ecclesiastical history hitherto, but the Tübingen School distinguished between what was speculative and what was historical. "It conceives of Christianity as a series of connected events, having a history... it does not enter the lists for or against this or that doctrine, but analyses it, tracing its growth and formation", and that was sufficient.[82]

Books and articles were one indication of Stanleyite development; their practical work in Oxford itself was another. Stanley, Jowett and Pattison became outstanding tutors and leaders of young men; they represented a new approach to learning and a new relationship between teacher and student. They hoped that the colleges would embody such changes and were drawn together more closely as an organised group with other liberals so that a programme of reform could be undertaken. Utilising some of Arnold's ideas, Jowett spoke in 1846 of his hopes that the universities, instead of representing the worst half of the clergy, might become a real link between Church and State. "Catch them young: you may undermine their fierce Tory and High Church principles at College": the change must be all-embracing.[83]

The *Christian Remembrancer* said indignantly that the liberal party in Oxford had forced reform on the university,[84] but the agitation dated from the 'twenties, when the Noetics proposed new schools of study and encouraged a high attainment in logic as some counterbalance to the poor examination record of most students. The University Reform Commission set up by Russell in 1850 was a liberal engine, with Samuel Hinds, Bishop of Norwich and former colleague of Whately, as chairman, Stanley as secretary, assisted by Goldwin Smith, and other members who included Powell, Liddell and Tait. Jowett, with Pattison, Stanley and others, sent the Prime Minister a memorandum of thanks, but the Tractarians were shocked at the partizan team of Commissioners and feared that the university's character would be transformed to resemble German models. Pusey said in his evidence that German disbelieving theology was the product of competing professors; he now felt that all the troubles of the Church since the Reformation could be ascribed to German professors. Jowett, as the English equivalent of such

[82] *WR*, April, 1857, pp. 327-363. Other major articles by Pattison in *WR* are April, 1861, pp. 403-418, January, 1862, pp. 169-200, October, 1863, pp. 483-531, and April, 1867, pp. 325-344.
[83] E. Abbott and L. Campbell, eds., *Letters of Benjamin Jowett*, p. 2.
[84] *Christian Remembrancer*, October, 1860, p. 304.

pedants, proposed an ambitious school of theology on modern lines in which the old authorities would be dethroned.[85]

In the event, the Oxford bill was not as radical as was feared, or hoped for: clerical fellowships were retained in some strength, fellows and scholars were required to be Anglicans. The Stanleyites petitioned Russell against this and supported Nonconformist protests in parliament. There was a second University Commission in 1854, and in the meantime the triumvirate of Jowett, Stanley and Pattison worked indefatigably for reform: one monument of this was the "blue book" of 1852 with its 800 pages and appendix of 47 recommendations, and another was the new examination statute of 1864. A statute establishing honours moderations and finals in history gave Jowett an opportunity to teach Hegel, while Pattison worked against Bishop Butler.

Pattison and Goldwin Smith were the two publicists for these changes. In commemoration of the new regime inaugurated in October, 1854, Pattison wrote jubilantly in the *Oxford Essays* of 1855 about the glorious opportunities now available. Oxford since the time of Henry VIII to the year 1804 had ceased to be a school of liberal culture, and though Copleston had restored classical studies the Tractarians had neglected these and only Hampden, in their period, understood Aristotelian philosophy. He equated the High Churchmen with medieval obscurantists, but their numerical superiority could not now halt the cause of university regeneration. Nowadays, the "really living power in Oxford lies, whatever indications may be thought adverse, at this moment, in the movement of speculative thought in this place". The speculative movement (he admitted) drew on German teaching, whereas their enemies had "less than a child's knowledge of the nature of German institutions", and it meant that teaching in higher education could no longer be dogmatic.[86] Goldwin Smith, in the 1858 *Oxford Essays*, repeated Pattison's argument that the Tractarian period had been an interruption in the movement of reform. The abolition of the "tyrannous" religious tests in the university was the next object, so as to bring Oxford once more "into direct connexion with the practical requirements and interests of the age".[87]

---

[85] *Report and Evidence upon the Recommendations of Her Majesty's Commissioners for inquiring into the state of the University of Oxford*, Evidence pp. 1-173. On reform issue generally cf. W.R. Ward, *op. cit.*, pp. 180-209, and C.E. Mallet, *A History of the University of Oxford*, III, p. 290 f.

[86] *Oxford Essays, 1855*, pp. 287-9.

[87] *Oxford Essays, 1858*, pp. 266-87.

The reformers' contacts widened, both in the university and outside. Stanley developed friendships in Cambridge, with Hort (as another Rugby man), Lightfoot and others; Pattison grew intimate with Hort and did parish duty for him.[88] Where extreme opinion existed at Cambridge it was on the matter of revelation, and by 1858 Jowett and Wilson were on close terms with Rowland Williams, the radical Fellow of King's. An argumentative Welshman, Williams had been in Cambridge for more than twenty years, first as a clever undergraduate and then as Classical Tutor of King's from 1845-50, and, though he was appointed Vice-Principal and Professor of Hebrew at St. David's College, Lampeter, in 1850, he retained his fellowship until 1859.

Williams did magnificent work at Lampeter, remodelling the college and giving it a new lease of life, but his theological singularity had its drawbacks: he was not typical of Cambridge men, and, perhaps, not typical of Broad Churchmen either, and he owed nothing to the forces which produced the Oxford radicals. His sense of isolation, heightened by his Welshness, increased over the years and made him a prickly partner in any enterprise. But he was a true reformer, and gave evidence before the Cambridge Commission of 1850 about overhaul of his own college, and he also possessed a good knowledge of German theology. He preached from Neander and Stier, liked Rothe and Tholuck, and praised the Schleiermacher school, though (he said) he disliked the subordination of reason and enquiry to the mere feeling of dependence. Hegel's philosophy of history deeply influenced him. Williams summed up his position as being the converging result of Neander, Bunsen, Stier, Jowett and F. W. Robertson, coming upon plentiful doses of Coleridge, with some study of the Christian Fathers, in the spirit in which they were unfolded by Bunsen in his *Hippolytus*. Bunsen was notorious for long windedness and opaqueness; Williams, similarly, with so many mentors to chose from, had not thought out his position completely, though he was more disposed to compromise than Jowett or Pattison, believing in a middle way in theology. He knew what he was opposed to: he criticised Mansel who preached in Cambridge "a solid fragment of Butler", and he thought that the 1858 Bamptons exposed the hollowness of the High Church position: "his argument tells *not more* against Rationalism than against Revelation... For if you supersede Nature, you ought to improve upon her". Like Jowett he felt that "Christ's religion is indeed the

---

[88] Hort, I, p. 378.

Natural one. He reveals the obscured truth of the God of nature".[89] It was understandable, therefore, that Jowett wished to make common cause with him, and Wilson enlisted him for the *Westminster*.

William's extreme views were shown first in 1854 in two Advent sermons at St. Mary's, Cambridge. Hort heard reports of them as "very heterodox and certainly very odd", and before the course was over Williams received a private hint that he had better not finish it.[90] Reaction stiffened his opinions; chosen as the Founder's Day preacher, at King's the following Lady Day, he searched for a provocative text and found Acts XXIV, 14, "that after the way which they call heresy, so worship I the God of my fathers". Subsequently published as *Rational Godliness* the sermon attacked all narrow and restricted views of revelation. Criticism had shown, said Williams, that the infallibility of scripture could not be maintained, yet faith had been reduced to holding this, removing God from life instead of seeing revelation in art, music and literature, not merely in "an image fallen once and for all from heaven; with no analogy in nature; with no parallel in history; with no affinity among the Gentiles; and (except for some special reason), with no echo to its fitness from the human heart". There was a "wonderful correspondence" between the spiritual judgments of the Gospel and the purest searchers after godliness elsewhere, for the Wisdom that took flesh in Christ came from the supreme and universal teacher of mankind. He criticised evidential religion and predictive prophecy and held that, instead, the Christian religion was in essence "attachment to Christ as a Person, and this can never mean to his name, or to his power... but rather to that goodness and that truth that he embodies".

The criticism of bibliolatry led the preacher to stress the Church, not as the Tractarians did but as a community of searchers after truth who, in due course, wrote their experiences down. "The Church was [there-fore] before the bible as a speaker is before his voice": the bible was not necessary to salvation. But this spiritual truth was not infallible, thus we could not be "fettered over much by the human accidents of our ancestors in the faith", and we must expect to find different stages of development in religion.[91]

Williams' major work, *Christianity and Hinduism* (1856), arose out of his essay for the John Muir prize which so pleased the Senate that he was

---

[89] Williams, I, pp. 347-8, 359, 361, 405. *Contemporary Review*, April, 1870, pp. 58-79.

[90] Hort, I, p. 299. W.H.B. Proby, *Annals of the Low Church Party*, II, p. 131.

[91] R. Williams, *Rational Godliness after the Mind of Christ and the Written Voices of His Church*, p. 377 f.

asked to produce a larger study of the subject and received the prize in its entirety. H. H. Wilson, the Sanskrit scholar, thought that the book would become the standard reference for the Hindu speculative systems. The argument took the form of a debate between various speakers. One held that the Gospel was superior to Hinduism and that Buddhism was not a divine revelation. But Williams himself was reflected in the view that the liberal Christian had "shifted the idea of revelation from its positive sense into a kind of spiritual growth, or something that more nearly resembles some Indian theories of a Divine spirit pervading and elevating humanity". Consequently, the Hebrew prophets were "full of that eternal Spirit of God which heathens in some measure possess through every well meant effort to realise righteousness on earth", and only predication, and not prediction, need be claimed for them.[92]

Apart from Williams, the Cambridge Broad Churchmen were slow in responding to these overtures. Hort thought that Jowett's scholarship was slipshod ("nearly always secondhand and often quite wrong", with the weightiest questions dashed off without work),[93] so did Lightfoot in a review of the Commentary in the *Journal of Classical and Sacred Philology*. But they seemed to be drawing nearer. Westcott's *Introduction to the Study of the Gospels*, in 1860, was indebted to "leaders of the extreme German schools", and held that criticism "even *without reverence*" might lay open mysteries for devout study; moreover, metaphysics was now contemplated from within, not from without.[94] He would not be so incautious again — *The Guardian* slashed the work for doing "nothing to promote a sober, reverent, and loving knowledge of the sacred writings", in the same vein that it dismissed another piece of liberal research as "Whately and water".[95] The two brothers Harvey and Charles Goodwin should also be noticed. The elder, soon to be Dean of Ely, did quiet, tentative but obviously "liberal" work on the gospels. Charles dissipated his energies more, as archaeologist, lawyer and bibliophile. He published a study of the hieratic papyri in the *Cambridge Essays* of 1858. But he knew German and developed in his theological convictions: this became critical for, after election as a Fellow of St. Catharine's in 1850, he felt that he could not proceed to orders and later resigned. Perhaps the rising discontent about "Niebuhrian evil",

---

[92] R. Williams, *A Dialogue of the Knowledge of the Supreme Lord*, pp. 311, 522, 529, 550, 554. Cf. *Dictionary of National Biography*, XXI, p. 451.

[93] Hort, I, pp. 315, 322, 437.

[94] B.F. Westcott, *Introduction to the Study of the Gospels*, p. viii.

[95] *G*, 5 December, 1860, p. 1070.

and the orthodox reviewers' discovery of "tendencies to rationalism" in his brother's books, finally convinced him.[96] Goodwin devoted each long vacation for nine years from 1851 onwards to geological researches: that was to have an obvious fruit in 1860.

These developments in England were increasingly noted in Germany in the 'fifties, to the gratification of Stanley, Jowett and Pattison, who had all claimed membership of a truly European movement. Jowett was now mentioned in the same breath as Arnold and Thirlwall, but the praise for the Commentary in Berlin, Göttingen and elsewhere was nearly matched by the welcome for Williams' two books. Lassen and Max-Müller saluted *Rational Godliness*, and Ewald thought that *Christianity and Hinduism* was the worthiest monument of English biblical scholarship since Archbishop Newcome. Bunsen said that this "perfectly framed Platonic dialogue", so like his own, was the most interesting book in English or German for twenty years: "no German could have written it".[97]

But the welcome at home was very different. Tulloch as well as Conybeare pointed out the dangers if churchmen did not give the more restless spirits their head, well knowing the trials experienced by other pioneers earlier. But the warnings went unheeded. There was conscious reaction in Oxford from the beginning. By 1855 the Stanleyites were being pilloried in the religious press. In answer, some became strident and over-assertive, and Powell and Williams, in particular, made more enemies for the cause in this way. The orthodox attitude about them developed in turn: from being troublesome individuals they had changed into a party pledged to use their influence to undermine the Church.

The Record, appropriately, had an early notice about activity at Oxford. In July, 1849, lamenting that German theology had been taken up at Cambridge, where it might be expected, *The Record* also found evidence of the same in the sister university, where it must be the counterpart of Tractarianism.[98] Thereafter, *The Record* kept a close watch on Oxford. Pusey, complaining to Wilberforce of the German tendencies in Wilson's Bamptons, said that the lecturer's doctrine had scandalised many of the heads of houses. Pusey spoke feelingly: he had been prevented from preaching by the bishop because of his views on the

---

[96] *Dictionary of National Biography*, XVIII, pp. 142-3. Cf. *G*, 4 April, 1860, p. 317, referring to "Mr C. W. Goodwin who, it may be remembered, gave up his Fellowship rather than take orders".

[97] F. Bunsen, *op. cit.*, II, p. 429. Williams, I, pp. 309, 314.

[98] *The Record*, 10 July, 1849, p. 6.

Eucharist. "You will be asked why they [the liberals] are allowed to officiate, I forbidden".[99] But the High Church party waited until 1855 to respond to the challenge: in 1851 they needed time to recover from the shock of the Gorham judgment. Wilson was opposed, however, in *The Record* for preaching "rationalism in the pulpit of the University of Oxford", and in various pamphlets. There was more dissension as Wilson continued his career in print. "Most dangerous" was Gladstone's comment on his essay, *Schemes of Christian Comprehension*, in 1857, and other readers felt similarly.[100]

Jowett, Powell and Williams were singled out after 1855; they were harried by preachers and chastised in print. Opposition took various forms and sometimes it was grievous. There seems little doubt that Jowett's views cost him the Mastership of Balliol in 1854, and he had to wait sixteen years while the conservative Robert Scott filled his place. Pattison also was disappointed in his first attempt at the Rectorship of Lincoln. When the Commentary appeared, Scott was asked to remove Jowett from the Tutorship of his college by, among others, the Bishop of Glasgow. A letter was also addressed to him in the *Morning Chronicle* which asked, "Are you doing right before God and man in upholding Mr Jowett in the position of Tutor?" Scott, to his credit, refused to act and also refrained from preaching against Jowett when asked to do so by the Vice-Chancellor.[101]

Jowett's friends began to be alarmed: Hort wondered if his conclusions might be "blank atheism"; others, as he made preparations for the second edition, counselled withdrawing the section on Paley since it was bound to offend traditionalists.[102] When the Unitarians spoke highly of the book, and the *Christian Reformer* described it as a manifesto of free thought, a plan was set afoot in Oxford to humiliate the author. C. P. Golightly, who had figured in other prosecutions in the university, together with MacBride, Principal of Magdalen Hall, asked the Vice-Chancellor to require his subscription to the Articles once more. The affront to the liberal conscience was deep; Jowett contrasted his plight with the liberty of T. H. Green who could say what he liked because he was a layman — but he signed.

The Vice-Chancellor's request to preachers from High and Low sections brought the Bishop of Oxford into the university pulpit to

---

[99] Liddon, III, p. 334.
[100] *The Gladstone Diaries*, V, p. 213.
[101] J.M. Prest, *Robert Scott and Benjamin Jowett*, pp. 10-13.
[102] Hort, I, p. 315. Abbott, I, p. 251.

answer Jowett, while Pusey also appeared, to warn against an undue stress on natural theology. Man's approach to God could only begin in faith, said Pusey, and faith was entirely the gift of God. The "province of reason is not antecedent to that of faith... Reason, unaided, cannot even penetrate into the sphere of the objects of faith... intellect, unenlightened by Divine light, intuitive as it may be in human things, is blind to the Divine... All its natural knowledge cannot decipher the very alphabet of the supernatural".[103] That was far from the spirit of the Commentary, and Pusey thought that only "religious feeling" enabled Jowett to avoid the consequences of his thought. Jowett was also punished financially. His stipend as Regius Professor of Greek was only nominal, but Pusey felt that a proposed endowment of £300 might advertise his views and become, as he said to Wilberforce, "a vote of honour" for "a sceptic denying all which a Socinian denies".[104] Jowett had to do without his extra income until the matter was finally settled in 1864 after much upheaval.

Stanley endured other vexations. When his appointment to the Ecclesiastical History chair was announced in 1857 he found that the atmosphere had appreciably hardened: only one letter of welcome awaited him — from Jowett.[105] The new professor's first essays in Church history were damned by The Guardian : "Theology, properly so-called, is as unfamiliar as it is probably repulsive to his mind... he recurs in effect to purely natural religion... the tendency of Dr Stanley's theology is unmistakeably in the negative direction".[106]

The Commentary on St. Paul by the two men was, of course, the main reason for many of these passions. A fierce notice in the Christian Remembrancer focused attention on the menace growing in the university. Stanley was dismissed for mistaking his vocation in becoming a biblical critic, but Jowett's volumes were the "outpouring of deep and serious thought", exhibiting a "refined, highly gifted, but unsettled mind". Jowett wrote with consumate skill for the young, high principled, intellectual and religiously disposed Englishmen of his day, but the beauty of his dissertations deliberately concealed opinions which, if barely stated, would cause them to revolt. "A beautiful feeling but a poisonous atmosphere pervades the whole".[107] The Hulsean lecturer for

---

[103] E.B. Pusey, All Faith the Gift of God, pp. 6, 17, 24.
[104] Liddon, IV, pp. 15-16.
[105] Prothero, I, pp. 500, 508-9.
[106] G, 4 May, 1859, p. 404.
[107] Christian Remembrancer, April, 1856, pp. 445-492.

1859, C. J. Ellicott, pointed out the Christological implications of Jowett's views. Jonah was an historical book (Jowett had suggested otherwise): to deny this meant that Christ "wittingly made use of a fabulous narrative to illustrate His Resurrection".[108] The Bampton lecturer for 1859 was George Rawlinson, Camden Professor of Ancient History at Oxford, who defended scripture's historical trustworthiness against the liberals: Moses' mother had probably met Jacob, who could have known Shem, son of Noah, and Shem was probably acquainted with Methuselah, who had known Adam, the first man.[109] This in the same year as *The Origin of Species*!

Professor Powell's development was described as scandalous by the *Quarterly Review* in October, 1859, while Pusey mounted the university pulpit once more to attack the erring scientist in a sermon entitled *Real Faith Entire*.[110]

The agitation caused by Williams' beliefs spanned the years from 1855 to 1860 and passed without a break into the prosecution over his article for *Essays and Reviews*. When *Rational Godliness* was published seventy petitioners asked Thirlwall, as Visitor of the college, to dismiss the Vice-Principal from his post at Lampeter. They were concerned about the effect of his teaching on ministerial candidates, though Williams made a vigorous defence of his methods and orthodoxy (listing the Fathers and Anglican divines quoted in his lectures) in *Lampeter Theology Exemplified*.[111] Thirlwall was in a quandary. He had some sympathy for Williams who was the only clergyman in the diocese with whom he could converse intelligently about foreign theology. He refused to require his assent to the Articles once again, to avoid a scene which would be as embarrassing to Thirlwall himself, as the translator of Schleiermacher's *Critical Essay on St. Luke's Gospel* in 1825, as to the radical professor. So he concentrated at great length on the theological issue, in his charge for 1857. He detailed the problems in a view of inspiration which only held that "the more spiritual a man's life the more inspired his writings", but, said Thirlwall, the sacred writers had peculiar functions apart from the ordinary experience of Christian men. Revelation as taught by Williams did not seem to differ from the ordinary work of the Holy

---

[108] C.J. Ellicott, *Historical Lectures on the Life of our Lord Jesus Christ*, p. 4.

[109] G. Rawlinson, *The Historical Evidences of the Truth of the Scripture Records*, p. 50. Rawlinson was praised in *G*, 11 January, 1860, p. 39, and *Christian Observer*, April, 1860, pp. 233-244.

[110] *Quarterly Review*, October, 1859, pp. 420, 423. E.B. Pusey, *Real Faith Entire*, pp. 93-4.

[111] J.C. Thirlwall, jnr., *Connop Thirlwall, Historian and Theologian*, pp. 222-4.

Spirit, and thus Christ could have entered the world's providential progress without any break in the natural sequence of events. Of course, such implications were in the letter of the book rather than in the author's consciousness; nonetheless, Williams in *Rational Godliness* left the impression that his desire was to efface the distinction between natural and revealed religion.[112]

Though he hoped that his action would cool hot tempers, Thirlwall did not gain much respite for Williams. This was partly because, having refused to act and having defended freedom of thought within the limits allowed by the Church, he then privately asked him to resign. The professor realised that the liberals could not build on the slender support suggested in the charge and his truculence returned. From Cambridge Williams issued *An Earnestly Respectful Letter* in which he spoke of the bishop's actions as a "masterly evasion".[113] Thirlwall was obliged to answer, and the reply, published in 1860, also avoided a solution: a "captious answer to the eccentric professor" was how the Bishop of London, Tait, described it.[114] But conservatives also lost patience with Thirlwall; an archdeacon absented himself in protest from a dinner attended by the bishop; others thought that he defended Williams. So there was some welcome for another Welsh bishop, Dr Ollivant, when he issued two addresses in which he condemned Williams' heresy.[115]

By 1855 a connection between radicals in the two universities was seen, by 1858 it was declared to be a single, organised movement. The *Quarterly Review* in December, 1855 contained a further but now more negative article on the Broad Church by Conybeare, entitled "The Neology of the Cloister", which dwelt on the similarities between Jowett and Williams. Rationalism in Germany had been superseded in some meaure by sounder writers, but "we find the errors against which they have contended gradually gaining ground on us at home; and we now have before us the works of two eminent Tutors of Oxford and Cambridge, which increase the mischief". Neither Jowett's Commentary nor *Rational Godliness* fully apprehended the absolute irreconcilability of Christianity and its modern enemies.[116] The *Christian Remembrancer* earlier praised *Christianity and Hinduism* but in October, 1859 ran an

---

[112] *Remains Literary and Theological of Connop Thirlwall*, I, pp. 292-308.
[113] Williams, II, p. 3.
[114] Davidson, I, p. 306.
[115] A. Ollivant, *A Charge delivered to the Clergy of the Diocese of Llandaff, August, 1857*, pp. 70-6.
[116] *Quarterly Review*, December, 1855, pp. 149-150.

article on "Modern Latitudinarian Theology" which criticised Powell's *The Order of Nature* and the second edition of the St. Paul; though different in many ways, the two books were on the same side, "and that side is opposition to the truths of Revelation".[117] The welcome for Powell's *Christianity without Judaism* indicated the "existence in the Church of England of a party more or less influential" — so held the *British Quarterly Review* in April, 1858, a few months after Bishop Ollivant in his charge had spoken of "a School of Theology rising amongst us", in reaction to Tractarianism, of which the chief representatives were Williams (in his *Westminster Review* articles as well as sermons), Jowett and Stanley.[118]

More daring and sweeping than these was Mansel's broadside in his Bampton lectures. For Mansel by 1858 pantheistic thought from Germany now had obvious advocates in England. Mansel could be comic about German theology. His drama, *Phrontisterion, or Oxford in the Nineteenth Century*, poked fun at the Reform Commission and its odd foreign notions of salaried professors, each with a "Frau Professorin" and brood of children, who needed five times as much pay as celibate dons. There was a chorus of cloudy professors, evidently Jowett and others, who sang a final hymn to the Infinite, celebrating Hegel, Strauss and Feuerbach, "in the land that produced one Kant with a k, and many Cants with a c"(!).[119] In the Bamptons he bracketed Jowett, Powell and Williams together as possessing a "morbid horror of anthropomorphism" and replacing it with a metaphysical exposition of God's nature and attributes. They also betrayed another consequence of the metaphysics of the Absolute — an opposition to miracle as the setting aside of universal law. But if the Incarnation be accepted as the greatest miracle of all, why could not the prophets be divinely inspired to predict the future? "Once concede the possibility of the supernatural at all", and the bible was restored to its rightful place.[120]

The Bamptons were greeted as the "commencement of a new era in Oxford" which would wrest leadership from the "fashionable and large party of rationalists" — that was the opinion of *The Guardian*.[121]

[117] *Christian Remembrancer*, October, 1859, p. 388.
[118] *British Quarterly Review*, April, 1858, p. 414. A. Ollivant, *op. cit.*, pp. 65-6.
[119] H.L. Mansel, *Letters, Lectures and Reviews*, pp. 399-403.
[120] H.L. Mansel, *The Limits of Religious Thought*, pp. 280, 285, 355, 390-1, 417, 427-8.
[121] *G*, 24 March, 1858, p. 237. Cf. *Christian Remembrancer*, April, 1859, pp. 352-387, noting Mansel's criticism of Jowett.

Williams himself recognised that the battle for belief would not be fought in his own university. He joined himself to the Oxford men in *Lampeter Theology Exemplified*, for "Bishop Hampden, Dr Arnold, Professor Powell, Mr Stanley, Mr Jowett, and such portions as I understand of Mr Maurice", had said nothing less than he held in *Rational Godliness*. Apart from Maurice he quoted hardly any contemporary Cambridge figures in his defence, evidently implying that the Cambridge Broad Churchmen would not force the issue.[122] But how would the battle be joined? — Mansel's lectures suggested no possibility of compromise, and Williams claimed that he had not even the rudiments of biblical criticism. "In all his volume not one text of Scripture is elucidated, nor a single difficulty in the evidences of Christianity removed".[123]

Identification of extreme opinions was damaging in another form. Powell's *The Unity of Worlds* was evidently read carefully in the G. H. Lewes-George Eliot household, and Lewes spoke highly of his "courage and candour".[124] The *Westminster Review* said that in *Rational Godliness* Williams saw "further than many of his brethren; he has a courage and power of expressing what he says", while *The Inquirer* thought that he was more clear than Maurice, more scholarly than Robertson, and more eloquent than either.[125] These were compliments from men who appreciated the Stanleyites' attempts to build a bridge between faith and honest doubt. But Jowett, in particular, suffered in churchmen's eyes as the praise mounted. Francis W. Newman, agnostic brother of John Henry, welcomed the Commentary in the *Westminster* in 1858 for being free of doctrinal presuppositions. His article began by equating new thought in the Church of England with the Broad Church movement. "It is the Broad Church to which alone a thoughtful and reasonable Anglican can look with pride". But who must direct it? The answer seemed to be, Jowett, the "foremost mind in the Anglican Church". Jowett showed that for the first time the combined learning, fairness, religious sentiment and profound theological thought of modern Germany were exhibited in an Anglican divine, and that with a directness and simplicity more English than German. There was also praise for Powell and heavy criticism of Mansel for attempting to set back this new thought. The reviewer did not expect the new "quasi-

---

[122] R. Williams, *Lampeter Theology Exemplified in Extracts from the Vice-Principal's Lectures*, p. 28.
[123] *ER*, p. 67 n.
[124] *The George Eliot Letters*, II, pp. 279, 382.
[125] *WR*, July, 1855, pp. 209-10. Cf. April, 1857, pp. 564-7.

Coleridgean school at Cambridge" to effect a lead: everyone asked of Maurice, "what *does* he mean?", whereas Jowett was all lucidity. In another number the Review said that Oxford and Cambridge were still waiting for a religious philosophy. The only candidate worth considering was Jowett's noble and true system, though the writer admitted that "it is so different from the hereditary Protestant doctrines, that the Oxonians cannot be blamed for looking askance and timidly at it".[126]

A staunch friend of Maurice, Catharine Winkworth admitted, nonetheless, that there was a "certain set of questions connected with the Bible which are puzzling men's minds now that he leaves on one side, and we want some one to grapple with them as well". She saw Jowett as the extreme alternative to Maurice; that was in 1863, after *Essays and Reviews*, and the choice seemed equally clear in 1860.[127]

"What is this nineteenth-century religion for which all things have been preparing?" R. W. Church asked wonderingly.[128] The Stanleyites, now variously identified by their opponents, though not by themselves, as a school, a group or a party, were convinced of the answer. What made them so confident, so singular, so different from their fellows, so contemptuous of tradition? In each case the intellectual biographies of Stanley and the rest show how liberalism came of a long development. In that evolution there were many factors and the most important, except for Williams, was their reaction to the Tractarian movement.

Since Stanley himself did not take the ultimate step of becoming an essayist, he may be noticed more briefly. As one of Rugby's most favoured pupils he predictably carried off many university distinctions and seemed set for a great career. His efficient secretaryship of the University Commission earned him plaudits even from conservatives. There is no doubt of Stanley's importance before 1860; had Jowett and Wilson taken his advice and not pressed ahead with the essays, his plans for a liberal theolgical review, and for conferences between opposing parties, might have matured. The problem about Stanley was that he could not understand the depth of orthodox conviction and the inevitability of conflict. For him liberalism was "natural"; he came from his home and from Rugby already formed. For this reason he saw Arnold through his own spectacles, as a peacemaker who, given twenty years more of life, would have led the new forces in Oxford, taming the

---

[126] *Ibid.*, January, 1858, pp. 150-3.
[127] M.J. Shaen, *op. cit.*, p. 240.
[128] Church, p. 202.

extremists and disarming the suspicions of the orthodox. Yet Arnold could hardly have avoided a battle with the Tractarians, whom he regarded as perverse, and despite Stanley's emollient nature, his own antipathy to them was real, as Pusey and others well realised.

Benjamin Jowett saw matters more clearly, or perhaps he had fewer illusions. Born in 1817 he went up to Balliol as a scholar from St. Paul's school in 1836, and became Fellow in 1838 and Tutor in 1842. As a brilliant undergraduate he already disliked dogmatism and sensed that Newman's ethos was different from his own. Consequently, he did not agree with or understand many of Newman's principles, as he admitted to W. A. Greenhill in 1838. He made two qualifications about this: Newmanism was useful because, like all reforming movements, it disturbed the stagnant waters of orthodoxy, and Jowett was all for disturbance. "In the ordinary divinity of the day", he told Greenhill, "far too much stress is laid on words; there is a sort of theological slang... a religious phraseology in laying aside which you are supposed to be undermining the fundamentals of the Christian faith". And, secondly, he feared the opposing dogmatism which would crush Newmanism and any other new movement. Jowett, even as an undergraduate, wanted free speech in the Church and an end to persecution. Later, in 1855, he was "rather proud of having helped to draw up a document abounding in Liberal sentiments", protesting against current attempts to silence Newman. That recalled Stanley's boast that the intervention of the liberals had saved the Tractarians from complete disaster. But Jowett could never see the Church as Newman did. He wrote in his notebook of 1841, "it is our duty ro remain in the Church... [but] it would be a pious fraud to hold our tongue". The Church must be open to criticism. Robert Scott, lecturing on Niebuhr, "first aroused in my mind doubt about the Gospels", and Tait, then Tutor, implanted in him a desire to read German theology.[129]

Jowett proceeded to deacon's orders in 1842 and was ordained priest in 1845, but supported the agitation from his undergraduate days onwards to free the universities from clerical control. He disliked subscription: he said in 1841, "we should be only obliged to take the test in the letter as we should obey a law... No one can say we are bound to carry out in its full spirit a law we conceive to be indefensible". He had high hopes that Whately's attempts to relax subscription in 1840 would succeed. Jowett's labours on behalf of the University Commission were

---

[129] Abbott, I, pp. 59 n., 69, 111.

immense and began in 1846 with a draft of questions, to be submitted to heads of houses on the question of reform, which he provided for the Dissenting M.P., Christie, who raised the matter in parliament. In 1848 he prepared for the Commission by issuing a pamphlet proposing revision of the examination statute. Jowett wanted a school of theology, so that religion might be studied on new lines instead of falling back on the old arguments. "Religious persons feel that the evidences of Paley or Lardner are not the reasons for their belief, or the answers to their difficulties".

One answer must be in a fresh approach to the bible, but "can it be said truly that much has been done in this place in the last twenty years for Scriptural interpretation?"[130]

Jowett seemed on the threshold of an outstanding theological career when his Commentary appeared: Maurice was for some a prophet and seer but Jowett was a religious thinker of a new kind. Yet the state of his belief aroused deep misgivings in Pusey ("what Jowett rebels against is not Tractarianism but mystery"[131]), at one end of the theological spectrum, and in Tait at the other end ("there is an obscurity over what he believes of the centre of Christianity... is this [St. Paul's Christianity] distinctly recognised by the writers of his school?"[132]), and the *Christian Remembrancer* said openly in 1859 that he had once been much nearer the truth.[133] Against that, Bunsen claimed that Jowett's was the deepest mind that he had met with in England.[134] Maurice himself in 1859, aware that Jowett was being compared with him, said that they differed greatly. "Nevertheless, I recognize in him one of the honestest and bravest of men, — honest and brave as few men are in this day, — in that he will not express more than he thinks, and that he will state what he thinks, without regarding consequences, — a quality all the more remarkable in one who evidently hesitates so much before he assumes a position". This must have a "salutary effect upon us all, seeing that one of our great temptations is to use 'unreal words', and to let our statements outstrip our convictions".[135] Thus Maurice showed his awareness of Jowett's position, and his own generosity of spirit.

Jowett's emergence as a Broad Churchman was interesting. He had

---

130 *Ibid.*, pp. 76, 175.
131 Pusey MSS, letter to Keble, 23 October, 1861.
132 Davidson, I, p. 281.
133 *Christian Remembrancer*, October, 1859, p. 389.
134 Abbott, I, p. 196.
135 F.D. Maurice, *What is Revelation?*, p. 213.

experienced nothing personally of the Latitudinarianism of the Noetics but felt that there must be an alternative to the two main parties, and so he called himself a liberal. Goldwin Smith said that Jowett's first impulse in conversation was always to deny whatever was advanced by the other person,[136] but Jowett also rejected dogmatism because he felt that it was impossible not to define any idea without bringing in its opposite: "Being both is and is not". He could never be a sceptic: liberalism meant honesty, refusal to countenance humbug, a sense of the moral imperative, the need for self-improvement. It meant forming oneself in the mind of Christ, though Christ by 1879 had become less an historical figure than the "idea of goodness". In its last stages Jowett's view of religion grew more simple, he had come to recognise the need for "mystery", and it remained consistently anti-clerical.

Frederick Temple had been chosen after the less adventurous Goulburn to follow Arnold and Tait at Rugby, and when he contributed to *Essays and Reviews* that (said the *Christian Remembrancer*) opened the eyes of parents to the "real tendency of the teaching which has prevailed at Rugby for the last thirty years".[137] The Devonshire youth who went up to Balliol in 1839 evinced a hatred of "parties instead of principles" and was, he told his mother, weary of the "aggresive theology" of the Tractarians. He was another deeply influenced by Tait and owned himself "terribly excited" by Coleridge. Private judgment, he said, was not only a right but a duty. There could be only two courses open to a man, to obey a Church infallible or to obey conscience. "Obedience to what?... to an internal monitor, or an external guide? And if the latter, why?... how these things weigh upon me". On another occasion he asked, "why do you believe in the bible? — because it agrees with your conscience".[138] He was struck by Maurice's description of conscience as a supernatural gift. The boy at Oxford, painfully working out his convictions in the midst of theological upheaval, was obviously the father of the man.

Temple achieved a remarkable double first in mathematics and classics in 1842, and in November of that year he succeeded W. G. Ward as college lecturer in mathematics and logic. An admirable lecturer, he had Aristotle at his finger tips and made havoc of the manuals in logic of Whately and Aldrich, while he introduced Balliol students to Kant and

---

[136] Goldwin Smith, *Reminiscences*, p. 83.

[137] *Christian Remembrancer*, October, 1860, p. 329.

[138] Temple Appreciation, pp. 54, 68-9.

Comte. By 1845 he was Junior Dean and in 1847 he was ordained priest by Wilberforce. With Jowett, who was Tait's successor as Tutor and four years his senior, Temple enjoyed a perfect intellectual companionship. Speaking of Temple's mental attitude in the early 'fifties, Jowett said "he seemed to me as free as air".[139] Temple was a staunch liberal in politics, serving on Gladstone's committee in the Oxford election of 1847. He welcomed the University Commission and gave evidence before it, justifying the right to interfere with Founders' wills which High Churchmen, in contrast, held to be sacred; but Temple saw it as a vital reform without which "all other reforms are likely as not to be mischievous".[140] He joined others to pay for the suit in the Queen's Bench to open the fellowships at All Souls to competition (1847) — with some success. At the age of 26, in 1848, Temple went to Kneller Hall, a brave new venture designed to produce masters for elementary schools. Temple was a good administrator, brusque, sure of himself, a natural leader, and it was not his fault that the scheme failed. He then became an Examiner in the Education Office and Inspector of Schools, from which he moved to Rugby.

Temple contributed an article on National Education to the *Oxford Essays* of 1856. He wished for a more practical use of financial resources, even if this meant overthrowing established endowments. His great concern was for the education of the middle classes — a force for the improvement of society which would be held back by the restrictions attached to grammar school foundations. If freedom demanded the end of these, he did not hesitate: "there is a point beyond which the denominational system ceases to be so much a security for religious as for doctrinal teaching" — that fateful distinction.[141] Temple did impressive work in setting up the local examinations system which gave the grammar schools their stimulus for producing university entrants. In January, 1860 he gave evidence before the Popular Education Commission.

Temple showed the emergence of a new professional clergyman, an administrator on whom the Church drew for its leaders for the next half century and more, an educationist with a role in the world, a headmaster who was a man of many parts and not simply a priest. It was a virtuoso role, and Temple played it perfectly. His wider learning took the form of

---

[139] Temple Memoirs, I, p. 78.
[140] *Ibid.*, I, pp. 82-3.
[141] *Oxford Essays, 1856*, p. 244.

an interest in science which he retained to his death. At Kneller Hall he lectured on physics and chemistry, and he encouraged such studies at Rugby. He was an appropriate figure to be asked to preach the opening sermon at the famous meeting of the British Association at Oxford in 1860. In that charged atmosphere Temple held that the two books of nature and revelation both came from God. The religious man "has no more right to refuse to accept what he finds in the one from what he finds in the other. The two books are indeed on totally different subjects, and the difference in their importance is derived from the difference of their matter, and not from any difference in their authority". The sermon, preached to what G. V. Cox called an ultra-liberal audience, became the basis of his essay, and it was criticised for its "sophisms".[142] Temple knew, even earlier than this, that he was being watched because of his wider interpretation of both ministry and education. His association with Jowett was discussed when his appointment to Rugby was being canvassed, "but I will not purchase Rugby at the cost of my right to think for myself".[143]

Mark Pattison, perhaps the most consciously intellectual of the reformers, was Tutor of Lincoln College and, after an initial disappointment, became Rector in 1860. Born in 1813 he was an undergraduate at Oriel from which he moved, despite a disappointing second class, to become a Fellow of Lincoln in 1839. Pattison was ordained priest in 1843 and was appointed to the Tutorship the same year. The *Christian Remembrancer*, in its character assassination of the essayists, said that he was "well known as one whose opinions on theological subjects have been entirely changed".[144] Pattison, lonely, impressionable, was — unlike Jowett and Temple — an undergraduate drawn to Newman, an habitué of the "monastery" at Littlemore, and lovingly mentioned in the *Apologia* as one of those last Anglican friends who gathered to say farewell on the eve of the conversion.[145] The parting had a profound effect on Pattison, for he experienced a revulsion of feeling about religion which coloured his attitude for the rest of his life. Pusey saw him as one of the casualties of the Newmania going beyond Tractarian principles, "a renegade Romaniser of the Ward school", as he told Keble.[146] H. H. Vaughan, another High Churchman turned radical, anticipated

---

[142] G.V. Cox, *Recollections of Oxford*, p. 461.
[143] Temple Appreciation, p. 210.
[144] *Christian Remembrancer*, October, 1860, p. 353.
[145] J.H. Newman, *op. cit.*, p. 213.
[146] Pusey MSS, letter to Keble, 23 October, 1861.

Pusey's comment when he said to W. G. Ward that for men like himself there was no mean between Newmanism on the one hand and extremes far beyond Arnold's on the other.[147] However unjust to Arnold, conservatives saw him as the historical relativism which Pattison espoused after 1845.

Pattison said that in his reaction his "faith and perception of divine things" was withdrawn. This affected him emotionally: he became morose and of uncertain temper. Though he never actually resigned his orders, he maintained merely the externals of religion and became an opponent of any church revival in his college. He was no more attractive to agnostics. Henry Sidgwick held that Pattison's life was an example of the dangers of disillusionment, "a moral fiasco which the orthodox have a right to point to as a warning against infidelity".[148] That was harsh, for the Rector believed in *something* to the end, and his own description of his liberalism, in the *Memoirs*, was of a sense of that higher development when "all religions appear in their historical light, as efforts of the human spirit to come to an understanding with that Unseen Power whose pressure it feels, but whose motives are a riddle".[149] It was not quite as nebulous as this in 1860, though it was obviously far removed from his previous dogmatic faith. A sermon in 1861 on education as the "cultivation of the intellect and the character, and not the communication of useful knowledge", put his case exactly, and explained why he should be both so interested in a new natural theology and also be a liberal pedagogue who wished to change the university into a place for research and investigation, rather than for the teaching of accepted doctrines.[150]

Pattison in 1859 followed up his recommendations to the University Commission by writing a large report on elementary education in Protestant Germany for the Commission on Popular Education. His comparisons were not quite so unfavourable as his previous contrasts between theology in Germany and England, but he saw little use for Church instruction in the schools. Pattison's intellectual stature was not, however, questioned, and his articles in the *Quarterly Review* on Scaliger, Huet, Montaigne and others, earned him respect. He was an outstanding examiner in the school of *literae humaniores* and, once the frowning cliffs of his reserve had been scaled, a teacher almost of the personal quality of Jowett.

---

[147] W.R. Ward, *op. cit.*, p. 113.
[148] A. & E. Sidgwick, *Henry Sidgwick, A Memoir*, p. 404.
[149] M. Pattison, *op. cit.*, pp. 327-8.
[150] M. Pattison, *Sermons*, pp. 44-71, especially p. 56.

Cambridge men never tired of underlining one of the defects of the Oxford system: the bitterness of party politics. Tractarian belligerence sent Jowett and Temple to find an alternative, but not in Evangelicalism which was just as dogmatic in its opposing assertions. Goldwin Smith, another who went through the same baptism, said that there could be only one way for such spirits — to coalesce with the "knot of original Liberals" who had remained from the Oxford of the 1820's.[151] The friend who effected the link was probably H. B. Wilson of St. John's. Fourteen years older than Jowett, Wilson was already a Fellow by 1825 and so knew the Latitudinarian developments in Oxford before the Tractarian onslaught. Tait was a comparable figure, except that he left Oxford in 1842 while Wilson remained until 1850, in time to help with the liberal resurgence after the High Church *débâcle*.

A faint air of mystery hung about Wilson. He became the editor of *Essays and Reviews* (i.e., he collected the articles together and sent them to the printer without alteration), but he was not really the prominent leader and man of action suggested in the prosecutions which followed the book. Perhaps his long tenure of a country parish obscured his talents, or perhaps he did not advertise himself. A High Church writer, speaking from "personal knowledge", said that there were few men living "on whose critical judgment of Plato and Aristotle we would more implicitly rely... as a classical scholar and a master of Grecian philosophy, he is, in the fullest sense, *'factus ad unguem'* " — but he was a recluse of the study, a "conscientious but very sensitive and nervous tutor of his college".[152]

Wilson undoubtedly had an effect on the young. R. B. Kennard, his pupil and friend, when preaching the funeral panegyric in 1888, spoke of the Bamptons of 37 years previously being attended by a "vast academical audience" which increased in numbers and enthusiasm. Kennard also described Sunday evenings at St. John's given over to private lectures on the epistles, which drew undergraduates.[153]

Jowett, who was not to be taken in, praised Wilson. He wrote to Stanley, Edward Caird and Charles Voysey, at various times between 1858 and 1870 on Wilson's qualities. To Florence Nightingale he said that, "Mr Wilson is a very able and powerful man (did you ever see his Bampton lectures?): if he had health and a little more knowledge of the

---

[151] Abbott, I, pp. 177, 273. Wilson and Jowett were on close terms by 1850 - cf. Abbott, I, p. 139.

[152] *Church Monthly*, January, 1861, p. 7.

[153] R.B. Kennard, *In Memory of Henry Bristow Wilson*, pp. 27, 36.

world, he would be very eminent indeed", while he told Caird that he had "great confidence in Wilson's ability and high principle".[154] Another tribute came from the honest doubters. Wilson did useful work in his theology and philosophy reviews for the *Westminster*, but withdrew in January, 1858, evidently because of criticism from churchmen or from the *Westminster's* own public. George Eliot wrote urgently to the publisher that this was a great loss: "I think ability and conscientiousness in the execution of the work undertaken, so much more important elements in a contributor than an unrestrained 'outspokenness', that I shall not cease to regret Wilson's alienation, until I hear that you have replaced him by someone who, being more undaunted, is equally well-informed and judicious".[155] Kennard went further: Wilson was for him the "natural leader of the liberal party in the Church of England". But that was a preacher's licence.

Wilson, born in 1803, was educated at the Merchant Taylors' school and became Tutor of his college in 1832. He filled several university offices, select preacher, public examiner in 1836 and 1850, and finally Professor of Anglo Saxon in 1839. Wilson's first published work, in 1841, was a letter to the Rev. T. T. Churton on subscription, which he wrote in reaction to Tract 90. His comments on the Tractarian position led Ward to publish a contentious pamphlet in reply.[156] A sermon in October, 1843, on *The Independence of particular Churches*, clearly foreshadowed his teaching in the Bamptons and essays: an ecumenical unity of Christendom was not yet possible because of national differences, but within a nation religious accord should be possible if the Church was comprehensive enough and allowed each man the right of private judgment.[157] Wilson supported university reform though, unlike Jowett and Pattison, doubted the wisdom of the German professorial system, in a pamphlet published in 1855. He was consistently an enemy of the traditionalists, and his action in joining Tait as one of the tutors who censured Tract 90 was never forgiven, as Pusey showed — Wilson was "an old opponent and heretic in his Bampton lectures".[158] That was also because, among other things, Wilson thought that Zwinglianism was

---

[154] Jowett MSS, ff. 35-9, letter to Florence Nightingale, July, 1862. Abbott, I, pp. 403, 442.

[155] *The George Eliot Letters*, II, p. 420. Wilson quickly resumed the reviews. Cf. also his larger articles, *WR*, January, 1857, pp. 134-172, and July, 1862, pp. 40-62.

[156] W.G. W[ard], *A few words in support of No. 90 of the Tracts for the Times, partly with reference to Mr Wilson's letter, passim.*

[157] H.B. Wilson, *The Independence of particular Churches*, pp. 4, 25-6.

[158] Pusey MSS, letter to Keble, 23 October, 1861.

the best approach to the Eucharist in the modern age, and he interpreted "This is my body" purely figuratively. But he did not commend himself to Evangelicals either, for Protestantism, he held, was "not any of the systems of doctrine set up at the Reformation period, in opposition to the Roman Church... but [consisted] in the vindication of the *natural* and Christian freedom of churches and individuals against the assumption of Rome to impose doctrine".[159]

The other bridge figure, though older, was Baden Powell, who outlasted all the original liberals and remained associated with Oxford until his death in 1860. Powell, born in 1796, became a Fellow of Oriel and an intimate of Whately (whose sister-in-law he married), and thus might be classed as a "Noetic". He graduated in 1817 with a first class in Mathematics and was ordained in 1820, returning to Oxford as Savilian Professor of Geometry in 1827. Powell's first reputation was in the scientific world for his work on optics and radiation, the most important publications in these fields being in the 'thirties and 'forties, and for his researches with Herschel, Babbage and Airy he was elected a Fellow of the Royal Society in 1824, while still a country vicar.[160] Powell served on the Council of the Society repeatedly, and he was also a Fellow of the British Association. Merz, in his *History of European Thought in the Nineteenth Century*, said that the decade 1835-45 in science was entirely dominated by the remarkable discoveries of Melloni, Powell and others on the nature of heat.[161] In fact, his range of interests in science was wide, from treatises on the Differential and Integrated Calculus, and the Geometry of Curves, to a work on the undulatory theory of light, and many reports for the Royal Society and British Association. Far from being a merely academic writer he also had a gift for popularisation, as was shown in his *History of Natural Philosophy*, in 1834, and in his public lectures. For these he made his own models, and one on comets became famous, as audiences flocked outside to see the heavenly bodies which had been graphically described to them.

The Savilian Professor was urbane, quiet in speaking, sedate in manner. But there was obvious energy. The Royal Society obituary spoke of the revolution worked in his subject at Oxford. He was the acknowledged representative of mathematical and physical science in the older university — "we may say the only representative", for when he

---

[159] H.B. Wilson, *The Communion of Saints*, pp. 134-7, 170-1.
[160] *Dictionary of National Biography*, XVI, pp. 237-8.
[161] J.T. Merz, *A History of European Thought in the Nineteenth* Century, II, p. 105.

was appointed science was at a low ebb. But by 1860 Oxford scientists were held in honour because of his efforts.[162] Powell was the friend of T. H. Huxley and, like him, a believer in the "great principle of orderly evolution". Darwin acknowledged that he gathered from Powell's work the logical weapons by which he reasoned on his collected facts.[163] Sir William Grove said that he had read through *The Unity of Worlds* nine times, while Robert Stephenson saw it as his "second bible", to which he owed the mental happiness of his life.[164]

Powell might have been a scientist who happened to be a clergyman, just as he might have rested his religious belief only on an objective, external reality like the uniformity of nature. But he was a religious zealot as well, and in his last years his grounds for faith seemed almost entirely subjective and interior. His scientific reforms were the counterpart of his Latitudinarian friends' attempts to revive theology in Oxford in the 'twenties. He could preach extempore sermons on the most intricate subjects without wandering from his theme. The clarity was applied unmercifully to traditional divinity. He supported Renn Dickson Hampden, the Regius Professor of Divinity, whom the Tractarians wished to depose for heresy, and the *British Critic* linked his name with Hampden's for teaching "fearful neologisms". But Powell asked whether the theological student "shall be taught and encouraged to think for himself, whether theology shall be propounded on the basis of rational enquiry?".[165] That was the basis of the quarrel and not necessarily an antipathy towards High Churchmanship: Powell opposed any conservatism, whether Evangelical or Tractarian, on the old Latitudinarian principle which became the new liberal tenet, that nothing should be closed to investigation, and God had willed it so. He quoted from Hampden to show how the Church had opposed Galileo, and in 1839, in *Tradition Unveiled*, he accused Newman of the same sort of bigotry.[166] The Tractarian J. B. Mozley, in a letter in 1844, included Powell among the aggressive liberals, "they hate us so", and Pusey dismissed him as a "rationalist of old, before the Tracts".[167] That was in 1861; at least it

---

[162] *Proceedings of the Royal Society*, November, 1860 — February, 1862, XI, pp. xxvi-xxix.

[163] C. Darwin, *The Origin of Species*, p. xx.

[164] W. Tuckwell, *Pre-Tractarian Oxford*, pp. 213-4, and cf. F. Bunsen, *A Memoir of Baron Bunsen*, II, p. 497, "Baden Powell's *Unity of Worlds* has been very helpful to me".

[165] *The British Critic*, April, 1834, pp. 415-434. B. Powell, *Remarks on a Letter from the Rev. H.A. Woodgate to Viscount Melbourne*, p. 5.

[166] B. Powell, *Tradition Unveiled*, p. 68, and cf. his *Natural Philosophy*, p. 182.

[167] *Letters of the Rev. J.B. Mozley*, p. 168. Pusey MSS, letter to Keble, 23 October, 1861.

suggested that Powell was consistent in his attitude. When Hampden vacated the Regius chair in 1847, Whately proposed that it be continued in the same Latitudinarian vein with either Samuel Hinds or Powell as the holder.

A liberal veteran, the professor advocated university reform — naturally: he served on the Commission and obviously thought that the bill did not go far enough. Hence he joined Stanley and others in a petition to the Prime Minister against the retention of clerical fellowships in such force. Powell was also a member of a deputation to parliament in 1855 asking for abolition of matriculation tests, so that Dissenters could be admitted to the university. He wrote an advanced tract on state education — a favourite theme of his —, with prevalent misconceptions on religious grounds in mind, in 1840.[168] In the midst of all this activity Powell still found time to become a highly proficient musician and painter. He rejoiced in a large family and married three times. There was evidently something about his personality which made him elastic and supple, a clerical scientist with a difference, whose liberalism was continuously developing. It was a pity that most churchmen knew him only as a fighter.

Jowett did not wish to become a leader, but his Commentary might suggest the direction in which the others were moving. It opened up new fields and was theologically far more advanced than anything that Powell, as the most notorious of the Oxford men, had written. The least notorious liberal, Temple, asked some pointed questions about the new St. Paul in a letter written in 1856. Temple evidently felt some disquiet about Jowett's work, if not Stanley's, and since the Commentary had been dedicated to him — Jowett spoke of the "blessing of a never — failing friendship" — he also shared some responsibility for it. The letter shows the wide differences existing in a group that its enemies thought was uniform and consistent. Temple admitted a good deal, the need for a new metaphysic, a fairly radical criticism of the bible, and, though no one could accuse him of cowardice, he wished to be circumspect rather than "over-honest". He preferred generalities rather than following up his conclusions. But he correctly pointed out Jowett's one-sidedness and his restricted view of the Atonement.

"You seem to me much too controversial and, when engaged in controversy, very unmerciful", Temple wrote. "I miss in you something

---

[168] B. Powell, *State Education considered with reference to prevalent misconceptions on religious grounds, passim.*

of that 'economy' whereby Maurice manages to express his doctrine in the phraseology of the Articles. You run to the opposite extreme and insist upon expressing all that you have to say in words as unlike those of your opponents as you can find". Jowett had attacked the word "sacrifice". But Temple thought it was hopeless to try to get rid of it, "it expresses to most people not merely the idea of satisfaction to Divine Justice but that of absolute surrender of self to love and duty". Jowett wrote of the Atonement from only his own experience, but many other people were impressed with a sense (which he denied) that "sin has a kind of prolific power working evil for ever after". Temple also thought that he had been unnecessarily hard on the epistle to the Hebrews. "It is always worth while if you are teaching men to give up a common interpretation to tell them what they must put in the place of it. This you have not done". "While you are negative you are in earnest, when you become positive you seem to get feeble and cold". He advised Jowett not to publish yet his projected essays on scepticism and prayer. "I think if you wait a few years you will better see what you have to deal with".[169]

Jowett, however, did not change his tone and, in any case, he had defended his method of argument with the essay on casuistry in the Commentary, which criticised overscrupulousness. He thought that the liberal movement was fragmented and certainly too muted. By 1858 he was talking of the next stage in their progress: a volume ten years ahead of its time.

---

[169] Jowett MSS, Box E, package δ, letter from Temple to Jowett, undated but probably 1856.

CHAPTER TWO

"THE CAUSE OF RELIGIOUS AND MORAL TRUTH"

The first and the last thing about *Essays and Reviews* was that it was quite unplanned. This was the fount of all its troubles. Despite what the religious newspapers said, the Stanleyites did not unite finally to lay waste the Church, though Jowett, at the other extreme, was certainly wrong in claiming that the authors only knew one another slightly.

The promoter of the scheme was not a theologian at all but the Oxford bookseller John W. Parker junior, whose speculation known as the *Oxford and Cambridge Essays*, begun in 1855 as the first fruits of the reformed universities, had come to an end after 61 essays had been published in four annual volumes. To fill in the interim he proposed publishing a further speculation, a combined volume. The American *Church Monthly*, stating "what we know to be the facts", believed that a deep design was involved; everyone in Oxford knew of preparatory meetings between four of the radicals, and much to-ing and fro-ing between Balliol and Rugby. So it was a Machiavelli-like Temple, "subtle, erudite, uncandid", who organised his colleagues for the assault.[1] But the figures actually responsible were the more unlikely ones of Wilson and Pattison who had worked together on the *Westminster Review* and saw the need (which that organ did not satisfy) for a "free treatment" but yet in "a reverential spirit" (Wilson) of theological and kindred subjects.[2] The beginnings were as small as this : though at that time, January, 1858, Wilson hoped that the volume would develop into an annual series (he had been editor of the *Oxford Essays*), there was no guarantee that this would be the case: the volume could have appeared quietly and been soon forgotten. But Wilson, in particular, canvassed his friends, among others, believing that a useful opportunity had presented itself.

Temple in later life exaggerated the fortuitous manner in which *Essays and Reviews* emerged, but his statement conveys his strength of feeling about the matter: "I did not even ask who was to be the editor; and did not know till he wrote to ask me for my paper. There was neither plan

---

[1] *Church Monthly*, January, 1861, p. 11.

[2] MSS Pattison 52, ff's 95-7. Cf. M. Francis, "Origins of *Essays and Reviews*", in *The Historical Journal*, XVII, 4 (1974), pp. 797-811.

nor organisation. The *Oxford Essays* had suggested the publication. And these new essays were supposed to be, and as regards composition actually were, as independent of each other as the different papers in the *Oxford Essays*".[3] Jowett said that the authors simply took the subjects which suited them, "without concert and without seeing one another's writing", and Wilson edited without alteration.[4]

In the first place, therefore, the essayists were guilty of lack of care and foresight; there was little preparation or consultation, and this suggested that they were mere opportunists. This was a lighthearted approach in a serious situation. But, secondly, *was* the book as undesigned as they claimed? The fact that by January, 1858, Wilson had recruited Williams as a contributor shows that he had a radical tendency in mind, and this is borne out by a letter which Jowett wrote to Stanley in the following August:

"Wilson wishes me to write to you respecting a volume of Theological Essays which he has already mentioned... The object is to say what we think freely within the limits of the Church of England. A notice will be prefixed that no one is responsible for any notions but his own. It is, however, an essential part of the plan that names shall be given, partly for the additional weight which the articles will have if the authors are known, and also from the feeling that on such subjects as theology it is better not to write anonymously. We do not wish to do anything rash or irritating to the public or the University, but we are determined not to submit to this abominable system of terrorism, which prevents the statement of the plainest facts, and makes true theology or theological education impossible".

The two friends had evidently had some discussion earlier about discretion, but Jowett pressed his argument:

"Pusey and his friends are perfectly aware of your opinions, and the Dean's, and Temple's and Müller's, but they are determined to prevent your expressing them. I do not deny that in the present state of the world the expression of them is a matter of great nicety and care, but is it possible to do any good by a system of reticence? For example, I entirely agree with you that no greater good could be accomplished for religion and morality than the abolition of all subscriptions; but how will this ever be promoted in the least degree, or how will it be possible for any one in high station ever to propose it, if we only talk it over in private?"

[3] Temple Appreciation, pp. 204-5.
[4] Abbott, I, p. 347.

Again he urged Stanley:

> "I want to point out that the object is not to be attained by any anonymous writing".[5]

Temple admitted, "I asked, before I agreed to write, what the probable line would be. I was told that it would be in the Liberal direction, but strictly within the limits allowed by the Church of England".[6] It was too late to speak of "dismay" when the book appeared, when the stipulation that "nothing should be written which was inconsistent with the position of ministers of our church", was shown to be empty. Temple suffered most from an editorial policy, or lack of it, which forced the writers, out of loyalty to one another, not to criticise opinions far more extreme than their own.

The famous preface is a *crux* here. The previous essays had borne an opening statement, as in the 1855 Oxford volume, that they were the product of no school: each author was "responsible for his opinions and for none but his own; and no attempt has been made to give a general unity of thought to the publication". The new collection was launched similarly:

To The Reader.

> "It will readily be understood that the Authors of the ensuing Essays are responsible for their respective articles only. They have written in entire independence of each other, and without concert or comparison.
>
> "The Volume, it is hoped, will be received as an attempt to illustrate the advantage derivable to the cause of religious and moral truth, from a free handling in a becoming spirit, of subjects peculiarly liable to suffer by the repetition of conventional language, and from traditional methods of treatment".

The importance of this preface for the writers was obvious. Like the essayists who preceded them, each stressed his individual character: there was no joint responsibility — everyone would see that as soon as the table of contents was perused. "It will readily be understood..." wrote Wilson or Jowett. Yet nothing was so misunderstood or overlooked in the succeeding controversy as the Address to the Reader. Thirlwall, who knew perfectly well that it was modelled on earlier ones, jeered at such "curious preliminary remarks". *The Guardian* said that it was obviously

---

[5] *Ibid.*, p. 275.
[6] Temple Memoirs, II, p. 605. Temple Appreciation, p. 204.

inserted "for legal purposes". The preface, in fact, failed conspicuously in its effect. This was partly because of its ambiguity — the second paragraph, unlike the first, admitted a conscious theme ("the cause of religious and moral truth", to be treated in unconventional language) — and also because a highly selective choice of authors resulted from Wilson's efforts. Critics drew their own conclusions. The preface was a smokescreen designed to hide the unity, the form of the book was deliberate — an haphazard structure unleashing on the public extreme views which a better-composed work would have qualified — and so was the order of contributions: Temple's mild essay was meant to draw the reader in, and he became more enmeshed until he finally reached Jowett's atheism.

Even the name had some deep meaning. Why was the title *Essays and Reviews* chosen? It was an important question. For the most controversial religious book of the nineteenth century it was a neutral, ordinary, not to say pedestrian, title. But might the reader be more seduced by seeing something so innocuous on the spine of a book — *Essays and Reviews* rather, than, for example, something like *Sesame and Lilies, Sartor Resartus,* or *Lux Mundi?* Of course this was nonsense: the fact was that the essayists did not even bother to spend time on choosing a title. But speculations of this sort showed how far the preface failed in its purpose; and its ambiguity and brevity again suggested the haste and lack of thought in the preparation of the volume as a whole.

The haste had immediate consequences as well as long term ones. Wilson could not find many contributors able to write without proper consultation; and those who did provided material already to hand, or wrote with a speed that they afterwards regretted. Stanley was the chief of those who had doubts about the project which could not be stifled. He wanted a theological review, or a whole series of volumes, and he feared the effects of an open alliance. So, to the chagrin of Jowett particularly, he sent a refusal. When the book appeared, Stanley felt that his caution was justified; he would have been linked with authors who were unpardonably rash, "throwing out statements, without a grain of proof, which can have no other object than to terrify and irritate".[7] Objections by Hort and Max-Müller, for much the same reasons, narrowed the circle still further. Alexander Grant was prevented by an Indian appointment. Bishop William Thomson and G. D., later Dean, Boyle escaped appearing in the volume because, intentionally or not, they did not get

---

[7] Prothero, II, p. 34.

their papers to the printer on time.[8] Wilson applied to Pattison to substitute for Hort, and at the last minute Temple and Powell were brought in to remedy other defections. As a result Temple wrote his essay in a few hours and it was, in fact, a revised version of an address that he intended for a British Association service, with unthinking statements and generalisations that he found difficult to defend. He sent it direct to the printer.

In Powell's case the results were more serious. He used part of a series of lectures given at a fashionable High Church in London when no one questioned, or perhaps understood, the "neology" contained in them, and these were in themselves a summary of his book which appeared in 1859. When the essay was published it only seemed as if Powell was confirmed in his errors; he had made no attempt to answer his critics or be more positive. Why should he repeat his views (men asked) unless he wished to make them more clear, more damaging? But perhaps the trend of *Essays and Reviews* would have been the same had time not been so pressing: Jowett adapted an article intended for the new edition of his Commentary, but too late for it, and its provocative tone owed nothing to a printer's deadline.

The wonder of *Essays and Reviews* is that chance should have brought such a team finally together. But it is equally startling that their joint work was sent to the press without more ado. Even Wilson, conscious that he preferred to include only strong liberals, must have halted at the spectacle presented by Parker's announcement in his Spring List for 1860. Did he have second thoughts? The contents were as follows:

The Education of the World, by Frederick Temple, D. D.
Bunsen's Biblical Researches, by Rowland Williams, D. D.
On the Study of the Evidences of Christianity, by Baden Powell, M. A., F. R. S.
Séances Historiques de Genève. The National Church, by Henry Bristow Wilson, B. D.
On the Mosaic Cosmogony, by C. W. Goodwin, M. A.
Tendencies of Religious Thought in England, 1688-1750, by Mark Pattison, B. D.
On the Interpretation of Scripture, by Benjamin Jowett, M. A.

---

[8] W. Tuckwell, *Reminiscences of Oxford*, p. 226. H. Kirk Smith, *William Thomson, Archbishop of York, His Life and Times*, p. 157. G.D. Boyle, *The Recollections of the Very Rev. G.D. Boyle*, p. 49.

(Goodwin — the only layman of the seven — was secured through the good offices of Dr Williams). It was certainly a united university production. At a stroke the most radical clergymen in the Church of England, save one or two, had apparently made common cause in one book. And all the controverted questions seemed to have been raised together — Genesis, Germanism, Atonement and eternal punishment, the alienation of the masses from the Church, the infallibility of the bible: hardly a vexed topic was left untouched.

However, and perhaps paradoxically, in the astonishment produced by the list of authors and contents may lie the justification for the hurry and an answer to the doubts concerning the book. Arnold and Hare, as the *Westminster Review* had once noted, had lived and died without making themselves heard; but that could never be the fate of the writers of *Essays and Reviews*. This had two effects. "You see what a crew I am going to take an oar with", wrote Williams. "Wish us *bon voyage*".[9] It did not matter if Jowett had little sympathy for Powell's tone and that, in a markedly Oxford volume, the Cambridge contributors looked isolated, nor that Williams also disliked the approach adopted by Powell, while Pattison's object was not clear to him. As Williams said, "the need is of fellowship", and that underlay everything. Secondly, in fellowship, they had spoken out. Suppression (that "abominable system of terrorism") had gone far enough, it now covered all opinion, and the liberals could no longer be cautious "as a condition of real usefulness", said Jowett.[10] Though he found one of the essays "most offensive in tone", Temple held that the book broke through the "mischievous reticence which was crusting over the clergy and damaging the very life of the Church". "Many, perhaps most, will think the price too high. I cannot think so".[11] They assented to the hopes of Bunsen, doyen of them all, when he said in 1857 that the tyranny and bigotry in Britain touching religious thought must be broken down, but "if we show that our apparent destruction is restoration... we shall be heard".[12]

Essays and Reviews was published on 21 March, 1860. Temple's essay came first, naturally. It was a work of theology, but "scientific", in making no prior assumptions. Examine the world, said Temple, and you will be convinced of the idea of progress; then you may draw religious

---

[9] Williams, I, p. 386. Williams originally wished to remain anonymous, MSS Pattison 52, f. 97.
[10] Jowett MSS, f. 23, letter to Florence Nightingale, September, 1861.
[11] Temple Appreciation, p. 215. Temple Memoirs, I, p. 285.
[12] *The Autobiography and Diary of Samuel Davidson*, p. 75.

implications. It was thus the best introduction to an important theme in
the essays, theology as a developing or progressive science. Temple had
believed in progressive revelation since at least 1843, i.e., as he began his
post-graduate career at Balliol and read German authors in earnest.[13] In
the background of the essay was F. W. Robertson's translation of
Lessing's "The Education of the Human Race", published posthumously
in 1858, while the analogy between mankind's intellectual growth and the
individual's development was familiar (though with important differences) from Hare, Arnold, Thirlwall and Niebuhr. Arnold long before
said, "The human species has gone through a state of less fullness of
moral knowledge, or less enlightened conscience, as compared with its
subsequent attainments, just as every individual has done".[14] The notion
of stages of development had a wide currency. "Have we not heard
something like this before?" asked *The Guardian*, recalling that Stanley
had "revealed to the world the fact that the Church was destined to pass
through three stages", and that brought to mind Bishop Hinds' "Three
Temples", the belief preached by Whately's Latitudinarian colleague in
1829 that "all revelation is progressive, but especially that whereby God
has revealed himself".[15]

Temple's argument was that the study of history disclosed how man's
conscience had been educated, a spiritual growth that was not the same
as material progress. "Man is a spiritual as well as a material creature",
and "must be subject to the laws of the spiritual as well as to those of the
material world". History was to be divided into stages, corresponding to
childhood, youth and manhood, to each of which certain races made
distinctive contributions. "First come Rules, then Examples, then
Principles. First comes the Law, then the Son of Man, then the Gift of
the Spirit. The world was once a child under tutors and governors until
the time appointed by the Father. Then, when the fit season had arrived,
the Example to which all ages should turn was sent to teach men what
they ought to be. Then the human race was left to itself to be guided by
the teaching of the Spirit within". The Hebrews disciplined the human
conscience in their conviction of the unity and spirituality of God. Rome
disciplined the human will, Greece the reason and taste, Asia the spiritual
imagination.

Progressive revelation brought with it a problem. A youthful mankind
needed examples, but if Christ's revelation had come to modern man,

---

[13] *ER*, pp. 1-49. Temple Appreciation, p. 82.
[14] T. Arnold, *Sermons*, II, p. 438.
[15] *G*, 4 April, 1860, p. 317. S. Hinds, *The Three Temples*, p. 1.

would his divinity have been as easily recognised? "The faculty of Faith has turned inwards", wrote Temple, "and cannot now accept any outer manifestations of the truth of God. Our vision of the Son of God is now aided by the eyes of the Apostles, and by that aid we can recognise the Express Image of the Father. But in this we are like men who are led through unknown woods by Indian guides. We recognise the indications by which the path was known, as soon as those indications are pointed out; but we feel that it would have been quite vain for us to look for them unaided". Modern man knew more than the early Christians the "precise outline of the truth", "they had not the same clearness of understanding as we", nor could the past sit in judgment on the "developed religious understanding" of modern man. But the apostles had a "keenness of perception which we have not, and could see the immeasurable difference between our Lord and other men as we could never have seen it. Had our Lord come later, He would have come to mankind already beginning to stiffen into the fixedness of maturity. The power of His life would not have sunk so deeply into the world's heart".

Temple held that man had now reached the last stage, both in the history of the world and the Church. As the individual developed, so the same law could be found in the growth of the Church. There had been no further revelation, and the "more advanced section" realised that the Church could not claim infallibility. "The Church, in the fullest sense, is left to work out, by her natural faculties, the principles of her own action. And whatever assistance she is to receive in doing so, is to be through those natural faculties, and not in spite of them or without them".

Thus, the dogmatism of earlier ages must be modified. The decisions taken then were, on the whole, right, but a vast number were now obsolete, and many doctrinal statements were plainly unfitted for permanent use. The career of dogmatism in the Church was in many ways similar to the hasty generalisations of early manhood. Logical statements to clothe the truth were necessary, but "it belongs to a later period to see 'the law within the law', which absorbs such statements into something higher than themselves". Another step in this advance was the Reformation and its main lesson was toleration, which "implies a confession that there are insoluble problems upon which even Revelation throws but little light". But, in obedience to the universal law of development, the lesson of toleration was best learned slowly. "The strongest argument in favour of tolerating all opinions is that our conviction of the truth of an opinion is worthless unless it has established itself in spite of the most strenuous resistance..." Evidently, that happy situation had now been attained. We had now also realised that an enlarged understanding of the world must accompany (modify?) the doctrine of revelation. "Creation is a new book to be read by the side of Revelation". "There are found to be more things in heaven and earth than were dreamt of in the patristic theology".

Temple dealt with conscience in his section on the bible. Logically, on his argument, the bible was a record of antiquity — but this was a gain, rather than a disadvantage. For scripture was not drawn up in precise statements of faith or detailed precepts of conduct — had it been, "we should have had no alternative but either permanent subjection to an. outer law, or loss of the highest instrument of self-education". But the bible, from its very form, was exactly adapted to the needs of the modern age. "It is a history; even the doctrinal parts of it are cast in a historical form, and are best studied by considering them as records of the time at which they were written". If there were conflicts of authority, "we use the Bible... not to over-ride, but to evoke the voice of conscience. When conscience and the Bible appear to differ, the pious Christian immediately concludes that he has not really understood the Bible". He admitted that it was the principle of private judgment which "puts conscience between us and the Bible, making conscience the supreme interpreter whom it may be a duty to enlighten, but whom it can never be a duty to disobey".

The essayist believed that the high value which (as a Kantian) he gave to conscience acted as a brake on any wild or irrational exercise of private judgment. He was, therefore, able to greet biblical criticism with open arms, as he identified the bible with the voice of conscience:

> "He is guilty of high treason against the Faith who fears the result of any investigation, whether philosophical, or scientific, or historical... Even the mistakes of careful and reverent students are more valuable now than truth held in unthinking acquiescence".

He concluded that "clarity was valuable above all things except godliness". "We are now men governed by principles, if governed at all, and cannot rely any longer on the impulses of youth or the discipline of childhood". The adult man learned "not to attempt the solution of insoluble problems and to have no opinion at all on many points of the deepest interest".

Temple was consistent in his thought. In the 1856 *Oxford Essays* he held that the extension of national education was urgent because of the progress of the human mind: the Church could no longer be too dogmatic.[16] His Bamptons of 1884 reconciled science and faith by an evolutionary theory. The imperfections of the world "are like the imperfections of a half-completed picture not yet ready to be seen".[17] But the college sermons of the 'sixties gave a more definite place to scripture. Though written in human language and subject to human thought, the bible (he said) had an indwelling divine authority unlike anything else that the world had ever seen. Yet the "unique power" of scripture lay in its being the voice of conscience, while its historical nature required one to search for the "unchangeable law of right and truth and goodness", that which was "above and beyond and beneath all that exists or can exist", and which could not (presumably) be equated with the outward written form of scripture.[18]

What influences caused Temple to think in this way? Temple saw the past in terms of "earlier" or "lower" stages to which the human race could not return. This involved him in some poor historical judgments: the middle ages must be a period of total dogmatism, while the Reformation, as the next upward step, must embody the principle of toleration, modifying the "early dogmatism by substituting the spirit for the letter, and practical religion for precise definitions of truth". Despite their view of the declension of history, the Deists also contrasted the medieval period and the Renaissance in this way, while it became a commonplace for Herder, von Treitschke and others who saw Luther as the liberator of the modern world, making man's conscience autonomous and laying the foundations of the ideal state. But the feeling of historical inevitability seemed to echo Lessing in whose scheme the Reformation figured as the epoch of toleration and unrestricted private judgment. The similarity between Lessing's title, in Robertson's recent version, and his own, and the resemblances in the argument, could not have been accidental. Temple did not see man's education simply as the "March of Mind", for that would have been merely utilitarian and it did not take sin seriously enough, but his emphasis on some factor, an ideal kernel like conscience, which would escape the solvents of history, looked back to Lessing. All the essayists thought similarly about this matter.

The second essay became an extended book review. Rowland Williams completed his work with great speed in the Christmas vacation of 1858. He had originally meant to write on Renan and would have caused even

---

[16] Oxford Essays, 1856, p. 244.
[17] F. Temple, The Relations between Religion and Science, p. 117.
[18] F. Temple, Sermons preached in Rugby School Chapel, 2nd series, pp. 34-6.

more controversy, for the *Vie de Jésus* was received with gasps when it appeared in 1863. But he turned to another foreign master. "Bunsen's Biblical Researches" caused much mystification. For which was Bunsen and which was Williams? The Dean of Arches complained about ambiguity; others spoke of Williams' gloss on Bunsen, or "The Chevalier Bunsen and his prophet Dr Williams".[19] He was accused of dishonest practice, of hiding behind another to propagate his own views; but the author only reverted to the form found in many of the previous *Oxford and Cambridge Essays*. That also explained the viewiness and generalised argument of the article, which might suit a book review but hardly the weighty volume which *Essays and Reviews*, under intense scrutiny, soon became.

Bunsen gave the professor an excellent platform as one who had written more for England than Germany in the last twenty years of his life, perhaps to remedy the century-long English indifference to exegetical study which he so much deplored. Long before Bunsen's arrival as Prussian ambassador in 1841 he had radical contacts. In 1833 he corresponded with Whately about Anglican liturgical reform and union with Dissenters. For him Arnold felt "all but idolatry", "so beautifully good, so wise, so noble-minded" (this to Hare and in similar tones to W. K. Hamilton), and in tribute named one of his daughters Frances *Bunsen Whately* Arnold.[20] The Baron signed his letters, "Yours sincerely in Plato and in Christ", and breathed his last saying, "gratitude to Niebuhr", by whose grave he was buried. Through Arnold Bunsen met Stanley, whom he introduced to the Prince Consort, and Stanley brought Jowett to him in turn; that was in 1844.[21] But Williams had a personal debt as well, for Bunsen had said of *Christianity and Hinduism* in 1856 that it was a book more nearly like his own than any other in England or Germany.[22] Bunsen, in literary retirement at Heidelberg, still remained a magnet: Williams made a pilgrimage in 1857, so did James McCosh in 1859, writing of an idyllic setting and the old lion as active as ever.[23] The dislike of conservative churchmen was in marked contrast, as they regarded Bunsen as one of the main influences in the dissemination of

---

[19] *G*, 23 May, 1860, p. 474, 25 June, 1862, p. 602.

[20] A.P. Stanley, *Life and Correspondence of Thomas Arnold*, I, pp. 303-4, II, p. 112. Cf. F. Bunsen, *A Memoir of Baron Bunsen*, II, p. 429.

[21] R.B. Kennard, "*Essays and Reviews*", Their Origin, History, General Characteristics and Significance, p. 53.

[22] F. Bunsen, *op. cit.*, II, p. 429, and cf. II, p. 497.

[23] J. McCosh, *The Supernatural in Relation to the Natural*, p. 365.

"Germanism". The *Christian Remembrancer* chided his *Hippolytus* in 1853; the *Quarterly Review* said of *Egypt's Place in Universal History* in 1859 that the credibility and scepticism of the author were alike extraordinary; and a cold obituary in *The Guardian* (the Baron died in November, 1860) spoke of his "intermeddling" which led to the Jerusalem bishopric (Anglican, Lutheran alternately) with all its anomalies.[24] It came as a shock, therefore, to have Bunsen erected as a kind of patron saint of theological scholarship, but it was (surely) all of a piece with everything else in *Essays and Reviews*. The act of homage, however, damaged his reputation still further.

Williams must have known that advocacy of Bunsen was a sensitive matter, for the French liberal de Pressensé had been harshly treated on this account some years before. But this did not deter him from a eulogy of one who "in our darkest perplexity has reared again the banner of truth", and ending with a couple of stanzas dismissed as either indifferent or ridiculous, depending on the temperament of the reviewer:

"Bunsen... My lips but ill could frame thy Lutheran speech,
　Nor suits thy Teuton vaunt our British pride —
But ah! not dead my soul to giant reach,
　That envious Eld's vast interval defied;
And when those fables strange, our hirelings teach,
　I saw by genuine learning cast aside,
Even like Linnaeus kneeling on the sod,
　For faith from falsehood severed, thank I GOD".

Despite extravagance of this sort, Williams wished to be helpful and to reassure the fearful that scripture came to new life under the hand of a modern German critic. No other author's work could furnish so pregnant a text for a discourse on the subject, he held. "It would be difficult to say on what subject Baron Bunsen is not at home".[25]

The understanding of revelation must be widened, said the Welsh professor. "There is hardly any greater question than whether history shows Almighty God to have trained mankind by a faith which has reason and conscience for its kindred, or by one to whose miraculous tests their pride must bow; that is, whether His Holy Spirit has acted through the channels which His Providence ordained, or whether it has departed from these so signally that comparative mistrust of them ever

---

[24] *Christian Remembrancer*, January, 1853, pp. 213, 281. *Quarterly Review*, April, 1859, p. 401. *G*, 5 December, 1860, p. 1071.
[25] *ER*, pp. 50-93.

afterwards becomes a duty". The "moral constituents of our nature, so often contrasted with Revelation, should rather be considered parts of its instrumentality. Those cases in which we accept the miracle for the sake of the moral lesson prove the ethical element to be the more fundamental".

The Baron had shown the way forward, completing in a grand synthesis the labours of Eichhorn, Ewald, Herder and Gesenius, so that there was truly a "pathway streaming with light " in Germany. All these writers replaced notions of external authority with an inner warrant based on "principles of reason and right, to which our heart perpetually responds, and our response to which is a truer sign of faith than such deference to a supposed external authority as would quench these principles themselves".

As for the source of man's inner authority, Bunsen ("as a countryman of Hegel") had spoken of the Spirit or Divine Thought bringing order out of confusion. On this ground he was able to say that the bible was inspired, for "the Bible is, before all things, the written voice of the congregation". The sacred writers were like us, and we were promised illumination from the same source. Discounting "supernaturalism", the essayist concentrated on re-interpreting the miraculous and infallible elements in scripture. The evidence of the canonical books showed principles perpetually true, "but not adequate to guarantee narratives inherently incredible or precepts evidently wrong". We were able to say this because we had within ourselves a "verifying faculty". Why should the least rational views of the gospels be the truest, or our faith have no human element and its records be exempt from historical law?

In contrast to those who would make Christianity a mere book religion, Bunsen laid the foundations of faith in the necessities of the human mind : "he believes in Christ, because he first believes in God and in mankind". And in Christ Bunsen found "brought to perfection that religious idea, which is the thought of the Eternal". If we were true to the witness within ourselves we, too, would recognise Christ, not the supernatural figure but the "moral saviour of mankind". Williams dealt at length with the reinterpretation of New Testament language that this claim implied, and he admitted that it was in a "philosophical sense".

The essayist reviewed Bunsen's most important works in turn, selecting their most original and startling features as he thought fit. Taken together, the Baron's writings demonstrated how the bible and church history could be set in a broader understanding of revelation. Williams spoke of the "law of growth traceable throughout the Bible as in the world", instead of (to quote his mentor) the "fiction of an external revelation". *Egypt's Place in Universal History* (English translation 1848 onwards) demanded that the narrow biblical chronology must be extended — perhaps even 20,000 years in regard to the emergence of civilised man. "The mention of such a term may appear monstrous to those who regard six thousand years as a part of Revelation. Yet it is easier to throw doubt on some of the arguments than to show that the conclusion in favour of a vast length is improbable". The traditions of Babylon, Sidon, Assyria and Iran were used by Bunsen to illustrate and confirm, though also to modify, our interpretation of Genesis. "Our deluge takes its place among geological phenomena, no longer as a disturbance of law from which science shrinks". As his *Egypt* sifted the historical data of scripture, so Bunsen's *Gott in der Geschichte* (1857) responded to its directly religious element, for example, in the belief that Moses intended to found a free religious society but was compelled to organise a sacerdotal system and formal religion because of the rudeness and hardness of heart of his people.

Williams particularly wished to defend the *Bibel-werk für die Gemeinde* (1858) which had received a poor welcome in this country. As for the *Hippolytus* (1853), he found this to be "pregnant and suggestive beyond any book of our time".

He admitted that Bunsen's writings showed a "vast induction on the destructive side". The command to Abraham to sacrifice Isaac, rather than coming from God, was given by the "fierce ritual of Syria, with the awe of a divine voice". The Pentateuch was not written by Moses, and the crossing of the Red Sea "may be interpreted with the latitude of poetry". The cursing psalms were hardly evangelically inspired; David did not foretell the Exile, nor were Psalms 22 and 23 prophecies of the crucifixion. Above all, the prophets were not divinely appointed to explain by a riddle the key to history. The Virgin Birth in Isaiah 7 was to take place in the reign of Ahaz, and the figure of the suffering servant in chapters 52 and 53 was better applied to Jeremiah. Micah's references to Bethlehem did not anticipate Christ's birth there. Daniel, "supposed to be specially predictive", was a history of past occurrences up to the reign of Antiochus Epiphanes. As for the New Testament, Hebrews was not Pauline, nor could II Peter claim apostolic authorship. All this demanded an adjustment to prevailing conceptions; yet not so large as was often supposed, for Williams quoted a plethora of authorities, including Luther, Calvin, Grotius, Butler, Bishop Chandler (who thought that only twelve passages in the Old Testament were directly Messianic), Coleridge, Arnold, Kidder and Keith, in support of Bunsen.

The essayist's language was often obscure. Bunsen himself had been likened to Maurice by the *Westminster Review* for building up vast edifices of words without any apparent meaning: Williams darkened the understanding still further by his slipshod speech. An example of this was his most notorious line, "the Bible is an expression of devout reason, and therefore is to be read with reason in freedom", in which he translated Bunsen's *"vernünftig"* as "devout reason". This would have been better omitted or given a whole sentence in clarification, drawing on Coleridge's version of "reason", which some of his readers would have readily understood. Such drawbacks — coupled with his strong criticism of adversaries — gave the essay a negative tone. However, Williams' concentration on the prophets, and on Isaiah in particular, reflected Bunsen's own interests. The bible was still modern man's best book, whatever respectful allusions were made to the first Buddhist *Sakya* and other writings of comparative religion, and he underlined his conclusions in *Christianity and Hinduism* on the function of prophecy in a universalist notion of revelation. Since there was "no chronological element in Revelation" (Bunsen), there could be no predictive element in prophecy. But Williams was more rash than Bunsen who retained some possibility of foresight or clairvoyance in certain prophecies. The prophets, like Christ himself, must be detached from their immediate historical antecedents; their importance lay in being teachers of moral truths, and they witnessed to Christ in the sense that, like him, they spoke of the values at the heart of Christianity which fulfilled the aspirations of all good men.

Powell died of thrombosis almost immediately after the publication of *Essays and Reviews*, in June, 1860, and the explanation of his last work was never forthcoming. Some thought it meaningless, but many regarded it as simply the summit of a career of scepticism. This was not fair to Powell who, on the Sunday before his death, had as usual both communicated and preached at the London church, St. Andrew's, Wells Street, which he attended, and who had also applied to preach the next Bampton lectures in Oxford in defence of Christianity. His essay, he wrote, was not intended to be controversial: "it is purely contemplative and theoretical", a "calm and unprejudiced" survey of the state of the argument about the Christian Evidences.[26]

Powell's first aim was to show the impossibility of miracle understood as a break in the law of nature, and this (he held) was a matter of clarification: it concerned the convictions and feelings of those who

---

[26] *Ibid.*, pp. 94-144.

thought that they "saw" the miracle. Among those convictions was the idea of "*a positive external Divine revelation* of some kind", which had formed the very basis of all hitherto received systems of Christian belief, and which found miracle necessary to authenticate it. But modern study only confirmed the earlier philosophical difficulty of appealing to evidential facts as variations of the natural order. And by making them matters of evidential facts present-day apologists must allow them to be investigated on critical grounds and supported by exact evidence. "When a reference is made to matters of *external fact* (insisted on as such) it is obvious that reason and intellect alone can be the proper judges of the evidence of such facts. When, on the other hand, the question may be as to points of moral or religious doctrine, it is equally clear, other and higher grounds of judgment and conviction must be appealed to". That division ran throughout the essay, and he criticised those who did not understand it. The appeal to the "sacredness" of an evidential fact only confused the issue.

The essayist went further: apologists alleged the historicity of the gospel miracles, as vouched for by the apostles' testimony, yet " from the nature of our antecedent convictions", the probability of some kind of mistake or deception somewhere in the records was greater than the probability occurring in the way described. Against the appeal to apostolic experience Powell brought in Hume: "a miracle is a violation of the laws of nature, and as firm and unalterable experience has established these laws, the proof against a miracle, from the very nature of the fact, is as entire as any argument from experience can possibly be imagined". A further argument, derived from an historical approach to doctrine, suggested that the apostles' contemporaries were circumscribed in the thought conditions of their time. With a firm belief in constant supernatural interposition they were as much blinded to the gospel as opponents to it had been since. Those who had living divine instruction were, nevertheless (said Powell), not superior to their times; there never existed an infallible age of exemption from prejudice and doubt. (But the Savilian Professor, no more than Hume, did not say that "evidence for the unusual cannot be entertained").

Once clarity had been established, the second aim was to define those "other and higher" grounds of judgment in moral and religious matters to which he had referred. Here Powell took up his theme of a faith which lay beyond historical accidents and had its exercise in the realm of spirit. "The more knowledge advances, the more it has been, and will be, acknowledged that Christianity, as a real religion, must be viewed apart from connexion with physical things". "In nature and from nature, by science and by reason, we neither have nor possibly can have evidence of a *Deity working miracles;*— for that, we must go out of nature and beyond science". Instead of a belief in the miraculous, as commonly understood, "it is rather in points of less definite character that any exercise of faith can take place". "The '*reason* of the hope that is in us' is not restricted to *external* signs, nor to any one kind of evidence, but consists of such assurance as may be most satisfactory to each earnest individual inquirer's own mind". "Many points of important religious instruction, even conveyed under the form of fictions (as in the instances of doctrines inculcated through parables) are more congenial to the spirit of faith than any relations of historical events could be".

The third aim was one found elsewhere in *Essays and Reviews*: to produce an historical pedigree for the liberal position, which would justify his distinction between inner and outer worlds. Powell's main authorities were Christian divines — Evangelicals, Tractarians (Tracts 18 and 85), and many others including Coleridge, Lyell, de Wette and Döderlein. In comparison with these authorities the evidentialist argument was weak, so he disparaged Paley for saying that "we are unable to conceive of revelations being made except by miracles", and for reducing the appeal for Christianity to a series of syllogisms. But Paley had also said, "once believe in a God, and all is easy" — thus, the attestation of miracles was not irresistible, and (a reference to Butler here), in the very uncertainty which remained, "the trial of faith lies", which implied that they must really rest upon some independent moral conviction.

If there was one theme in the essay, it was the need for theology to speak to the modern world. Powell stressed that there had been a change in the appeal to miracles: they were the rule formerly, and no difficulty was felt in speaking of them; but now that they were felt to be the exception, the evidential argument had assumed a far larger and more isolated importance than it deserved. But this raised deeper questions about the change in the understanding of theism and of revelation itself, consequent upon the new intellectual climate in Europe and America:

> "Thus considerations of a very different nature are now introduced from those formerly entertained; and of a kind which affect the *entire primary conception* of 'a revelation' and its authority, and not merely any alleged *external* attestation of its truth. Thus any discussion of the 'evidences' at the present day, must have a reference equally to the influence of the various systems, whether of ancient precedent or of modern illumination, which so widely and powerfully affect the state of opinion or belief".

Paley, as the symbol of outdated evidential logic, would soon be totally neglected. But Powell's target were his modern advocates who "betray an almost entire unconsciousness of the advance of opinion around them". Here the five references to Archbishop Whately were significant. "No man has dwelt more forcibly on miraculous evidence", even to becoming one of the "would-be philosophers" who argued that exceptions in science allowed the possibility of miracle, and that what was dismissed as impossible by one generation, because contrary to experience, might be accepted by another which had fuller knowledge. But the essayist turned the tables on the logical archbishop. His exceptions only pointed to the opposite — the "real and paramount dominion of the rule of *law* and *order*". The "far-famed" *Historic Doubts relative to Napoleon Bonaparte* only proved that the bible narrative was no more miraculous than the marvellous exploits of Napoleon or the paradoxical events of recent history, while Whately's theory of civilisation, intended to support Paley and the credibility of revelation, could be reversed completely by reading Darwin. But even Whately must see the difference between miracles as mere wonders and as "signs", and he would reject a Christ whose external attestation of his mission conflicted with his moral teaching. Powell meant to suggest how little a clever or "rhetorical" presentation of Christianity counted in the face of the deeper doubts and spiritual questions of the age. And nothing that Whately said could stand against his reiterated distinction between testimony and fact — whatever testimony alleged, the "fact" was that miracles did not occur, and all the witnesses in the world could not alter it. "No testimony can reach to the supernatural".

Stanley held that the essay represented the "common view of the religious world much more nearly than they like to admit",[27] and it was true that after 1860 the argument from miracle rapidly lost ground. J. B. Mozley in his Bamptons for 1865 valiantly restated the orthodox position, but Powell had already summed up the ordinary person's difficulties and proposed a new area of discussion. He also had the advantage of speaking as a practising scientist. In *The Spirit of the Inductive Philosophy* in 1855 the Savilian Professor described how the scientist generalised from the phenomena of a particular kind which he examined and, by use of analogy, established that all the phenomena of that kind were similar. "The process derives its whole force from the discovery and acceptance of sound and well-framed *analogies*" (hence),

---

[27] Prothero, II, p. 34.

"THE SOUL OF INDUCTION IS ANALOGY". The extension of inductive analogy and the law of continuity brought one finally to the conclusion that nature was totally uniform. "All induction begins and ends in the conception of order". No miracle could interrupt this nor, since uniformity must extend to the future as well, could any be postulated on the grounds of our yet incomplete knowledge.[28] In *Essays and Reviews*, with Faraday in support — his *Lectures on Mental Education* spoke of the consideration of natural laws and extended analogies correcting the errors of sense — the triumph of the inductive principle was complete.

The essay needed to be read alongside *The Order of Nature* (1859) for any proper appreciation of its aim. In this vast work Powell spoke of his moral objections to the old theories: thus, the argument from design used the model of a personal agent, whose contrivances were limited by the conditions of the case and the nature of his materials, and pursued by steps corresponding to human plans and operations, an "approach leading only to the most unworthy and anthropomorphic conceptions".[29] Mansel in his *Metaphysics* in 1857 had also warned of the limitation of arguments from design which confined the proof of design to instances of adaptation of means to a perceptible end — a demonstrated God who was a creature of the human imagination, adding nothing to the experience of his existence and encumbering theology with feeble arguments. Mansel quoted Waterland, "mischief is often done by pretending to strict and rigorous demonstrations" which only brought into question what was before unquestionable.[30]

Again, in the essay, Powell held that " 'creation' is only another name for our ignorance of the mode of production", and coupled this with praise for Darwin's "masterly volume which must soon bring about an entire reconstruction in favour of the grand principle of the self-evolving powers of nature" — a reconstruction that he had anticipated in 1855 in announcing that the "introduction of new species was a regular, not a casual phenomenon", and no species was essentially and inherently immutable, i.e., man did not appear suddenly, as in Genesis, and higher beings than man might yet evolve.[31] Most men thought that this meant that God had not created the world, but Powell's theory depended on a fine distinction between physical and moral causes which he only explained in the earlier volume. Nature, he held, did not show a first,

[28] B. Powell, *The Spirit of the Inductive Philosophy*, pp. 18-19.
[29] B. Powell, *The Order of Nature*, p. 238.
[30] H.L. Mansel, *Metaphysics*, p. 279.
[31] B. Powell, *The Philosophy of Creation*, p. 359.

efficient or moral cause, but only phenomena and their sequences. However, the vast system of universal law, unity and design suggested, by analogy, "mind". Professor Owen proposed a similar view at the British Association in 1858 — indeed, Powell quoted him in the essay — but he was godly, and no one drew sinister implications as they did when Powell reinterpreted creation as a doctrine of revelation and a matter of faith, not science.

The essay also lacked Powell's defence of his scientific position which he made in *The Spirit of the Inductive Philosophy*. Consequently, Hume loomed larger than he might have intended. The celebrated essay on miracles was, he admitted, basic. Mozley, for one, saw this as an advantage in opening up the Savilian Professor's argument. Hume unadorned had a clarity not possessed by Hume in the trimmings of nineteenth-century Idealist scientists like von Humboldt, Oersted and others whom Powell quoted earlier. Mozley asked whether the reasoning was as "scientific" as he claimed. When Powell appealed to experience he meant Hume's definition of it, but the uniformitarianism there was more philosophical than the product of pure research. The principle of analogy could only be functional, not speculative, and when it determined past, present and future, then the motivations of pure science had been exceeded. In addition, deductive logic might give total certainty, but inductive logic only suggested probability. Yet in using inductive logic Hume claimed that there was a certainty, not a probability, of miracles not occurring.[32]

Hume also emerged in Powell's statement that testimony "is but a second-hand assurance; — it is but a blind guide; testimony can avail nothing against reason". He failed to add the qualification that he had given, following Lyell, in *The Order of Nature*: he agreed with Hume that the credibility of a miracle could not be established on human testimony, but not, because as Hume said, human testimony was fallible, but "because human testimony is not the proper proof". Mozley could only comment, in a letter to Church in 1861, "Baden Powell's tacit argument is that a thing is not a fact because it rests upon a ground of faith in addition to ordinary testimony".[33]

To these criticisms Powell's reply seemed to be a principle of ambiguity: a man might think of miracles on a theological level, not a scientific one, which suggested that he might affirm one thing while

---

[32] J.B. Mozley, *Eight Lectures on Miracles*, p. 46.
[33] B. Powell, *The Order of Nature*, p. 287. *Letters of the Rev. J.B. Mozley*, p. 249.

meaning another. This cast doubt on the unity of one's experience and on the claims of religion on the external world; but it was a modern answer and could be found in various books on the relations of science and faith after 1860. And Powell was surely right to point out in *The Order of Nature* that the critical spirit which Hume and others represented was akin to the habit of mind encouraged by the Renaissance and Reformation. Churchmen should realise that the "speculations of the Rationalistic school, which create so much offence in the minds of orthodox Protestants, proceed on no other principles than those which dictate their own critical rejection of the ecclesiastical miracles" claimed by the Roman Church.[34]

H. B. Wilson's essay began not with a reference to German theology but Swiss, and with the introduction of an odd-sounding word, "multi-tudinist". As Wilson used it this was not the same as the French *multitudiniste*; he meant it as a contrast to individualist, a term which denoted a narrow sectarian view of the Church.[35] The full title was, "Séances Historiques de Genève — The National Church", and Wilson showed how the Swiss city, as evidenced in recent lectures, now questioned the individualist principle of its origins under Calvin. The essayist did not mention it, but the "Low Churchman", de Gasparin, was answered on lines like his own by the liberal, de Pressensé, in the preceding lectures.[36]

The essay was intended as a hit against the Evangelical party and its belief in eternal punishment.[37] Such a doctrine might be feasible when a small element in society was alienated, but it lacked cogency when a majority of the population were religiously disaffected on a scale previously unimagined. Nor was it justified by the threats facing the Church, for Wilson was optimistic about the coming changes. Men doubted only for sincere reasons; their difficulties were a native growth, not a "disease contracted by means of German inoculation" but a spontaneous recoil from the doctrines preached in church and chapel. "The sceptical movements in this generation are the result of observation and thought, not of passion", said Wilson.

---

[34] B. Powell, *The Order of Nature*, p. 419.

[35] Geoffrey Faber suggests that Bungener probably invented the word "le multitudin-isme", and this was translated directly as "multitudinist" by Wilson; *Jowett, A Portrait with Background*, p. 238. Cf. *Quarterly Review*, January, 1861, p. 479, "Wilson's absurd nomenclature, multitudinism".

[36] *Le Christianisme au Quatrième siècle : Séances Historiques données à Genève en Mars 1858, par Gasparin, Bungener et de Pressensé* (Geneva, 1858).

[37] *ER*, pp. 145-206.

In regard to the "heathen", "in what relation does the Gospel stand to these millions? Is there any trace on the face of its records that it even contemplated their existence?" "As to the necessity of faith in a Saviour in these peoples, when they could never have had it, no one, upon reflection, can believe in any such thing — doubtless they will be equitably dealt with. And when we hear fine distinctions drawn between covenanted and uncovenanted mercies, it seems either to be a distinction without a difference, or to amount to a denial of the broad and equal justice of the Supreme Being". Why not see men as germinal souls who would attain perfection in some after life — in the bosom of the "Universal Parent"? Instead of an imminent End and millenarian expectations, we must contemplate a "long future" which would extend to "worlds to come". Development must, therefore, have a *post-mortem* significance.

Thus placed at the opening of a new epoch, men must recognise the true nature of the English Church and its relation to society. In his Bampton lectures in 1851 Wilson had allowed that the political society and the spiritual occupied the same area, concerned the same individuals and had the same aims. Yet Christianity must not be seen simply as an instrument for accomplishing ordinary social and domestic ends (instead of raising a universal population into a condition truly Christian), for that would involve reproducing the absolute co-extensiveness of the spiritual and temporal societies, and, in the past, churches which had been so bound up with the body politic left no adequate room for the play of their moral influence. He had modified this by 1857, in the *Oxford Essays*, to hold that the only limit to toleration in a Church was the exclusion of those who excluded themselves on doctrinal grounds. [38] He now said (1860) that when the "office of the Church is properly understood", its objects would be seen to coincide nearly with those of the state. In fact, Church and State were only the nation considered under different aspects.

The essayist enlarged on this idea : public security and order must be upheld, but, conscious of its highest purposes, the state would desire that all its people should be brought under a moral influence which would supply motives of conduct, nobler, stronger and purer than those which imposed only an outward restraint. For the fulfilment of this desire, the nationalty "will throw its elements, or the best of them, into another mould", and out of them "constitute a spiritual society" to exercise such

[38] H.B. Wilson, *The Communion of Saints*, pp. 270-1. *Oxford Essays, 1857*, p. 128.

an improving influence. This society was the national Church. But the purpose both of Church and State would be defeated alike by "errors and mistakes in defining Church membership, and by a repulsive mode of Church teaching". The Church's teaching must be confined to matters in which both Church and State had a common interest, and the state could have no concern in a "system of relations founded on the possession of speculative truth".

> "Speculative doctrines should be left to philosophical schools. A national Church must be concerned with the ethical development of its members. And the wrong of supposing it to be otherwise, is participated by those of the clericalty who consider the Church of Christ to be founded, as a society, on the possession of an abstractedly true and supernaturally communicated speculation concerning God, rather than upon the manifestation of a divine life in man".

In turn, the Church's ministry need have no supernatural basis. The first aspect of ministerial calling must be the functions of a public teacher. Since it was a public office, the ministry must be recruited from the whole of the nation. It was clear that the service of the national Church "is as properly an organ of the national life as a magistracy, or legislative estate ... in a different light from the service of a sect". Thus, "to set barriers before the entrance upon its functions, by limitations not absolutely required by public policy, is to infringe upon the birthright of the citizens". Building upon Coleridge's notion of the "nationalty", Wilson held that the Church's endowment represented the circulation of a certain portion of the real property of the country, and the public interest demanded that such circulation should be released from all unnecessary limitations and restraints — speculative (i.e., doctrinal), antiquarian, and the like. The clergyman must be set free.

The new Coleridge produced an historical argument to justify his claim that the Church of England was multitudinist in character. The Judaism from which Christianity sprang had a great deal in common with other national churches, with their concern to penetrate the whole public and domestic life with a religious sentiment. The glory of the Gospel would be partial otherwise. Christ and St. Paul approved of the multitudinist principle. The apostolic churches were multitudinist and exhibited the worst defects of that form.

Wilson's further remarks showed how much he opposed the Tractarian doctrine of the Church: indeed had he, and not Keble, preached the Assize Sermon in 1833 he would have conceded the proposition denied there, that by a simple act of parliament the government could limit the powers of the Church, i.e., reduce the Irish bishoprics. His essay implied that the state had such prerogatives because of the multitudinist character of English religion. The Tractarians, he said, reverted to medieval forms of doctrine and practice which were "neither of the essence of a national Church, nor even of the essence of a Christian Church". But the Church must be comprehensive, it must embrace those who held aloof because of its dogmatism (the honest doubters) and also the great body of Dissenters. "Nor is a multitudinist Church necessarily or essentially hierarchical, in any extreme or superstitious sense; it can well admit, if not pure congregationalism, a large admixture of the congregational spirit".

Paradoxically, Wilson had now to argue that his suggestions did not conflict with the Articles. Newman had advocated a Catholic interpretation of the Articles; Wilson claimed that the doctrinal freedom which he proposed was permitted by their liberal spirit. "It is more difficult than might be expected, to define what is the extent of the legal obligation of those who sign them", he wrote, "and in this case the strictly legal obligation is the measure of the moral one. Subscription may be thought even to be inoperative on the conscience by reason of its vagueness". No part of the essay caused more offence. *The Guardian* remarked, in a comment on the memories of 1841, "We have no desire to be uncharitable, but we must say that the famous Tract 90 contained no special pleading if these observations do not".[39]

The key to the essay lay in Wilson's principle of ideology. Human knowledge was relative, but a new national Church, allied to the state and forsaking all claims to absolute knowledge, could ensure the survival of Christianity. That meant that the bible on which the formularies were based did not refer to historical certainties, nor did the formularies themselves demand this, for the sixth Article did not hold scripture to be supernaturally dictated, nor did it define inspiration, and the Word of God was not co-extensive with scripture. The bible should be interpreted "ideally", not as a statement of literal fact. The essayist summarised his position in language very like Powell's: "Jesus Christ has not revealed His religion as a theology of the intellect, nor as an historical faith; and it is a stifling of the true Christian life, both in the individual and in the Church, to require of many men a unanimity in speculative doctrine, which is unattainable, and a uniformity of historical belief, which can

---

[39] *G*, 23 May, 1860, p. 473.

never exist. The true Christian life is the consciousness of bearing a part in a great moral order, of which the highest agency upon earth has been committed to the Church".

Society itself must, of course, witness to this great moral order, and the essayist here employed a common stock of ideas held by Broad Churchmen concerning the state. Hooker lay behind the belief in a natural order of society in which religion had a fundamental place — though to speak of the Church as "a society which is in it [the state], though in a sense not of it, which is another, yet the same", did not suggest the "real" difference between the two required by Hooker. There was also a French tradition of thought which influenced the original lectures at Geneva and was familiar at Oxford through the teaching of Comte, reacting against Chateaubriand, de Bonald and de Maistre, and republishing in a different form the eighteenth-century vision of a world-wide humanity. The essay contained an echo of Saint-Simon's theories of a spiritual power and a temporal power in the state, and the transfer of the former from the priests to the "men of science" (*savants*), and the latter from the nobles to the propertied class. Wilson went no further: his Bamptons were delivered in the light of the revolution of 1848 and held that "Christian influence is... capable of counteracting the tendencies to socialism in more ways than one", though he admitted that there was no safe resting place for society when it denied the claims of all and each to an equal partition of goods, as of right, unless it made some approach to a distribution of these goods according to merit.[40]

The more obvious source was the work of Coleridge and Arnold. Coleridge drew on German Idealism and a Romantic conservatism to portray society as a whole and, as in Herder, relate a nation's institutions, including the Church, to the needs of the national culture. But Coleridge, in speaking of the "idea" of the state, which preceded and gave form to it, "the conception of a thing which is given by knowledge of its ultimate aim", allowed no confusion between the Church of Christ and the national Church, otherwise "many and fearful mischiefs" would ensue. "The true Church *of* England is the National Church, or Clerisy. There exists, God be thanked!, a Catholic and Apostolic Church *in* England", which was not an estate of the realm, had no nationalty entrusted to its charge, and formed no counterbalance to the collective heritage of the state.[41] The notion of "usufruct", of "public religion" being developed "by reason of tendencies inherent in their nationalty",

[40] H.B. Wilson, *op. cit.*, pp. 232-3.
[41] S.T. Coleridge, *On the Constitution of Church and State*, pp. xi, 107.

and of national churches not even needing to be Christian, were all derived from Coleridge, while the essayist's proposed new ministry was like Coleridge's clerisy of public instructors. But in the thirty years since *The Constitution of Church and State* had appeared, Coleridge's abstractions had become dimmed; for Wilson the state had become more moral, more concerned with health, welfare and education, and, correspondingly, the Church needed (as was suggested by the 1851 census) to become less doctrinal, less narrow. Wilson also differed from Arnold's *Principles of Church Reform* in one obvious respect, though he too saw the state as an ethical creation: Arnold's scheme comprehended Dissenters on the basis of the common possession of agreed doctrine, and thus excluded Unitarians. Wilson saw unity in moral terms only, so there was no difficulty in comprehending Unitarians.

The historical relativism suggested another source for his ideology. Observers at the time saw its author in Schleiermacher's pupil, Richard Rothe, whose great work, *Die Anfänge der Christlichen Kirche*, was published in 1837. Though it was unfinished and untranslated, the *cognoscenti* were well aware of Rothe's thesis: Arnold read the book in 1838, though it was too late to alter his opinions in any marked way, and he rejected Rothe's views on the origin of episcopacy.[42] Rothe showed how Church and State could be lifted into a higher understanding. The Church as a mere doctrinal body could have no permanency as the spiritual evolution of history proceeded, but in its ethical form it grew alongside the state. As the Church shed its former prerogatives, so there would be a corresponding development of feelings, opinions and principles in the state, tending towards a final identification of secular and religious, natural and divine. The resulting body would be one in which the individual's energies would be fully expressed, the highest point of reason, the supreme development of the spirit of man. As in Bunsen's *Constitution of the Church of the Future*, which Wilson may also have reflected, it was necessary to excite the religious interest and cooperation of the numerous "unconscious" Christians (a theme in the 1851 Bamptons), and that also required ecclesiastical organisation to be simplified and reduced to a minimum, for religious and civil communities finally to coalesce.[43] Wilson made no reference to Rothe but a kinship seemed apparent.

---

[42] A.P. Stanley, *op. cit.*, II, pp. 92-3. Cf. *Aids to Faith*, pp. 158-9, and F. Lichtenberger, *History of German Theology in the 19th Century*, p. 524.
[43] R. Rothe: *Die Anfänge der Christlichen Kirche*, p. 51, and cf. C.C. J. Bunsen, *The Constitution of the Church of the Future, passim*.

C. W. Goodwin, in the fifth essay, wrote a radical comment on the many attempts in the 1850's to reconcile Genesis and geology, and pronounced them unsuccessful.[44] The problem was more profound (he said) than the obvious conflict between the evidence of fossils and the Mosaic account of creation. We had to deal not only with scientific and historical criticism but also with the delayed impact of the Copernican revolution. For, somehow, seventeenth-century theology had been able to overlook the discrepancies and integrated the idea of the earth revolving round the sun into a traditional system which still portrayed creation as less than 6,000 years old. The Latitudinarian or liberal attitude of mind which arose in the earlier epoch was (naturally) the only one which answered the difficulties of clergy and the intelligent laity successfully.

Much of Goodwin's essay was technical, and for some of the church people who read it the "Mosaic Cosmogony" was probably their first detailed encounter with the results of modern geology. He painted a stark picture of a small, lonely world whirling through vast space, one startlingly different from the biblical universe centred on Israelite man and his maker. However, the fears were groundless: the answer was plain for all who had eyes to see. Religion, said Goodwin, was the study of the "dealing of God with man as a moral being". If we were dismayed by the modern scientist's presentation of the facts of the universe, then we had mistaken the purpose of revelation, which did not concern matters of fact. Physical science was not what the Hebrew writers professed to convey; so why should we hesitate to recognise their fallibility on this head? Genesis itself could not be strict revelation, a consistent whole, for the essayist sharply distinguished between the first and second chapters as containing two separate and irreconcilable accounts of creation. So here, as elsewhere in *Essays and Reviews*, biblical criticism was used in the service of a theological argument.

The "wondrous first chapter" of Genesis was not poetic, a riddle or an allegory, but a plain statement of fact given from a standpoint entirely different from our own. It was the best and most probable account which could then be given, but we could only accept it now, not as an "authentic utterance of Divine knowledge", but as "a human utterance which it has pleased Providence to use in a special way for the education of mankind". Respect for a "narrative which has played so important a part in the culture of our race" was the attitude which he recommended

---

[44] *ER*, pp. 207-253.

towards the bible as a whole, instead of the popular attitude which assumed that scripture, bearing the stamp of divine authority, must be complete, perfect and unimpeachable in all its parts. Admittedly, a bible which contained only spiritual truth must occupy a much smaller place in man's thought:

> "...the humble scholar of truth is not he who, taking his stand upon the traditions of rabbins, Christian fathers, or schoolmen, insists upon bending facts to his unyielding standard, but he who is willing to accept such teaching as it has pleased Divine Providence to afford, without murmuring that it has not been furnished more copiously or clearly".

Goodwin believed that the "Hebrew Descartes or Newton" who wrote Genesis 1 would be sympathetic to this wider view of the universe. But his modern orthodox defenders were guilty of casuistry or worse in claiming that he wrote in advance of his time. The essayist passed in review Horne's *Introduction to the Holy Scriptures* (1856), which postulated the perfect harmony between bible and geology, Buckland's Bridgewater treatise, Hugh Miller's *Testimony of the Rocks*, which held that the "days of creation were not natural but prophetic days", and Pusey's citation of the Fathers to show that the days were meant to represent indefinite periods of time. He asked, with some truth, where a theology which maintained such elaborate deceptions would end. But he also realised the perplexity of a man like Ruskin who spoke of the doubts brought on by the "clink of those dreadful hammers". "If only the geologists would let me alone I could do very well".[45] (Pusey, also, in correspondence with Newman, was much less confident than he appeared in public. "I quite feel what you say about Buckland's *Reliquiae*", wrote Newman in 1858. "It has made me distrust every theory of Geology since"[46]).

For Goodwin the best defence of Genesis must lie in some moral aspect, and he suggested that it was a useful first guess at the great truth established by nineteenth-century science, the universal sway of law, "the highest revelation of modern inquiry — namely, the unity of the design of the world, and its subordination to one sole Maker and Lawgiver". However, the essayist implied that the Mosaic account confused moral and physical worlds by portraying creation in such a grossly physical

---

[45] E.T. Cook, *The Life of John Ruskin*, II, pp. 19-20.
[46] Liddon, IV, p. 78.

form. Ruskin might have protested: there was more poetry in Genesis than Goodwin allowed.

Written at a distinctly lower temperature, Mark Pattison's study of eighteenth-century thought applied the principle of development to the theology of the period.[47] The essay was the one obvious academic work in the collection : according to Merz, it fixed in the mind of nineteenth-century man the "meaning of the word Thought as the most suitable and comprehensive term to denote the whole of the inner or hidden life and activity of a period or nation".[48] But it had a practical aim, to show that (in Pattison's words) "there is a law of continuity in the progress of theology which, whatever we may wish, is never broken off". So the Victorian Church could not neglect "those immediate agencies in the production of the present". For instance, biblical criticism was no novelty but had its beginnings in the previous century, while the rational approach to theology which reigned then had influenced the Evangelicals to make Christ's death part of a concrete scheme of redemption. Again, the anti-rationalism of the Tractarians was not a traditional Catholic trait but a reaction against the eighteenth century. But the *Seculum Rationalisticum* lasted from 1688 to 1830, and Pattison clearly thought that the Oxford Movement was a mere interval until the true heirs of rational English divinity (the Broad Church radicals) emerged.

Pattison's main argument was reasonable enough: everyone criticised eighteenth-century religion, but divinity before 1750 was very different from that which followed it; it was not all "Old Bailey" theology, as Dr Johnson called it, though it was entirely concerned with the importance of reason in matters of religion. Nor was rationalism anti-Christian; rather, it was an attempt to "prove the truth" of Christianity, without considering overmuch what use should be made of religion when it was proved. Thus, the Kantian philosophy only gave scientific form and a recognised position to a principle which had long unconsciously guided all treatment of religious topics both in England and Germany.

Pattison illustrated the difference between the first and second stages of eighteenth-century theology in various ways. Reason was first offered as the basis of faith, but gradually became its substitute. The mind never advanced as far as the stage of belief, for it became increasingly engaged in reckoning up to it. In the first period men showed that the facts of Christianity were not incredible, but in the second the whole burden of

---

[47] *ER*, pp. 254-329.
[48] J.T. Merz, *A History of European Thought in the Nineteenth Century*, I, p. 25 n.

proof was shifted to the evidence that the facts had actually occurred. The first stage, in its quest for interior attestation, raised some momentous problems, but the second, in concentrating on external evidences, knew nothing of spiritual intuition. Pattison saw one great defect arising out of this — the neglect of the historical argument, which was surely as important as the philosophical. Only Herbert Marsh's lectures at Cambridge showed honest and critical enquiry into biblical origins, yet "that investigation, introduced by a bishop and professor of divinity, has scarcely yet obtained a footing in the English Church", and the present inconsistency in argument, which professed that religious belief rested on historical evidence yet refused such evidence to be freely examined in open court, was clearly a reflection of the eighteenth-century attitude. The Tractarians had disinterred the remains of Christian antiquity but failed because they had neither the critical tools to work with nor the historical materials to work upon. Theology had almost died out; and then Coleridge came; "the evidence-makers ceased from their futile labours all at once, as beneath the spell of some magician".

Approaching the eighteenth century in the proper historical manner — instead of using some preconceived, non-critical approach — enabled one to obtain a fresh view of the period. In particular, it restored to favour the "father of English rationalism", John Locke, whose treatise on *The Reasonableness of Christianity* dominated his contemporaries. Locke saw man's religion as the fruit of an intellectual process. Reason was natural revelation; special revelation was natural reason enlarged by a new set of discoveries communicated by God immediately, the truth of which was vouched for by reason, by the testimony and proofs given. "So that he that takes away reason to make way for revelation puts out the light of both". Natural religion was the first stage of the journey, and its sufficiency was the basis of the debate between Deists and the exponents of special revelation. The deference paid to natural religion was also an attempt to establish *a priori* the *necessity* of a revelation, and Locke, especially, had warned against our liability to attribute to reason much of moral truth that (in fact) derived from revelation.

The essayist rebuked Evangelical critics who said that these divines were "Arminian" because they were alleged to have dropped the language of justification and sanctification in favour of the terminology and ideas of the moralists. But, though the dynamic nature and interior working of faith was unknown to such thinkers, their attempt to make morality practical was justified. This was an age when abstract speculation was brought down from the heights and compelled to be intelligible. The popular appeal to reason was the first effort of English divinity to find a new basis for doctrine which would replace those foundations (infallible Church and the inner light) which had failed it. Locke put it succinctly, "God has furnished men with faculties sufficient to direct them in the way they should take". And common sense, whatever its demerits, was still necessary in religion, "as at the present day when a godless orthodoxy threatens, as in the 15th century, to extinguish religious thought altogether, and nothing is allowed in the Church of England but the formulae of past thinkings, which have long lost all sense of any kind".

At this point Pattison became vehement as he contrasted Locke and his followers with the stagnant condition of current theology, as religion became stiffened into phrases which were the objects of reverence but not of intelligence, as it blocked the road, the useless encumbrance of the past, and as it became an "unmeaning frostwork of dogma, out of all relation to the actual history of man". This system was equally fatal to popular morality and to religious theory. "It locks up virtue in the cloister and theology in the library. It originates caste sanctity, and a traditional philosophy".

> "The ideal of holiness striven after may once have been lofty, the philosophy now petrified into tradition may once have been a vital faith, but now that they are withdrawn from public life, they have ceased to be social influences. On the other hand, the 18th century exhibits human attainment levelled to the lowest secular model of prudence and honesty, but still, such as it was, proposed to all men as their rule of life... It did not substitute a factitious phraseology, the pass-words of the modern pulpit, for the simple facts of life, but called things by their right names".

In later life Pattison described the essay as innocuous, it was simply a "scientific history of the self-development of opinion", and not a party manifesto. As such it had been used by Dorner in his study of the doctrine of the period.[49] The defence of Locke, in the current religious situation, was, however, startling. As Pattison said, "every flippant High Church reviewer has learnt to fling at Locke", and there were Evangelical strictures as well. They disliked *The Reasonableness of Christianity*, but Pattison's thesis really depended on Locke's *Essay Concerning Human Understanding*. "Self-development" meant that Locke was the product of the preceding intellectual evolution, going

---

[49] M. Pattison, *Memoirs*, pp. 314-5, and cf. I. A. Dorner, *History of Protestant Theology, particularly in Germany*, II, p. 496 n.

back to the Renaissance, while the true theology of the nineteenth century could only be one which took him as the norm or developed further along the path marked by him.

Pattison's theory is best analysed here rather than later, for to treat him in the context of the essays controversy generally is to risk neglecting him — the essay was often ignored or relegated to the world of scholarship where it belonged. In any case, Mansel had already anticipated it in a lecture some years before which objected to such a simplistic account of intellectual evolution. For Mansel, Locke was not the norm but a departure from the classical Anglican tradition which had not altered in the Reformation. Locke had challenged the philosophy of innate ideas, but this had serious consequences for the doctrine of God. Older theologians had declared the essence of God to be mysterious and incomprehensible, and they meant, not the "real essence", but the logical essence comprised in attributes and expressed in definitions, which Locke called his nominal essence and which Toland, claiming to rest on Locke, said *could* be known. They held that the analogies drawn from the attributes of man were imperfect, as the attributes could not exist in God as they did in man; in man they were many, in God they were one. Stillingfleet recognised Locke's innovations in this regard when he complained about "the new way of ideas".[50] Mansel's criticism could, of course, be answered; but the point remained. Pattison defended Locke because, once his intellectual stature was acknowledged, his practical consequences — above all, Latitudinarian terms of communion — would be difficult to resist. The epistemology was less important than that which followed from it.

Pattison cloaked his final question — whether the inherited doctrines of revelation matched the new ones proposed by the liberals — in a mysterious paragraph. This, and his technical approach generally, meant that the essay failed to make the impact for which he had hoped. This was not the case with the final essay, Jowett's tract on the interpretation of scripture, which raised the same issue in a more popular form.[51] It was an appropriate conclusion to the book, warmly written and crystal clear in intention. Jowett gave the full statement and elaboration of the essayists' attitude to the bible. He intended to be extreme and provocative. The second edition of the Commentary was published in October 1859 and excited more hostility than ever. The essay was partly written

---

[50] H.L. Mansel, *Letters, Lectures and Reviews*, pp. 306-17.
[51] *ER*, pp. 330-433.

during a visit to the Tennyson's the same winter, and one incident illustrated his mood. He asked his hostess, "can the truth do any harm?" She replied, "it can surely do no harm to tell the truth". But Jowett said, "that is the verdict of the simple mind". According to Tennyson's biographer Jowett moderated his tone on the Laureate's advice, yet he knew that there were few simple minds any longer who would read impartially anything he had written.[52]

The connection with the Commentary was plain. Jowett had approached St. Paul as a man writing out of his own experience, and this suggested a way of understanding the bible as a whole. Scripture, in Jowett's eyes, had a life of its own, detached from the use of it made by the Church, and the task of the modern interpreter was to discover this. In so doing he found the original meaning of the text and its permanent value for humanity, whereas the commentators "seem rather to reflect the changing atmosphere of the world or the Church". As time passed commentary and bible had become so firmly connected that it required an effort of thought to appreciate the extraordinary nature of the phenomenon. The history of interpretation would indicate "the causes which have darkened the meaning of words in the course of ages; it would clear away the remains of dogmas, systems, controversies, which are encrusted upon them".

Jowett's analysis of the allegorical, logical and philosophical methods of interpretation was lengthy. But he disliked the rhetorical most of all, because of the preacher's tendency to "exaggerate or amplify the meaning of simple words for the sake of edification", which had an unfortunate influence on interpretation. "For the preacher almost necessarily oversteps the limits of actual knowledge, his feelings overflow with the subject; even if he have the power, he has seldom the time for accurate thought or enquiry". Jowett saw accurately that the bible when preached was out of the hands of the critic, its sacredness emphasised. But he pointed out that there was nothing sacred about methods of interpretation however hallowed by use—mystical and logical approaches had been practised on the Vedas and the Koran as well as Jewish and Christian scriptures — and the New Testament was written in a language known with tolerable certainty. (That language exhibited a world of difference between scripture and creeds and demanded that the bible should be allowed to speak for itself).

Why, then, in the present state of biblical scholarship, were the old

[52] Abbott, I, p. 276.

methods so emphasised? It must be to uphold received meanings, not the true and original one, of the bible. But we had a duty to ask what scripture actually meant, not what it could be made to mean by ingenious scholars dedicated in advance to a particular point of view.

> "In natural science it is felt to be useless to build on assumptions; in history we look with suspicion on *a priori* ideas of what ought to have been; in mathematics, when a step is wrong, we pull the house down until we reach the point at which the error is discovered. But in theology it is otherwise; there the tendency has been to conceal the unsoundness of the foundation under the fairness and loftiness of the superstructure... many principles have imperceptibly grown up which have overridden facts. No one would interpret Scripture, as many do, but for certain previous suppositions with which we come to the perusal of it".

Jowett dwelt on these suppositions: "There can be no error in the Word of God"; the human interpreter was a thousand times more likely to err than the inspired writer; prophecy could not fail; the inspiration of the New Testament was set at nought by inquiring too closely into the origin of the gospels. When a critic protested that this meant that the bible could never be approached objectively, he was told, "God speaks not as man speaks", and investigation was forbidden by appeal to the limits of human inquiry. But, "it is better to close the book than to read it under conditions of thought which are imposed from without". Whether these conditions were the tradition of the Church or the opinions of the religious world made no difference. "They are inconsistent with the freedom of the truth and the moral character of the Gospel".

Passing from protest to argument, Jowett claimed that inspiration itself was open to different meanings. "Nor for any of the higher or supernatural views of inspiration is there any foundation in the Gospels or Epistles" — their authors were not free from error or infirmity. Inspiration could be judged only by examining the writers and their context, and the judgment must take into account the well ascertained facts of history and science. "Neither is there any ground for assuming design of any other kind in Scripture any more than in Plato or Homer. Wherever there is beauty and order, there is design; but there is no proof of any artificial design, such as is often traced by the Fathers, in the relation of the several parts of a book, or of the several books to each other. That is one of those mischievous notions which enables us, under the disguise of reverence, to make Scripture mean what we please". He thought that these matters would be clarified by examining the origins of the first three gospels, "an inquiry which has not been much considered by English theologians since the days of Bishop Marsh". "We can no longer speak of three independent witnesses of the Gospel narrative", said Jowett: to allow a common oral tradition would dispose of many alleged difficulties at one stroke.

The essayist could hold such views because he believed in an understanding of revelation which was far wider than anything held in the past. "The great differences of opinion about the interpretation of Scripture run up at last into a difference respecting revelation itself, whether given besides the human faculties or through them, whether an interruption of the laws of nature, or their perfection and fulfilment". But the New Testament itself pointed to the solution proposed by liberal theologians by a "principle of progressive revelation", which admitted imperfect or opposite aspects of truth, variations of fact, inaccuracies of language. Scripture was spirit, not law; its words were those of a "man talking to his friend", and he contrasted the "extraordinary and unreasonable importance attached to single words, sometimes of doubtful meaning", concerning divorce, the personality of the Holy Spirit, infant baptism, original sin, and episcopacy, with the neglect of Christ's views on riches and poverty — a contrast between Christ's religion and the Church's. And that belief in the damnation of the heathen or of Catholics should ever have prevailed implied a strange forgetfulness of such passages as, "Who rewardeth every man according to his work". The same habit of silence or misinterpretation extended to words or statements of scripture in which doctrines were thought to be involved.

The habit of viewing the bible through centuries of interpretation was not only untrue to the spirit of scripture, it was now critically assailed, and the common people, mechanics and artisans, for whom the bible was intended, read the critics. Jowett now proposed the method that would answer all the difficulties and restore the original meaning:

> "*Interpret the Scripture like any other book.* There are many respects in which Scripture is unlike any other book; these will appear in the results of such an interpretation. The first step is to know the meaning, and this can only be done in the same careful and impartial way that we ascertain the meaning of Sophocles or of Plato. The subordinate principles which flow out of this general one will also be gathered from the observation of Scripture. No other science of Hermeneutics is possible but an inductive one, that is to say, one based on the language and thoughts and narrations of the sacred writers".

Jowett stressed that, on this level, the bible was to be approached like any other piece of literature, without the exercise of any special gifts:

"...it would be well to carry the theory of interpretation no further than in the case of other works. Excessive system tends to create an impression that the meaning of Scripture is out of our reach, or is to be attained in some other way than by the exercise of manly sense and industry. Who would write a bulky treatise about the method to be pursued in interpreting Plato or Sophocles? Let us not set out on our journey so heavily equipped that there is little chance of our arriving at the end of it. The method creates itself as we go on, beginning only with a few reflections directed against plain errors. Such reflections are the rules of common sense, which we acknowledge with respect to other works written in dead languages; without pretending to novelty they may help us to 'return to nature' in the study of the sacred writings".

The essayist listed these rules: first, that scripture had one meaning, "the meaning which it had to the mind of the Prophet or Evangelist who first uttered or wrote, to the hearers or readers who first received it". Secondly, we should interpret scripture from itself, "like any other book written in an age and country of which little or no literature survives, and about which we know almost nothing except what is derived from its pages". " 'We cannot understand Scripture without becoming familiar with it'... The intelligent mind will ask its own questions, and find for the most part its own answers". These principles held with all acknowledgment of the different aspects and styles in the sacred writings, their depth and inwardness, their infinite and inexhaustible character.

Jowett was aware that his approach accorded best with the bible in English, and that the strength of traditional interpretations was their alleged faithfulness to the Hebrew and Greek texts. He also smarted under the criticism that his linguistic scholarship, in the Commentary, was faulty. But he doubted whether, as against historical studies, "any considerable light can be thrown on the New Testament from inquiry into the language", and there followed the most revealing comment in the essay:

"Scripture has an inner life or soul; it has also an outward body or form. That form is language, which imperfectly expresses our common notions, much more those higher truths which religion teaches".

Here was another solution. Jowett saw its vindication in the degeneracy and decay of the Greek language at the time when the New Testament was written. "That is a more important revolution in the mental history of mankind, than we easily conceive in modern times, when all languages sit loosely on thought, and the pecularities or idiosyncracies of one are corrected by our knowledge of another... That degeneracy was a preparation for the Gospel... the beginning of another state of man, in which language and mythology and philosophy were no longer to exert the same constraining power as in the ancient world". Grammatical exactness was, therefore, misplaced, nor did it realise that the decay of a language could be a creative principle also. Jowett pointed out, correctly, that the early Christian experience was powerfully expressed in a new and non-classical Greek. So "words must not mean too much", and ignorance of Greek in the modern reader "was more excusable than ignorance of the nature of language". We must distinguish between the superficial connexion of words and the real connexion of thoughts. "Christian truth is not dependent on the fixedness of modes of thought", nor on any sharp difference between figure and reality. We must look for the common element throughout scripture — the universal truth which "easily breaks through the accidents of time and place in which it is involved". "The world changes, but the human heart remains the same; events and details are different, but the principle by which they are governed, or the rule by which we are to act, is not different".

Discussion of Jowett's own theory of interpretation belongs elsewhere,[53] but the implications of his essay are obvious. Jowett complemented the views of his fellow writers and unified the whole work which would otherwise have remained a collection of startling fragments.

The bible was the final justification for the liberal approach, said Jowett. Rather than treating it as a handbook of doctrine, it should be used as an "element of liberal education". Nor were its contents miraculously ordered: the essayist agreed with Baur that the canon was not a law or rule of belief but only a list of writings. The Church had decided what constituted scripture, so Jowett in some sense put the bible into the history of the Church — but the Church for Jowett was not a supernatural body but a human society, evolving like any other institution. Jowett protested with some justice about the current unworthy views of scripture — "it is not a useful lesson for the young student to apply to Scripture principles which he would hesitate to apply to other books" — and, despite what his critics said, he cared deeply for the New Testament: as he had read Sophocles "hundreds of times", so he knew the epistles off by heart.[54] His great desire was that the bible should be read with freedom, and then it could make its own appeal to the unprejudiced enquirer. If this meant that the subjective needs of the

---

[53] See below, p. 314f.
[54] Abbott, I, p. 264.

individual came first and scripture's own authority and the Church's role as interpreter came second, that was no great drawback.

As with Powell, J. B. Mozley made some apt comments on Jowett : he asked what was the "aboriginal Christianity" which the essayist dug up beneath no end of strata but "as perfect an *arcanum disciplinae* as ever invented by tradition? If the letter of Scripture is a veil, and Christianity is Jowett beneath the veil, one does not feel very secure".[55] Jowett would have replied that in stressing the individual he was being true to the principles of the Reformation. Chillingworth had said, "the Bible only is the religion of Protestants", and Jowett added that "the Bible is Christendom", meaning that it supplied a common language to educated and non-educated alike, "in which the best and highest thoughts of both are expressed; it is a medium between the abstract notions of the one and the simple feelings of the other. To the poor especially, it conveys in the form which they are most capable of receiving, the lesson of history and life". "There is no such treasury of instruments and materials as Scripture", and its disappearance would alter human discourse to a scarcely conceivable degree.

This was, of course, a mainly literary approach to the bible, but Jowett did not accept that he had narrowed Christianity down to a book. For him scripture was able to stand alone; there was no need to say with Dr Hawkins, "the Church to teach, the Scripture to prove".[56] Jowett could not conceive of a situation in which the bible would be unknown to the great mass of the public while the Church was still active and doctrine continued to be taught.

The attitude to language in the essay needed constant reference to the Commentary. There Jowett had described the inversions in the meaning of words between St. Paul's age and ours and the consequent hazards for interpretation. Westcott said that he magnified the difficulties: "lan–guage is a condition of our being", it determined the conception as well as the communication of ideas, and writing introduced no limitation into the representation of truth which did not already exist in the first conception and expression of it. To suppose that words and cases were convertible, that tenses had no meaning, and forms of expression were accidental (Jowett implied all this), "is to betray the fundamental principles on which all intercourse is based".[57]

---

[55] *Letters of the Rev. J.B. Mozley*, p. 245.

[56] E. Hawkins, *A Dissertation upon the Use and Importance of Unauthoritative Tradition*, p. 33.

[57] B.F. Westcott, *Introduction to the Study of the Gospels*, pp. 12, 14, 33.

Jowett, however, did not accept that a disbelief in the exactness of language was a prelude to philosophical scepticism. The "externals of interpretation" against which he declaimed had been shielded too long by mere textual study. The root of this attitude originally was, perhaps, his Evangelicalism: it was Henry Venn the elder who spoke of "a thing so immaterial as an accurate investigation of the Hebrew text", when "all things necessary to be known are the same in every version as in the original".[58] Another cause, according to Leslie Stephen, could be found in his befuddled Hegelianism.[59] The essayist's biographers saw a temperamental characteristic: Jowett felt acutely the problems attending his abstract idealism, of connecting the idea to the concrete individual.[60] Whatever the cause, Jowett's passionate denunciation of the tyranny of the grammarians and long-dead interpreters arose from deep convictions. Jowett did not think that men were sufficiently concerned with the truth; they lazily accepted on trust words which they thought were unchanged when, in fact, they had changed greatly. Thus, a kind of theological slang was used to obscure a situation of great complexity and challenge — the bible was not a whole but a mixed collection of books, its language was capable of many different meanings, and we no longer understood much of its terminology: in other words, the world of scripture was far removed from our own. The bible was uncertain. It was not easy to say "what is the meaning of 'proving a doctrine from Scripture' ".

How, then, could we arrive at the truth? By examining every received opinion sceptically, by using the historical method rigorously, and by trying to recover the experience underlying the words, even if this meant in some cases inverting the language and changing its meaning entirely. We must not mistake the symbols for the reality that they pictured, the terminology for that which it expressed. The notion that the truth of Christ had to be concealed under the cloak of sacred language must be abandoned. None of the other essayists said this as pungently as Jowett; yet his approach summed up theirs. All disliked theological catch phrases, the worship of words instead of a proper examination of them.

In attempting to establish a connection between these separate contributions which together make up *Essays and Reviews*, the preface exists as

---

[58] H. Venn, *The Life and a selection from the Letters of Rev. H. Venn*, p. 537.
[59] L. Stephen, *Studies of a Biographer*, II, p. 136.
[60] Abbott, II, p. 411.

a warning: the essayists themselves wished to be considered as independent, individual authors; each had a strong theological character of his own which owed little to anyone else, and there were, for example, deep differences between Powell and Pattison, while Temple's was always a more orthodox viewpoint. The critics who dismissed the preface and treated the seven as a team did them injustice and usually provided a crude and superficial analysis of the book.

Nonetheless, with these qualifications in mind, it is possible to speak of a theology in *Essays and Reviews*, if not a theological system. The essayists never retracted anything that they said. That is one reason for attempting to discover whether any *leitmotifs* ran through the book. Again, their background in the previous five years had been similar; if they themselves had discovered some fellowship in their witness to truth, then some common purpose was implied when they appeared together within the covers of a single book.

Bishop Wilberforce demonstrated their alleged unity by simply juxtaposing statements of Temple with Wilson, or Williams with Jowett, and saying, "Behold the similarities". Anything resembling such a method will obviously be out of the question. Nor is it possible to compare the essays with their promised supplements, the further volumes which never appeared, though Wilson had them in mind, and which would have explained the positions that they took up in the book.

However, the essays were not isolated. One can claim that they crystallised ideas which their authors had stated elsewhere, in larger works and other articles, and that these to some extent present a consistent point of view. So cross-references are possible, as in the case of Temple who exhibited a continuity in his thought from the *Oxford Essays* of 1856, through the essay of 1860 and the sermon on *The Present Relations of Science to Religion* which lay behind it, to his Bamptons for 1884, when he was Bishop of Exeter. In middle age he still held that the seat of religious authority lay in man's moral faculty; so there could be no real conflict between science and faith. Moral nature like phenomenal nature was subject to law. In Jowett's essay the background was supplied by the articles on natural theology and on St. Paul's use of language, in the Commentary, while the evolution of Powell and Wilson from their earlier work has already been suggested. Wilson made a clear reference to Williams' *Rational Godliness* at the beginning of his essay.[61] When seen in this light various things in *Essays and Reviews* fell into place. And

---

[61] *ER*, p. 148.

though the authors were vague about some momentous questions, when it came to subjects about which they held decided views, or which they wished to oppose, their basic agreement was not difficult to find.

There are two great matters in *Essays and Reviews*: the nature of the Church, and the nature of revelation itself. Wilson dealt with the first in an extreme fashion and has often been dismissed for being odd and perverse. Yet, with Jowett's, his was the most important article in the book and, like Jowett's, its point of view was shared by all the Stanleyites in one way or another.

What did the essayists consider to be the nature and function of a church? Powell, in a sermon in 1850 on *The State Church*, expressed it well: the object, historically, was to provide "some outward form of religion of which the mass of the community may freely avail itself, and the Establishment so framed is a territorial Church; and as such reckons as members all who do not openly dissent. Its characteristic function, in one word, may be that it provides a form of religion for those who have none of their own". This establishment was instituted and kept up by the state for the benefit not of the Church, nor of religion, but of the community at large. The whole aim ought to be comprehension, and all reformation in liturgy and formularies should be solely in the way of omissions.[62]

Wilson suggested that the assumptions beneath this view were largely naturalistic ones: the religious body was part of society, evolving as society itself evolved and answering to human needs and aspirations, and not founded on abstract, divinely communicated revelations about God (hence the ministry, also, must be altered). Arnold's was a similar sociological approach: analyse society, and its moral and spiritual wants, particularly the need for unity and cohesion, defined the Church's *esse*, without having to seek for the latter in some supernatural or miraculous factor.

A model for such a religious communion existed: the Church best suited to the new conditions of the nineteenth century was — the Church of England. It was unique, though having a parallel in the recent German Church unions and in the liberal nature of primitive Christianity. This was the true national Church, "the freest, most learned, most rational Church in the world" (to quote Stanley),[63] a Church which opened her boundaries wide because she was "nearly, if not quite, the most tolerant

---

[62] B. Powell, *The State Church*, pp. 14-15.
[63] Prothero, II, p. 38.

religious body on the face of the earth" (thus Temple in the 1856 *Oxford Essays*). "In this toleration lies her greatest strength". "The custom of our church refuses to draw a precise line between those who belong to her and those who do not; and that custom is to thousands the greatest of blessings".[64] The purpose of the Church of England was to represent the nation's approach to God. Hence it was not a denomination, and the state should not be misrepresented as "allying itself with one out of many sects" (Wilson)[65]. For this reason also the Church of England was by its nature "not High nor Low" (both sectarian tendencies) but "Broad" (Stanley again): Connop Thirlwall said in 1866 that she had the advantage, "such I deem it — of more than one type of orthodoxy... Each has a right to a standing place, none to exclusive possession of the field".[66] Equally, the Church could not be narrowly dogmatic, nor even narrowly Christian. Wilson spoke of national churches not even needing to be Christian, for "religious and moral truth" must come before everything else. "The Church to which we have the happiness to belong, allows us to acknowledge the ambiguity... of the word Church and of the word Salvation".[67]

Jowett expressed these hopes with that peculiar blend of urgency and spirituality that was his own. "The real facts and truths of Christianity are quite a sufficient basis for a national Church", he wrote to Dean Elliot — and the Church of England did not insist on anything more.[68] He explained to Florence Nightingale, in July, 1862, why the essayists could not leave the Church and reconcile their consciences. "I believe that there is upon the whole greater freedom in the balance of the parties in the Church of England than there can be in any small community even of Unitarians or free thinkers; as to unity there is no possibility of the semblance of unity in any other body. I cannot give up the hope that this great organisation may be one day used for far higher purposes". It was not a forlorn belief — the Calvinist Church in Holland had changed overnight and become liberalised.[69]

The speculations are interesting, but their practical application to the Victorian Church seems impossible. Wilson's essay, at times, is pure

---

[64] *Oxford Essays, 1856*, p. 242.
[65] *ER*, p. 195.
[66] C. Thirlwall, *Letters to a Friend*, p. 57.
[67] H.B. Wilson, *op. cit.*, p. 245.
[68] Abbott, I, p. 348.
[69] Jowett MSS, f. 39, letter to Florence Nightingale, July, 1862. Cf. *ibid.*, "I feel I should be denationalised and sectarianised if I separated".

fantasy, and, though he had a large county parish, he seems to have lost touch with the realities of life. But perhaps that is the measure of the failure of *Essays and Reviews* to work any revolution in the Church. The concept of English national religion, of Church and State as the nation considered under different aspects, has disappeared in the twentieth century, but the radicals thought that it was capable of infinite expansion in the nineteenth. In view of the Church Rate bills and more minor agitations, could anyone in 1860 forecast the future? Lacking a sense of the Church's agelessness, and more aware of its vulnerability at the hands of time and circumstance, the liberals saw a transformation round every corner.

There were two other reasons for their conviction. As a challenge to the narrow Tractarian view of the Church were the older Latitudinarian tradition and the Reformation itself. Burnet, Hales, Tillotson, Balguy and Clarke, were all invoked by the essayists as their forefathers, as well as Arnold and Coleridge. Motives of toleration had framed the Articles, maintained Wilson in 1851 as he did in 1860. "And herein, as I humbly conceive, consists the wonderful felicity of the Church to which we belong" — her dogmatic declarations were suspended on scripture, not on interpretations of it, and were not final, according to the exegesis of one year or century, but provisional, until men should agree in the sense of scripture.[70] The point was similar to Hampden's in his Bamptons of twenty years previously: there was an evident contrast between scriptural truth and credal propositions, and the Anglican formularies were modes which might be explained by different thinkers in different ways: controversy would only arise if one insisted on them.[71] Jowett only went beyond Hampden in restricting the truths of the bible to more general aspects. Furthermore, the Articles were repealed in the Comprehension Act of 1689, which was passed by the Commons though rejected by the Lords. Burnet and others had said at that time that the requirement of subscription was a "great imposition".[72] Reformation was a continuous process; the original ideals had become moribund by the eighteenth century and were denied by the Tractarians; they must be revived.

Secondly, there was the evidence for this comprehensiveness in the national life itself. Maurice was an illustration of it: he had said some years before that the Church of England was a witness for that universal

---

[70] H.B. Wilson, *op. cit.*, p. 74.

[71] R.D. Hampden, *The Scholastic Philosophy considered in its relation to Christian Theology* (1 ed.), p. 376.

[72] A.P. Stanley, *Essays chiefly on questions of Church and State*, p. 109 f.

redemption which the Scottish Presbyterians had declared to be incompatible with their confessions.[73] A generous example of the larger goodwill was F. W. Newman, of whom Powell made so much in his essay; he held Newman up as a light and seemed to echo his own spiritual development, to the scandal of the orthodox. Even Bradlaugh grudgingly preferred the Church to sect. Commenting in 1860 on the Nonconformist agitation to abolish the Church Rate, he declared: "Some say that if we overthrow the Church we have to encounter a greater amount of bigotry at the hands of the Dissenters; and they urge, with truth, that the Church is more tolerant than the Chapel". When Bradlaugh went on to demand that the churches be used for enlightening the country, instead of preaching dogma, and "so causing the Church to be converted into a useful, national institution", he said no more than the radicals, although they would have resisted his call for complete secularisation.[74]

Finally, the state was vitally concerned in this subject. Wilson said in the *Westminster Review* in 1870 that *Essays and Reviews* grew more directly out of the Gorham judgment than most people realised. Some of the writers pondered the possibility of applying its principles (protection of width of opinion, etc.) to "some more important subject matter" than baptismal regeneration itself.[75]

The essayists approached these questions from the standpoint of historical criticism. That was why they were interested in the national and social aspects of religion instead of the eternal verities of a supernatural Church, the phenomenal instead of the essential. The historical method was the much-vaunted novelty in *Essays and Reviews*, and explained its preoccupations and emphases. It was to be spoken of in absolute terms, according to Pattison: its findings, as with the inductive method in physics, were not invalidated by errors in its application. Doctrine could now be accounted for by the "general laws applicable to the whole history". So one could fairly speak of the "judicial supremacy" of the method, "its claims to decide without appeal on what is... it is, in short, a positive science, repudiating theory".[76] The positivism was emphasised by Jowett: he held that the historian's investigation was

---

[73] Maurice, I, p. 183. Cf. *ER*, p. 187 for a similar claim by Wilson.
[74] *National Reformer*, 16 June, 1860, p. 4.
[75] *WR*, October, 1870, p. 469.
[76] *Ibid.*, April, 1857, pp. 343-4.

"above controversy, of which it traces the growth, clearing away that part which is verbal only".[77]

To set *Essays and Reviews* in its cultural context is to see it as a religious counterpart of those historically-dominated studies (Buckle, Maine, etc.) which proposed to explain society and its institutions by their historical origins, an evolutionary process from lower to higher, from simpler to more complex forms. Powell showed in *The Order of Nature* how much he was influenced by Buckle's *History of Civilisation*, though the essayists' interests were narrower because they saw "history" mainly in terms of criticism of the bible: "the claim of philology as the only key to history has been gradually established", announced Pattison. All this meant a "vast induction on the destructive side" (to quote Williams), as the essayists wrestled with the bible and with that "extreme and too exclusive Scripturalism" from which so many evils had flowed to the people of England (Wilson).[78] It was easy to see why biblical criticism so dominated *Essays and Reviews*. Their task was to interpret those scriptural doctrines which collided with the historical point of view, above all, revelation itself understood as something delivered once and for all, out of any connection with the *Zeitgeist* of the time, validated by prophecy and miracle, personified in the supernatural Christ. What did man know about God? How did he know? Revelation was a problem.

The low estimate of the Old Testament in *Essays and Reviews* was a clear example of an historically-conditioned approach to revelation. Williams' critical point that the Pentateuch was not written by Moses but rather "indicated his mind", led to a theological conclusion: the truly Mosaic was not the Judaic but the essentially human, "and it is not the Semitic form, often divergent from our modes of conception, but the eternal truths of a righteous God, and of the spiritual sacrifices with which He is pleased, that we ought to recognise as most characteristic of the Bible". Powell referred to Schleiermacher in claiming that the Jewish belief in miracles was relative to the thought of their day. Wilson doubted the Jews' uniqueness, for both the religious element and the understanding of theocracy were much stronger (he held) in other peoples than older scholars supposed, while Hebrew conceptions of Jehovah were obscured by figurative representations. Wilson added, "all things sanctioned among the Jews are certainly not to be imitated by us, nor all pagan institutions to be abhorred". But though the Hebrew writings

---

[77] Epistles (2 ed.), II, p. 570.
[78] *ER*, pp. 69, 177.

represented law as against gospel, they could not be ignored, and even Wilson, who so emphasised their ideological content, allowed that the Hebrew approach to the deity was far superior than in other national religions. Jowett naturally thought that Plato's teaching about God was higher, but he provided a solution with his theory that the revelation in scripture was progressive; it began in the earliest books with the truth of the unity of God, and proceeded from that basis. "It is a notion of value to the interpreter, for it enables him at the same time to grasp the whole and distinguish the parts. It saves him from the necessity of maintaining that the Old Testament is one and the same everywhere".[79]

To be historically-minded also meant that revelation must be separated from the miraculous. Wilson predicted confidently in his Bamptons that, "as civilisation advances, the domain of the preternatural recedes, law is found to embrace continually more and more, the exceptional and occasional is found to be less and less frequent; and at length the conviction arises clear and well-defined, that in the Divine creation, all is subject to law".[80] Goodwin, with a reference to the argument from induction, could not accept that creation was miraculous as described in Genesis. Temple thought that the appeal to miracle belonged to man's childhood. So did Jowett; "what is progressive is necessarily imperfect in its earlier stages, and even erring to those who come after".[81]

The historical method put the traditional doctrine of revelation in a new and unflattering light. Scientific discovery and advance were not, strictly speaking, part of revelation. The case of Galileo, said Goodwin, had shown that "those things for the discovery of which man has faculties specially provided are not fit objects of a divine revelation". What the old divinity professed was "of little use in satisfying those who would know how and what God really has taught mankind, and whether anything beyond that which man is able and obviously intended to arrive at by the use of his natural faculties". The "definition and idea" of divine revelation must, therefore, be modified.[82] Powell made the same contrast in 1829: "The object of a divine revelation must be to teach divine things [not] the laws and structure of the material universe". On the latter reason was brought to bear, and it was "idle to suppose that revelation be directed to the same end" — an argument which he completed in his

---

[79] Ibid., pp. 62, 116, 170, 171, 387.
[80] H.B. Wilson, op. cit., pp. 120-1.
[81] ER, pp. 40, 251, 348.
[82] Ibid., p. 209.

essay : "the boundaries of nature exist only where our *present* knowledge places them... the inevitable progress of research must, within a longer or shorter period, unravel all that seems most marvellous".[83] Authority could not be insisted on in those matters which were merely the product of historical evolution and not "revealed".

But the essayists avoided Lessing's conclusion that human reason would, in due course, discover everything. History had a purpose in actually eliciting the nature of revelation, and man's inherent faculties could never have attained to this alone. According to Jowett, historical study finally showed that amid all the different modes of thought and speech in different ages, "there is a common element in human nature which bursts through these differences and remains unchanged, because akin to the first instincts of our being". Here revelation had its domain, the interior castle of the heart, the seat of conscience — Williams quoted Bunsen's dismissal of "this fiction of an external revelation". Thus, revelation concerned a primary truth which "easily breaks through the accidents of time and place in which it is involved" (Jowett).[84] The childlike and simple possessed it, but the mature man, when his mind was cleared of former confusions — and disregarding the later interpretations and accretions fastened upon the truth — also came to understand it.

For Jowett, Christ most fully revealed this eternal truth : his teachings were seen to be the part of scripture most immediately and universally applicable. "The reason is that they are words of the most universal import. They do not relate to the circumstances of the time, but to the common life of all mankind". Only nineteenth-century man understood why Christ said that we must become as children to enter the kingdom of heaven. As Temple held, there was a relation between the "inner law of mature life and the outer law of childhood", which he described in another way as "the link of sympathy which binds the present with the past, and fills old age with the fresh feelings of childhood". That was why the essayists in the old age of the world advocated a return to the bible, as it appeared fresh from the labours of liberal critics. It was "a history; even the doctrinal parts of it are cast in a historical form" (Temple), so it could be seen as the record of the childhood of man, or as the "book for the heart" (Jowett). It was unsophisticated, even barbaric, full of contradictions and difficulties, but it allowed the universal truth to speak

---

[83] B. Powell, *Revelation and Science*, pp. 11-12. *ER*, p. 109.
[84] *ER*, pp. 92, 411, 412.

with a directness lacking in the creeds. That also was why they looked back to the "democracy" of the early Church.[85]

The centre of interest in revelation had obviously moved from God to man. God was the "Universal Parent" (Wilson), immanent rather than transcendent, "Eternal" rather than "Lord" (Williams); his involvement in the world of mere matter was in some doubt. Both Jowett and Powell opposed the teleology of the argument from design. And how could one pass from the idea of a first cause to that of a Creator? — all that the world suggested was Hume's sequential rather than causal relationships.[86] Man was the nineteenth-century being, equipped with the "greater cultivation of religious understanding" (Temple), who possessed within himself the verifying faculty, his own moral tribunal, the right of appeal to which was superior to all miracles — "the human mind is competent to sit in moral and spiritual judgment on a professed revelation" (Powell).[87] Private conviction, not law, mattered.

There was a curious eighteenth-century flavour about this anthropology. As the truths of revelation were eternal and changeless, so human nature itself was essentially static. Wilson spoke in the Bamptons of the "constant possession by the human race, under all its varieties, of substantially the same faculties and the same tendencies, wherein... unity did and does really exist". That was another reason for denying exclusive revelation. The moral nature of man was "substantially one and the same always and everywhere" — and Hume had said no less, of course: "Mankind are so much the same, in all times and places, that *history informs us of nothing new* or strange in this particular".[88] Such a humanism had no place for teaching about original sin. "The world changes, but the human heart remains the same", said Jowett. Man might be ignorant, but he could not be aboriginally evil, and all the essayists rejected the Calvinistic tenet of human depravity.[89]

Christ was seen, not from the side of God, not the phantom figure of Chalcedon, but as man. In the received theology Christ's self-knowledge was both infused and experimental, but the radicals insisted on its experimental aspect. Wilson, describing in his Bamptons how Christ shared the same consciousness as ourselves, obviously preferred to think

---

[85] *Ibid.*, pp. 39, 40, 44, 86, 413, 428.

[86] Epistles (1 ed.), II, p. 407. *Oxford Essays, 1857*, p. 187.

[87] *ER*, p. 122.

[88] H.B. Wilson, *op. cit.*, pp. 76, 184. Cf. D. Forbes, *The Liberal Anglican Idea of History*, p. 123.

[89] G. Faber, *op. cit.*, p. 407.

of it as participation rather than abstract endowment.[90] When Williams, in *Rational Godliness*, held that Christianity meant attachment to Christ as person, and not to his name and power, he added a footnote that this issue was "vitally critical and pregnant". Men came to Christ by acknowledging the authority of things pure, lovely and of good report. The apostles reasoned upward (not from the power and authority of Christ): they "felt goodness and inferred God". "Such a mode of thought has the advantage of starting more from the purer moral instincts of our nature".[91] Powell, in *The Order of Nature*, held that the resurrection of Christ should be dwelt on in its "doctrinal spirit" rather than the physical letter, "not as a physiological phenomenon but as the cornerstone of Christian faith and hope".[92] Naturally, his critics took this to mean that the Resurrection had not actually happened.

Wilson's essay suggested that doubts of this kind were not to be treated as worse than a morally defective life. "We do not find the Apostle excommunicating those Corinthians, who said there was no resurrection from the dead. On the other hand, we know it was only in an extreme case that he sanctioned excommunication for the cause of immorality. And upon the whole, if we cannot effectually compare the persons deficient in a true belief of the resurrection, with an immoral or evil liver — if we can only say they were both bad Christians — at least we have no reason to determine that the good liver who disbelieved the resurrection was treated by St. Paul as less of a Christian than the evil liver who believed it". From this Wilson concluded the "at least equal value of the Christian life, as compared with the Christian doctrine", and he thought that in upholding such a view St. Paul might have been influenced by the Buddhist *Dharma*. The New Testament did not teach a consistent doctrine about Christ, and we could not altogether reconcile the picture of Jesus in the synoptic gospels with those in St. Paul and St. John. "At any rate, there were current in the primitive Church very distinct Christologies".[93]

Jowett, of course, taught a number of Christological radicalisms, questioning the Virgin Birth and the historicity of the miracles, and proposing, like Williams, a thoroughgoing moral interpretation of the Atonement. It was no longer an external substitutionary act offered to

---

[90] H.B. Wilson, *op. cit.*, p. 225.
[91] R. Williams, *Rational Godliness after the Mind of Christ and the Written Voices of His Church*, p. 377 f.
[92] B. Powell, *The Order of Nature*, p. 458.
[93] *ER*, pp. 164, 179.

the Father but an inward matter of men following the words of Jesus. In Jowett, more than anyone else, occurred that momentous change from Easter to Christmas, from Christ as Atoner to the preacher of reconciliation who appealed to the spiritual faculty inherent in man. By 1865 he could no longer accept the fact of a physical resurrection.[94]

The drawbacks and advantages in *Essays and Reviews* were equally many. However fair their hopes were for a national Church, it was liberal writers who suggested why they could not be realised. Thirlwall, in particular, as a living embodiment of the old Latitudinarian tradition, refused to believe that the ideal of Burnet and Tillotson saw its fulfilment in the terms of communion proposed by Wilson. Their greatest weakness lay in the attempt to replace doctrine with morals, without realising — "with what seems to me a strange neglect of patent facts" — that they must allow "equal latitude in ethical as in theological speculation".[95] Hort and Maurice wrote similarly. The essayists had not solved what R. W. Church said in 1870 was the difficulty of "combining a National Church with a Church having the *raison d'être* of a religious society, believing in a definite religion, and teaching it".[96] They made too much of a universal moral sense: show a working man the ethical reason for religion and he will immediately recognise it. That assumed that most men had the same gifts of education as themselves, and it hardly touched the social and economic reasons for the alienation of the masses, who would not be satisfied by doctrine merely shorn of its offensive intellectual items.

With this attitude went also a low view of the Church. Wilson and Jowett held that the Church had borrowed many of its ideas and practices from the pagan models of the time; if they were swept away in an instant, the "spiritual organisation", priesthood, etc., would be quickly reconstructed. The "unreasonable importance" given to episcopacy and other institutions, rites and practices was beyond Jowett's comprehension. It was not now possible, he said (and how soon he was proved wrong) to revive the interest in baptismal regeneration found in the Gorham controversy.[97] Admittedly, the Latitudinarians had proposed toleration, admission of Dissenters, and idealistic programmes for reform of the Church. But this was something more. It marked the

---

[94] Jowett MSS, f. 127, letter to Florence Nightingale, 16 April, 1865.
[95] *Remains Literary and Theological of Connop Thirlwall*, II, p. 45.
[96] Church, p. 226.
[97] *ER*, pp. 169-170, 358-9, 421.

acceptance by religious thinkers of that retreat from the Church, its admission of a subordinate role in society, which has become so obvious in the twentieth century.

Did this also suggest that authority lay ultimately with the state? Wilson, in answering the Tractarian view of the Church, seemed to fall into the hands of Thomas Hobbes: for the sake of the reaction upon its own merely secular interests, "the nation is entitled to provide from time to time, that the Church teaching and forms of one age do not traditionally harden, so as to become exclusive barriers in a subsequent one, and so the moral growth of those who are committed to the hands of the Church be checked, or its influences confined to a comparatively few".[98]

The great omission in *Essays and Reviews* was any article on Christ himself. It could have been an excellent exercise in modern theology, uplifting the faint-hearted and providing a human and devotional core to a book that was sometimes depressingly abstract to read. The seven shared all the motivations of the nineteenth-century quest for the historical Jesus. Their work was quickly overshadowed by Seeley's *Ecce Homo* and Renan's *Vie de Jésus* but, like them, it separated Jesus from the distinctions and formularies of the Church. The interest in his psychology (for instance) was implicit. Renan claimed that Christ's tone of thought was a psychological result of his surroundings, and Jowett wondered in later life, "could I write as well as Renan?"[99]

All the essayists honoured the historical Jesus. Williams sought to reassure the "sincere Christian [who] now asks, is not then our Saviour spoken of in Isaiah?" about their method. Though there was no historical fulfilment of prophecy, yet truth and patience, grief and triumph, had their highest fulfilment in Christ.[100] But what did Williams actually mean? They magnified Christ as a teacher of ethics but did not disclose the secret of his authority. Jowett stressed his universality, yet even that had to be understood carefully. Jowett asked, "Are the accidental circumstances of the first believers to become a rule for us? Is everything, in short, done or said by our Saviour and His Apostles, to be regarded as a precept or example which is to be followed on all occasions and to last for all time? That can hardly be, consistently with the changes of human things".[101] Their critics seized on the implication: Jesus might

---

[98] *Ibid.*, p. 194.
[99] Abbott, II, p. 243.
[100] *ER*, p. 74.
[101] *Ibid.*, p. 357.

finally be left behind in the historical process; like scripture itself, the outward form would be abandoned for the inner meaning. Temple, indeed, suggested that the outward form would be unrecognised as divine by later ages. Christ's understanding of revelation was obviously limited.

The Christological defects followed, at least partly, from their understanding of revelation. The essayists seemed to devalue the facts at the basis of Christianity, preferring to see it as a body of ideas which needed no particular rooting in time or place.

The question of the miraculous was certainly answered too easily. Despite his claims, Powell went beyond anything suggested in Coleridge or Arnold, and for the first time in English divinity a complete divorce between faith and science was apparently proposed. The nature and content of faith were not entirely clear. Volumes seemed to be suggested by Wilson's statement on "how great [an] extent the history of the origin itself of Christianity rests ultimately upon *probable* evidence". What, then, should the believer resort to? — it seemed to be a subjective world where religion must be "viewed apart from connexion with physical things", where faith concerned "points of less definite character", and ended in "such assurance as may be most satisfactory to each earnest individual inquirer's own mind" (Powell). The individual learned not to expect "copious or clear" teaching from revelation (Goodwin), so that he would have "no opinion at all on many points of the deepest interest" (Temple).[102] Perhaps what the essayists lacked most was a sense of the supernatural. They concentrated on treating religion from within.

Jowett said in the Commentary that "formulas of reconcilation" must be found. There was no better defence of *Essays and Reviews*. The honest doubters, floundering in their "chaos of faith, half pantheism, half atheism", as A. S. Farrar put it,[103] needed such a gesture from the Church. Jowett went further: "The Christian religion is in a false position when all the tendencies of knowledge are opposed to it. Such a position cannot be long maintained, or can only end in the withdrawal of the educated classes from the influences of religion". Those who held the possibility of a reconciliation or restoration of belief wished to preserve the historical use of Scripture as the continuous witness in all ages of the higher things in the heart of man, as the inspired source of truth and the way to the better life. "They are willing to take away some of the external supports, because they are not needed and do harm; also, because they

---

[102] *Ibid.*, pp. 34, 128, 144, 202, 252.
[103] A.S. Farrar, *Critical History of Free Thought*, p. 508.

interfere with the meaning".[104] In 1860 as in 1855 he urged his readers to take note of the crisis facing the Church:

> "[It is impossible] to keep the level of knowledge at one point in Germany, at another in England... The truth seems to be, not that Christianity has lost its power, but that we are seeking to propagate Christianity under circumstances which, during the eighteen centuries of its existence, it has never yet encountered".[105]

Goodwin spoke of theology maintaining a "shivering existence... bemoaning itself for the hostility which it encounters. Why should this be, unless because theologians persist in clinging to theories of God's procedure towards man, which have long been seen to be untenable? If, relinquishing theories, they would be content to inquire from the history of man what this procedure has actually been, the so-called difficulties of theology would, for the most part, vanish of themselves".[106] Goodwin meant that the new historical and scientific methods were God's gift to man; why not, then, use them as others were doing? And if the orthodox complained that revelation had become invested in generalities and the distinctive nature of Christian truth was lost, the reply was that "testifying for liberty and the love of truth and tolerance is a sufficient creed". A friend spoke these words of Stanley and for all who were called by his name.[107]

In conclusion: if the book had a unity, radical conclusions could be drawn from it. *Essays and Reviews*, consciously or not, seemed designed for the situation described by Conybeare and others. It accepted and practised biblical criticism with candour and without fear; it deferred to German scholarship and proposed an altogether wider understanding of revelation. Positivistic science dominated the world of fact. The principle of development or evolution unlocked the secrets of knowledge. Darwin's book was a "masterly volume", said Powell, while Jowett also made a passing reference to *The Origin of Species*.[108] By appealing to a new sort of natural theology, the seven solved to their own satisfaction the problems of Church and State, sacred and secular, religion and the world, even if this reversed the traditional order. And as a domestic

---

[104] *ER*, pp. 374-5.
[105] Epistles (2 ed.), II, pp. 447, 519.
[106] *ER*, pp. 211-2.
[107] Church, p. 203.
[108] *ER*, pp. 139, 349. Williams, however, thought that Darwin was "negative and painfully materialistic", Williams, II, pp. 277-8.

matter they suggested a return to that liberal idea of the Church of England which the Latitudinarians represented and which the Tractarians repudiated. They would be willing to lead the movement but they thought that the immediate aim was to mobilise the liberal forces in the Church To that end the reiterated cry above all others in *Essays and Reviews* was: release the clergy, remove the shackles of subscription. Once the clergy were liberated, great things would follow, among them "an age of research in which Christianity would be free".[109]

The situation by 1860 needed to be resolved. The liberals in Oxford must have combined sooner or later. And perhaps, as Pusey held, *Essays and Reviews* or some similar work was the natural outcome of the new Latitudinarianism. Jowett's teaching by 1855 was, Pusey told Keble, part of a larger whole — a "systematic attempt to revolutionise the Church of England".[110] Six years later, in a letter to *The Times*, he saw the publication of *Essays and Reviews* as "a challenge to admit that teaching, as one of the recognised phases of faith, in the English Church".[111]

R. W. Church said that it was an odd collection for such purposes — the writers had not got their thoughts together into such an order and consistency as to warrant their coming before the world with such revolutionary views; indeed, he spoke of the "guerilla way in which these men write, each man fighting for his own hand".[112] Temple held for that reason that no one supposed the essays would live: "they were not of that texture".[113] But their significance was seen within the month, and within the year *Essays and Reviews* had convulsed the Church.

---

[109] *ER*, p. 91.
[110] Pusey MSS, letter to Keble, October, 1855.
[111] Liddon, IV, p. 29.
[112] Church, pp. 186, 188.
[113] Temple Appreciation, p. 205.

CHAPTER THREE

THE LITERARY DEBATE

Rowland Williams offered Fenton Hort a place in *Essays and Reviews*, but Hort had a premonition and refused. When he saw the list of other contributors, he realised that the welcome would be very different from the Cambridge essays in which he, Harvey Goodwin, Ellicott and others had taken part. Williams asked him to write on Justin Martyr, a favourite Father with the radicals (in *Essays and Reviews* Justin was praised for his "utmost evangelical freedom and simplicity of thought"[1]), but Hort, surely, would have interpreted Justin's alleged universalism differently, and he could never have agreed with Williams that the Fathers regarded prophecy as merely "spiritual", i.e., non-supernatural.

Hort believed that the scheme would bring on a crisis. Various influences were (he said) acting quietly on orthodox but rational men which would bear good fruit in due time, but a combined open assault would frighten many back into a mere traditionalism. "As a mere matter of prudence, it seems to me questionable to set up a single broad conspicuous target for the Philistines to shoot at, unless there is some very decided advantage to be gained. Moreover I must confess a strong repugnance to any measure likely to promote anything like a party organisation".[2]

That was in October, 1858. Though Williams allowed no one the gift of clairvoyance, Hort predicted exactly the events following on *Essays and Reviews*. The united appearance of the most notorious clergymen in the Church of England caused a tumult. Conservatives used the book as a stick to belabour new theology. The Broad Church, magnified (or reduced) to a party, suffered grave damage.

The reaction to *Essays and Reviews* took two forms, one a literary controversy, the other a battle in the Church courts. High Churchmen wielded their pens furiously in the former, so it is suitably introduced here by H. P. Liddon, Pusey's disciple and a strong orthodox thinker, who has the earliest notice, in the theological biographies of the time, of

[1] *ER*, p. 64, n. 5.
[2] Hort, I, p. 399.

having read the essays. Liddon had finished the book by 31 March, 1860, and sent a letter to Keble on that day:

> "There is a volume of 'Essays and Reviews', published by J. W. Parker, which has just appeared, and which seems to go further in the race of Rationalism than anything which I have yet seen. Between Jowett's and Wilson's essays the Gospel history simply evaporates, as Jowett considers the first three Gospels to be merely three forms of one tradition, but not 'three independent witnesses' to our Lord's sayings and acts (an exaggerated development of Bishop Marsh?), and Wilson sees in St. John an element of legendary and ideal embellishment, which contrasts disadvantageously with the predominant moral element of the 'Synoptic' Gospels. Certainly nothing nowadays seems to 'make a sensation' excepting only the Catholic teaching, as if the principle of rationalism had been generally admitted and it was merely a question of degrees. This book has already sold largely in Oxford".[3]

The hard tone of the letter anticipated the turmoil to come, and Liddon soon took other steps. By Easter he had sent the essays to Walter Kerr Hamilton, Bishop of Salisbury, urging him to take action against Williams. Liddon remarked to Pusey how different Temple's essay was from Newman's "beautiful sermon on 'The Submission of the Reason and the Feelings to the Revealed Word' ".[4]

Hort quickly followed on Liddon and showed how a liberal thinker responded to the essayists' challenge. Towards the end of April he recommended the book to his friend John Ellerton, the hymn writer. He was obviously more favourable, but he breathed a sigh of relief at his escape. He had not read Powell or Wilson, Goodwin was "poor", "R. Williams on Bunsen is R. Williams all over, and quite worth reading". He continued:

> "Temple's is at least powerful and interesting. Mark Pattison's is, I think, very good, and likely to be of use to you. He almost ignores Clark, W. Law, and the Cambridge Platonists; but as to the general current of religious thought he seems to me quite right. Jowett is provoking as usual. I suppose he will do good to some in forcing honesty of criticism upon them, though there is perhaps not a single thought new to you or me; but his blindness to a providential ordering of the accidents of history is very vexatious. It is curious to see how completely he is leavened with J. H. Newman".[5]

---

[3] J.O. Johnston, *Life and Letters of Henry Parry Liddon*, p. 63.
[4] C.P.S. Clarke, *The Oxford Movement and After*, p. 240.
[5] Hort, I, p. 417.

Hort meant there that reaction and counter-reaction in Oxford were obviously mirrored in the pages of *Essays and Reviews*. Another early reader was Max-Müller. He wrote to a correspondent on 6 May of his surprise that it should have been written by clergymen.[6]

Private notice soon gave way to public notoriety. *The Guardian* had a quick reference in April to the work of the "Peelites" of the Broad Church party and promised clerical readers a broadside to come. But the first literary review was written by a non-Churchman, in *The Spectator* for 7 April, 1860, and the heading was significant — "Open Teaching in the Church of England". *The Spectator* and papers like it kept up a lively interest in the essayists between 1860 and 1864. Their theological attainments naturally interested the reviewer less than their stand as "new men" who were "eminently brave and courageous", furnishing a precedent in new developments of faith which allowed free enquiry and open expression of opinion. They were benefactors and not enemies to the Church: old and time-honoured convictions must be modified when faced by recently-discovered facts, otherwise a "cowardly consciousness" only destroyed all intellectual activity and paralysed moral and social activity. The language was very like the essayists' own, so was the call to encourage new thought. "Free speech is indeed not the truth, but it is the condition of serving truth". The clergy must be set free: it was useless to ignore the movement, pusillanimous to lament it, and tyrannous to attempt its suppression.[7]

The *Literary Gazette* printed a review on 14 April. William Stebbing, a correspondent of Pattison, wrote to him about it, since the reviewer praised the essay on the eighteenth century but criticised the general tone of the rest. Its prediction of popularity for Pattison did not, however, come true.[8]

These outsiders' views were in marked contrast to the almost universal condemnation by the Church press, and they became a barometer for the hardening opinion in the country at large as the essayists presented the apparent spectacle of martyrs for the truth. *The Times* began by noticing *Essays and Reviews* as an item of general interest but by 1864 held that thoughtful men were being repelled from the Church as bishops encouraged their clergy and as "a hundred pulpits ring with futile invective

---

[6] *The Life and Letters of Friedrich Max-Müller*, I, p. 235.

[7] *The Spectator*, 7 April, 1860, pp. 331-2.

[8] MSS Pattison 53, f. 150, letter of William Stebbing, 26 April, 1860. Cf. f. 271, "there are many clergy and gentry in whose reading clubs to my knowledge the Essays are in circulation" (J. Earle, 1 August, 1860).

against the cringing infidel". The prosecution of Jowett in Oxford in 1862 was put down to the "*odium theologicum* of a few infatuated dignitaries" fighting for the "interests of religion and piety against those of truth and justice". Church leaders were "short-sighted men with a rooted distrust of the power of truth to abide the ordeal of free inquiry".[9]

If *The Times* felt so strongly it was not surprising that the *Saturday Review*, under Philip Harwood — no friend of the Church of England — kept up a continuous sniping at clerical scolists. But the essayists were clergymen as well, which did not commend them; their book had "a conservative as well as a destructive side, which it is not fair or wise to overlook". Stanley, for daring to defend them and add credit to the Church, was publicly rebuked. Jowett thought that there was little malignity in the newspaper accounts generally, but he made an exception for the "subtle genius" of the *Review* which, by 1863, was prophesying that the Church would be wrecked in the storm.[10]

The layman's point of view was put, rather self-consciously, by *Fraser's Magazine* in a long sympathetic article in August, 1860. Ruskin in *Modern Painters* was held to say much the same about the bible as Jowett, and was it not true that "the importance of a text may generally be measured by its intelligibility"?[11] The *British Quarterly Review*, however, on the "New Movement from Oxford", had few hopes about a free approach to scripture.[12] *Macmillan's Magazine* was polite but lukewarm while the *National Review*, expectedly, was far more enthusiastic.[13] The *Dublin University Magazine* said that the seven were *not* united: it spoke of "antagonism in *Essays and Reviews*".[14]

The *North British Review* questioned the preface : "the combination... of men, most of whom are recognised as leaders of the Broad Church, can hardly be accounted accidental". There was even a meaning in the order of the contributions. This "surpliced infidelity" harmed the Broad Church. "There was not a little in the position and character and aims of that party, when it arose into public prominence, that gave promise of good... But when from the duty of censors of the opinions of opponents the Broad Church party proceeded to set forth those teachings of their

---

[9] Liddon, IV, p. 28.

[10] Abbott, I, pp. 296, 349.

[11] *Fraser's Magazine*, August, 1860, p. 236.

[12] *British Quarterly Review*, January, 1861, pp. 3-80.

[13] *Macmillan's Magazine*, May, 1861, pp. 41-8. *National Review*, January, 1861, pp. 151-189.

[14] *Dublin University Magazine*, May, 1861, pp. 513-50, and cf. April, 1861, pp. 385-404.

own in which they are peculiar, it has been otherwise; their success has not been gain, but loss".[15]

However, the real reputation of the book rested on three other periodicals, and the essayists eagerly looked forward to reading these. Support from even one would have gained them entrance into many homes, approval from two would ensure their success. They did not expect much from the *Quarterly Review*, but the *Edinburgh*, which had featured Conybeare, and the *Westminster* must surely praise the essays. Williams' review of Rawlinsons' Bamptons was given prominence in the July number of the *Westminster*; the lectures were written, said Williams, "as if nothing had been done from Bishop Marsh to Dr Baur", and could only be the consequence of the irrationalising judgment displayed in Mansel's Bamptons.[16]

But they received a great shock, and the greatest came in the following issue of the *Westminster*. A brilliant article by Frederic Harrison, entitled "Neo-Christianity", treated the essays as the *reductio ad absurdum* of the Broad Church position. Harrison appeared first, and the others followed suit; Wilberforce in the *Quarterly* was blatantly hostile, Stanley — on the face of it, an excellent choice — wrote a painfully ambivalent article in the *Edinburgh*.

Harrison was only 23, and his university career, a flight from Christianity to agnosticism, mirrored that of J. A. Froude, W. E. H. Lecky and others. Consequently, he was impatient with any accommodation to honest doubt. He had heard Wilson's Bamptons and Mansel's "agnostic dialectics" but was more influenced towards doubt by the "men in between", like F. W. Robertson and "dear old Maurice stammering through the story of Dinah" and demolishing any remaining orthodoxy.[17] *Essays and Reviews* was true to type: it was radical but still wished to use the name of Christian. Harrison had no use for such ambiguity and set out to expose it. The book did not convert honest doubters to Christianity. The article shocked the growing numbers of churchmen who had read, or heard reports of, the liberal manifesto. *The Guardian* remarked, "many hard things have been said about *Essays and Reviews*, but nothing so damaging to the authors has ever appeared in

---

[15] *North British Review*, May, 1861, pp. 281-329, August, 1860, pp. 159, 161.
[16] *WR*, July, 1860, pp. 33-49.
[17] B. Willey, *More Nineteenth Century Studies*, p. 162.

print as the eulogy in the *Westminster*". (Jowett, however, was just; he befriended Harrison and never dismissed the article).[18]

Harrison gave the essays uniqueness and — most damagingly — a single point of view, a common identity:

> "A book has appeared which may serve to mark an epoch in the history of opinion. The latest phase of religion at length has developed its creed. The vigour and candour of this volume would raise it above the dust of theological strife; but its origin gives it a place in the record of religious thought. The subject, the form, and the authorship are alike significant. It is no work of a single or isolated thinker; nor of unconnected thoughts upon secondary opinions. It is the combined work of several of the leaders of thought in our seminaries of religious and useful learning; and it deals, not without some method, with the central topic in which all religious inquiry is now summed up. Of the seven essays, four are wholly occupied in treating of the authority or value of Scripture; two of the other three deal chiefly with the same topic. A book like this is not a collection of pamphlets bound up into one volume; or the farrago of a few kindred minds. It would be equally idle to pretend that each writer is not morally responsible for the general tendency of the whole".

The historical method and the concept of development were the key to the book. But how could the essayists remain in their half-way house, he asked. If it was to be retained as holy writ, the bible must be defended as a miraculous gift to men and not reduced to the position of the Apocrypha, while the Koran was equally inspired on their theory.

Another of Harrison's most telling points concerned the effect on the young. The essays demonstrated the parlous situation in Oxford — more than "mouldering scepticism" was found in those cloisters. "They are honeycombed with disbelief, running through every phase from mystical interpretation to utter atheism". *Essays and Reviews*, as the product of this, was in direct antagonism to the whole system of popular belief, and it must have serious consequences. It was an aggressive book whose object, spirit, method and details, as well as design, contradicted the faith of the Christian public and the broad principles on which the Englishman's Protestantism rested.

All attempts to show that these opinions were in accordance with scripture, the Articles, the liturgy, or the Church, had little practical value and did no small practical harm, said Harrison. "Such reasoning may ease the conscience of troubled inquirers; but is powerless to

---

[18] *G*, 17 October, 1860, p. 915. E. Abbott and L. Campbell, eds., *Letters of Benjamin Jowett*, p. 14.

persuade the mass that *that* is, after all, the true meaning of what they
have been taught and have believed..." He added: "What becomes of the
Christian scheme when the origin of man is handed over to Mr Darwin;
and Adam and Eve take their seats beside Deucalion and Pyrrha?... in a
word, from one end of this book to the other the same process is
continued; facts are idealized; dogmas are transformed; creeds are
discredited as human and provisional; the authority of the Church and
of the Bible to establish any doctrine is discarded; the moral teaching of
the Gospel remains; the moral sense of each must decide upon its
meaning and its application... It may be that this is a *true* view of
Christianity, but we insist in the name of common sense that it is a *new*
view". Religion to regain the world must have a doctrine, but "that end
will not be attained by our authors, by subliming religion into an
emotion and making an armistice with science. It will not be attained by
any unreal adaptation, nor by this, which is of all recent adaptations, at
once the most able, the most earnest, and — the most suicidal".[19]

The effects of Harrison's antithesis could be seen in the articles in the
Quarterly and *Edinburgh* reviews: Wilberforce said that the essayists had
been exposed by their fellow rationalists, Stanley quoted a plethora of
faint liberals to place them in respectable company. The article quickly
became the received tradition about the essays — which was unfortunate
for (as Maurice and others implied) Harrison had transferred his own
nemesis of faith at Oxford, and his now equivocal relations with liberal
tutors like Jowett, to the larger scene of religion in England and so could
not give an impartial study of the book. Nor did Harrison notice that
some men of science and honest doubters did appreciate the gesture of
the essayists. Some months later, T. H. Huxley and others subscribed to
a *Memorial to the Rev. Dr Temple*, supporting his cause against the
bishops. "Feeling as we do that the discoveries in Science, and the
general progress of thought, have necessitated some modification of the
views generally held on Theological matters, we welcome these attempts
to establish religious teaching on a firmer and broader foundation".[20]
But most churchmen knew nothing of Huxley's attitude and only too
readily accepted Harrison's version of events: in particular, that the
essayists formed a united band.

Bishop Wilberforce's attack in the *Quarterly Review* for January, 1861,

---

[19] *WR*, October, 1860, pp. 293-332. Cf. *ibid.*, April, 1862, p. 530 f., for a more
favourable attitude.

[20] Imperial College, London, Huxley Collection 2263.

had to be reprinted four times. The clergy in their thousands read his judgment as coloured by Harrison:

> "It is not indeed a 'neo-Christianity', but it is a new religion, which our Essayists would introduce; and they would act more rationally, more philosophically, and, we believe, less injuriously to religion, if they did as their brother unbelievers invite them to do, renounce the hopeless attempt at preserving Christianity without Christ, without the Holy Ghost, without a Church".

The article was unsigned but reports of Wilberforce's authorship soon circulated, and the proceeding, and the tone with which it was carried out, caused much comment. Tait deplored the article, while Maurice thought it "very shocking" that, firstly, he should attack his own clergy anonymously and, secondly, that he should utter vulgar jokes about Bunsen, whom he knew and for whom he had professed esteem.[21] The article did Wilberforce's reputation little good and, in fact, he was a far kinder man than his words suggested. Why was he so bitter? It was obvious that the essays, or Harrison's interpretation of them, shocked Wilberforce, and he wrote with intense personal feeling. But Wilberforce was not a private individual; and the *Quarterly Review* was no polite magazine but one of the organs of the Conservative party. It was inevitable that the article was taken as a declaration of war against the Oxford reformers by the bishop of the diocese and also, since he was a leading member of the bench, as a statement of the "official" attitude towards radical theology. Wilberforce, only a little less than Harrison, bore responsibility for the subsequent debate which concentrated on the errors of the seven and ignored their positive aims.

He, too, put forward the essays as a united work; he stressed resemblances, found common themes, and would not allow Temple to escape responsibility for the extreme views of the others. No defence which disclaimed joint responsibility was possible, said Wilberforce. "The same purpose is before every writer; the same general tone of writing pervades the whole book... the verdict of the English public will be unanimous and clear... the book must be taken as a whole".

Much of what Wilberforce wrote was repeated in the Church press and need not be quoted. As a theological analysis it was, also, superficial and adopted knock-down arguments. The language was hostile: Jowett made obvious mistakes which were "as discreditable to a scholar as to a

---

[21] Maurice, II, pp. 382-3.

divine". His New Testament difficulties could be answered by learning no deeper than Doddridge's Family Expositor or Matthew Henry's Commentary. Williams "resolves the Incarnation into a set of misty words". Powell manifested a scarcely veiled atheism; "if there is meaning in words [he] gives up the very being of a God". Wilson was a stammering, equivocating subscriber. Temple's figure of the education of the human race ("this laboured similitude") contained an implicit denial of the fall of man and hence of redemption; but if all history became a progressive rise or gradual improvement, this led to the notion that faith consisted in principles of right and reason and "disobedience to God's external authority", in order that men by that disobedience might more completely obey reason.

In searching for a principle that would explain the essayists' unity Wilberforce seized on the importance given to private judgment. "The idea of this 'verifying faculty' — this power of each man of settling what is and what is not true in the Inspired Record — is THE idea of the whole volume, the connecting link between all the writers". But this must lead to the utter destruction of all notion of inspiration, he held; all that was left instead of scripture was a residuum of earlier legends, oral traditions, poetical licences, and endless parables. Wilson's ideological principle meant that the "already well nigh unlimited power of explaining away the letter of the Word of God is increased to the uttermost".

Wilberforce wished to isolate the writers and so minimise their importance. "All the schools of theological opinion amongst us are opposed to the Essayists". They provoked this reaction because they had abandoned the traditional study of English theology: "their whole apparatus is drawn bodily from the German Rationalists". The party through their love of naturalism was blind to the plainest rules of fair critical enquiry.

The final shaft concerned their status as clergymen. It was their position, and not the subjects that they raised, which caused public interest in them, the rare and startling paradox that men of such eminence should put forth doctrines incompatible with the bible and the Christian faith as the Church of England received it. "The attempt of the Essayists to combine their advocacy of such doctrines with the retention of the status and emolument of Church of England clergymen is simply moral dishonesty", he declared. Wilberforce stressed the clerical element: the claim for liberty was much greater than Newman's in Tract 90 (he did not spare Wilson, the Tutor who had once signed the Protest against Tract 90). "They believe too much not to believe more, and they disbelieve too much not to disbelieve everything". His last word was on the present position of the authors and the probable effect of their theories:

> "...we have felt bound to express distinctly our conviction that, holding their views they cannot, consistently with moral honesty, maintain their posts as clergymen of the Established Church. We see more danger in the shape of widespread suspicion and distrust likely to arise from their continuance as teachers of that Church, whilst clearly disbelieving her doctrines, than from their lucubrations themselves".[22]

Wilberforce's threat of persecution made defence urgent, and no one was better qualified than Stanley to provide it. He was a leader of the Germanists and privy to the plans for *Essays and Reviews*. The surprise that he did not appear in the volume was tempered by the belief that he would reveal all in his article. Whatever they thought of his theology, few doubted his courage: "next to Garibaldi, you are the bravest man in Europe", Max-Müller told him when he read the *Edinburgh Review* for April, 1861.[23]

Yet Stanley misjudged his case and his audience. In view of the claims of Harrison and Wilberforce he thought that an eirenical approach was the best — mollifying opponents, underplaying the essayists' novelty, emphasising the comprehensiveness of the English Church. He knew that he had to steer a middle course between the "bottomless Charybdis of the *Westminster* and the barking Scylla of the *Quarterly*". But, first, he had to overcome his own reservations. "For seven men, without real agreement of view, to combine as if they had, and to combine, moreover, when the name of almost every one of the set would add weakness instead of strength to the others, appears to me to be a practical blunder, of which I cannot conceive how men of ability could be guilty". That was to the editor of the *Edinburgh*. He defended Temple's work and thought that Jowett's was the next best; "too negative and antagonistic, of course, but wonderfully fertile of thought". The others were strangely crude, and Powell's was a "mere *rechauffé* of his (to me) unintelligible argument..." Williams and Wilson were, he thought, guilty of unpardonable rashness, Pattison was imperfectly cooked.[24]

These doubts came to be reflected in the article and compromised its aim; in particular, though he did not intend this, Stanley minimised the

---

[22] *Quarterly Review*, January, 1861, pp. 248-305.
[23] *The Life and Letters of Friedrich Max-Müller*, I, p. 246.
[24] Prothero, II, pp. 31, 34.

theological importance of the essays, though not their importance as expressions of free speech by the clergy.

The eagerness with which the article was awaited, and the disappoint-ment that it caused, was obvious in various quarters. Tait said that a great opportunity had been thrown away. "Take counsel with your friends before writing", he expostulated, and he wrote in his diary that the article was "quite powerless, its logic very poor".[25] *The Guardian* sneered, "very bad is the case which seems to admit of no better defence".[26] Thirlwall disliked the comparison between Schleiermacher and the seven; Maurice was as depressed by the "smartness" of the reply as by Wilberforce's article. Hort felt similarly.[27] Williams made a comparison with Wilberforce to Stanley's hurt: "the half-friendly tone of the *Edinburgh* will do us more harm than the *Quarterly* with its avowed hostility". Stanley was "ridiculously unfair", he had dropped "Wilson and myself in the mud, particularly poor me".[28] The *Christian Remembrancer* agreed: Stanley was content to throw the rest overboard, "if only he can save the first and the last of the seven writers".[29]

Stanley admitted that the book contained a "disparaging tone through-out... Conclusions arrived at by the life-long labours of a great German theologian are pitchforked into the face of the English public, who never heard of them before, with hardly a shred of argument to clothe their repulsive forms". But the public had been misled into thinking that there was an identity of sentiment, when no such identity existed. (Stanley did not emphasise this sufficiently). And Articles, Bible and Church were far wider than their opponents held. "The questions raised by the Essayists, with very few exceptions, are of a kind altogether beside and beyond the range over which the formularies extend". Moreover, "no passage has ever yet been pointed out ...which contradicts any of the formularies of the Church in a degree at all comparable to the direct collision which exists between the High Church party and the Articles, between the Low Church party and the Prayerbook". The reformers in the sixteenth century were wiser in their generation than the bishops of the nineteenth. There was no Article on the inspiration of the bible or on the definition of miracle. Wilson's remark on the "unhappy" Athanasian creed was compared with Tillotson's well-known "wish that we were well-rid of it".

[25] Davidson, I, pp. 307, 310.
[26] *G*, 1 March, 1861, p. 475.
[27] Prothero, II, p. 42. Hort, I, p. 375.
[28] Williams, II, pp. 39-40.
[29] *Christian Remembrancer*, July, 1862, p. 157.

His belief that virtuous heathens would be saved was no less (or more) repugnant to the Eighteenth Article than St. Peter's declaration that "in every nation he that feareth God and worketh righteousness is accepted of Him", and the numerous confirmations of that inspired truth down to the present Bishop of London.

The liberals were, therefore, committed to maintaining their position for the good of the Church, said Stanley. To withdraw now would mean that "Truth was made for the laity and Falsehood for the clergy... Against this godless theory of a national Church we solemnly protest". It would mean a heavy blow to biblical study, a breach between religion and science, devotion and truth, the repulsion, already sufficiently alarming, of the higher intelligences and more generous spirits among the young from the ministry : finally, it would reduce the national Church "to the level of an illiterate sect or a mere satellite of the Church of Rome".

Against Wilberforce he doubted the essayists' alleged challenge to the supernatural. They had tried to show how miracles could be removed altogether out of the sphere of logic to that of faith. They wished to place Christianity,

> "beyond the reach of accidents, whether of science or criticism; to rest its claims on those moral and spiritual truths, which, after all, are what have really won an entrance for it into the heart, not merely of the highly educated, but of the poor, the ignorant, the afflicted, in every age of the world".

All built alike, not on any outward signs, but on the immutable relations between the moral law of God and the moral conscience of man. Stanley did not answer Wilberforce's contention that the seven had transferred authority from external law to the individual's private opinion, but he denied that they were isolated from the mainstream of orthodox Christianity. "Nor is it the more latitudinarian divines who must be ignored to represent the Essayists as revolutionaries and atheists. The Fathers of the Church of England, the Fathers of the Church Catholic, nay, even some of the modern champions of rigid orthodoxy, have committed themselves irretrievably to the doctrines which in the recent agitation have been so recklessly condemned". Arnold (with passages verbally coincident), Coleridge Westcott, Alford, Milman, Burnet and others all pointed in the same direction. Butler lay behind Temple : "if in Revelation there be found any passages the seeming meaning of which is contrary to natural religion, we may most certainly conclude such seeming meaning not to be the real one" (Stanley misread Butler).

The intention was good, but Stanley showed his superficiality by lumping German divines with English and by making no distinction between the Cambridge and Oxford schools. Tait, for one, felt that he had been badly compromised. "Men are... greatly irritated by being continually told by you that they [and the essayists] all mean the same thing... that they are fools for supposing they differ from the so-called negative theology, when they, according to your showing, in truth agree with it".[30] But the reader was not meant to linger over the details; Stanley's vivid way of writing pressed him towards the conclusion: the future lay with the essayists. The great opportunity which they presented must not be neglected:

> "There have no doubt been cold Latitudinarians... But history has again and again recorded the noblest examples of Christian life and teaching amongst those who offended and rose above the theological prejudices of their contemporaries... if the Church of England is to hold its place as a national institution, — if Christianity is to hold its place as the religion of the world, — it must be by the fulfilment of hopes such as that which breathes through the Chief Essay of this now celebrated volume".[31]

The tone was admirable, but who was convinced by it? What Stanley lacked was the moral wrath displayed by Harrison and Wilberforce.

Whatever the merits of the article, it only brought unwelcome attention to Stanley himself. His mother thought that his hopes of becoming a bishop were now ended, while the *Church and State Review* said that he was unfit to be religious adviser to the Prince of Wales.[32] But Stanley's troubles only became part of the general liberal travail. By April, 1861 the essayists were reading, not the polite notices of newspapers and literary men, but the daily diatribes of the religious press, and their indignation and alarm mounted. There was only one exception: *The Guardian* in due course became liberalised (to Pusey's and Keble's disgust), though only mildly, as it turned out. But the earlier *Guardian* gave the first large-scale review of the essays, and in its hostility and lack of sympathy anticipated the rest. The article, on 23 May, 1860, was longer than for any other book in that year, not excepting *The Origin of Species*, with which it coupled the essays, and showed that reaction from churchmen was

---

[30] Davidson, I, p. 312.
[31] *Edinburgh Review*, April, 1861, pp. 461-499.
[32] *Church and State Review*, October, 1863, p. 56. Cf. W. Brock, *Infidelity in High Places*, p. 55.

immediate and critical. Words like "atheism", "subversion" and "rash–ness" were freely used.

For the *Guardian* writer, the publication was a sign of the times but a portentous one. If it were the production of an individual, it would still be sufficiently remarkable, for such ventures did not appear "without a sort of consciousness that appreciation at least, if not welcome, awaits them... not only as an exposition of the sentiments and conclusions of certain thinkers, but as an index also of the thoughts which are working in the minds of men about us". The issue turned on the relationship of Church and scripture, so cavalierly treated in the volume:

> "They utterly ignore, we fear they deliberately despise, those functions of the Church as subsidiary to holy writ, when we speak of her as witness and keeper. If her witness is set aside... nothing whatever remains to check the idiosyncracies of the individual. He may, as the writers before us evidence with melancholy force, find by one device or another anything he pleases in Scripture — or, if he prefers it, nothing definite whatever".

Prosecution was already in the mind of the writer; he doubted whether the essayists retained "any real hold upon those truths which are the very characteristic of our holy religion", and the question about Jowett's repeated subscription to the formularies was "painful".[33]

The *Christian Observer* followed suit in June. It saw the book as the Tract 90 of the Broad Church school: Tract 90 was meant to establish the principle that a man might retain the orders and benefices of the Church without believing the Articles — the essayists held that they might retain them without believing the bible. "This is the worst and most perilous case of the two...the Church must cleanse itself from this sin or find its very existence endangered". The reviewer found sinister implications in a title page which was the "quietest, most modest, most unpretentious which our readers ever saw".[34]

The Record was, predictably, quick off the mark. On 21 May, 1860, it said that, unless challenged, *Essays and Reviews* "will produce more evil than anything which has been produced by the press for a long period". Week by week it treated readers to a separate dissection of each essay. In November there was another attack on the "effrontery of the Oxford essayists".[35]

---

[33] *G*, 23 May, 1860, p. 473; a preliminary notice appeared on 4 April, 1860, p. 317.

[34] *Christian Observer*, June, 1860, pp. 372-398.

[35] *The Record*, 21 May, 1860, p. 2, 4 October, 1860, p. 4, 10 October, 1860, p. 4, 16 November, 1860, p. 4.

The technique of character assassination, familiar from *The Record*, was copied by otherwise respectable journals : Williams, said *The Record*, showed a sad decline from the days when he was regarded as the "foremost classic in Cambridge". *The Guardian* saw him as an example of the proverb *corruptio optimi pessima*. In October, 1860 the *Christian Remembrancer* said that his rapid "intellectual and moral career" since his book on Christianity and Hinduism was "fearfully instructive". The latter article set *Essays and Reviews* in the atmosphere of unbelief shown at the British Association meeting in Oxford in 1860. A book, "however weak or vapid it may be, which contains a smart attack on scripture, will command larger attention when this setting prevails". As for the writers themselves, with the exception of Temple and Pattison, "we have never met with so flagrant a case of dishonesty within the pale of the Church of England, not excepting Tract 90 and Ward's 'Ideal of a Christian Church' ". *Essays and Reviews* contained a profound ignorance about the religious opinions of the Catholic world, and (a point which Harrison was simultaneously making), "we confess our utter inability to comprehend the intermediate position in which the essayists stand". Jowett's proposal for a union of Christendom based on the modern interpretation of scripture, leaving open all doctrines, the rule of religious opinion being allowed to vary, "is the wildest chimera that has ever been seriously proposed for the adoption of churchmen". A separate article rebuked Powell:

> "If we encounter a complete acceptance of Darwin by an ordained priest of the Church of England, and in a volume not professedly devoted to physical science but one which is 'an attempt to illustrate the advantage derivable to the cause of religious and moral truth' — then indeed we are perplexed. Mr Darwin at any rate said nothing about the cause of religious and moral truth. He says take it or leave it, but Professor Powell goes on to apply it to theology and belief in God".[36]

There were many similar criticisms. When warned on all hands about the criminal volume, the Church public naturally rushed to buy it. The surest sign of the notoriety of *Essays and Reviews* was the vast sale from January, 1861 onwards. The total printed in 1860 was 3,000 copies; the first edition of 1,000 had been exhausted by June, the third edition was in the shops by November. But between January and June, 1861, 13,000 copies were sold. The fourth edition was out of print within a month of

---

[36] *Christian Remembrancer*, October, 1860, pp. 327-360, April, 1861, p. 469.

Wilberforce's article in January, and a fifth edition of 2,000 went in a fortnight. A *Guardian* correspondent wrote indignantly of seeing copies selling like hot cakes one February afternoon in an S.P.C.K. bookshop. The withdrawal of the publisher John W. Parker — either because of orthodox pressure or because of the death of his son who had originally promoted the volume — made no difference to the situation: Longman's took over the book, and it absorbed all their energies. The sixth, seventh, eighth and ninth editions of 3,000 all came out in March. The sixth edition was sold off in six hours, and a bookseller bought up 700 copies of another edition in one order. The tenth edition was issued in cheaper form for the wider circulation. A year after their quiet appearance the essays bore a very different complexion. R. W. Church told his American correspondent that there would be a row over Darwin, "if there were not a much greater row going on about *Essays and Reviews*".[37]

How could the radicals' offensive be answered? *Ought* it to be answered? Maurice thought that the replies did little good, and certainly the level of debate in the newspapers and magazines was poor. In fact, by 1865, some *400* books, pamphlets and articles had been written about *Essays and Reviews*.[38] The best way of replying, and so meeting the essayists' contentions, lay in some lengthy analysis of their theology. Yet the most serious volume out of the 400 was itself a collection of essays — *Aids to Faith*, which had as many levels of competence as the offending book. It, too, contained a preface disclaiming mutual responsibility, and so making a virtue out of the fact that most of the writers "did not know their coadjutors": only the editor had seen the whole, and each had written independently. Ewald was astonished; how could the English imagine that proper discussion could be conducted by such means?[39] Yet three leading publishers were promising replies in this form by March, 1861, and expected great things from them. Without much depth or penetration, the volumes were also generally hostile to the essayists' point of view. *Aids to Faith* was already projected in August, 1860, and its direction could be seen. Hort was asked to contribute but said that he could not join any "orthodox protest" which (he implied) substituted polemics for reasoned thought.[40]

After some delay *Aids to Faith* was published in the summer of 1861.

---

[37] Church, p. 188.
[38] J.F. Hurst, *History of Rationalism*, p. 400.
[39] *Göttingische Gelehrte Anzeigen*, 24 July, 1861, pp. 1161-1180.
[40] Hort, I, p. 428.

Its separate articles answered the essayists one by one, and the contributors included both Low and High Churchmen. A.C. McCaul, Professor of Hebrew at King's College, London, and George Rawlinson, the Camden Professor, between them wrote the most tendentious essays, ridiculing evolutionary views of the Old Testament, and subscribing to the Mosaic authorship of the Pentateuch, the universality of the Deluge, and the creation of man as taking place less than 10,000 years before the latter event. Goodwin was dismissed because he did not know Hebrew. The editor, William Thomson, Bishop of Gloucester and Bristol, had escaped being one of the seven. Consequently, he stressed his orthodoxy and exposed Jowett for speaking of "Gregory of (*sic*) Nazianzen", and for drawing on F.C. Baur for a solitary patristic reference in support of lax views of the Atonement which, if quoted in full, would have confounded him. Jowett ought to have taken more seriously the New Testament which preached an objective Atonement consistently.[41]

Any book in which Mansel appeared must obviously be considered. His Bamptons had criticised Powell generally; he now dealt with the Professor's misconceptions about the miraculous in a long and difficult essay.

Mansel agreed that miracles were admissible only as supplementary adjuncts of a faith already believed. But they were indispensable to such a faith, if seen as due to the introduction of a new element into nature which was superior to it, a different cause from the ordinary causes in nature. After all, the exercise of human free will brought about changes in nature, showing that mind was more powerful than matter. Mansel thought that the truest idea of God was of Him as Mind, though he failed to notice Powell's distinction between physical causation, "or the action of *matter* on *matter*, and moral causation, or the action of *mind* on *matter*", which suggested the same approach. Powell had misunderstood Butler's teaching that miracles as evidences of revealed truths were to be rejected only if contrary to the previously known truths of natural religion.

Powell's use of Hume was Mansel's main target. Hume's theory was "just as strong or just as weak as the day when it was written as at the present time". It had received no extra support from the progress of science since Hume: indeed, how could the "evidence of a firm and unalterable experience", if such existed at any time, be capable of being made stronger? But experience, confirming the impossibility of vio-

---

[41] *Aids to Faith*, pp. 214, 232, 284, 327, 346.

lations of the laws of nature, was not so monolithic as Hume thought. No scientific thinker in the previous century doubted that the sensible phenomena which came under his experience were owing to *some* natural cause acting by *some* natural law, whether the actual cause or law were known or unknown. The nature of this conviction was not altered by any subsequent increase in the number of known as compared with unknown causes, and "experience" must be wide enough to contain all discoveries anticipated in the future. Advancing scientific investigation even strengthened the supernatural claims of Christianity: while eliminating the number of unknown natural causes of alleged marvels, it would leave the real miracles unexplained. In that case only two alternatives were possible. "Either the recorded acts were not performed at all... or they were performed, as their authors themselves declare, by virtue of a supernatural power, consciously exercised for that very purpose". If one chose the first alternative, Christianity as a religion must be denied, said Mansel. If miracles were impossible, Christ was not resurrected or ascended; and without a supernatural Christ as its moral basis the Christian life became a mockery. So much for the belief that morality and human progress were not dependant on orthodoxy.[42]

It was difficult not to be swayed by the logic of the argument. But there was one obvious drawback. Mansel held that it was necessary to *prove* Christianity. But Powell by denying this had placed the discussion on a different level. The reader who had been convinced by the Professor of Geometry would hardly go back to the Professor of Logic.

The most interesting section of the essay concerned his opponents' debt to foreign authors. McCaul, with a brace of references, had shown Williams' likeness to Schleiermacher. Mansel, who had made similar references (more than twenty to Schleiermacher) in his Bamptons when writing about Jowett, Powell and Williams, added more in *Aids to Faith*. When Powell said that "Christianity must be viewed apart from con-nexion with physical things", Mansel saw the same fatal division between the "external accessories" and the "essential doctrines" which was contained in section 14 of Schleiermacher's *Der Christliche Glaube*. Indeed, to show Schleiermacher's similarity of thought (though not, of course, suggesting that Powell had learned from him directly), he translated a relevant passage.[43]

F.C. Cook, a Canon of St. Paul's and Inspector of Schools, also

---

[42] *Ibid.*, pp. 1-40.
[43] *Ibid.*, pp. 5, 18, 112, 120.

spoke in disparaging terms of Schleiermacher. To his system "may be traced that aversion to what is called dogmatism, which distinguishes many of our own writers who, without adopting all his views, have passed through his school". *Essays and Reviews* was true to type; "we consider it a fortunate circumstance that on the first appearance of Ideology [in England] so much of its true character has been disclosed" — i.e., its basic pantheism, its belief in the absorption of the individual consciousness in the Infinite Spirit, its *a priori* assumption that all miraculous interventions were impossible. The claim that the future of theology lay on the path marked by German thought also cast light on the demand for clerical freedom:

> "In the writings of all schools of rationalism and neology, a prominent place is assigned to the vindication of absolute liberty of sceptical speculation, not merely for students but for professors of theology".

Jowett described Cook as the only man in England who could be called really learned.[44] But Cook could see only one conclusion to the essayists' thought — the atheism and rationalism of Strauss, de Wette and others.[45]

Williams' predecessor at Lampeter, E. Harold Browne, now Norrisian Professor at Cambridge, wrote a mild essay which traced the innovators' approach to scripture back to Coleridge's belief that "whatever *finds* me bears witness that it has proceeded from a Holy Spirit". But he asked, sensibly enough, where did this stop: we discovered more which "found" us in Baxter's *Saints' Everlasting Rest* than in the second book of Chronicles. The fault lay in not distinguishing between objective and subjective revelation or between supernatural illumination and the inspiration of all good men. Fathers, schoolmen and reformers all saw that there was a difference between what we knew of ourselves and what was revealed. Inspiration was of the nature of a miracle and was questioned only by those who had doubts about the miraculous itself.[46]

C.J. Ellicott, Dean of Exeter, in his reply to Jowett questioned the supposed constant element beneath the surface of scripture, so that — however much interpretation itself changed — the basic meaning of the bible was unaltered. Why should the nineteenth century be superior to all other ages in discovering this basic meaning? Jowett (he held) was too

---

[44] Abbott, I, p. 271.
[45] *Aids to Faith*, pp. 147, 149, 150, 157, 165.
[46] *Ibid.*, pp. 287-321.

subjective, and he also ignored the other requirement in interpretation: it must be grammatical, historical, contextual, and minute, but it must also be exercised according to the analogy in faith, in the light of the understanding and experience of the Church.[47]

Aids to Faith went into four editions and also provoked an answering literature of its own. Browne was attacked by extreme literalists as an temporiser and even as an ultra-liberal.[48] Bishop Thomson was criticised for mis-reading Anselm's Atonement theory in *Cur Deus Homo* and, from a different angle, for his reservations about the doctrine of vicarious suffering: the Mauricians J. Llewelyn Davies and Francis Garden said that his essay contained "startling language on God's wrath".[49] A "Bachelor of Divinity" wrote 138 pages in *An Answer to the Archbishop of York on the subject of Endless Torments* (Thomson succeeded to the northern primacy in 1863). A blast from the Methodist Thomas Jackson was directed at Bishop Fitzgerald (writer of an essay on the evidences) for his censure of Wesley and the Evangelicals for neglecting the proofs of religion.[50] Thomson's omnibus was a disappointment and particularly to those who expected an official answer that would be a panacea for theological ills. But there was no coherence in orthodoxy itself, no formulated doctrine of biblical authority which would satisfy both a McCaul and a Browne, and it could not be found in a volume which brought such strangely assorted companions together. *Aids to Faith* had much less unity than the essays themselves. The disturbing picture that it gave of the divisions in the Church was pointed out by both *The Rambler* and the *Westminster Review*.[51]

The second volume of this type, *Replies to "Essays and Reviews"*, edited by Wilberforce, confirmed the impression made by *Aids to Faith*. Here the more rigid, conservative wing had their say. It was less a scholarly product than a straight opposing of the liberal writers' teachings in turn. But Gilbert Rorison described the Mosaic cosmogony as an "inspired hymn of creation", in an essay on Goodwin, and this would have been denounced as a betrayal by McCaul in the companion work. Wilberforce seems to have anticipated that anomalies would occur and astutely wrote his preface before reading the book.[52] His hard words — the essays were

[47] *Ibid.*, pp. 371-469.
[48] G.W. Kitchin, *Edward Harold Browne, A Memoir*, p. 213.
[49] Anon. ("A Catholic Layman"), *Anselm Scriptural and Catholic*, p. 12. J. Llewelyn Davies and F. Garden, *The Death of Christ*, Tracts for Priests and People XIII, p. 4.
[50] T. Jackson, *Aids to Truth and Charity*, p. 6.
[51] *The Rambler*, 1861, p. 408. *WR*, April, 1862, p. 530f.
[52] *Replies to "Essays and Reviews"*, p. ix.

a preparation for Antichrist, a tricked-out pantheism, he said — were exceeded by Christopher Wordsworth, whose vituperations about Jowett shocked readers.[53] For him inspiration simply meant infallibility. "If the documents are not free from error, we have no authority for the doctrine contained in them". But the future Bishop of Lincoln was more intellectually able than this: fear about the public effect of *Essays and Reviews*, and the agitation now at full height among the clergy, made him lose his balance.[54]

If that were possible, Wordsworth's points were made more violently by J. W. Burgon, whose article, written in characteristic vein — "wielding the jawbone of an ass", someone facetiously said — attacked all seven writers as infidels. Other contributors were Henry John Rose, who chose Hengstenberg as a representative German in place of Bunsen as championed by Williams, C. A. Heurtley, Lady Margaret Professor at Oxford, and E. M. Goulburn. Heurtley dwelt on Powell's "hateful principle" — his admission of necessary ambiguity into theological discourse, so that a thing could be true as a matter of theology, while false scientifically. "Woe to the Church in which it gains currency!"[55] Dr. Goulburn, as his predecessor at Rugby, was set to answer Temple on the Education of the World. W. J. Irons provided one of the better analyses of Wilson. The Act of Toleration, he pointed out, had formally registered the fact that the Church was no longer national. Wilson's scheme alarmingly resembled the facts of the present religious life of the nation, a Church without supernatural claims, depending on the bible alone, but a bible deprived of its divine warranty — this (said Irons, an old opponent of Powell) would never accomplish regeneration of the national life.[56]

Both the *Westminster Review* and *Fraser's Magazine*, significantly, praised the most substantial essay in the book, A. W. Haddan's reply to Pattison.[57] Haddan, more than twenty years before, had been Newman's curate at St. Mary's, but he now questioned the evolutionary approach to doctrine, or, at least, Pattison's version of it. Pattison, he said, exhibited as the grounds of faith what were, in truth, the causes of its corruption, the character and mental condition of each successive age.

---

[53] *WR*, April, 1862, p. 539.

[54] *Replies to "Essays and Reviews"*, pp. 409-500.

[55] *Ibid.*, p. 144.

[56] *Ibid.*, pp. 199-276.

[57] *WR*, April, 1862, p. 539. *Fraser's Magazine*, August, 1862, p. 206. Pattison described Haddan as "one of the best representatives of the enlightened Tory and Anglican section", *Memoirs*, p. 246.

But men did not see the eternal verities only through the past world of thought, and it was possible to speak of infallibility, though not the exaggerated papal notion of it. Haddan obviously thought that Pattison's revulsion from Tractarianism had impaired his judgment: he had been driven to believe that if no living infallible voice was possible then no infallibility at all was possible. But was that philosophically tenable ground for denying the possibility of religious faith at all? "Because moral evidence is not in itself formally infallible, is it impossible that *some* moral evidence shall bring within the reach of men truths which *are* formally infallible?" The bible was evidence of a past infallible revelation, and the basic understanding of that revelation had been preserved by the instrumentality of man himself, "not with mathematical demonstration or rigorous precision, but with moral certainty and with substantial truth". In the flux of historical uncertainty some firm ground was, therefore, possible, nor did Pattison's claim that the Hanoverian divines supported him bear much examination. They were not so far gone as to speak of a verifying faculty, and Butler's *Analogy* was an elaborate depreciation of the supremacy of reason.[58]

Butler was frequently quoted as the classic defence against Deism old or new. But in another volume, entitled *Faith and Peace*, William Lee needed 109 pages to mould Butler as a suitable *riposte* to Powell.[59] This indicated the difficulties in answering essays, which were usually far longer than the offending work itself, if they were not to be plain negatives. The editor, Archdeacon George Denison, became the great adversary of the essayists in Convocation and elsewhere. As editor he aimed high, and *Faith and Peace* would have been important had Keble and Pusey written for it as he had intended. But Pusey had reservations, and Keble supported his friend and kept silent.[60]

The blueprint of some other essays is tantalising, for the authors would surely have grasped the opportunity missed in *Aids to Faith*. B. F. Westcott of Cambridge tried influencing R. W. Jelf to stem the "reckless assaults" on the radicals, but already felt by the end of 1860 that a "mediating volume" was needed, putting forward the values proclaimed by Jowett and his friends but also those things which in a misdirected zeal they had neglected. The Cambridge trio saw their own position becoming unpopular, so Hort and Lightfoot joined in, chose a

---

[58] *Replies to "Essays and Reviews"*, pp. 347-408.
[59] *Faith and Peace*, essay 4.
[60] Pusey MSS VI, f. 280, letter of Denison to Pusey, 8 March, 1861. f. 281, letter of Pusey to Keble, March, 1861.

title — *Revelation and History* — and a scheme: Lightfoot was to take the "preparation of the Gospel", the stages of Jewish history, the work of the different nations of antiquity and the special calling of Israel. Westcott's subject was the "witness of God in His Son", the Incarnation as an historical revelation of God, and the question of miracle; and Hort was to treat of the development of doctrine within the New Testament and in the historical epochs since the close of the canon. Hort wrote to Westcott of the "extreme importance" of that side of truth which the essayists represented. They seemed to him to "*believe* very much more of truth than their (so-called) orthodox opponents, and to be incomparably greater lovers of truth". So the volume must obviously be as much sympathetic as antagonistic to them. "For Jowett himself, much as he vexes me with his lazy taking on trust of objections... I find I have an increasing love. There are things in his essays (not in *Essays and Reviews*) which meet the real *ultimate* difficulties better than anything I know".[61] That was an astonishing tribute, and the beleagured seven badly needed such gestures of affection and support.

But the scheme came to nothing: the strains of the outside world ruffled even the calm of Cambridge. There was a "sad defection" on Lightfoot's part; he pleaded pressing commitments but evidently found Hort's opinions too advanced for his comfort. Westcott expostulated: a reaction more perilous than scepticism was setting in, he said. "Of all the cares, almost the greatest which I have had has been *Essays and Reviews* and its opponents. The controversy is fairly turning me grey. I look on the assailants of the essayists from the Bishops downwards as likely to do far more harm to the Church and to the truth than the essayists".[62] *Revelation and History* would have been a courageous book, and Westcott and Hort must command our respect accordingly.

The replies sold well, but the essays themselves outpaced all: by March, 1862 the eleventh edition was out, making 20,000 in print; a year and two editions later it was 22,250 copies. As opposition grew, so did the sales. This provided a parallel with the Deists: the 79 works written against Collins's *Discourse of Free Thinking*, or the 115 against Tindal's *Christianity as old as Creation*, only popularised the heresy. The similarities multiplied as the outcry grew larger. Writers recalled Swift on Woolston:

> "He does an honour to his gown,
>   By bravely running priestcraft down",

[61] Hort, I, pp. 428, 437-9, 442-5, 448.
[62] A. Westcott, *Life and Letters of Brooke Foss Westcott*, pp. 213-6.

which fitted Wilson or Jowett nicely,[63] just as, 50 years later, Ronald Knox's lines on William Temple's contribution to the modernist *Foundations* would have done for his father's work in *Essays and Reviews* :

> "His name suffic 'd to leave th' insidious tome,
>   A household word in every English home".[64]

Of books produced by individual authors at this time, two deserve most comment. The first was by Pusey, and it shows that his attitude to *Essays and Reviews* was more complicated than his admirers or detractors allowed. In a sense, Pusey's situation was very like Newman's : both had backgrounds which made them sensitive to some of the issues raised by the essayists. In Pusey's case it was his early involvement with German theology. He adopted a rather cumbrous way out of the dilemma, firstly by distinguishing between the positive aspects of foreign theology and the merely sceptical, and secondly by refusing to join *Faith and Peace* and other volumes because they were not scholarly or serious enough. He explained his stand in a letter to *The Guardian*. Several topics in the essays (he said) required whole books in answer ; in any case, there was the random scepticism of the book as a whole which could not be met by simple replies. "The writers, in their own persons, rarely affirm anything, attempt to prove nothing, and throw a doubt on everything. If any of us had dogmatised as to truth as they do to error, what scorn we should be held up to !". A proper acquaintance with the foreign sources of this unbelief was necessary, and this could not be given systematic expression in a brief space or any one treatise or volume.[65]

Pusey concentrated his energies, therefore, on his large commentary on the book of Daniel. But when this appeared in 1864 Pusey seemed to have fallen into the trap of the other orthodox opponents. The work was scholarly, but his distinction between positive and negative teachers was often unreal, and his anxiety to avoid the taint of German heresy underlay everything. He explained the change in his position since he was 27. "I say this, because some are fond of quoting an early work of mine, the remaining copies of which I withdrew some 30 years ago". The reference was to the *Historical Enquiry*, which he had written against Hugh James Rose in 1828 in defence of German Protestantism, and

---

[63] H.L. Mansel, *Letters, Lectures and Reviews*, p. 295.
[64] F.A. Iremonger, *William Temple, Archbishop of Canterbury*, p. 159.
[65] *G*, 6 March, 1861, pp. 214-5.

which he now admitted was over-sanguine about the restoration of faith
then beginning in Germany; moreover, he had left some things purposely
unexplained, while others were crudely said. But, "nothing which I wrote
had any bearing on the English Articles, whose positive teaching I ever
valued, or any part of the Catholic faith, in which (as I acquainted myself
with Rationalism as a duty) God ever, in His goodness, preserved me,
without any temptation to part with any of it".[66]

Perhaps, as the tone suggests, Pusey would have done better by
avoiding publication. The "Germanists" consistently misunderstood
him. Thirlwall said that the book was a "painful enigma" : such resolute
and passionate one-sidedness in a man of extensive learning must, he
thought, be "a reaction against inward misgivings kept under, as
suggestions of the Evil One, by a violent effort of the will".[67] And the
commentary, despite Pusey's desire for objectivity, was dominated by the
essays crisis. It was too quarrelsome, filled with too many voluminous
foot-notes arguing the small detail of the controversy, and too anxious to
be of much help to the student or exegete.

Pusey approached the prophecy of Daniel as one especially fitted to be
a battlefield between faith and unbelief. "It admits of no half-measures.
It is either divine or an imposture". Against Rowland Williams he held
the book to be by Daniel, on the ground that Christ himself believed this;
further, since Christ understood the prophecies to refer to himself, the
integrity of the book also concerned the question of predictive prophecy
as a whole. The moral qualities of the prophets were subservient to their
witness to the Coming One. The commentator spoke on behalf of a
supernatural understanding of the bible; Daniel was not the record of
some natural anticipation of the future (such as Schleiermacher held) but
of divinely communicated truth about the Lord. He condemned the
naturalism, or Pelagianism, of the essayists, as of Ewald, Samuel
Davidson, and various other figures, with a side-thrust at Tait for his
part in the Privy Council judgment which exonerated Williams and
Wilson from charges of heresy. Pusey impugned the radicals' motives:
they shrank from stating explicitly as their own the unbelief which they
suggested to others. "They undermined men's faith without denying it
themselves in such definite terms as would materially risk their offices or
positions".[68] Pusey also issued a new edition of Tract 90 in 1861 to

---

[66] E.B. Pusey, *Daniel the Prophet*, p. xxvi n.
[67] *Letters Literary and Theological of Connop Thirlwall*, p. 245.
[68] E.B. Pusey, *op. cit.*, pp. iii, 1, 5, 110, 222, 232, 470.

counteract Wilson's argument about the Articles, and he brought the discussion up to date in an historical preface.

The other outstanding book was the *Critical History of Free Thought*, the Bamptons of 1862, given by A. S. Farrar. A lesser man would have made the subject a tirade against rationalism, but Farrar mentioned the essays only in passing. His courage was remarkable and suggested his later development as a liberal thinker and friend of the Broad Churchman, Edwin Hatch. Only the historical-critical method provided a proper insight into the genesis and growth of free thought, he said. To analyse unbelief as a species of psychological or moral lapse, or, as van Mildert had done, as the work of Satan, was only "strictly theological, and removes the enquiry from the province of human science". "Scientific rigour" demanded an attitude of fairness to those who manifested the symptoms.

Farrar thought that the dangers to faith in the modern world were exaggerated, and he proposed a novel view of free thought based on Buckle's notion (*History of Civilisation*, I, 4) that civilisation depended upon the progress of intellect, and scepticism, therefore, was an almost unmixed blessing. "Free thought has had an office in the world", under the administration of a benevolent Providence, and it had strengthened the Christian faith. "While therefore fully appreciating the reverent wish of Christian men to defend the truth with sacred tenacity, which leads them to regard all doubt with alarm; we can frankly allow the function and use of the phenomenon of doubt in history when viewed as an intellectual fact. The use of it is to test all beliefs, with the view of bringing out their truth and error". Farrar criticised rationalism for being only a partial expression of the "teaching of scripture as expressed in the dogmatic teaching of the Church". But he emphasised the complexity of modern free thought, when represented by writers as diverse as John Stuart Mill, James Martineau, Theodore Parker, Francis Newman, Sara Hennell and others, all of whom must be approached with understanding. The Church must not draw in upon itself, and it must not silence the clergy who represented the movement within its ranks.

"The prevention of the expression of doubt is not the extinction of feeling", said Farrar, "and such acts of repression cannot reach the laity of the Church, even if they touch the clergy". Instead, the clergy should be trained to "supply the intellectual cravings of the present day, they must be placed on a level with its ripest knowledge, and be acquainted with the nature and origin of the forms of doubt which they will encounter". The "opposite stratum of society" could be reached only by the "delicate gifts of intellect, and by the ripest learning".[69]

Annual series like the Bamptons naturally reflected the debate, though other lecturers were less circumspect than Farrar. Edward Garbett, editor of the *Christian Advocate*, proclaimed aloud the novelties of *Essays and Reviews* when he gave the Boyle lectures for 1861:

> "The production of such a volume, from persons holding the official positions of the writers, might unhappily be paralleled in Germany, but is, I believe, without precedent in the history of the Church of England".[70]

Unlike Farrar, Garbett eschewed the historical-critical method, and he had forgotten the Deists. The Hulseans for 1862 were rather more favourable, the lecturer being J. S. Howson, joint author with W. J. Conybeare of a life of St. Paul.[71]

The public appetite was not, of course, satisfied by these works, and the publishers applied to more authors. The easiest course was to turn a publication meant for another purpose into a dissertation on *Essays and Reviews*. This was the method chosen by George Moberly, headmaster of Winchester and future Bishop of Salisbury, as early as October, 1860, when he added a pugnacious foreword to a book of sermons on the Beatitudes. As an educationist almost as distinguished as Temple, Moberly was worried about the effects on the young. The essayists' error was that the "nude scripture, the merest letter of the sacred volume, is spoken of as if in it and in it alone resided the entire revelation of Christ and all possible means of judging what that revelation is". But the new Testament was written to men who already knew Christian truth, and it was historically and notoriously erroneous to suppose that the Church and its traditional doctrines were either literally founded upon the written words of scripture or that they could impart no illustration nor help in the interpretation of those words.[72]

J. W. Burgon went one better. He had returned to Oxford in 1860, after being English Chaplain in Rome, to find himself appointed select preacher. He now prefaced his sermons, which were on Inspiration and Interpretation, with 200 pages in answer to the essays.[73]

---

[69] A.S. Farrar, *Critical History of Free Thought*, pp. ix, xiii, 465, 484, 488, 492, 497, 510.
[70] E. Garbett, *The Bible and its Critics*, p. iv.
[71] J.S. Howson, *Five Lectures on the Character of St. Paul*, p. xii.
[72] G. Moberly, *Sermons on the Beatitudes*, pp. iv-xxxix.
[73] J.W. Burgon, *Inspiration and Interpretation*, pp. ix-xxxv especially.

Then there were the pamphlets. Moberly's foreword was 58 pages long, an ideal size, and was quickly issued as one of the many tracts which kept printers busy between 1861 and 1864. These constitute a *genre* of their own and equal anything, in virulence and variety, in the history of theological controversy. A few spoke up for the essayists. R. B. Kennard and G. J. Wild, two clergymen of the Salisbury diocese, published several pamphlets, much to the pain of their bishop.[74] Stanley drew up a catena of extracts, 72 pages long, to show Jowett's orthodoxy, which was at once dismissed by Wilberforce.[75] In turn, Goldwin Smith, in *The Suppression of Doubt is not Faith*, chided Wilberforce for his article in the *Quarterly* and his sermons at Oxford against teachers who led young men astray (the second sermon contained an extraordinary passage on the 'Doubter's Death' which achieved a large sale for it).[76] J. M. Ludlow also published criticisms of Wilberforce.[77] Under the heading, *Conscience and the 'Quarterly'*, the Rev. Henry Jones wrote a plea for fair play towards the essayists. The Rev. Robert Ainslie, of Christ Church, Brighton, published a total of eleven discourses in support of the book.

But most of the pamphlets were unashamedly hostile and gave no quarter when dealing with neology. Their titles showed this, thus: *Jesus Christ and the Essayists contrasted*, *The Essayists judged out of their own mouths*, *"Essays and Reviews" compared with Reason and Revelation*, *Catholicity and Reason* (they accepted 9/10ths of F.W. Newman's system — why not all?), *Another Gospel Examined, or the Essayists exposed*, *Worn-out Neology*, *A Crystal from Cloudland* (named thus, because the radicals' theology was airy-fairy), *Two Great Heresiarchs* (Williams and Wilson), and *Anti-Essays*, a title which had various permutations. The essayists were seen to constitute a mystic number, so some writers described them with images from the book of Revelation, "The seven extinguishers of the seven lamps of the Apocalypse", or "Seven Stars in a new constellation", and a common title, parodying Aeschylus was, *"Septem Contra Christum"*.

---

[74] R. B. Kennard, *"Essays and Reviews", Their Origin, History, General Characteristics and Significance*, pp. 17, 49, 50, and cf. his *The Late Professor Powell and Dr Thirlwall on the Supernatural*. G. Wild, *A Brief Defence of "Essays and Reviews"*. Wild was criticised in *G*, 5 April, 1861, p. 333.

[75] *Statements on Christian Doctrine and Practice extracted from the published writings of the Rev. Benjamin Jowett, passim*.

[76] *The Suppression of Doubt is not Faith*, p. 22 in particular.

[77] J.M. Ludlow, *A Dialogue on Doubt. The Sermon of the Bishop of Oxford on Revelation*. Tracts for Priests and People VI, pp. 29-30.

Some writers became lyrical. A composition in verse entitled *The Grievance and the Remedy* was followed by another, *The Last Regret*, defending revelation. A clerical dramatist set a conversation piece in a drawing room in Russell Square. Another dialogue ran to 457 pages, with the players showing no sign of wilting. Even more ingenious was a pamphlet on *Milton's Prophecy of "Essays and Reviews"*, which contended that the poet, in the *Areopagitica*, had foreseen the controversy and had warned the English nation beforehand. But this was on the fringe; so was a tract by Charles Girdlestone, issued towards the end of 1860, arguing for liturgical revision on the ground that the prayer book could not meet the negative theology now revealed or satisfy the aspirations of the new age.[78] More representative were furious broadsheets written by Evangelical mission agencies, claiming that their work in industrial areas had been hampered beyond measure since the detestable volume appeared.

It was to be expected that liberal opinions and writers, however remote from the essayists, would be included in these condemnations. Thomas Arnold, denounced as the father of neology in one tract, had to be defended by H. A. Woodgate in another. *"Essays and Reviews" Considered* took pains to establish Arnold's orthodoxy.[79] George Eliot was understood to be the author of *"Essays and Reviews" Anticipated* which implied that Schleiermacher and his English translator Connop Thirlwall were the real inspirers of present-day rationalism. Why should the "royal road to orthodoxy" be open only to bishops, when some of them had a heterodox past like Thirlwall?[80] *The Spectator* favourably noticed the pamphlet and probably expressed the view of many people who thought that Thirlwall's attitude was inconsistent, if not actually dishonest. It was an embarassing situation for the bishop, but he had to reply. Thirlwall's defence was that he had translated Schleiermacher as a lawyer and not as a clergyman, but "I shall never consent to the narrowing by a hair's breadth of that latitude of opinion which the Church has hitherto conceded to her ministers".[81]

Among the better pamphlets was a series by another group of liberals who needed to make their position clear. Bearing the old name of *Tracts for Priests and People*, these were put out between 1861 and 1863 by the

---

[78] C. Girdlestone *Negative Theology an argument for Liturgical Revision*, p. 16.

[79] H.A. Woodgate, *"Essays and Reviews" Considered*, p. 28.

[80] *"Essays and Reviews" Anticipated*, p. 6.

[81] *The Spectator*, 20 April, 1861. Cf. *Letters Literary and Theological of Connop Thirlwall*, p. 234.

Christian Socialists led by Maurice, Ludlow and Thomas Hughes (they were called the "Hughesian tracts" for this reason), and they soon occupied a middle position between critics and defenders of the essays. Maurice had difficulties in explaining this *via media*, not simply because of his own chequered career in regard to radical opinions but because most people were impatient of his complicated and subtle mental processes which made him distrust the essays and yet refuse to join the agitation against them. A quick analysis was preferable, and Maurice failed to convince. But Maurice's judgment on the essays controversy must be taken very seriously.

Maurice had reservations about the Christian Socialist tracts at the beginning: he did not want his comments to be construed as a condemnation of the radicals, and he disliked the answering volumes: "how fearful are these denials of denials!" He considered Strauss and Feuerbach as the appointed destroyers of philosophical and religious *systems*; the essays were also, perhaps, weapons of divine vengeance. The efforts to repress them were, he told Stanley, "mere struggles to keep off the question, 'What dost thou believe? dost thou believe anything?' which must be forced upon each of us, the bishops included". The unbelief of the time was more wide and deep than those who complained of *Essays and Reviews* had any notion, while orthodoxy was simply a covering for atheism — what he called the "devil worship of the religious world". It must be broken through, and whether it was done by the essays or in any other way was a matter of indifference, "though it is not a matter of indifference whether the Church shall be committed to a new persecution which must make the new reformation, when it comes, more complicated and terrible".[82]

In *The Mote and the Beam* Maurice put his reservations and qualifications about both the essayists and their opponents into print. The result was a tract which probably failed to convince anyone as a piece of argument but which lifted the issue onto a higher plane. No one else made the essays into a subject for examining one's conscience and motives and the need for faith which High and Low Churchman, conservative and radical alike, must feel. Theology and science must be reconciled, said Maurice; too often they were presented as antagonistic principles and powers. The essayists wished to counteract this:

> "But they are not quite sure whether the counteraction is to come from more liberal notions, or from a deeper and more earnest faith. They vibrate

---

[82] Maurice, I, p. 349, II, pp. 383, 391.

between the two conclusions; when they see how afraid those who profess orthodoxy are of investigation, they incline to the former. Oh, let them be sure that that terror is itself the consequence of faithlessness; that it is faith we need, one and all. The orthodox need it, and show that they need it by the shrieks with which they fill the air when any doubt is stirred. The liberal need it, and show that they need it by their incapacity to encounter any of the real problems of the world except by vague generalities".

In the deepest doubts of the nineteenth century, as of the sixteenth, there was a demand for faith deeper than that of monarchs or priests who wanted only to crush the expressions of unbelief. "Let only a few men at Oxford declare that they believe in such a God, that they are sure His Kingdom is indeed established and will have no end, and the voice... will reach a thousand hearts". Maurice ended on the same stirring note:

> "I doubt not every movement in Oxford has been an effort for this reform. But it has been a reform *manqué*, because so much of opinion worship has been mixed up with the worship of God. The clear distinction must be made, the full reform must come. But who will stand in that day? Which of us will bear the light of it?"

Conservatives, therefore, found little to cheer them in Maurice. But the seven must also live up to his demand. Temple came off worst. "What makes this Essay so disappointing, almost heartbreaking, to those who had hoped so much from it?" The Jewish people, as embodying the childhood of man, were represented only as the teachers of monotheism to the world, a far stonier conception, telling mankind not to worship a great many gods. "Oh! miserable result of law, history, prophecy! Miserable substitute for the revelation of the living God... how entirely has Dr Temple defeated his own admirable convictions... he might have justified that conviction if he had followed the living lessons of Scripture instead of giving us this scholastical figment in exchange for them". Pattison's essay was simply negative, "a conclusion in which nothing is concluded", Powell's suggested that faith and reason were complete opposites. As for Jowett, "no essay leaves on my mind such a sense of an inward belief, of an honesty, a devotion which words cannot express which must come forth in the life of a man. No essay causes me more perplexity — leads me to ask myself oftener, 'Does the Scripture then mean anything, everything, or nothing?'". Jowett had written the best essay and also the worst.[83]

---

[83] F.D. Maurice, *The Mote and the Beam. A Clergyman's Lessons from the Present Panic*. Tracts for Priests and People II, pp. 11-17.

Others in the series criticised opponents like Wilberforce. In a controversy which was predominantly clerical, Thomas Hughes put out a useful pamphlet entitled *Religio Laici*, and J. M. Ludlow wrote *Two Lay Dialogues* on the laws of nature and positive philosophy. Two of the longer tracts were by C. P. Chretien, on the evidences, and R. H. Hutton on *The Incarnation and Principles of Evidence*. The Hughesian tracts suggest what pamphleteering — had it been more sensibly conduced — might have achieved. But, perhaps, this may be doubted. Even Maurice with his wonderful appeal, as always an exception to the general run of Victorian Church life, may have done the seven a disservice by agreeing to write for the series at all.

The ample volumes of "Lives and Letters" of the Victorians contain many allusions to the controversy from men and women in all walks of life. One of the most intelligent of the High Churchmen, J. B. Mozley, in his frequently amusing and perceptive letters on contemporary events, deserves to be quoted. He found Powell's work puzzling. "His view of course *admits* of the Scripture miracles being true as *facts*, though not as miracles — *i.e.* mutations of law. But he nowhere expressly states this truth as fact. It is all jumble and confusion when he comes to this point, which is, of course, the turning point of the whole: a 'region of faith', as he calls it (*i.e. not* of sight, as he must expect to be interpreted) — not of real fact".[84] Others found Powell an enigma but did not describe it so well as this. A more liberal churchman than Mozley, Charles Kingsley, another member of the Christian Socialist group, was equally critical of the radicals. He agreed with Maurice in rejecting the view that the bible was a human history containing a gradual discovery of God. In sermons on the Pentateuch in 1863, Kingsley scrutinised the notion of God – consciousness. Why should this be any less fallible and corrupt than any other part of human nature?[85]

More hot-tempered than Hort or Maurice, Kingsley expressed the annoyance felt by the Cambridge party. "What the plague had these men to do, starting a guerilla raid into the enemy's country on their own responsibility?" he asked Stanley. There was nothing in the volume which Cambridge had not gone through already — "doubts, denials, destructions — we have faced them all till we are tired of them. But we have faced them in silence, hoping to find a positive solution. Here comes a book which states all the old doubts and difficulties... Here are men

---

[84] *Letters of the Rev. J.B. Mozley*, p. 249.
[85] C. Kingsley, *The Gospel of the Pentateuch*, p. xi.

still pulling down, with far weaker hands than the Germans, from whom they borrow, and building up *nothing* instead".[86] But Kingsley, to his credit, refused to join in the memorials to the archbishops and all such clerical follies.

The Scottish Broad Churchman, George Gilfillan, who had suffered for his beliefs, was dismayed when he read the volume. "The Essays do not appear to me fair statements of perplexity but, on the contrary, a dogmatism on the part of sceptics which is truly absurd".[87] That harsh judgment was echoed by another Scotsman, Thomas Carlyle. Evil remained triumphant in the world, despite the claims made for progress, so he intensely disliked the optimism of the writers, and he thought that, by continuing to be clergymen, they were playing with their consciences. "Jowett has no charms for me; I saw Jowett twice over; a poor little good-humoured owlet of a body — 'Oxford Liberal' and very conscious of being so; not knowing right hand from left otherwise. *Ach Gott!*"[88] He vented his exasperation to J. A. Froude and also to Wilberforce, whose diary for January, 1868 included the following remarkable entry: "rode with Carlyle... against the essayists on dishonesty ground and atheistic".[89] Jowett himself realised Carlyle's antipathy; he summed up his attitude as, "seven sentinels — deserted their post — ought to be shot".[90]

John Ruskin bought *Essays and Reviews* as he had earlier bought Jowett's Commentary. His lectures *Sesame and Lilies* in 1864 contained a clear reference to the prosecution of Williams and Wilson when he spoke of the relationship of Shakespeare and Dante to Church authority. "They were both in the midst of the main struggle between the temporal and spiritual powers. They had an opinion, we may guess. But where is it? Bring it into court! Put Shakespeare's or Dante's creed into articles, and send *it* up for trial by the Ecclesiastical Court".[91]

For James Martineau, the Unitarian scholar, the essays showed the intellectual part of Anglican society in revolt against the received forms of Christianity and snatching at something deeper and truer.[92] But W. F. Hook thought that they had abused freedom of enquiry. "If the

[86] *Charles Kingsley: His Letters, and Memories of his Life*, II, p. 127.
[87] R.A. and E.S. Watson, *George Gilfillan, Letters and Journals*, p. 418.
[88] A. Carlyle, ed., *Thomas Carlyle: New Letters*, II, p. 200.
[89] R.G. Wilberforce, *Life of the Rt. Rev. Samuel Wilberforce*, III, p. 8. J.A. Froude, *Thomas Carlyle: A History of his Life in London 1834-1881*, II, p. 263.
[90] Jowett MSS, f. 21, letter to Florence Nightingale, 28 August, 1861.
[91] J. Ruskin, *Sesame and Lilies*, p. 77.
[92] J. Drummond, *The Life and Letters of James Martineau*, I, p. 397.

writers had resigned their preferments they would have at least proved their sincerity, but what we object to is their obtaining an extensive hearing for their opinions from the circumstance of their being English clergymen — their opinions would otherwise have been comparatively harmless, except to themselves".[93]

Gladstone was already reading the pamphlets attacking *Essays and Reviews* by 26 April, 1860, and on 10 May he started on the book itself. He spent a good deal of time on the symposium *Replies to "Essays and Reviews"* and Wilberforce's article in the *Quarterly Review*.[94] But he made no public pronouncement about the volume. Though he looked at the essays with "strong aversion", he told W. K. Hamilton that they were a rude shock to the mere scripturism that had too much prevailed.[95]

However, in private, Gladstone did not hide his feelings. His copy of *Essays and Reviews*, in St. Deiniol's Library in Hawarden, contains some strong comments, written down as he read the book. When Jowett said that criticism did away with the supposed conflict between reason and faith, Gladstone replied, "this narrows Salvation to those who can reason". Jowett's teaching, which placed us in the position of the first Christians, before the New Testament was written, elevated "the Old above the New Dispensation". His views on inspiration were similarly rebuked. "Surely there is necessity to examine into a deduction from Inspiration when it may be unlawful to question the Inspiration itself". "What is the better mind of the World" (that Jowett so emphasised)? "There is none that doeth good". The concluding sentence on the love of truth also provoked Gladstone. "How can a man Love the truth who loves not the Lord Jesus Christ". Jowett said that everyone needed to make war on their prejudices, and Gladstone put in the margin, "none more than the writer of this essay". His final footnote was, "a cold vain barren Philosophy, ending with the Grave here. The sport and Triumph of devils hereafter".[96]

Both Gladstone and Disraeli moved significantly and, in some respects, similarly on the matter of Church-State relations as a result of *Essays and Reviews*, Gladstone always more apprehensive of theological niceties, Disraeli more circumspectly because of the need to carry his Conservative colleagues with him. The controversy revealed traits in

---

[93] W.R.W. Stephens, *The Life and Letters of Walter Farquhar Hook*, p. 534.

[94] *The Gladstone Diaries*, V, pp. 483, 486, 540, VI, pp. 5, 8, 20, 63, 89.

[95] D.C. Lathbury, ed., *Letters on Church and State of William Ewart Gladstone*, I, pp. 201, 406, II, p. 337.

[96] Gladstone Papers, St. Deiniol's Library.

Disraeli's character unsuspected by most people, and these obviously intrigued his biographers, Buckle and Monypenny.[97]

As a statesman, Disraeli opposed heterodoxy because secure religion was important to the civil magistrate, and as a Tory he was no friend of the social repercussions of *Essays and Reviews* which might follow from the political sympathies of Jowett and the others. Victorian England had become an unrivalled empire, but its base was the character of the English people. "Now, I want to know where that famous character of the English people will be if they are to be influenced and guided by a Church of immense talent, opulence and power, without any distinctive creed". The union of the country's wealth and luxury with such a church would lead to a dissoluteness of manners and morals which prepared the tomb of empires. Accordingly, in the election of 1865, he based the claims of the Conservatives to the confidence of the country, first and foremost, on their defence of the Church.

Disraeli also spoke as a churchman and a Jew, by race if no longer by conviction. Some found his defence of the Old Testament against new-style Latitudinarianism difficult to swallow. Froude described the out-landish figure cut by Disraeli at the Oxford Diocesan meeting in the Sheldonian in November, 1864, the orator who claimed to be on the side of the angels (against Darwin's apes), addressing the university and country clergy, "in a black velvet shooting coat and wideawake hat, as if he had been accidentally passing through the town".[98] But, in spite of the posturing, Disraeli was sincere, though he could not resist jibes at Bishop Colenso, for introducing his obsolete discoveries with the wonder and disingenuousness of his own savages, and Maurice as a nebulous professor who in his literary style had revived chaos. From the point of view of Judaism he criticised the essayists for unsound scholarship ("their learning is always second-hand", and, moreover, Hebrew scholars like Astruc and Simon had long anticipated the German critics), and for vaunting the nineteenth century above everything else. The whole form of Europe had changed since 1789, but what had now happened? When the turbulence was over, mankind bowed again before the Divine truths entrusted to the promulgation and custody of a chosen people!

As a churchman, Disraeli put the opinion of the intelligent laity. He told the Commons in 1863 that the bill to relax subscription to the

---

[97] On the following see G.E. Buckle and W.F. Monypenny, *The Life of Benjamin Disraeli*, IV, pp. 360-74.

[98] *Ibid.*, IV, p. 375.

Articles was one "in favour of the priesthood, and not of the laity", who had a right to expect that a man appointed to expound doctrine should not, instead, invent it. The charge was well made: *Essays and Reviews* was, in some ways, an absurdly *clerical* book. Addressing the Oxford Diocesan Conference in 1862 he claimed that a true interest in the laity would lead to a national Church far better than Wilson's model. Like Wilson Disraeli deprecated any suggestion that the Church was a sect (so he opposed High Churchmen's cries for disestablishment), for she showed her nationalty by extending her influence over those millions who were religiously indifferent. In this way the existence of a national Church could be reconciled with the principle of civil and religious liberty on which English society was based. He, too, advocated national education and greater participation by the laity, even in Convocation, but, unlike Wilson, he also showed interest in a rejuvenated parochial system, the extension of the episcopate, and closer relations with colonial churches.

Convinced that the Church could align herself to the new situation, Disraeli was accommodating in parliament. The Tories realised that Dissenters must be given relief, and the compulsory Church Rate was abolished in 1868, when he was premier. In 1865 he voted for the amended subscription bill since it now met his requirements. In contrast to this pursuit of sound political principles he found the essayists' proposals a mere surrender. It would end only in an infidel Church, and he could not understand why they should still be "sworn supporters of ecclesiastical establishments, fervent upholders, or dignitaries, of the Church". He wagged his finger playfully at Stanley. "Pray remember, Mr Dean, no dogma, no Dean", but respected him for having the wit not to become one of the seven.

The essays reached the highest circles. Stanley was at Windsor in December, 1862, and was summoned after dinner by the queen. "There was a good deal of conversation, about *Essays and Reviews*, about the Apocalypse, the Psalms — most interesting".[99] The queen was sympathetic. She told the Tennysons that Oxford, in denying him his extra salary as Professor of Greek, had used Jowett shamefully.[100]

A significant aspect of *Essays and Reviews* was the publicity given by writers abroad, particularly after the episcopal censure of February, 1861. For such writers the book was obviously important. Was England

---

[99] Prothero, II, p. 125.
[100] Abbott, I, p. 342.

now to lead Europe in theological speculation? The prospect was intriguing and unfamiliar, and the interest in Jowett and Williams which already existed was intensified. However, welcome and opposition were just as mixed as at home. Among German journals the most bitter attack, as might have been expected, came from Ernst Wilhelm Hengstenberg's article in the *Evangelische Kirchen Zeitung* for January, 1862. The Evangelical Gazette was the widest selling clerical review in Germany and for forty years was edited by Hengstenberg in the fashion of Veuillot's Ultramontanist *Univers*, so that personalities were the main business of its polemics. The battle with Oxford radicalism had, however, been joined by the essayists themselves in Pattison's criticisms of Hengstenberg when discussing German theology in the *Westminster Review* in April, 1857. Hengstenberg was an old friend of Pusey and his ally against liberalism. In his view the millenarian kingdom had commenced with Charlemagne and lasted until 1800, since when the Church had been witnessing the events preceding the end of the world and the last Judgment.[101] Understandably, he felt the essays to be a portent of Antichrist.

Hengstenberg saw the home of the book as Germany itself, but his point was not quite the same as Pattison's, for he saw no continuity between present-day radicalism and Luther's alleged belief in toleration and freedom of conscience. And by dismissing the native genius of the writers — "they are mere parrots and the only difference between them is their varying powers of imitation" — he consolidated his argument that the volume was part of a world-wide movement of unbelief. It need not, therefore, be discussed as a work of theology or a legitimate development of historic faith. It was only necessary to expel it from the Church. Let the English Church, by exercise of her ancient rights, act as judge for the rest of Christendom (*The Guardian*, not surprisingly, had the review translated and used it as ammunition to support synodical proceedings against the seven[102]). Powell was a conscious atheist, Williams was too dependant on Bunsen, the "know-all" who had betrayed true German theology, others used "the same sort of devious language which the Rationalists used while they were still uncertain of their ground". The master of this game of hide and seek was Jowett. Alone of the reviewers Hengstenberg saw the reason for Jowett's

---

[101] F. Lichtenberger, *History of German Theology in the 19th Century*, p. 213. Cf. C.H. Cottrell, *Religious Movements of Germany in the Nineteenth Century*, p. 26, and *WR*, April, 1857, p. 357f.
[102] *G*, 26 March, 1862, pp. 303-4.

depreciation of the divine ordering of scripture. And why, did he distinguish between the inner and outer meaning of scripture? "With what careful fatherly provision Jowett works for the denial of revelation and of the God who has made his name by the deeds of his righteousness, substituting instead a rationalistic anonymity with serpent-like cunning!" That was a fair sample of Hengstenberg's wording.[103]

From the liberal side, Ewald noticed the essayists sympathetically in a long review in the *Göttingische Gelehrte Anzeigen* in July, 1861. He found, instead, a "noble spirit". The writers were attempting something new and they admitted the deficiencies in English scholarship. Pattison's essay was important for Germany also. Wilson showed that a Church, without ceasing to be a genuine Christian body, must nevertheless be a people's Church. Temple's work was linked with Lessing and praised for its beautiful sentiments, though Ewald was not convinced by the analogy of the life of man standing for the human race; he thought that this was better applied to single nations; and surely Christ was more than an example or pioneer? Jowett's essay was the most important. "One should be very content that a university like Oxford, where the more precise researches have lain fallow for so long, should possess such a man, especially because he belongs to the younger generation and we can expect much of him in the future". The book showed that Germany had now returned the debt that she owed two centuries before when England possessed the best minds in the field of theology. But he feared "silly and unfair" prosecutions which gave undue importance to these "indeliberate pages", and he thought that the volume itself was an inauspicious start, because of its essay form, for a new theological era. Too many things were dealt with in *Essays and Reviews* in a condensed way which forbade proper discussion. He criticised Jowett for this and also Wilson whose ideological principle ("this strange foreign term"), insufficiently explained, implied that the historical element evaporated — which was not a matter of indifference, as Wilson thought it was. The distinction between ideal and historical must be made more carefully: why could not matters of an historical nature also be ideal?[104] Ewald repeated this criticism when he visited Williams in 1863.[105]

The *Protestantische Kirchen Zeitung* reported unfavourably on the controversy in England, noting the support given by the secular press to

---

[103] *Evangelische Kirchen Zeitung*, January, 1862, pp. 85-98.
[104] *Göttingische Gelehrte Anzeigen*, July, 1861, pp. 1161-80.
[105] Williams, II, p. 75.

the essayists, who had "only made use of their rights as Protestants to pursue free research", in contrast to the hostility of the bishops.[106]

In France the *Revue Chrétienne* welcomed the essays, and protested against the bigotry condemning them, but this was to be expected since the editor, de Pressensé, held like views.[107] The *Revue des Deux Mondes* had an article by Edmond Schérer, which placed the book in the context of the "Crisis of Protestantism" as a whole, and found its key in the principle of private judgment, which had only one outcome: "The bible can keep its place in our religious life on one condition, that it no longer exercises, as previously, a kind of despotism over the human spirit, but, instead, should identify itself with the voice of conscience within us".[108]

There was swift and — apart from the Unitarians — unfavourable notice of the essays when they appeared in the United States in the summer of 1860. A 51-page review in the *Christian Examiner* in November, 1860, was followed by 84 pages of comment in the *American Quarterly Church Review* for July, 1861. The *Church Monthly*, the *Princeton*, and the *North American* reviews and the *New Englander* for 1861 were peppered with references to the "new Oxford school".[109]

One figure, above all, who stood outside the Church of England and regarded the controversy keenly was John Henry Newman. He had left a church ill-prepared for the onrush of liberalism, and in Oxford itself in 1845 there were clear omens of the future. Newman had evidently purchased the essays soon after their appearance. In his *Memoirs* Mark Pattison recorded one of those human situations which vivify Victorian Church history, the radical essayist entering the Oxford train at Paddington and horrified to meet his former leader in the same compartment. What would Newman say of *Essays and Reviews*? In fact, either Pattison pretended not to know Newman or he had genuinely forgotten what he looked like: Newman charitably assumed the latter and made himself known. Pattison wrote thankfully, "my fears were quickly relieved". Newman thought it wrong to throw speculations broadcast upon the general public, for it unsettled their faith without offering them anything else to rest on, but, addressed *ad clerum*, the

---

[106] *Protestantische Kirchen Zeitung*, 13 April, 1861, p. 362.

[107] *Revue Chrétienne*, 1861, pp. 390-2, 1862, p. 483.

[108] *Revue des Deux Mondes*, 1861, pp. 403-424.

[109] *Christian Examiner*, November, 1860, pp. 351-401. *American Quarterly Church Review*, July, 1861, pp. 257-358. *Church Monthly*, January, 1861, pp. 6-12. *Biblical Repertory and Princeton Review*, XXXIII, 1861, pp. 59-84. *North American Review*, 96, 1861, pp. 177-216. *New Englander*, XIX, 1861, pp. 84, 161, 323, 541.

essays would have been a different matter. Then it would only have been a debate between scholars.[110]

But Newman was soon called upon to make more public declarations. Anglican friends applied to him for a defence of the faith. Cardinal Wiseman roundly asserted that Newman had written three volumes vindicating revelation which were now in the press. Newman was perplexed that everyone expected him to do something. The controversy threatened to open up old wounds: he said that he was still being grossly misrepresented twenty years after the Tractarian events, and the essays would be used as an excuse for further attacks. "All these German theories will come before us and have to be answered. The answer requires a great deal of previous discussion, and Catholics must first learn many controversial principles and facts, which at present they shrink from. If I began to attack the German school, I should at once be attacked in my rear by some narrow-minded disputant of our own Creed. This is the difficulty of our position, and time alone will overcome it". He demurred over congratulating Pattison on his election as Rector of Lincoln in 1860, since it might be taken as approval of the essayists. He was well aware of Pattison's change in belief, "but much as I feel for his state of doubt and discomfort, I cannot stomach his joining such men as Baden Powell and others — What has he in common with such men? They have said a great number of bold things, which I suppose he would not say, but for which he has made himself virtually answerable... it is very painful that Pattison, not only should not be a Catholic, but should have thrown himself into the first rank of the assailers of revelation". But he wrote to the new Rector in due course and criticised those, Tait in particular, who mixed up Pattison's name with the others.[111]

Newman's correspondence shows that *Essays and Reviews* was, for him, a judgment on the bibliolatry of popular religion in England. He made a distinction between this and the traditional teaching of the Church of England on scripture, but his Anglican correspondents found it a thin one. The remedy for *Essays and Reviews* (Newman implied) could only be the Catholic Church which was not committed to plenary inspiration. By striking a blow at the inspiration, veracity and canonicity of the bible, the essayists (he said) aimed at "whatever there is of Christianity in this country. It is frightful to think where England would be, as regards Revelation, if it once got to disbelieve or to doubt the

---

[110] M. Pattison, *Memoirs*, pp. 315-6. J.H. Newman, *Letters and Diaries*, XX, p. 63. The meeting took place on 18 July, 1861.

[111] J.H. Newman, *op. cit.*, XIX, pp. 455, 477, 480, 500, XX, p. 29.

authority of Scripture. That is what makes the Volume so grave a matter — and the responsibility of those who have to do with it is great". The party was not new, but whereas the Deists' arguments fell on unpropitious soil, "now everyone is alive to religious subjects". Yet Newman realised why the radicals felt that they must speak out — "it is not right to keep up shams" — and he still called Pattison his friend, while for two of the essayists (presumably Temple and Jowett) he felt great respect.[112]

The state of Oxford troubled Newman. Malcolm MacColl, then a curate at St. Barnabas, Pimlico, told him that the intellect of the university was at Jowett's feet, and many wished him to reply, particularly in view of the fact that "at least two of the Essayists became sceptics in consequence of the recoil which followed from their having lost, in you, their intellectual head". Newman answered that he had anticipated such perplexities, "and it was one of my severest trials in leaving it, that I was undoing my own work, and leaving the field open, or rather infallibly surrendering it to those who would break down and crumble to powder all religion whatever". "A dreadful battle is coming... If I had thought that the weapons which Anglicanism gave me were equal to meeting it, I never should have left persons and scenes so dear to me". Charles Crawley told him that his prophecy of the fate of Oxford years before was now being too truly verified. "They crushed Number 90 and its associates *then* — and now they have to deal with Neology and Rationalism".[113]

Not surprisingly, a rumour got about that the former Tractarian leader would soon return to Oxford and meet unbelief (and Jowett) in person. Jowett himself was delighted; Newman was the only adversary worth considering[114] — so he was intrigued to find Newman one September day in 1862 on the train between Birmingham and Oxford. "It *was* Jowett I came up with. I did not know I had ever known him *personally*. He was so vigorous in his demonstrations (of countenance) that at last I asked him some indifferent question. On which he at once came and sat next to me — and said that he had known me in the Long Vacation of 1840. We had a good deal of conversation. He got out at Oxford".[115]

But Newman and Jowett only appeared together as names cited in a correspondence battle in *The Times*. Maurice wrote a letter criticising

---

[112] *Ibid.*, XIX, pp. 480, 482, 487.

[113] *Ibid.*, XIX, pp. 453, 487.

[114] Jowett MSS, f. 89, letter to Florence Nightingale, 4 November, 1864.

[115] J.H. Newman, *op. cit.*, XX, p. 275.

Pusey's suit against Jowett in the Vice-Chancellor's court at Oxford and held that Tract 90 asked for no less width of comprehension in interpreting the Articles than did the essayist. He disagreed with the sense that Jowett put on the formularies, but "I have no reason to suppose that he considers it in a non-natural sense". When Pusey heatedly denied that he advocated subscription save in the literal grammatical sense, Maurice replied that Newman, who imputed to the writers of the Articles a slippery and dishonest intention and said that it could only be defeated by slippery and dishonest practice on the other side, "was doing just as much to undermine our faith in the Articles as Mr Jowett has done". Newman and Jowett coupled by Maurice! Newman was forced to act, though reluctant to do so: he vindicated himself in *The Times* and elicited an apology from Maurice.[116] But Newman's reserve was noticeable; he was concerned only to set the record straight, not to defend Anglicanism against Jowett.

The last reference to the controversy over the essays was in Newman's *Apologia Pro Vita Sua* in 1864. Without mentioning the book itself, his assault on radicalism generally — "my battle was with Liberalism; by Liberalism I mean the anti-dogmatic principle and its developments" — was coloured by it. Newman cast his mind back to Whately's Latitudinarianism as a precursor of the essayists, a theological school, "dangerous as opening the door to evils which it did not itself either anticipate or comprehend", and to Hugh James Rose's warnings of the perils to England which lay in the biblical and theological speculations of Germany. Rose saw in the Whigs' distribution of Church patronage the authoritative introduction of liberal opinions into the country, and Newman referred to his own change in the face of this challenge. He claimed, what Pattison had admitted, that the Tractarian movement had broken that first assault, quoting his reply to Hampden's pamphlet, "Observations on Religious Dissent". "Since that time Phaeton has got into the chariot of the sun; we, alas! can only look on, and watch him down the steep of heaven".[117]

Less complicated than Newman, H. E. Manning condemned *Essays and Reviews* roundly, and he was thankful that he had left a church which "gives *pabulum* to every heresy".[118] The *Quarterly Review*, with other papers, accused Manning of being in ecstasies, of exulting and uttering

---

[116] *The Times*, 20 February, 1863, p. 9, 23 February, p. 5, 24 February, p. 9, 25 February, p. 8, 27 February, p. 9. Cf. J.H. Newman, *op. cit.*, XX, pp. 413-5.

[117] J.H. Newman, *Apologia Pro Vita Sua*, pp. 45, 54, 62, 233-4.

[118] J.H. Newman, *Letters and Diaries*, XIX, p. 503 n. 5.

"wild paeans and savage joy" over the Privy Council judgment acquit-
ting Williams and Wilson. Manning denied this but said that the
judgment revealed the absence of all discernment, certainty and authority in the Church of England. The alternative was between
"Rationalism or Rome... either the human certainty of history and
criticism, or the divine certainty of Catholic tradition".[119] Cardinal
Wiseman spoke similarly. He instanced the essays as the latest of a
number of cases of uncontrolled liberty of thought which the established
Church was unable to suppress. The parting shot was that, "this
supposed teaching body feels within herself that want of power to act
outwardly".[120]

Avoiding Manning's too obvious contrasts, which seemed to allow no
place to history or criticism whatever, a highly intelligent review was
provided for *The Rambler* in March, 1861 by H. N. Oxenham, a convert
from the Tractarians. He went one better than Harrison and headed his
article "Neo-Protestantism". For Harrison criticism led to Rationalism,
for Oxenham the Protestant principle itself, when taken to its logical
conclusion in *Essays and Reviews*, had the same result. The fact that no
one yet had effectively answered the book showed how its basic
convictions permeated the Anglican (Protestant) mind. He saw *Essays
and Reviews* as marking an epoch in religious thought: the book gave
form and name to sentiments widely spread; it was, he said, "a kind of
touchstone by which the hearts of many are revealed". The new Oxford
volume was no domestic or merely academic work for *The Rambler* but a
sort of digest of the national mind. The writers, therefore, had passed
from being clergymen or ecclesiastics to being representative figures like
Tennyson. But that passage revealed how much of Christianity had been
given up in the face of the solvents of the nineteenth century:

> "Did we ask whether the writers hold such doctrines as the Trinity, the
> Incarnation, or the Resurrection, which they seldom name except to suggest
> some new definition, or disparage some old one, we should probably be met
> by an indignant refusal. But they would hardly deny that the terms convey
> to their minds a very different meaning from that put upon them by the
> great majority of Christians. That they do not believe in miracles, prophecy,
> inspiration, original sin, or eternal punishment, is not an inference from
> their statements, but a summary of them".[121]

---

[119] H. E. Manning, *The Crown in Council on the "Essays and Reviews"*, p. 19, and cf. his
The Convocation and the Crown in Council, pp. 3, 30.

[120] *G*, 6 July, 1864, p. 664. Cf. *Chronicle of Convocation*, 1864, pp. 1798-9.

[121] *The Rambler*, March, 1861, pp. 287-314.

Oxenham's clarity of mind which enabled him to deal more effectively with *Essays and Reviews* than most of the ponderous Anglican replies arose from his conviction of an opposed religious system, the Catholic Church. For similar reasons Unitarian and Free Christian reviewers treated the essays perceptively. No writer exposed the unity of the book better than the Boston Unitarian who spoke of the "phenomena" when no collisions or inconsistencies occurred. "Most strange of all, neither one of them affirms any important point which any other has denied; nor does either one of them assail as a heresy the boldest conclusions yielded by the rest".[122] Others more agnostic than Harrison followed his example and sneered at a church which harboured radicals in her bosom and discovered them when it was too late. Thus, Hermann Bernard's selections from Lessing were reissued by his brother in 1862 under the title *Cambridge Free Thoughts*, and were intended to do damage to the Church through the essayists' own use of Lessing.[123]

But the fiercest light cast on *Essays and Reviews* came from militant anti-Christian organisations who found the volume a heaven-sent piece of propaganda. Speakers in Convocation gave various examples of this, such as the American lecturer who took the book with him on a tour of northern manufacturing towns as evidence of the coming end of orthodox religion, or the "atheists" in Leeds who circulated passages from it: that showed the evil tendency of *Essays and Reviews* more than anything else, said good Dr Jelf.[124] These organisations represented an anticlericalism far older than the serious or reluctant doubt disclosed in the *Westminster* or *National Review*, and they were interested only in demolition. The *National Reformer* opened its first number on 14 April, 1860, with the pronouncement, "To suppose that Christianity could be necessary to the virtue and happiness of mankind — to suppose that God could think it so, and yet make it known to so few, and to those imperfectly and so late, — is folly and blasphemy". So it welcomed the essays and mourned the death of Powell, the "ablest and most liberal" clergyman of all, while featuring his essay, as well as Temple's, in the course of an argument against the Church. (Bradlaugh did not find his way completely smooth, however: extracts from the Savilian Professor,

---

[122] *Church Monthly*, January, 1861, p. 10, quoting *The Christian Examiner*, November, 1860, pp. 351-401.

[123] H.H. Bernard, *Cambridge Free Thoughts and Letters on Bibliolatry, passim*.

[124] *G*, 27 February, 1861, p. 188. Cf. *Quarterly Review*, January, 1861, pp. 284-5.

that "ornament to the clergy", were read at Bradford, but Christians in the audience shouted out that they had heard enough of Powell).[125]

Bradlaugh and his noisy paper did not signify much, and the academic and wordy *Essays and Reviews* would not affect working men who had already been alienated from bourgeois Christianity, but churchmen who felt threatened on all sides were scandalised at this fresh prominence given to the seven.

The literary controversy surrounding *Essays and Reviews* is most significant for what it reveals of the state of orthodox theology. A good deal of rubbish was written by Wilberforce, Denison and the Recordites, and Burgon, for instance, was heavily criticised by *The Guardian* for conducting a campaign of "terrorism" and for his extreme fundamentalism in his sermons on Inspiration and Interpretation. The "sneers, insinuations and hard words" in these ill became a Christian, said the reviewer.[126] Denison, of course, held that such means were necessary. When trying to persuade Pusey to write for *Faith and Peace* he said that constructive work was "inadequate to meet the special exigencies of the case without the destructive part also; what is wanted for the masses is first to 'clear the ground' of the perilous stuff".[127]

Avoiding destruction, but unable to rise to Maurice's height, the intellectual conservative concentrated on defence. That was Mansel's tactic: his rigorous examination of Powell was to show that orthodoxy was superior in clarity of mind and sureness of technique; but it was still a restatement of the traditional position, and he failed to meet Powell's ultimate challenge.

Defence was necessary in two matters: first, in regard to the essayists' dislocation of fact and faith, caused by their historical outlook which seemed to make all truth relative; and secondly, in regard to the authority of the bible now that it was treated as a human record and not as direct revelation. R. W. Church, doubting the wisdom of Moberly's preface to his sermons on the Beatitudes (only a "tolerably complete answer", not a pamphlet, would do), said that the book raised, and "very painfully handled", the necessity of having any historical truth to believe in at all. "...We must meet them on a ground which has become inevitable

---

[125] *National Reformer*, 30 June, 1860, p. 4, 10 November, 1860, p. 7, 1 December, 1860, p. 1.

[126] *G*, 23 October, 1861, p. 974. Cf. *WR*, October, 1861, p. 545, and E.M. Goulburn, *The Life of John William Burgon*, I, p. 260.

[127] Pusey MSS, VI, f. 280, letter of Denison to Pusey, 8 March, 1861.

almost, that of actual historical criticism ...their power lies in their being left alone in possession of it".[128] The *Westminster Review* said that the critics found it easier to run down the Hegelianism in *Essays and Reviews* than to answer the historical criticism, and there was some truth in that.[129]

F. C. Cook, in *Aids to Faith*, dealt with the first by claiming that Wilson's ideological principle was the obvious conclusion of the essayists' historicism. Cook admitted that the human mind recognised the discrepancy between events as they occurred in secular history and the absolute ideas or principles which all events exemplified and represented. Thus, "whenever we read a narrative, in which the ideal and real are presented in perfect accordance, we are all but irresistibly impressed with the conviction that it must be fictitious". He drew a modern distinction between sacred and profane history, for the latter did not teach momentous and necessary truths such as the unity of God, the unity of man, the universal principles of morality, or the systematic development of the purposes of an almighty and loving will. "Sacred history teaches them all, and teaches them not by mere abstractions, but by the representation of events in which our conceptions of what is right, reasonable and desirable, find a perfect satisfaction. Our only postulate is one which cannot be denied on rational grounds by any but atheists — that God has the will and the power of making Himself known to His creatures". Thus, in sacred history, the ideal became actual — but in the life and person of Christ this was also part of human history.

The argument has since become familiar, but this union of ideal and actual in Christ was ably demonstrated by Cook. When he read the gospels the ideologist (Wilson called him the ideologian) thought that he was listening to a beautiful dream, but the Christian realised that "every fact in the life of our Master is in accordance with a spiritual principle which it actually and completely represents". For both the choice was the same, between the ideal and the historical; the ideologist could not believe that the account of Christ's life referred entirely to "fact", but Cook asked him to consider the possibility, and also that the historical event preceded the myth, and not *vice versa*.

But Cook had to include writers like Fichte under the blanket of "atheism", and, more importantly, his argument depended on a conservative approach to the bible. Thus the fourth gospel was much earlier

---

[128] Church, p. 186.
[129] *WR*, April, 1862, p. 534. (Part of a theology review by Wilson).

than the second-century date assigned by Wilson, and (attacking him by way of Strauss) scripture must be approached differently from other ancient writings:

> "The question is simply this: are the same principles applicable to secular history and to the records of a scheme which is professedly one of divine interpositions? We see perfectly well that if they were applicable, the conclusions of the ideologist could scarcely be controverted. To one who does not view the sacred narrative as a thing apart, not merely in certain details, but in its entire construction, resting altogether upon different principles from those which he is accustomed to apply in historical investigations, its facts, whether or not what is commonly called miraculous, have *prima facie* this characteristic of fiction".[130]

That suggested how urgent the second matter, defence of the bible, had become. One way was to take up Cook's (as Mansel's) point about the essayists' presuppositions. It was fairly certain that the radicals' denial of inspiration arose not so much from their critical position as from their rigid separation of physical and spiritual worlds. But that affected all religious knowledge and not merely the biblical writers' veracity: such knowledge could be founded on no evidence, since there was no apparent communication between the two worlds, and it could only result from "certain convictions of the mind, wholly incapable of being tested as to their truth". So warned *Aids to Faith*.[131] In any case, the question of inspiration did not present only irreconcilable alternatives. The Church of England had never defined it (Tait), or had allowed two different theories to be held (Thomson); the essayists opposed phantoms of their own making.[132]

E. Harold Browne proposed other grounds for discussion. With arguments derived from Butler, Lardner, Paley and others, he held that the question concerned the credibility of the biblical witnesses rather than the inspiration of writers. "All the history, and even all the great doctrines of the Gospel, might be capable of proof, and so deserving of credence, though we were obliged to adopt almost the lowest of the modern theories of inspiration". If the apostles were twelve common men, of common honesty and intelligence, and if they could not have been deceived or had any intention to deceive the world, then surely (he

---

[130] *Aids to Faith*, pp. 140-3.
[131] *Ibid.*, p. 305 n.
[132] W. Thomson, *A Pastoral Letter to the Clergy and Laity of the Province of York*, p. 14. *Aids to Faith*, p. 404.

held) their testimony must be accepted as true and, therefore, Christ must have lived and taught and worked miracles, and risen from the dead, an accredited witness sent from God.[133]

But Browne gave up more than he intended: avoiding the scriptural writers' inspiration by stressing the integrity of the apostolic witness, played into the hands of Powell who suggested that, however sincere and well-intentioned the apostles' contemporaries may have been, the probability of some mistake or deception somewhere was greater than the probability of a miracle occurring. No one really answered Powell's contention about the miraculous tongues alleged among the Irvingites, a matter of contemporary "testimony", yet no "sober-minded person, except those *immediately interested*, or *influenced by peculiar views*, for a moment believes these effects to be *miraculous*".[134] Nor did Browne's theory deal with claims that the apostolic testimony had of necessity to be expressed in terms of myth. Mansel contented himself by showing the essayists' one-sidedness because they relegated Butler and Paley to a dry logical era and formally ruled out the possibility of miracle.

Another way was to expose the essayists' mere scripturism. But the bible had never been held in classical theology to be the only source of man's knowledge of God. Hence, there was a fresh assertion of the Church's authority as the guardian of scripture. This had obviously always been a Catholic position, but High Churchmen had descended to an astonishing literalism like most others in the 1850's, as Newman implied. Moberly, in his preface to his *Beatitudes* sermons, showed how the essays opened their eyes to the dangers of this situation and to the neglect of a truly Catholic and Anglican understanding of the bible. This did not meet the radical objection that Church and tradition were, like everything else, subject to the law of development, but it was not merely an argumentative ploy and could have been expanded (perhaps in Hort's projected essay) into a constructive theology of tradition. The nearest approach to this was not found until *Lux Mundi*, thirty years later, when plenary inspiration was rejected but the creative instincts of the first century Christians were emphasised, as also the importance of the patristic witness for interpreting scripture.

One gesture from the conservative side which harmonised scripture and development was found in T. D. Bernard's Bampton lectures for 1864 on *The Progress of Doctrine in the New Testament*. The communi-

---

[133] *Aids to Faith*, pp. 301-321.
[134] *ER*, p. 108.

cation of the truth by God in apostolic times was obviously not the same as man's apprehension of that truth in subsequent periods, leading to the present, said Bernard. The apprehension exhibited a progress. "He who looks back upon the tortuous and agitated course of thought perceives that the truth is not only preserved, but in some sense advanced, the definitions of it becoming more exact, the construction of it more systematic, and the deductions from it more numerous. Thus the history of the apprehension of Christian truth by man which commences within the New Testament, is continued in the history of the Church to the end of time; and still, while it is continued, it is in some sort a history of progress, and one in which the Spirit of God mingles, and one which the providence of God moulds".[135] But the New Testament was essentially factual, and the only fundamental development took place within the covers of the book itself.

The clearest answer to the essayists' reappraisal of the authority of scripture was given by James Fendall, prosecutor of Wilson in the Court of Arches, and it allowed very little latitude. Fendall denied Jowett's contention that there was no more design in the bible than in Plato or Homer; scripture was not an historical record but actual revelation itself and showing a design from beginning to end. The fact that it was written at different periods by human writers did not alter this, for it was conceived of as a whole by God himself in eternity and so was the "work of the master mind of the world's Creator". Thus, the notion that man's spirit used the bible, as it used any other source, for searching out truth which it itself evaluated and judged, must be rejected. If the claim was well founded that the bible was the direct communication of God, "we shall surely not dare to analyse God's word in the same way as we should the works of Sophocles or Plato".[136] There was no answer to that; if the bible was unique, then man's new-found spiritual hegemony was totally checked.

Otherwise, there was little initiative in the replies. Some of the solutions were simplistic. Theological definitions carefully made in the past were forgotten, surprising ignorance was revealed. Some writers criticised Jowett for speaking of the Mosaic law as a mixture of moral and positive commands, on the grounds that the Ten Commandments were just as "positive" as the ceremonial, but Jowett was merely using the old

---

[135] T.D. Bernard, *The Progress of Doctrine in the New Testament*, p. 13.
[136] J. Fendall, *The Authority of Scripture*, pp. 80, 82.

academic distinction that a "moral precept is a precept the reason of which we see; a positive precept the reason of which we do not see".[137]

Damaging admissions were made in other ways. In a statement on the heresies in the book, the Convocation of York held that, on the principle of the verifying faculty in man, the "fundamental and distinguishing truths of Christianity must in all consistency be rejected", and these included the Trinity, the Incarnation, and the Resurrection of the body, which were mysteries not capable of being received by any verifying faculty, "but only in submission of the mind to a reasonably attested revelation from God".[138] The use of the phrase "in all consistency" was dangerous: were the great doctrines totally irrational? "Submission of mind" might mean that the York clergy were quoting, or misquoting, Mansel, but it also suggested obedience to an infallible Church.

There was also the additional possibility (which Newman, for one, feared) that the replies might actually be a dissuasive to belief, for strong assertions could give more away than was intended. There was the spectre of Mansel's "nescience", for instance: some saw it glancing over *Aids to Faith* as it had done in the Bamptons. Mansel questioned Powell's assertion that the study of physical causes was the sole real clue to the conception of a moral cause, and that physical order, so far from being opposed to the idea of supreme intelligence, was the very exponent of it (the earlier Powell said this more clearly than the later). But Mansel asked, in a sentence already quoted, whether matter was the true image of God. The class of phenomena which required that kind of cause which we denominated a deity was exclusively given in the phenomena of mind, he said: "the phenomena of matter, taken by themselves, do not warrant any inference to the existence of God". The remaining prop left by Powell thus seemed to have been knocked away by his orthodox opponent. The startled reader at least found Powell's universal theory positive.

What did Mansel offer in return? He asked for clarity. To speak of a Supreme Mind evinced in the laws of matter was to use terms which had no meaning until we understood what 'mind' was from the consciousness of the mind within ourselves. "The personality and, as implied in the personality, the moral nature of God, is not... an isolated conception, derived from a distinct class of facts, and superadded to another conception of a Deity derived from the order of nature", wrote Mansel.

---

[137] Epistles (2 ed.), II, p. 509.
[138] Quoted in *WR*, October, 1861, p. 551.

"It is the primary and fundamental idea of a God in any distinctive sense of the word... To speak, in the language of modern pantheistic philosophy, of a Reason or Thought in the universe, which first becomes conscious in man, is simply to use terms without a meaning; for we have no conception of reason or thought at all, except as a consciousness".[139] Powell's separation between the two sources of theology was oversimplified, but did Mansel's sophisticated argument suggest that man could not conceive of God as mind *at all* from the witness of the physical world?

The answers to the essayists' Christology were traditional. When Jowett implied that Christ might have been mistaken in seeing the Old Testament as inspired, Mansel and Pusey said that this was impossible. The alternative was to hold that he knowingly made use of erroneous scriptural statements, which cast doubt on the purity of his moral character. When the integrity of the miracles was questioned, the reply was similar: Christ must have had divine knowledge; he knew that he could work miracles, and he did so. Another omission concerned the doctrine of the Atonement. There was no spirit of compromise when dealing with the more subjective restatement of the work of Christ proposed by Maurice and others, not to mention the essayists' own disposal of penal substitutionary and "Calvinistic" views.

The reaction of 1860-1864 did not, therefore, provide any means of theological advance. Its main discovery, apart from the theological innovations of the book, was the existence of an organised neological party within the Church. The preface was dismissed. The party had published a manifesto and would go on to do other things — Harrison's telling point about their work among and influence on the young suggested more implications — while behind them stood a larger movement of supporters — the illusion of a "conspiracy against Revealed Religion" (Stanley).[140] Consequently, the positive aspects of *Essays and Reviews* were disregarded. Though both Powell and Jowett had protested against the rhetorical presentation of Christianity, the treatment of the matter was entirely rhetorical: the essayists were opponents, the setting a court room, it was not a question of private conviction but of law. Religious authority, represented in a man like Bishop Wilberforce, could not accept that there was any other method of dealing with it. The essayists could never be seen as mere individuals.

The two doctrines particularly affected by this hardening or regression

---

[139] *Aids to Faith*, p. 27.
[140] Prothero, II, p. 34.

were, not surprisingly, those on which Williams and Wilson were acquitted by the Privy Council — the infallibility of scripture and everlasting punishment. Everything was felt to depend on them. Agitation over the bible and its authority can be understood, in view of the confused situation which obtained in the Church in 1860. The debate about scripture continues, though the crude fundamentalism which made Burgon say that even the consonants of the English text were infallibly inspired has passed into history. But eternal hell-fire as a theological issue is now dead, and there is little chance of it being resurrected. It is certainly less easy to understand. Why was it insisted on with such ferocity by 1864, to the indignation of rationalists and doubters who thought that believers were far more immoral in this regard than notorious sinners? But to the orthodox churchman it was as necessary to know that the wicked would not escape in the end as to believe that the bible was the inerrant word of God. Even Catholics, who had everything to gain, and nothing to lose, from *Essays and Reviews*, placed them together; in a reference to the essays judgment in 1864, Cardinal Wiseman said that they were "vital doctrines of the sacred deposit", and therefore not to be tampered with.[141]

The saintly Keble was even prepared to defend hell-fire before biblical infallibility. At the Bristol Church Congress in October, 1864, he read a paper on the matter :

> "It was an all-important subject, even more important in its practical bearings perhaps than that most solemn subject of inspiration. Never was its practical aspect set before him more forcibly than when talking to an old woman in his country parish, a poor woman. She had a son who was a great trouble to her from his wicked habits. He (Mr Keble) told her about this — about the awful doctrine of eternal punishment being called in question. He had told all what he thought of the matter to forewarn them. The poor woman was terribly alarmed to hear of any doubt on this solemn truth, and said, 'Oh, what an effect it will have, when my son hears it, on him. What will become of him?' ".

Keble sat down, "amidst tremendous applause".[142] The point was that these "practical bearings" (if men were not afraid of hell, they would be worse than ever) allowed no theological doubts after the essays judgment, if they had been possible before.

Pusey held that distinctions must become more rigid. If "everlasting

---

[141] *Pastoral Letter of H.E. Cardinal Wiseman on Trinity Sunday, 1864*, pp. 14 and 15.
[142] W. Lock, *John Keble, A Biography*, pp. 179-182.

punishment" did not mean "eternal" but only "long enduring" then, he told Keble, "one is not bound to the received meaning of any word whatsoever". The far-spread perversion of words adopted by the "new, compromising school of unbelievers", must be opposed, otherwise Arianism (the Son's begetting from the Father "from everlasting" might only mean "a long time ago") would be let in, as well as Pelagianism.[143] On these definitions Pusey condemned, as well, Maurice who, with the Cambridge school generally, held that "everlasting" did not mean "eternal". Maurice protested that the *Oxford Declaration of the Clergy* in 1864 actually brought in a new test of belief, supplementary to the Articles, which were deliberately wide, and this not only concerned hell-fire, but inspiration, Atonement and other matters.[144]

The narrower definitions were forced on Church leaders. In March, 1864, the Archbishop of Canterbury, harassed by Pusey, Keble and Phillpotts, sent this statement to *The Guardian*:

> "I wish it to be generally understood that, in assenting to the reversal of the Judgment of Dr Lushington on the subject of Eternal Punishment in the case of Mr Wilson, I did so solely on technical grounds; insomuch as the charge against him on this point was so worded that I did not think it could be borne out by the facts.
>
> "The Eternity of Punishment rests, according to my mind, exactly on the same grounds as the Eternity of Blessedness; they must both stand or fall together; and the Church of England, as I maintain, holds both doctrines clearly and decidedly".[145]

Thomson of York, similarly pressed, said that the doctrine of the terminable punishment of the wicked found no countenance whatever from holy scripture.[146] Pusey (according to Pattison) spoke of agonizing screams echoing along the lurid vaults of hell, Wilberforce of the demons' tormenting in hell of the lustful man by the instrument of his lust — both felt that the faith was now protected.[147]

The regression produced one other casualty. When convictions could be felt so strongly about hell-fire, that suggested that any movement of conciliation or mediation would be difficult. Tait wanted to lead a party of compromise, Maurice hoped for it, the Hort-Lightfoot-Westcott

---

[143] Liddon, IV, p. 48.

[144] *Ibid.*, IV, pp. 57, 59, 61.

[145] *Ibid.*, IV, p. 49.

[146] W. Thomson, *op. cit.*, p. 20.

[147] *WR*, April, 1867, p. 342. Pattison is probably referring to Pusey's sermon on "Everlasting Punishment", preached in Oxford on Trinity XXI, 1864.

scheme — or Farrar's Bampton lectures — could have been its beginnings. But most churchmen saw the situation only in terms of Harrison's Either-Or. Either, you must believe everything, or, you will believe nothing. On this basis they readily accepted his confusion between faith and blind acceptance and his claims that the essays were in direct antagonism to the received tradition of belief. The Broad Church proposal for a scholarly movement which united men of good will only saw an ironic outcome in the High Church — Low Church pact, which would collapse once the volume was abjured. As Henry Venn asked, "Do we and the Tractarians mean the same thing by the 'inspiration of Scripture'? I think not".[148] The practical effects of a policy of no compromise meant that the essayists' hopes were dashed, of clerical liberty, of an alliance between science and religion, of a new reformation equal to anything in the sixteenth century. But the personal effects were most marked on the reconcilers themselves. That was why Lightfoot withdrew from the projected peace-making volume *Revelation and History*, and why Maurice found his position terribly limited. Tait realised that the clergy of the London diocese suspected him because of his association with Jowett.

> "The candid incline to surmise of late
>   That the Christian faith proves false, I find;
> For our Essays-and-Reviews' debate
>   Begins to tell on the public mind,
> And Colenso's words have weight".

So wrote Browning in 1864 in his volume *Dramatis Personae*. Browning did not like *Essays and Reviews* because it taught an irreligious optimism, opposing the fact of original sin, that "Corruption of Man's Heart", which he, as a poet, understood well enough.[149] But Browning could have had no sympathy with the clamour of the debate, which was at its height when he wrote the poem. The sheer amount of literature about *Essays and Reviews* is, indeed, startling. To examine the periodicals, books and pamphlets also becomes an exercise in the pathology of Victorian religious thought which has nothing to equal it. Amid the hysteria and fear of crisis sensible men lost their heads, and sarcastic writers preferred to use invective. There is very little humour. Yet one last voice deserves to be heard:

---

[148] W. Knight, *Memoir of the Rev. Henry Venn*, pp. 329-30.
[149] R. Browning, *Dramatis Personae*, p. 77.

> "Denounce Essayists and Reviewers,
>   Hang, quarter, gag them or shoot them —
> Excellent plan — provided that
>   You first of all refute them".

Essays and Reviews and the answering volumes provided ready-made material for *Punch*. The trivia and the panic were too obvious to miss, while the *volte-face* of Bishop Hampden, the erstwhile heretic who now denounced the liberals and protested against Sunday rail excursions, and the inconsistency of Pusey who joined with his former persecutors to persecute others, were tellingly reported:

> "Still scarred with Oxford's missiles freely thrown,
>   What hand as PUSEY'S fit to cast a stone?
> What he may want in spirit or in skill,
>   He will make up in venom or ill-will.
> It only needs to drive the lesson home,
>   That NEWMAN should be summoned back from Rome,
> And HAMPDEN called in to complete the trio,
>   JOWETT'S indictment to conduct con brio".

This little rhyme of 7 March, 1863 *Punch* entitled *"De Haeretico Comburendo"*. The campaign against Jowett's salary increase called forth another verse, "In Re Jowett", and a mock report of the "Small Debts and Heresies Court", in which Pusey appeared as accuser and "The Fathers", brought in seven cabs (a tart reference to Pusey's habit of voluminous citations), were called as witnesses. "Transportation to Natal" (i.e., Colenso's diocese) was the decision of the court, unless Jowett apologised to Pusey.[150]

But perhaps only *Punch* smiled. By March, 1863 the literary argument, however loudly it was conducted, no longer troubled the essayists as before; they were faced by a greater threat.

---

[150] *Punch*, 7 March, 1863, p. 100. Cf. J.C. Thirlwall, jnr., *Connop Thirlwall, Historian and Theologian*, p. 228.

CHAPTER FOUR

CONTROVERSY IN THE COURTS

The summer of 1860 was the worst in the nineteenth century,[1] and as it dragged its course through gales, storms of hail and incessant rain, it matched the darkening mood of the essayists. At first, Jowett was optimistic: the heresy hunts in the religious press only made the book more popular, he said, so that sweethearts shared it on train journeys ("God help them!"), and when a Quaker synod passed a condemnation the young Quakers read it more avidly.[2] But the essayists' opponents also realised this, and began to see that other action was necessary. Archdeacon Denison, indeed, listed four ways of dealing with neology, and, for effectiveness, placed argumentative treatises like *Aids to Faith* at the bottom.[3] What was needed was a determined move by *Ecclesia Anglicana* herself; so Jowett and company had premonitions of persecution and an attempt to drive them from the Church.

"Let not the essayists imagine that reaction is a thing unknown", warned the *Christian Remembrancer*.[4] C. J. Vaughan, instituted as vicar of Doncaster in November, read the XXXIX Articles in public, an almost unheard of proceeding which *The Times* saw as part of a general desire to return to dogmatic instruction.[5] Williams, returning from a holiday abroad, found in his postbag reports of clerical agitation in Derbyshire.[6] The shape of things to come was clearly suggested in December. Max-Müller, a friend of the essayists, was defeated by the more orthodox Monier-Williams for the Sanskrit professorship at Oxford. The Masters of Arts turned out in force to lobby against the Germanists, and, before returning to their country parishes, they held a meeting about the book. From this emanated a committee to organise a monster petition — the first of the "Protests of the Clergy" with which Oxford chastised the essayists. At Cambridge, Lightfoot's election to the

---

[1] Mrs Grote, *The Personal Life of George Grote*, p. 247. *Charles Kingsley: His Letters, and Memories of his Life*, II, p. 112.
[2] Abbott, I, p. 352.
[3] *Faith and Peace*, p. vi.
[4] *Christian Remembrancer*, April, 1861, p. 486.
[5] *The Times*, 10 November, 1860, p. 12.
[6] Williams, II, p. 18.

Hulsean chair, vacated by the conservative Ellicott, was as critical, but to Hort's relief he was appointed.[7]

If things got worse, who would protect the radicals? The state was bound to come to their aid eventually. The Judicial Committee of the Privy Council had defended George Gorham against his bishop, Henry Phillpotts, in 1850, and compared with that obscure Evangelical minister the essayists were among the most respected churchmen in the national life, with connections in high places. Pattison made much of this in an article in the *National Review*. The Church of England, he held, had always cherished the educated man, and the state could not permit any change which left the essayists at the mercy of a religious mob, for this would reduce the established Church to an approximation to Roman Catholicism with its dead level of democratic orthodoxy, stripped of men of knowledge and attainment, who had hitherto checked the tendency of the congregation to legislate doctrinally.[8] Pattison magnified the essayists — they were not quite the liberal aristocracy that he claimed — but he was right to see all the signs of a clash between Church and State. Such a crisis did, in fact, occur in 1864 when the Convocations condemned *Essays and Reviews* after the Privy Council had acquitted Williams and Wilson of the charges brought against them by churchmen. From the lawyers there was talk of secret courts, *cabals* and *praemunire*, while clerical leaders like Wilberforce answered that the Church must settle its own affairs and discipline erring writers who were in orders.

But in 1860 state aid seemed a long way off. If reaction took a serious turn, the essayists realised that they must look for support in other quarters. For a time, at the beginning, they hoped that they might find it in the bishops. It was plain that both enemies and friends could not leave the book alone (the wiser course was only realised in later years), but the bishops could deflect attention from the authors themselves.

Jowett and Temple visited Tait at Fulham, in January, 1861, and made their anxieties known. "Tait was very kind, and on the whole even gave me the impression that he agreed with me", claimed Jowett.[9] The following month Stanley also asked for assurances from Tait when he heard that the bench was meeting to discuss *Essays and Reviews*. "You also gave me to understand when I was at Fulham (and thus effectually prevented me from taking any active step in the matter) that no measure

---

[7] Hort, I, p. 448.
[8] *National Review*, January, 1863, pp. 187-220.
[9] Davidson, I, p. 300.

could be taken by the Bishops except a general recommendation to the clergy to preach the truth more actively".[10]

But the three friends had not reckoned with the busy pen and tongue of Wilberforce, nor had Tait. As soon as he understood the drift of feeling about the essays, the Bishop of Oxford acted promptly. Speaking at High Wycombe, in November, 1860, he turned the conclusion of his deanery charge into an appeal to a national audience, as Disraeli, Lord John Manners and the journalists present realised. His subject was "Rationalism":

> "Are there not signs enough abroad now of special danger to make us drop our lesser differences and combine together as one man, striving earnestly for the faith? When from within our own encampment we hear voices declaring that our whole belief in the Atonement is an ignorant misconception, when the history of the bible is explained away by being treated as a legend and its prophecy deprived of all supernatural character by being turned into a history of past or present events... when in words, so far as opinion privately entertained is concerned, the liberty of the English clergyman appears to be complete, when we are told that they may sign any Article of the national Church, if it is only their opinions which are at variance with them... when, I say, such words as these are deliberately uttered by our ordained clergy, and who still keep their place in the national Church, is it not time for us, laying aside our suspicions and divisions about small matters, to combine together in prayer and trust and labour and love and watching, lest, while we dispute needlessly about the lesser matters of the law, we be robbed unawares of the very foundations of the faith?"[11]

Wilberforce saw the essays as an act of disloyalty in a beleagured church. His gesture towards the Evangelicals was clear: the Broad Church must be crushed. As Stanley said, a "powerful ecclesiastical influence" was now at work, and the bishop's intervention was followed up by his article in the *Quarterly Review* in January.[12]

Given such a lead, what would be the attitude of the other bishops? The best guide lay in the liberal members of the bench. However, Tait, Thirlwall and Hampden, instead of standing firm, chose Wilberforce's method of a charge to the clergy, and they were not reassuring. Richard Whately, on the Irish bench, was similarly compromised.

Tait delayed making his views known until his charge of December 1862, and this took 27 pages to describe the present difficulties of the clergy. "We must not be alarmed if we find free enquiry", said Tait: legal

---

[10] *Ibid.*, p. 284.
[11] S. Wilberforce, *Charge to the Diocese of Oxford, November, 1860*, p. 67 f.
[12] *Quarterly Review*, January, 1861, pp. 248-305. See above pp. 108-111.

prosecutions would not protect faith, and dogmatic denunciations only irritated intelligent laymen and excited the evil. But, while allowing their positive truths, he thought that the publication of the essays was a mistake.[13]

Tait was less timid than the essayists believed, but Thirlwall was certainly more aggressive than they expected. They emerged from his charge, delivered at great length in December, 1863, as a unified band who had made a mockery of the liberal nature of the English Church. In particular, he criticised Temple who was usually regarded as the mildest of the writers and unfairly yoked with the rest.

Thirlwall said that Temple's theory of development was not innocuous: the essay opened the broadest room for an assault on the foundations of Christianity without setting up any defence against it; it contained language directly suggestive of the most perplexing doubts. Temple's friends expostulated — Thirlwall, however, refused to withdraw. The essayist (he said) surely realised the conclusion of his theory — that the later development of the race was superior to the earlier — but the bishop dismissed his proposed reconciliation which held that the vision of childhood would recommend itself to the adult mind because of its freshness. Thirlwall asked tartly, why should it?

> "Those who have been taught that the age in which they live is one of independent thought, in which conscience is invested with supreme authority, and which is distinguished from former periods in the history of the world, not only by larger knowledge, but by superior clearness of view, must find it hard to reconcile this advantage with the requirement that they should look at a phenomenon of the past with the eyes of its contemporaries, whose 'vision' had not attained to the same degree of keenness as their own. They must think it strange that they should be asked to recognise our Lord's Divinity, not upon any evidence directly offered to themselves, but on the grounds of an impression made by His example on witnesses who, through the general imperfection of their development, were much less capable of accurately discerning the things presented to them, and, above all, of correct inferences from the seen to the unseen".

Thirlwall held to the idea of the education of mankind, and of the bible as the record of the moral and religious stages of this, but not the scientific, which came later.[14] But he parted company with Temple, as he

---

[13] A.C. Tait, *A Charge delivered in December 1862 to the Clergy of the Diocese of London*, pp. 14, 16.

[14] *Letters Literary and Theological of Connop Thirlwall*, p. 255.

had done earlier with Williams, over the uniqueness of the bible. As for the others, he deplored their unclerical conduct: if they wanted clerical liberty, why hesitate halfway? He agreed with Powell that science had no claim on faith, but if faith was restricted to its own sphere there could be no contact between the two, except by miracle, which the essayists rejected. But Christ knew that he worked miracles; to suggest otherwise was to cast a shade on the purity of his human character. In the new national Church of Wilson, Christ would only be revered as a teacher whose influence was adapted to the nonage of the world; he could not be an object of personal faith. "In a word, their Christology is one which will not bear to be prayed". But Thirlwall did not abandon all his previous unorthodoxies; he was less opposed to Jowett and refused any proposal to define the inspiration of scripture.[15]

Hampden held, like other writers who knew far less than he did, that behind the essayists was "their great text book, *Leben Jesu*". This had come later than his own Bamptons, and he could shrug off any supposed paternity for the new Oxford liberalism. His charge, delivered to the diocese of Hereford in 1862, was unpublished, perhaps because he found it difficult to make up his mind.

What did the writers allow as a residuum of historic fact, asked Hampden — if a totally evolutionary view of doctrine was allowed, where did certainty exist? Powell in using Hume had not distinguished between statements open to correction from enlarged experience and those relating to positive facts. No contradictory statements could be admitted about the latter without casting doubt and suspicion on the author. The accounts of miracles might seem like the former, so that what was held to be miraculous in one age was not so in another. But the scripture miracles "are not given as explanations of the events related in them according to the laws of nature then known, but as simple events out of the course of those laws, particular instances of exception from those laws and, of course, presupposing those laws from which they are exceptions, according to the then state of knowledge". The inspired writer simply stated in each instance an effect produced at the moment; and if the miracle was rejected it could not be on the grounds of his ignorance of physical laws known only by modern man. "He does not attempt to explain it; he merely says that a wonderful effect took place; and we, in that case, must reject his testimony altogether as false, as stating a particular event to have taken place which did not take

---

[15] *Remains Literary and Theological of Connop Thirlwall*, II, pp. 28-53.

place".[16] The point was tortuously made and he did not answer Powell's contention about testimony, but Hampden questioned whether the essayists had immersed themselves in the "world of scripture" as seriously as they claimed.

Dr Whately's charge, entitled *Danger from Within*, was the weakest of the four and suggested his declining powers. The noetic archbishop had taken umbrage at the rejection of Paley in the essays and, indeed, he held that a "very considerable and most important part of the publication" was meant as an answer to his edition of Paley published in 1859 (so he coupled the charge with a fresh edition of Paley and a postscript criticising the radicals): but the archbishop himself seemed to be the only person aware of this, as *The Guardian* unkindly pointed out. Whately was out of date even for orthodox churchmen.[17] The charge included a rebuke for Coleridge and for any subjective notion that religion was altogether a matter of feeling. The Christian, said Whately, quoting Paley, "endeavours not to seek and embrace a religion conformable to his character but, on the contrary, to make his character conformable to his religion... when it has been laid down that miracles are not all needed for the establishment of the claims of the gospel, it is very natural to proceed to the denial that they were ever wrought". The two Irish primates followed this with a letter to clergy and laity warning them away from the book.[18]

Perhaps Whately's hard words dispelled the illusion of liberal episcopal support which might have remained after the other elaborate theological analyses cloaked the real feelings of Thirlwall and Hampden. Some people were shocked that Whately should have spoken so bitterly of Powell.[19] If they had reservations, the remaining bishops shed them and began to emulate Wilberforce's example. One charge after another followed in 1861 and 1862 attacking the essays. They argued that their clergy expected them, and some would have said that they harmed no one. The liberals, however, unused to diocesan politics, were dismayed at the hostility in public of men who were charming in private. Stanley, on holiday in Constantinople and Mount Athos in 1861, spoke of "Sarum

---

[16] H. Hampden, ed., *Some Memorials of Renn Dickson Hampden*, pp. 210-18.

[17] *G*, 20 November, 1861, p. 1071.

[18] R. Whately, *Danger from Within*, pp. 18, 25. *The Times*, 8 March, 1861, p. 5.

[19] R.B. Kennard, *"Essays and Reviews", Their Origin, History, General Characteristics and Significance*, p. 64. Wilberforce reported Whately's strong feelings about Powell in *Chronicle of Convocation*, 1861, p. 466.

and S. Oxon combining with Winchester and Carlisle to tear the Church to pieces and render a quiet faith impossible".[20]

W. K. Hamilton of Salisbury was, predictably, antagonistic. He accused the essayists of disloyalty. "However comprehensive may be the limits within which our tolerant Church allows her clergy to exercise their ministry, those limits must exist somewhere".[21] The essays were seen by Charles Sumner of Winchester as an example of the malaise among the clergy, which was also reflected in the large decline in graduate candidates for the priesthood.[22] For Samuel Waldegrave, Bishop of Carlisle, the book was "not so much the inroad of a new and foreign element of mischief, as the outbreak of an infection which has long been stealthily at work amongst us".[23] The Bishop of Bath and Wells was early in the field, in May, 1861, speaking of "erroneous statements tending towards infidelity".[24] Prince Lee of Manchester followed the trend, to Westcott's chagrin, and avoided the middle course expected of him; no more pernicious or corrupting book had appeared for three centuries, he said.[25]

Episcopal initiative might have remained on this individual level, except that the dioceses demanded more. By the opening of the new year (1861) the bishops were in a quandary: some answer must be made to the memorials and addresses now pouring into Lambeth, but what action *could* the bench take? Archbishop Sumner called his colleagues to a meeting on 1 February, and they debated the matter. The only guide to the discussion is a memorandum left by Wilberforce and freely used by his biographer, to the annoyance of Davidson and Benham, who wrote the life of Tait. They felt that it was indiscreet and only gave Wilberforce's side of the picture.[26] The memorandum obviously defended his role, but it seems an accurate enough guide to the divided feelings of the bishops.

According to Wilberforce, Hampden was the most opposed, moving that they should prosecute, since it was a question between "Infidelity and Christianity... a question of Christianity or no Christianity". Thirlwall deprecated putting the matter into the hands of Convocation,

[20] Prothero, II, p. 49.

[21] W.K. Hamilton, *Charge of the Bishop of Salisbury, 1861*, p. 63.

[22] C. Sumner, *A Charge delivered to the Diocese of Winchester, 1862*, pp. 22-3.

[23] S. Waldegrave, *Charge delivered to the Diocese of Carlisle, October 1861*, p. 33.

[24] *Charge of the Bishop of Bath and Wells, 1861*, pp. 13-14.

[25] Charge quoted in *Protestantische Kirchen Zeitung*, 13 April, 1861, p. 362. Cf. A. Westcott, *Life and Letters of Brooke Foss Westcott*, p. 212.

[26] Davidson, I, p. 283 n. 1.

others doubted whether a court case would succeed and suggested that legal advice should be sought. Tait proposed taking no action at all; the literary debate would sufficiently answer the essays, showing their hollowness, and pointing out the great doctrines which they undervalued. Two of the writers (evidently Temple and Jowett) were his dear friends, while Pattison's essay was (he said) "unobjectionable". "He did not agree with the argument that it was a reflection on the Church of England that her Articles did not meet every form of evil. He thought that false doctrine must be endured". Hamilton explained with deep feeling his reasons for admitting Williams into his diocese, and he implied that he would take steps against the essayist as his bishop. That would have provided a way of escape for the rest of the bench, except that the primate insisted that some collective statement must be made. Others demurred; if this was the only course that could be followed it was unsatisfactory. Thirlwall warned that a mere declaration by the bishops, unless followed by action, would be an admission "that we had no means of repressing prolate heresy". Wilberforce represented himself as putting forward another point of view; by such action the bishops would originate, and, secondly, they would be condemning the essayists unheard. "The Bishop of Winchester supported him, and, replying to the Archbishop, who had said 'that the addresses did not ask what we were going to do, but what our opinions are', said : 'The addresses must mean what are you going to do, how are we to stop after a declaration? our present position is very difficult, it would then be worse — there are difficulties on both sides' ". Prince Lee was also opposed.

If the memorandum is correct, the primate bore the heavy responsibility for what followed: the document that they finally adopted was, in fact, the declaration of opinion, with all its anomalies. But did the gentle Sumner ride rough-shod over the rest? The entry in Wilberforce's diary is curious. Despite his stand on the other side, Wilberforce, "at the entreaty of Bishops, drew up an answer to addresses, which they all adopted, and sent it out". That was on 2 February, at Fulham, where he had spent the night, "very much tired" after the meeting, with London, Rochester and Carlisle.[27]

Wilberforce was further implicated. Sumner was evidently not present when the form was adopted, and he had been called away early from the previous day's meeting. The lapse of time between the meeting and the date borne by the letter when it was published in *The Times* (12

---

[27] R.G. Wilberforce, *Life of the Rt. Rev. Samuel Wilberforce*, III, pp. 2-4.

February) suggests that the rest were canvassed for their general assent to the letter, the precise form of which was left to the Bishop of Oxford. One or two diocesans received a shock when they discovered what stood above their names in *The Times* that morning: Wilberforce was not over-scrupulous. Henry Phillpotts of Exeter quickly wrote a disclaimer to *The Guardian*, saying that he was misinformed about the nature of the letter or he would have withheld his name.[28] There was more confusion when the newspapers on the first publication of the document did not carry the memorial to which it replied.

Such was the "secret history of the episcopal letter", to use Thirlwall's term. The greatest drawback lay in the manner of its appearance. On three previous occasions the bishops had acted in concert to meet a pressing situation. In 1842 they censured the High Church opponents of the Jerusalem bishopric; in 1847 they denounced the elevation of Hampden (whom they then regarded as a heretic) to the see of Hereford; and in 1851 all but two signed a protest against the re-establishment of the Roman Catholic hierarchy in England. The unanimity in 1861 was most striking of all. Yet this was, in effect, a "condemnation which oozed out in a private letter to a newspaper" (Denison), having been sent to *The Times* by the country clergyman (H. B. Williams) who first received it. *The Spectator* thought this "extraordinary", *The Times* said that it was "libellous", and Stanley felt that the procedure was without precedent in the history of the Church of England.[29]

No one was satisfied; the letter did nothing to allay the popular panic; aggressive clergymen said that it was cowardly; and it came as a complete surprise to the essayists. Jowett suspected moves in Convocation and already knew on 8 February that Dr Jelf would propose a hostile motion, but of episcopal action — "this apparition of the 25 bishops" — he knew nothing.[30] Of course, he imagined some deep motive in the roundabout method that the bench adopted.

The protest which was the immediate cause of the letter came from a rural deanery in Dorset and invited episcopal vigilance particularly in regard to undergraduates and ordinands. The test for belief must be stricter — which might mean that the bishops had been too lax in their examination of candidates:

> "We wish to make known to your Grace and to all the Bishops the alarm we feel at some late indications of the spread of rationalistic and semi-infidel

---

[28] Williams, II, p. 32.
[29] *Letters Literary and Theological of Connop Thirlwall*, p. 235.
[30] Abbott, I, pp. 345-6.

doctrine among the beneficed clergy of the realm. We allude especially to
the denial of the atoning efficacy of the Death and Passion of our Blessed
Saviour Jesus Christ, both God and Man, for us and for our salvation, and
to the denial also of a Divine Inspiration, peculiar to themselves alone, of
the Canonical Scriptures of the Old and New Testaments.

"We would earnestly beseech your Grace and your Lordships, as faithful
stewards over the House of God, to discourage by all means in your power
the spread of speculations which would rob our countrymen, more especially the poor and unlearned, of their only sure stay and comfort for time
and for eternity. And to this end we would more especially and most
earnestly beseech you, in your Ordinations, to 'lay hands suddenly on no
man' till you have convinced yourselves (as far as human precaution can
secure it) that each Deacon who in reply to the question, 'Do you
unfeignedly believe all the Canonical Scriptures of the Old and New
Testament?' answers, 'I do believe them', *speaks the truth* as in the sight of
God".[31]

The protest did not mention *Essays and Reviews* and was obviously
concerned about the wider aspects of unbelief among the parish clergy.
But the reply concentrated on the offending volume. The primate wrote:

"Reverend Sir, — I have taken the opportunity of meeting many of my
Episcopal brethren in London to lay your address before them. They
unanimously agree with me in expressing the pain it has given them that any
clergyman of our Church should have published such opinions as those
concerning which you have addressed us. We cannot understand how these
opinions can be held consistently with an honest subscription to the
formularies of our Church, with many of the fundamental doctrines of
which they appear to us essentially at variance.

"Whether the language in which these views are expressed is such as to make
their publication an act which could be visited in the Ecclesiastical Courts,
or to justify the Synodical condemnation of the book which contains them,
is still under our gravest consideration. But our main hope is our reliance on
the blessing of God, in the continued and increasing earnestness with which
we trust that we and the clergy of our several dioceses may be enabled to
teach and preach that good deposit of sound doctrine which our Church
teaches in its fulness, and which we pray that she may, by God's grace, ever
set forth as the uncorrupted Gospel of our Lord Jesus Christ".[32]

The signature was Sumner's but the language came from Wilberforce.
The Times made the matter more oblique, for its version had "their" for
"these" opinions; was it a slip or deliberately meant? But that was a
minor question. The letter meant a change for the worse in the essayists'

---

[31] *G*, 20 February, 1861, p. 166.
[32] Davidson, I, pp. 281-2.

situation. They could not rely on the bishops for protection. Indeed, the bench itself, manoeuvred by Wilberforce, had raised the question of legal proceedings. The essayists had further been compromised by the method of publication; was the letter a censure or judgment or not? — the uncertainty was one more reason for starting a prosecution. As Dean Inge said in a later situation when liberals felt a sense of loss and betrayal: "What wretched guidance the bishops have given — *Essays and Reviews*, Colenso, and now the Old Testament miracles!"[33]

The equivocations arose, of course, from the role that bishops were expected to play in both national and church life. It was doubly difficult when they were former liberals or academics, or both. Tait, in particular, was an example of the paralysis which could afflict a man of great resoluteness and power. Only an agony of mind allowed him to support the essayists in the episcopal meeting while, in totally contradictory fashion, he was preparing to sign Wilberforce's letter — and then to feel surprise and hurt when his friends misunderstood his motives.

The travail can be illustrated from Tait's diary and letters. 1860 was, he wrote, the most painful year of office yet. The folly of the publication of *Essays and Reviews*, Stanley's ill-judged defence, and then the Colenso madness, had so effectively frightened the clergy that there was no bishop (except, perhaps, Thirlwall, now "awakened as from a dream and to have shaken off Oxford's influence") who could prevent the widespread alienation of the middle class. He expected little from anyone else; the Archbishop of York had, by a tendentious charge concerning Colenso, entirely forfeited favour, Vaughan of Doncaster manifested a "strange and mysterious failure", and the bishops generally only gave the clergy a mere echo of their own addresses. His own vocation was clear, to prevent the Evangelicals from tyrannising over the Broad Church and coalescing with the High Church to exterminate the other party. He intended, God willing, to promote the formation of a new party, for "the liberals are deficient in religion, and the religious are deficient in liberality" — though he feared that, in the alarm, almost all those who would have formed it had deserted.

Tait knew that his own clergy mistrusted him ("they have made no move to give me an opportunity of saying anything", he wrote in his diary). But the mistrust spread to higher persons. Tait believed to the end of his life that his stand over the essays had cost him his influence with Palmerston. The prime minister had ceased to consult him over ecclesias-

---

[33] A. Fox, *Dean Inge*, p. 263.

tical matters because he was "too much inclined to liberal ideas", and he
saw Shaftesbury's hand in this. "Latterly all appointments seemed to be
made by Palmerston with no idea than that the person appointed was
safe as regards the *Essays and Reviews*". (Jowett naturally thought that
men were promoted to higher places simply for writing against *Essays
and Reviews*). Tait obviously felt this deeply for, as he said frequently, he
was no supporter of the book itself. "I deeply deplore and indeed
execrate the spirit of much of the *Essays and Reviews*". Williams' essay
seemed even worse than when he first read it, and he did not wonder at
the outcry and alarm.[34]

Jowett, he felt, had developed away from him by 1861. The old
comradeship had gone. He wrote in his diary on 20 January, 1861:
"Jowett has been with me two days. The unsatisfactory part of his system
seems to be that there is an obscurity over what he believes of the centre
of Christianity. As to the outworks, the conflict there is of comparatively
little importance; but the Central Figure of the Lord Jesus, the central
doctrine of the efficacy of His Sacrifice — in fact St. Paul's Christianity
— is this distinctly recognised by the writers of his school?.,. [They must
state] what is the *positive* Christianity they hold".[35]

A "very painful" correspondence took place with Temple when the
episcopal letter was published. Stanley wrote as soon as he read *The
Times*, "I do not know when I have been more startled... What can I say
in your defence?", but Tait replied that episcopal action was necessary
because the essayists allowed edition after edition to appear without any
change. Could not the copartnery (the association of Jowett and Temple
with the others) be dissolved?[36] But he dreaded receiving the post from
Rugby, and he wrote in his diary, "fear of misunderstandings with old
friends".

Temple spared him nothing. "What you did had not the intention, but
it had all the effect, of treachery". "If you do not wish to alienate your
friends, do not treat them as you have treated me... You will not keep
friends if you compel them to feel that in every crisis of life they must be
on their guard against trusting you". Tait asked Temple to consider the
unsatisfactory and ambiguous nature of a preface in which the authors,
on one hand, disclaimed united responsibility and, on the other, held that
they had a common object and collectively approved of the spirit in

---

[34] Tait MSS, Diaries Miscellanea 1828-79, ff. 40, 148, 150, 152-3, 213, 219, partly
reproduced in Davidson, I, p. 325.

[35] *Ibid.*, f. 151. Cf. Davidson, I, p. 281.

[36] Davidson, I, pp. 284-5.

which each tried to promote that object. Temple would have none of this and another letter spoke of more mischief done to him by Tait's remarks in Convocation. In his liberal days Tait had urged the critical study of the bible. But freedom was the necessary condition of that study. "To tell a man to study and yet bid him, under heavy penalties, come to the same conclusions with those who have not studied, is to mock him... You complain that young men of ability will not take orders. How can you expect it when this is what befalls whoever does not think as you do?" The minds of the laity would be poisoned, for they would think that those who remained in the ministry did so out of fear.[37]

Temple raised a deeper aspect: the bishops appeared to place the authority of the Church against the freedom of the theologian and thinker. A student had the right, he said, to claim, first, that the limits put upon him should be known beforehand, and, secondly, that he should be given a fair open trial by men practised in such decisions. Tait attempted a reply, but in his address to the Rugby staff Temple was even more outspoken about the bishops' competence. The censure was unjust because men who had not gone into the difficulties of the question condemned others only on the strength of their general impressions or traditional beliefs; "and it is also unjust that any one writing on such subjects should have hanging over him the possibility of a censure from a body of men who are guided by no fixed or plain rule of doctrine".[38] The chasm between faith and intellect seemed to yawn more widely if the bishop himself was a man of learning.

Now committed to their letter, the bishops stayed together. Like the essayists they had to defend their collective action. The essayists, in turn, hardened their hearts. Tait continued to hope for a recantation, or even breaking of the partnership. In Convocation he asked Jowett and Temple to declare that they were not responsible for every word in the book, as a gesture to the bishops.[39] Others tried to separate the two from the rest. James McCosh said that "seated on their academic heights" they did not weigh the destructive effects of the combined book on those beneath. "Whatever Mr Temple or Mr Jowett may have meant, we may see — unless it be counteracted — the proper result of the whole movement in once living faiths groaning, bleeding, and dying in that stony, arid and horrid plain which Mr Baden Powell has provided in his exclusive

---

[37] *Ibid.*, I, pp. 289-93.
[38] Temple Memoirs, I, p. 224.
[39] *Chronicle of Convocation*, 1861, p. 460.

naturalism, in his mechanical law, and physical causation".[40] Thirlwall was sceptical — he gauged more accurately the feelings of Jowett who rebuked Tait for "calling upon us to disavow our companions in distress", and resisted a plan of Stanley's, in that same month, February, to sign an explanatory letter to the Bishop of London; he preferred the friendship of Wilson, who had just written warmly to him.[41] Adversity drew them closer to one another, and this even overcame Williams' sense of isolation. The bishops realised the lesson and turned more easily to the other side. Understandably, the large majority of churchmen encouraged them. So did some Nonconformists. "Let the Bishops avail themselves of all the means at their disposal for uprooting error and heresy: if they succeed, well: if otherwise, let them proceed to the legislature for fresh powers". So wrote the *British Standard* in June, 1861.[42]

The appointment of a new primate in the summer of 1862 made no difference to the situation; indeed, Stanley became embroiled in a correspondence battle with Archbishop Longley. The primate said in a Lords debate that the essays were a united production, and Stanley wrote to ask what he meant. The essayists, he said, had no communication and were mostly unacquainted with one another; their contributions appeared in the order in which they were received (Stanley was almost certainly wrong in this), and no regular design was involved. The idea of a "liberal theological review" was contained in the book, but that only strengthened its likeness to any review of a particular political or theological complexion. Longley replied promptly : if the essayists were "associated in a common undertaking" and then denied the concert, "they would hardly be thought to be making a fair use of language," and if they were not associated in a common undertaking, how could the essays have found their way to the same publisher and possess the "obvious and acknowledged design of illustrating the advantage of a free handling of sacred subjects, instead of being of the heterogeneous character of the usual articles in Reviews?" Stanley protested, "will you allow me to make my meaning quite clear?", but a second letter from the primate insisted that there must have been some previous communication with some other person, "and it must have been understood among them all that there was one common object, one common design which their respective essays were to promote". In any case, the question

---

[40] J. McCosh, *The Supernatural in Relation to the Natural*, p. ix.

[41] Abbott, I, p. 346. E. Abbott and L. Campbell, eds., *Letters of Benjamin Jowett*, p. 172. Wilson criticised Tait similarly in *WR*, July, 1861, p. 227.

[42] *The British Standard*, 21 June, 1861, p. 41.

of moral responsibility remained, for their association continued after publication in a manner injurious to the cause of Christianity. To this Stanley made only an ineffective reply.[43]

How could the bishops' disapproval be strengthened? Maurice argued that it had gone far enough, but Wilberforce and Denison thought that other churchmen, in some official capacity, should be given a voice. They realised that the perfect organ lay to hand in the newly revived Convocations. On 26 February, therefore, ten days after publication of the letter, a debate was initiated in the lower house of Canterbury. No one quite knew what the outcome would be. Would Convocation risk the perilous precedent of the condemnation of Bishop Hoadly in 1717? The anti-liberal party thought that they knew the mood of the assembly and they were proved right. Until Stanley was appointed Dean of Westminster in 1862 the essayists had few friends in the lower house, while Tait and Thirlwall veered between support and dislike in the upper house. The uncommitted members were more anxious about the "sacred and elevated" character of Convocation itself than about protection of suspicious books. In such an assembly a body of determined men could always provoke an issue; even in 1891 Denison threatened an upheaval over the "dangerous error" in *Lux Mundi*,[44] and in 1861 he had far more support. The condemnation party kept the question going until they were finally victorious.

The first debate confirmed the rigorists' tactics. Members were disgruntled when, having been called to discuss the 29th Canon, they were drawn onto *Essays and Reviews* by Denison and R. W. Jelf, Principal of King's College, London, and they responded with a compromise solution. But readiness to talk about the book was obvious, once the discussion was initiated, and the themes which were to occur again in the following years were introduced one after another. Most of the speakers criticised the volume, others were shocked that clergymen should have written it, others wondered about the state of the un-iversities. The articles in the *Westminster* and *Quarterly* were obviously in their minds. On the matter of the theology in the volume the main discovery was the parallel with the Deists. This was repeated *ad nauseam* in later debates, even by those who ought to have known better — Thirlwall, for instance, compared Chubb's *True Gospel of Jesus Christ*, for a correspondent, and held that the Deist could have been inserted

---

[43] Longley MSS, vol. 4, ff. 222, 224, 227, 231.
[44] G.A. Denison, *Supplement to Notes of my Life*, p. 143.

into the essays without additional scandal. The main difference was (he wrote) that Chubb spoke plainly and bluntly, and did not affect to use the technical terms of a theology which he regretted, "and that he was not a clergyman".[45] The less acquiescent voices were heard more loudly than on later occasions; they doubted the wisdom of any show of repression, either because of the effect on the world outside or because the episcopal action still seemed sufficient enough. Others disliked the width of Jelf's motion and any judgment only on the basis of extracts from the book.

The resolution eventually agreed to was put by Christopher Wordsworth and entertained an "earnest hope that, under the divine blessing, the faithful zeal of the Christian Church in this land may be enabled to counteract the pernicious effect of the erroneous opinions contained in the volume". Wordsworth wished to be fair; the essayists could not defend themselves in Convocation, though he was quite prepared to meet them with the bitterest words outside.

Denison was dissatisfied with the resolution but bided his time. With suitable references to Tom Paine and other infidels, Denision said that the whole world was waiting for the Church of England to do something about the book, particularly for the sake of the young who were tainted, corrupted and almost thrust into hell by it. Jelf's opening speech pointed to the future most clearly of all. He asked that an address be sent to the primate and bishops, "with a view to synodical action". Jelf was no stranger to prosecution: he was implicated in Maurice's dismissal from King's, over his teachings on the Atonement, in 1853, but he was also one of the six heads of houses who had condemned Pusey's sermon on the Eucharist in May, 1843. Jelf indicted the essayists on nine counts, including "Ideology, that frightful principle wholly inconsistent with objective faith".[46] There was obviously little sympathy for the essayists' recasting of theology. Hort, when he read the "unreal and absolutely unsatisfactory" discussion, realised that Convocation would not repair the deficiencies which would shortly be revealed in *Aids to Faith* and other books. He could only comment indignantly to Ellerton, "surely this wretched paltering with great questions must soon come to an end, or else the Church itself".[47]

---

45 *Letters Literary and Theological of Connop Thirlwall*, p. 236.
46 *Chronicle of Convocation*, 1861, pp. 364-413. *G*, 27 February, 1861, pp. 188-91, 194-5. Cf. J.H. Overton and E. Wordsworth, *Christopher Wordsworth, Bishop of Lincoln*, pp. 172-3.
47 Hort, I, p. 443.

The upper house asked for the views of the northern bishops before making any decision. A hostile speech from the primate showed why as a Calvinist Dr. Sumner found the book "full of the most dangerous views". He called his colleagues together on 13 March to consider the reply from York, but in the meantime repeated his criticisms. On 12 March a petition, signed by over 8,000 clergy, was presented at Lambeth asking for action against the volume. The archbishop said that it had his sympathy: "I cannot be surprised that the clergy should unite in desiring to clear themselves from the reproach which may be cast against the Church itself, when some of her members 'holding', as is justly stated, 'positions of great trust', shall have published a volume the tendency of which is to undermine the very foundations of Christianity".[48]

The petition was the first of two "Protests of the Clergy" occasioned by *Essays and Reviews*. 11,000 signed the second, in 1864. It was carried by a large deputation led by W. J. Irons and A. C. McCaul, the High Church and Low Church joint secretaries, and in the list of sponsors the names of Dr Pusey and Dean Close were linked. *Ecce Signum!* The alliance asked for by Wilberforce in his charge was thus consummated, and there were other instances of the uniting effects of the essays (but in a way quite contrary to Jowett's hopes) before long. The complaints were typical of the protest letters which now filled episcopal mailbags. The tendency of the book, it was held, was to annihilate the authority of the bible as the Word of God, to reject all miracles, including Christ's, and to undermine faith in God as creator. The essayists were clergymen holding positions of great trust and possessing opportunities favourable in no ordinary way for the diffusion of error. "We therefore earnestly entreat your Grace to take counsel with other members of the episcopate and devise such measures as may banish and drive away from our Church all such erroneous and strange doctrines". Then followed the thousands of names.

Hare, long before, had protested about the "shameful touting for signatures. In what other class of men could such a thing happen?" R. B. Kennard who reported this added a story about a rural dean who said, "it is an awful book", but admitted that he had read only the extracts sent round with the petition and Wilberforce's article. His companion said, "I sign everything, but I have not read them".[49] But the petitions were valuable propaganda for their organisers. Westcott and

---

[48] *G*, 13 March, 1861, p. 250.
[49] R.B. Kennard, *op. cit.*, pp. 158-9.

Hort thought that the liberals must put up an answering show of unity.
So they proposed a counter declaration:

> "We, the undersigned clergymen of the Church of England, desire to protest
> publicly against the violent and indiscriminate agitation now being directed
> against a book called *Essays and Reviews*, and against the authors of it.
> Believing that the suppression of free criticism must ultimately be injurious
> to the cause of truth and religion, we especially regret the adoption of a
> harsh and intolerant policy, which tends to deter men of thought and
> learning from entering the ministry, and to impel generous minds into
> antagonism to the Christian faith".[50]

But this was another project which remained stillborn in their
correspondence; and could it ever have commanded thousands of
signatures?

On 14 March attention was fixed again on Convocation, the lower
house being crowded in anticipation that the bishops, reinforced by the
northern bench, would now act. They did so by agreeing to a gravamen
from the lower house asking for the appointment of a committee to make
extracts from the book and report back. This time Denison and others
got their way, and protests in the lower house were stifled. Among the
bishops Tait suspected the work of the pressure group and asked what
good previous synodical condemnations had done. But their lordships
were swayed by Thirlwall who took a different line and pressed for
synodical action. "Everyone is asking the same question. What is the
Church of England going to do? It is something absolutely required for
maintaining the character, I would almost say, the very being of the
Church as a Church". Thirlwall seems to have thought that the essayists'
"defiance" is not dissolving their partnership called for disciplinary
action, while other speakers felt that their continued silence needed an
authoritative condemnation. The result of the voting was 8:4 in favour of
Wilberforce's motion requesting the lower house to appoint its committee and report on the volume.[51]

It was an odd procedure in which the bishops desired to be guided by
the theological learning of the inferior clergy, and the lower house took it
to mean that Denison was justified. He was voted in as chairman of the
committee, and the report was therefore engineered as an outright attack
on the radicals and their principles. But the body wished to preserve at

---

[50] Hort, I, p. 439.
[51] *Chronicle of Convocation*, 1861, pp. 458-472, 551-572. *G*, 6 March, 1861, pp. 230-2, 20
March, 1861, pp. 281-3.

least the appearance of fairness, and it sat for twelve days and spent 70 hours in drawing up its report, "so that you may be assured full care has been taken". Within a few weeks the document was completed.

The 17 closely printed pages of the report found three leading errors in *Essays and Reviews*:

> "(1) That the present advanced knowledge possessed by the world in its 'manhood' is the standard by which the educated intellect of the individual man, guided and governed by conscience, is to measure and determine the truth of the Bible.
>
> (2) That where the Bible is assumed to be at variance with the conclusions of such educated intellect, the Bible must be taken in such cases to have no divine authority, but to be only 'a human utterance'.
>
> (3) That the principles of interpretation of the Bible, hitherto universally received in the Christian Church, are untenable; and that new principles of interpretation are now to be substituted if the credit and authority of the holy Scriptures are to be maintained".

In addition, the essayists denied many statements and doctrines of scripture, including historical facts of the Old Testament referred to by Christ himself; they also held that the creeds might be put aside as out of date in the advanced intellectual condition of the world, and that the formularies could be subscribed to without belief in them according to their plain and natural meaning. The report continued: "We notice in many parts of the volume the absence of that spirit of humility and reverence with which human reason ought ever to approach the study of divine truth... We notice also a confusion of the dictates of the natural conscience and Divine grace, and, in some places, the substitution of those dictates for Divine grace". The conclusion was:

> "It appears to us that, whilst the professed intention of the volume is the 'free handling, in a becoming spirit', of religious subjects, the general tendency and effect of the volume is unduly to exalt the authority of human reason; to lower the authority of Revelation in regard to things divine and spiritual; to unsettle faith; and to consign the reader to a helpless scepticism".[52]

Offending passages were attached, to prove the committee's case. The list, in fact, — despite the essayists' protests that they were being misrepresented — became the standard reference and was used even in the legal actions. There could be only one result of the examination,

---

[52] *G*, 19 June, 1861, pp. 581-3.

Essays and Reviews was a unity; its teachings were heretical and must be condemned by the Church.

Having done their work, the committee pressed for this decision within a day of the report being presented to the lower house. Only a third of the members was present, and Wordsworth and others protested, "for Christian charity's sake", that no hasty steps should be taken and that the essayists should be allowed to defend themselves. A two-day deferment was secured, and then for a further two days the report was debated at a fever pitch of excitement. Jowett complained that this "august body of nonentities" was "determinedly set against all the intellectual tendencies of the age", and he asked the prolocutor, Dean Elliot, to publish a letter uttering some useful truth which might restrain his members.[53] But, as a piece of conservative theology, the report was better than anything which had so far appeared on *Essays and Reviews* : it was not so opinionated as Wilberforce's article, and its air of apparent objectivity was only dispelled if the reader noticed how every negativism had been faithfully reproduced, while the more constructive aspects of the book were passed over. Armed with the report the conservative speakers talked a great deal about theological novelty, about startling new theories of biblical interpretation which would present every preacher with great problems, and about the harm done to the laity if they began to discuss the essayists' arguments among themselves. The other members listened and did not think to challenge the theological competence of the committee. Amid all the amendments and calls to order one thing was clear — the essayists could expect help only on the grounds that the tone of the debate was beneath the dignity of the house. This objection had some weight, for at the end of the debate Denison secured his original resolution by 31 votes to 8, a figure which suggested some abstentions. Nonetheless, the resolution which was duly transmitted to the upper house (22 June, 1861) was a resounding one: "... that in the opinion of this house there are sufficient grounds for proceeding to a synodical judgment".[54]

The story of *Essays and Reviews* and the Church might have ended there; the condemnation needed only the assent of the bishops, who had already expressed their disapproval of the book, to make it actual. The rigorist party had given Convocation the character that it hoped for. The bench rested content. The primate did not wish for further action,

---

[53] Abbott, I, p. 348. E. Abbott and L. Campbell, eds., *Letters of Benjamin Jowett*, p. 176.

[54] *G*, 26 June, 1861, pp. 605-611.

certainly not a case in the Church courts which were far too encumbered with technicalities.[55]

There remained, however, the Tractarian conscience of Bishop Hamilton of Salisbury, and by the date of the Convocation resolution he had already taken other steps. Hamilton had been applied to by Liddon, among others, as the one bishop whose Church principles ought to lead him to do something and, in addition, he felt a sense of personal betrayal at Dr Williams' conduct. Williams, to his chagrin, had proposed a move to the diocese in November, 1858, having accepted the college living of Broadchalke when South Wales became too much for him. Hamilton had read *Rational Godliness* and "other bad things" and knew of Williams' "constitutional love of disputation". He wondered whether he could legally refuse to institute him, but, when Williams assured him that he would not take the matter to law, the bishop felt charitable in return and stifled his doubts.[56] Williams was duly installed. When the essays appeared Hamilton immediately regretted his action and now did not hide his feelings about Williams. "What a very dangerous man he is, and his temper is vile; no self-control".[57] Hence, when the bishops met in February, Hamilton (according to Wilberforce's note) warned his colleagues that he felt he must prosecute. The projected Convocation resolution did not lessen this sense of responsibility.

But what form should prosecution take? Denison suggested that the bishop should try the essayist in his own consistorial court.[58] But Hamilton wanted something larger and feared lest he would not be thought objective. He began to look for some suitable procedure. The search did not take long, and he found what he wanted in the Church Discipline Act of 1840. Accordingly, on 1 June, after publication of a warning letter in *The Times*, he took the action which instituted the second stage of the proceedings against the essayists. Hamilton sent Letters of Request to the Court of Arches, under the rules of the Act, asking that Williams be tried on the ground that he had infringed the formularies of the Church of England. Williams felt that he was about to ·become a martyr, leader writers called the bishop a persecutor. Hamilton certainly bore responsibility for the events now set in motion, and he could not have been surprised when a second request was addressed almost immediately to the court concerning Wilson. Bishop Turton of

---

[55] Cf. R. Wilberforce, *op. cit.*, III, pp. 7, 22.
[56] Phillimore Papers, letters of W.K. Hamilton, 7 June, 1861, 3 January, 1862.
[57] Journal of W.K. Hamilton, 1858, f. 83.
[58] Pusey MSS, letter of Denison to Pusey, 8 March, 1861.

Ely, in whose diocese Wilson's parish lay, was unwilling to commence proceedings but he allowed James Fendall to take action as a private clergyman. The two cases were thereafter conducted as one. Within a few days, therefore, the position of the writers had materially altered. As the only essayists who held livings, Williams and Wilson were to be offered up in restitution for the sins of the others — though no one doubted that the book as a whole was on trial.

In fact, Wilson had already begun to feel the effect of restrictions before this. In May, 1861, he was due to preach at St. Chrysostom's, Everton, but Bishop Graham of Chester sent a monition to the vicar, John MacNaught, forbidding him to allow Wilson his pulpit and invoking a legal ruling that a clergyman not licensed in a diocese was bound to obey a bishop's inhibition. Wilson did not mount the pulpit and MacNaught read the sermons instead. They were then published with a note explaining the manner of their appearance. As examples of radical preaching the sermons were not, in fact, remarkable: Wilson noted variations in the Genesis stories, proposed moral objections to the notions of total depravity and hell-fire, and held in his usual vein that forms of church government and creed were not perpetual but depended on the state of conviction in men's minds.[59]

The Dean of Arches accepted the case, and briefs were prepared. The other essayists lent support to the two as the hearings drew near: they contributed to a "Williams and Wilson Appeal Fund" which Stanley (of course) assiduously organised. But, though spared a court, they experienced hostility in other ways. There was the spectacle of an enormous placard being carried about in Oxford displaying the bishops' letter with the offenders' names picked out in large type.[60] Temple, as a Queen's Chaplain, was not subject to ecclesiastical or academical discipline, but his staff at Rugby held anxious discussions and the trustees debated whether to dismiss him. A young Cambridge man refused a post at the school when the book appeared. Temple received letters from panic-stricken parents, and the *Christian Observer* encouraged them to get rid of the infidel headmaster; the school would be emptied unless he withdrew his work.[61] The boys themselves supported Temple to the hilt, but that worried him more than anything else: "I

---

[59] H.B. Wilson, *Three Sermons composed for the opening of a new organ at St. Chrysostom's Church, Everton*, pp. ix, 8, 18. Bishop Graham and Bishop Hamilton were criticised in *WR*, October, 1861, p. 550 and *National Review*, January, 1862, p. 113.
[60] Abbott, I, p. 324.
[61] *Christian Observer*, September, 1860, p. 637.

made a blunder in one respect, and in one alone. I ought not to have done anything which would encourage those boys to plunge into critical speculations before their time". So he warned the VIth Form not to read the book and asked the masters to judge him by his sermons in chapel.[62] These Temple published in due course, though without any implication that they were meant to counteract the essays. Temple showed obvious signs of strain as the controversy wore on. He had an exchange with the aged Bishop Phillpotts who implied (he said) that the essay on the Education of the World was at variance with the fundamental doctrines of the Church of England. The letters in *The Times* did Temple no good: Phillpotts wrote a "clever" reply (Newman) maintaining that the book as a whole was an attack upon Christian beliefs and a contributor who did not disassociate himself could not escape responsibility for the rest.[63]

Pattison's preferment was a donative one and not subject to episcopal institution, but he did not escape odium. He had a troubled correspondence with Edward Hawkins, Provost of Oriel, who set out to defend him and then realised that Pattison was not as innocent as he had first supposed. Hawkins preached against Colenso's use of Pattison's remarks and then sent the writer a copy of the sermon, since he "supposed that he [Colenso] had misapplied them to a purpose which you did not intend". But, to make sure, and since Pattison was under a cloud at Oxford because of his connections with the others, Hawkins asked him to publish something "distinctly recognising the leading Christian doctrines". The mystery deepened: Pattison thought that Hawkins wished to revive the controversy; Hawkins began to ask awkward questions, for instance, what religious phraseology was meant by Pattison's reference to "godless orthodoxy"?[64] The Provost was not an obscurantist, but he showed how the older leaders of thought in Oxford, once held to be liberal, were disturbed by rashness. Pusey, a good deal less inhibited, preached against Pattison in the university pulpit and warned undergraduates away from him.

Hard personal things were said about all the essayists, including Powell who had been removed from "the evil to come", as Kennard put it. This aspect entered their daily life. Williams found in Salisbury, after a protracted removal from Lampeter ending in August, 1862, that people

---

[62] Temple Memoirs, I, p. 220.
[63] *The Times*, 4 March, 1861, p. 10. J.H. Newman, *Letters and Diaries*, XIX, pp. 474-5.
[64] MSS Pattison 112, ff. 69, 72, 74.

would turn round in the streets to stare at him; Salisbury, where "the bishop's frown was looked upon as a social anathema".[65]

Most of all, Jowett found his prediction of the hard lot of the courageous critic coming true for himself. Sitting in church at Freshwater, when staying with the Tennysons, he was called "Judas Iscariot" from the pulpit by the local clergyman. He spoke ironically, of Dr Vaughan's fulminations, that he imagined being burned in Doncaster churchyard.[66]

In Oxford itself there were other vexations. At the beginning the authorities demurred about doing battle with Jowett again; they smarted under the criticisms of the *Saturday Review* which had spoken of the "lynch law" at Oxford. Jeune, the Vice-Chancellor, even held that faith would gain from open discussion, when Evangelical petitioners pressed for action.[67] But Harrison's exultant article referred to decay under the walls of Oxford, and the university would be a laughing stock unless some action was taken. Jowett could not be proceeded against on ecclesiastical grounds, but enquiries were made by Pusey and others as to whether he could be prosecuted in the Vice-Chancellor's court as a professor resident in the university. His essay was held to be at variance with the doctrine of the Church of England concerning inspiration and also contradicted the Eighth Article. The Savilian Professor had gone to a higher tribunal, Jowett still remained. The advice of Dr Phillimore, Queen's Counsel and an expert in such matters, was sought, and a suit was opened in February, 1863. *The Times* was aghast that such a "rusty engine of intolerance" could be put into motion, and no one was surprised that it failed on technical grounds after some months of uncertain existence. But Pusey stood by it as a rebuke to Jowett. While there was hope of success he was prepared to work with men who had once been his antagonists. Thus Heurtley and Ogilvie, who in former times had both pronounced that Pusey's own doctrines were contrary to the Articles, became his partners[68] (He also joined with them in an address to the Archbishop of Canterbury about the essays as a whole).

Pusey kept Keble closely informed about the case — Keble who himself admitted to the Bishop of Cape Town to joining a "sort of coalition" with Low Churchmen against current heresy.[69] But the two

[65] Williams, II, p. 64.
[66] Abbott, I, pp. 323, 347, 350.
[67] W.R. Ward, *Victorian Oxford*, p. 239. Cf. *G*, 13 March, 1861, p. 247.
[68] Liddon, IV, pp. 23-31.
[69] H.L. Farrer, *Life of Robert Gray, Bishop of Cape Town*, II, p. 428.

men shrank from being leaders in the campaign and found that others were also reluctant. Pusey wrote to Keble, "you and I had better not... else it will be ascribed to party. But are there no religious men who will, for the sake of the Faith, institute proceedings?"[70] Pusey was not too adept in these matters — or too sensitive — and it took from February, 1862, until the following November to find names. He bewailed the prevarications, particularly since Bishop Colenso's books were now aggravating the situation. Pusey told Stanley that he did not know what single truth he and Jowett held in common, "except that somehow Jesus came from God, which the Mohammedans believe too".[71] Such a teacher must be condemned, as he said to Keble: "I used to maintain, and do maintain, that the Church must bear with much, for fear of worse evils. But she must not bear with this naked denial of our Lord, the Atoner, and of God the Holy Ghost Who spake by the prophets".[72]

Keble offered £100 towards the expenses of the case and wrote encouraging letters to the Hebrew Professor. More, he defended the action in *The Guardian*. The prosecution, said Keble, was designed to protect the university and the Church, and the souls committed to them both, from "desolating opinions". He showed a flash of the old spirit of 1833. "Why are these over-liberal opinions... so rife in that once faithful body? One reason unquestionably is that there in an especial manner the hand of authority has been busy in discouraging, and as far as might be silencing and banishing, those who had been first to sound the alarm". Keble meant, as Pusey did, that the anti-Newman reaction had let in rationalism, and the outcome now faced them all: "whether the University of Oxford now is, and means to be hereafter, a believer in the Bible or no?" Oxford would be injured and the whole world scandalised if false teaching went unpunished.[73]

It was still the old story, what Keble called "the old academical feeling", of the parties in the university vying with one another for the allegiance of undergraduates. "All might have been saved if Newman had remained with us", wrote Liddon,[74] but he and Pusey did their best. Jowett complained of "confessions and Sunday evenings" at Pusey's rooms and of undergraduates becoming fanatics. In 1863 Pusey instituted "levees" to discuss biblical criticism: those who felt difficulties

---

[70] Pusey MSS, letter to Keble, 12 October, 1862.
[71] Prothero, II, p. 163.
[72] Pusey MSS, letter to Keble, 6 November, 1862.
[73] Liddon, IV, pp. 25-6.
[74] Prothero, II, p. 169.

sent in notice of them and they were answered at the next meeting. With this party Pusey went through Colenso's first volume on the Pentateuch, and "never met with anything more stupid, or narrow, or blundering".[75]

Jowett was infuriated at these tactics. An undergraduate society now met at Balliol calling itself "the Brotherhood of the Holy Trinity", and a very fat member occupied rooms below him, performing noisy devotions and Gregorian chants at midnight. His pupils (he told Miss Nightingale) were "whipped off to the Confessional, and then no amount of personal kindness weighs a feather against their fanaticism. They lose all sense of loyalty or regard... This is one of the unpleasantnesses of Oxford at the moment. I think that the best way is to ignore it and treat them as if I did not know that they go and repeat what I say to Pusey and Liddon".[76] Beneath the quaint horror of "the Confessional" (for Jowett could not imagine that sin meant *so* much), there was an insecurity and fear that liberalism and all its ideals might cease to attract the young. But Pusey held that Jowett employed similar tactics and had no reason to complain. "He is professedly living to propagate his infidelity", he wrote sorrowfully to Keble. "He works indefatigably for the young men, even to late at night, with this end. He lays himself out for the clever men, and the tutors of Oxford pass through his hands, the clever men, on this pure competitive system, becoming the Fellows of other colleges. Alas, if all this energy had been for God's truth!"[77] Jowett admitted as much to Florence Nightingale.

The struggle over Jowett had become, said Pusey, a life and death struggle over the future of the university as a place of religious learning and of the Church of England as an instrument of God for the salvation of souls. He spoke of this in relation to a second matter in which Jowett suffered vexation. Since 1858 the question of augmenting the purely nominal salary of the Greek Professor had hung fire. If the salary were increased, would that suggest that the university approved of his views? The salary and the essays became closely bound together, particularly when the suit in the Vice-Chancellor's court finally failed in the autumn of 1863. On 8 March, 1864, exactly a month after the Privy Council's judgment on *Essays and Reviews*, the university Convocation — swelled by country clergymen summoned by Denison — rejected the statute proposing the increase by 467 votes to 395. The meaning was plain: if one avenue was closed, the essayists' opponents would try some other

[75] *Ibid.*, II, p. 160.
[76] Jowett MSS, f. 146, letter to Florence Nightingale, 23 July, 1865.
[77] Pusey MSS, letter to Keble, 24 July, 1862.

way to injure them. But Jowett's prominence meant that his treatment was no longer a domestic concern. When the statute was defeated a second time, the two primates threatened to come to Oxford in person and vote for the increase; they feared that the intransigent group would harm the Church.

Pusey himself began to draw away from the bigots, the "Conservative party", as he called them : "they seem to me to sacrifice everything to their wretched Conservatism".[78] In fact, he was accused by the extremists of temporizing, just as his book on Daniel, because it was not a total refutation of the essayists, was called a Germanizing work. Denison warned him in a letter in *The Guardian* — "You throw yourself, with some confiding friends, into the arms of the revolutionists" — and, in public, the Archdeacon said that churchmen's faith and confidence had never been so shaken as when they saw Pusey resorting to expediency.[79]

Pusey, of course, had not changed: the real test of the university's faithfulness had been the prosecution against Jowett, the intrigue over the salary merely demeaned the Church. Help only came eventually when the Christ Church chapter, on "grounds of general expediency", raised the extra endowment from their own revenues, and Jowett finally got his larger pay in February, 1865. Pusey received no thanks; he had to defend his action in *The Times*, which had been very critical of the campaign in Oxford. Truth would stand, said Pusey, "but it is true also that individuals, to their own great loss, are led away by their teachers from it". But readers were unconvinced that "prosecution is not persecution", and the correspondence columns buzzed for weeks.[80] Jowett himself said that the conservatives were quite correct, "as if I had got the money I intended to have done all the mischief that I could with it". That was in a letter to Miss Nightingale; when the increase arrived he told Mrs Tennyson that the mischief could now begin.[81]

The Dean of Arches took eighteen months to consider his judgment, but the delay only seemed to bolster the sales of *Essays and Reviews*. The publishers issued a cheap edition and then, in the 12th and 13th editions, inserted quotation marks showing the passages on which the indictments were based. The first American printing, handled by a Boston Unitarian firm, was exhausted by October, 1860, and a second soon appeared. A Tauchnitz edition was on sale by 1862. The essays were exported to

---

[78] Liddon, IV, pp. 33-6.
[79] *A Letter from George Anthony Denison to Edward Bouverie Pusey*, p. 4.
[80] Liddon, IV, pp. 28-9.
[81] Jowett MSS, f. 73, letter to Florence Nightingale, March, 1864. Abbott, I, p. 326.

France and Germany, a French translation was prepared, and a Parsee was despatched from Bombay to render them in his own language. Circulating libraries loaned out the volume and its answers at 2d per day; it was displayed on railway bookstalls and hawked by newsboys along with *Punch* and *The Times*.

Preachers found that they could be sure of good congregations if they took Jowett and company as their subject. Stanley wrote sarcastically, "meetings of clergy were held to condemn the book which most of them had never read. Preachers, rising from a Saturday's perusal of the *Quarterly*, denounced the writers the next morning from the pulpit as Atheists".[82] E. M. Goulburn, Temple's conservative predecessor at Rugby and a contributor to one of the opposing volumes, was billed to preach at St. John's, Paddington, and found the church packed to overflowing.[83]

In reaching his verdict the octogenarian Dean read through *Essays and Reviews* (literally) twenty times. If that was not enough, he also had the lengthy arguments of the defendants' counsel to consider. Williams' case took nine days, Wilson's four, to plead, and the defence, conducted by James Fitzjames Stephen and James Parker Deane, contained much historical material. Stephen went into the case *con amore*. "If I stay 51 years at the Bar, I shall never have another which will interest me so much", he said.[84] In essence, his argument maintained that the English clergy were not compelled to hold to the absolute infallibility of the bible, and the matter should not have been sent to the court at all unless there was specific and concrete evidence of heresy. This did not portend an easy case for Phillimore, who appeared for Bishop Hamilton, while the Dean of Arches affirmed ("*ad nauseam*", as he put it) that the court's function was very limited: it was only to pronounce whether the statements complained of were inconsistent with or contradicted the prayer book and Articles, not whether they were true or false, or edifying or dangerous. "A book like *Essays and Reviews* may contain much deserving of censure, and yet the law of the Church may not reach it". The statement was a rebuke to those who expected a modern Star Chamber. That was why Denison declaimed against the judgment, "a single judge trembling under the responsibilities of his position; shrinking from dealing with the case in the only way which can satisfy the

---

[82] *Edinburgh Review*, April, 1861, p. 466.
[83] Williams, II, p. 36.
[84] *Ibid.*, II, p. 51 n. 2.

right".[85] But Lushington did not tremble: he merely pointed out that the Church of England lacked the means (detailed Confessions of Faith and canons) by which trials of belief could be conducted.[86]

On this basis, the Dean of Arches rejected either wholly or partly nine of the 22 charges against Williams and Wilson (25 June, 1862), and the reformed charges were reduced to three, being brought in on 12 September, 1862. On the charge that Williams had denied the predictive element in prophecy, the judge held that this opinion, though contrary to that commonly received in the Church, was not contrary to the formularies. But he found the statement that the "Bible is an expression of devout reason", and the "written voice of the congregation", was a violation of Articles VI and VII. Williams had contravened Article XXI in saying that "propitiation is the recovery of that peace, which cannot be while sin divides us from the Searcher of hearts", and Article XI with his statement on justification. Lushington complained of Williams' ambiguity: "if the author had studied to express his statements so, he could not have been more succesful". On the charge of universalism alleged against Wilson, the decision was that, "Mr Wilson does not say that men will be saved by the law they profess. He neither avers nor denies that they will be saved by the name of Jesus Christ". It was held, therefore, that he did not contradict Articles IX and XVIII, though the tendency of what he said might seem to be inconsistent with them. So also an implied denial of the genuineness of the second epistle of St. Peter was held not to be contrary to Article VI, the purport of which was canonicity, not authorship. The charges allowed against Wilson were that he denied that the bible was written by the special interposition of the Almighty Power (Articles VI and XX); that he denied any distinction between covenanted and uncovenanted mercies (Article XVIII); and that in the concluding two paragraphs of his essay he held that a hope must be entertained of an intermediate state after death, and that finally all would escape everlasting damnation, which was inconsistent with the doctrine of creeds and formularies. The sentence of the Court (15 December, 1862) in each case was suspension *ab officio et beneficio* for one year only, costs being given against the defendants.[87]

The prosecution had succeeded, on a limited basis, as a gesture.

---

[85] *Faith and Peace*, p. xii.

[86] *G*, 15 January, 1862, pp. 61-7, 22 January, 1862, pp. 85-90. Cf. Fitzjames Stephen, *Defence of the Rev. Rowland Williams*.

[87] *G*, 25 June, 1862, pp. 602-3, 606-7, 2 July, 1862, pp. 638-9, 17 December, 1862, pp. 1193-4.

Hamilton had been vindicated in taking the step, and in due course he would think about provision of services at Broadchalke during Williams' suspension. The weight of the judgment was particularly felt in the scale of the costs. Williams and Wilson would have been beggared had not a fund existed for their defence.

What did the trial actually achieve? Pusey thought that the decision had shown up Williams. "It ought to be very damaging to Dr Williams, in English opinion, to get off on the ground of not speaking plainly, especially when the courage of the *Essays and Reviews* has been so lauded".[88] In a letter to Florence Nightingale, Jowett was gloomy about the whole proceeding. Religion suffered when brought into court; his friends in the previous six months had not remonstrated with him about not speaking the truth but had murmured about prudence, the need to be aware of public opinion, and so forth. Consequently, the idea of truth had become "childish, ridiculous, impertinent". He hated the legal atmosphere. "Law applies definite words to definite facts; here are indefinite and even contradictory words applied to the everlasting shades of opinion. Lawyers don't seem to me aware that they require to be theologians even to be able to try words by their legal standard"[89].

But liberals were right to regard the judgment as qualified in some important respects. "It is to the Broad Church what the judgment in the Gorham case was to the Evangelicals", said Jowett in the same letter. Williams went much further, "my Master has done by me a work which will abide", and he taunted orthodox clergymen in the *Daily News* that their position had worsened; literary misrepresentation of the bible was now checked. "Glory be to the Father..."[90] (Jowett sniffed, "Dr Williams is a good and self-denying man, but he has the misfortune to be a Welshman"[91]). The bible emerged from Lushington's remarks less of a whole, less self-sufficient, more composite, more like any other piece of literature. Wilson seized on the Dean's admission that it was "open to the clergy to maintain that *any* book in the Bible is the work of another author than him whose name it bears". Again, the statements of scripture as to historical facts might be understood in a wholly figurative sense, without violating the "declaration of belief in the truths of Scripture".[92] Stanley, wondering, spoke of

---

[88] Pusey MSS, letter to Keble, 28 June, 1862.
[89] Jowett MSS, ff. 35-9, letter to Florence Nightingale, July, 1862.
[90] Williams, II, p. 69. Cf. *Daily News*, 28 June, 1862.
[91] Jowett MSS, ff. 35-9, letter to Florence Nightingale, July, 1862. Cf. Abbott, I, p. 353
[92] *WR*, October, 1862, p. 526.

Lushington's fortieth Article of Religion.[93] The standard work on the laws relating to Church and Clergy was quickly issued in a new edition in 1863 to show that "rational and dispassionate" discussion of topics previously debarred from the clergy was now permitted.[94]

Bishop Hamilton was not triumphant long. Fitzjames Stephen had warned the lower court that if the case went against them he would appeal to the Privy Coucil. The Judicial Committee had been established to deal with ecclesiastical matters; notoriously, it had given Gorham protection against his bishop in 1850. If the Dean of Arches had dismissed so many of the charges, why did he press ahead with the rest? There was room for reversing the decision. Accordingly, in June, 1863, the Privy Council was asked to intervene. The offensive now passed to the essayists.

The Committee considered the case in the summer. Seven members, presided over by Lord Chancellor Westbury, met to hear the appellants and their counsel. Williams created a most favourable impression, and Wilson's speech, later published, took three days to deliver. Wilson went back to the Church Fathers to show how liberal they were, and he made good use of Whately's *View of the Scripture Revelation Concerning a Future State*.[95] The shafts went home. Before the hearing ended the Committee suggested, without objection from the other side, the withdrawal of the charge about covenanted and uncovenanted mercies against Wilson and the charge based on Williams' interpretation of propitiation.

Hamilton's supporters drew obvious conclusions. Pusey wrote urgently to Tait, "I am afraid of lawyers... day by day, since I heard the rumour of the impending judgment, the thought of it has haunted me. It is the greatest crisis the Church of England has ever gone through... many are praying in regard to the issue, and I yet hope that God will hear us, and that He will incline the hearts of the judges not to allow His truth to be denied".[96] It was obvious that Pusey hoped to influence Tait, a member of the Committee, and also that he mistrusted him. Tait wrote anxiously in his diary the night before the judgment, "a most important matter for the Church", and was moved to prayer, "O Lord, grant that all may be overruled for good, that no stumbling blocks be thrown in the

[93] *Edinburgh Review*, July, 1864, p. 278.

[94] H.W. Cripps, *A Practical Treatise on the Laws relating to the Church and the Clergy*, p. 838.

[95] *G*, 24 June, 1863, pp. 594-5, 1 July, 1863, pp. 618-20. Cf. H.B. Wilson, *A Speech delivered before the Judicial Committee of Her Majesty's most honourable Privy Council*.

[96] Davidson, I, p. 314.

way of earnest Christians, and that thy blessing may watch over and guard thy Church".[97] Tait's involvement was, indeed, even deeper than Pusey realised.

The court's decision was announced on 8 February, 1864, and Stanley, who had a gift for such matters, best described it — and recalled how similar it was to the Gorham hearing in the public excitement, the clamour of the crowded court. "I saw at once, from the absence of the two Archbishops and the fallen countenance of Phillimore, that we were safe". Westbury's legendary mode of delivery gave the judgment the maximum effect, "till at the close not one [of the charges] was left, and the appellants remained in possession of the field".[98]

The Lord Chancellor began cautiously, on the Committee's limited powers and its reference only to a "few short extracts" from the book. If the essays were mischievous or baneful, they would retain that character whatever the court decided. But the court did not feel that the extracts about biblical inspiration were contradicted by or inconsistent with the formularies. The Eleventh Article was wholly silent as to the merits of Christ being transferred to men. "We cannot say, therefore, that it is penal of a clergyman to speak of merit by transfer as a fiction, however unseemly that word may be". Williams was allowed his version of the modern way to understand justification by faith, since the Committee believed that he did not advocate *only* what the charge alleged. On the charge that Wilson had denied eternal punishment, it was held that he had not denied a judgment at the end of the world, and the effect of allowing the charge would be to restore the 42nd Article withdrawn in 1562. The question of the eternity of future punishment was "mysterious"; "we do not find in the Formularies... any such distinct declaration of our Church upon the subject as to require us to condemn as penal the expression of a hope by a clergyman that even the ultimate pardon of the wicked, who are condemned in the day of judgment, may be consistent with the will of Almighty God". Westbury summarized the Committee's findings with the words, "on matters on which the Church has prescribed no rule, there is so far freedom of opinion that they may be discussed without penal consequences". The principle was established that "the caution of the framers of our Articles forbids our treating their

---

[97] Tait MSS, Diaries Miscellanea, 1828-79, small note book, ff. 88-9.
[98] *Edinburgh Review*, July, 1864, pp. 271-2. Prothero, II, pp. 43, 158. On Gorham judgment cf. F. Bunsen, *A Memoir of Baron Bunsen*, II, p. 246.

language as implying more than is expressed". The appeals were allowed with costs.[99]

Westbury went down in history as the judge who had "dismissed hell with costs".[100] There was no doubt of the importance of the decision, not least for the appellants themselves. The Church of England was never the same after February, 1864, and *Essays and Reviews* passed into the annals of the national life.

In this manner, the futility of the court proceedings against the essayists was demonstrated. The liberal side had won a resounding victory. Stanley had not actually expected "anything so clean and clear... the Bible may be really read without those terrible nightmares. Thank God!"[101] *The Times*, like Stanley, felt that the teaching of the essayists had been, in a sense, officially recognised. "The broad fact remains that a book which aroused the greatest public dissatisfaction and which was almost judicially condemned by the Bench of Bishops has been found practically unassailable in point of law... Right or wrong; the question is definitively settled, the members of the Church are released from all legal obligation to maintain a higher authority for the Scriptures than that claimed for them in *Essays and Reviews*".[102]

For the orthodox, however, the judgment was grievous. Pusey half expected it but that did not lessen the feeling of shock; he spoke of a "hidden blasphemy", "a soul-destroying decision".[103] *The Record* cried scandal, others said that a new national apostasy had been committed.[104] Some great principle of faith was lost.

The judgment is most interesting for its unspoken implications. One aspect, in particular, is worth examining. The Law Lords had supported the essayists. Did this mean that the state put as little value on doctrine as the radicals did? The answer was obviously not, since Williams and Wilson were acquitted for not breaking the law, not because they were not heretical. But the problem was the bishops' presence on the Committee. Many were perplexed at this and understood it to mean that

---

[99] G.C. Brodrick and W.H. Fremantle, *Collection of the Judgments of the Judicial Committee of the Privy Council in Ecclesiastical Cases relating to Doctrine and Discipline*, pp. 247-90. Cf. *G*, 10 February, 1864, p. 141. P. Hinchliff, *The One-sided Reciprocity*, pp. 16-34.

[100] F.W. Knickerbocker, *Free Minds, John Morley and his Friends*, p. 99. T.A. Nash, *The Life of Richard, Lord Westbury*, pp. 73-9.

[101] Prothero, II, p. 44.

[102] *The Times*, 10 February, 1864, p. 9.

[103] Liddon, IV, pp. 51-2.

[104] *The Record*, 25 April, 1864.

the Church was Erastian, ordering its beliefs at the whim of the secular power. Why had they not been able to protect the Church? The archbishops had been present at all the deliberations, while Tait throughout sided with the lay lords (and had the largest hand in constructing the judgment), who thus were "able to shield themselves behind the authority of an ecclesiastical judge, a ruler in the Church". So bewailed *The Record* on the "defection of the Bishop of London".[105]

The confusion continued for some months and was only partially removed by two pastoral letters which the primates issued explaining that a condemnation could not be enforced because of the obscurity in the defendants' language. But they denied that the Church was party to the final decision. "I do not acquiesce in the terms of the judgment, and therefore I am not responsible for the words [of acquittal]", declared Archbishop Longley in Convocation. That was three months after the judgment, and he had to answer Tait's charge why he had not made it known sooner.[106]

The Archbishop of York adopted a more roundabout method. Stanley said that the essayists' position had now been vindicated and "fixed for ever", but Thomson held that "the so-called Judgment" was only a statement for the guidance of the public of the grounds upon which the Advice to the Crown would be based.[107] There was something in this; the Advice to the Crown would form the real verdict on *Essays and Reviews*, and it might be far more negative and confined than Westbury's statement in open court.

Tait made no apologia for himself at the time; he believed that the bishops served a useful purpose on the Committee, and he did not see any evil results flowing from the decision. But he did not want the primates to absolve themselves of involvement too easily. He suggested that Thomson's argument was academic; most people understood Westbury's statement, widely publicised as it was, to constitute a judgment, and when appeal was made to the "Gorham judgment" it was always to the elaborate statement made by the court and not some private document sent to the queen. He agreed, however, that no opportunity was given to the spiritual peers to state their opinion in court, and thus they were held responsible for the statement as a

---

[105] Davidson, I, p. 319.
[106] *Chronicle of Convocation*, 1864, p. 1666.
[107] W. Thomson, *A Pastoral Letter to the Clergy and Laity of the Province of York*, pp. 6-8.

whole.[108] Stanley was wrong, therefore: the primates had not come to the essayists' aid, and Tait realised their predicament, while he had no sympathy for their protestations.

Tempers ran high in the weeks after the judgment. Could something be rescued from the wreckage? There were three possibilities, and these were canvassed one after another in High and Low Church camps. Pusey, after the first shock was over, thought that the only course was to minimise the weight of the judgment. A distinction must be drawn (he said) between legal and ecclesiastical aspects, for on any purely doctrinal consideration Williams and Wilson would have been found wanting. But the mere lawyers on the Committee would not have understood this. So he assiduously enquired of those among his circle who were lawyers *and* churchmen. Pusey realised that a divine who appeared before a legal tribunal as a defendant would be given the benefit of the doubt ("*The radical evil of Law Judges is their bias to acquit the accused*", he told Liddon — a statement which was not as extreme as it first appeared). But this need not count for anything with the Church, and the defendant's guilt remained. The opinions of the Attorney General, Sir Roundell Palmer, and Sir Hugh Cairns, on this matter convinced him — though they did not coincide entirely with his views — and Pusey published these together with a preface on the legal force of the judgment, minimising its importance for the Church.[109]

Secondly, something could be built on the distinction between legal and moral aspects drawn by the Court of Appeal itself, both in its awareness that the spiritual peers sat on it, but also in Westbury's own statement which repeated what the Dean of Arches had said earlier. As Westbury emphasised, the question with which the Committee was concerned was the purely legal one of contravention of the formularies, and that on the basis of a few "meagre" extracts, and its members refused to pronounce on the character of the volume. It might even be held, and *The Times* so argued in its leading article on the judgment, that had the court considered the essays as a whole it might have come to a different conclusion. In that case, the writers only escaped penal consequences by the skin of their teeth. "The Court took especial care to guard itself against being supposed in the slightest degree to disturb or differ from the very general censure which has been passed on the book... The great care and emphasis with which the Court guards

[108] *Chronicle of Convocation*, 1864, pp. 1666-70. *A Pastoral Letter addressed to the Clergy and Laity of his Diocese by Charles Thomas, Archbishop of Canterbury*, p. 4.
[109] Liddon, IV, pp. 85, 87.

itself against misconstructions indicate more than a merely legal cautiousness, and it will probably be felt that they imply a strong feeling on the points reserved".[110]

The defendants themselves may well have felt that the Lord Chancellor's speech did not show the complete triumph of the secular over the ecclesiastical principle. Years later it still rankled with Wilson, and he bracketed Lushington and Westbury together when he wrote about the matter in the *Westminster Review*. He spoke of the strong atmosphere of personal disapproval in the Court of Arches, while in the Privy Council Committee "there was a tone of Apology hardly consistent with the dignity of the Judgment Seat".[111] For opposite reasons, therefore, Wilson misunderstood the nature of the court as much as Denison and his supporters did.

The third course demanded that churchmen should face their responsibilities. The judgment showed that the state would not aid a doctrinaire religious policy or penalise clergymen for coming to conclusions (of not too extreme a kind) which other men had long adopted. The Church of England, judged only as a national church, a comprehensive religious body, must allow more liberty to those who professed its beliefs than Roman Catholics or Dissenters, as sectarian bodies, could, and it was in the national interest that it should do so. But Westbury said nothing about the Church putting its own house in order. As Pusey saw, and as Wilberforce and the primate now affirmed, recalling their warnings before the prosecutions commenced, the judgment put the case against the essayists firmly back where it belonged in the first place. The question of synodical condemnation, left unresolved by the bench after recommendation from the lower house of Convocation, must be considered again. The situation seemed to demand it. *The Times*, in the same leading article, expected that episcopal or public action would follow, indeed, there was a need for it. And if, as some believed, the Privy Council had allowed the appeals thinking that there was a larger body of liberal opinion than, in fact, existed, the mistake must be corrected by the Church itself.

What happened next was, therefore, curious or, to radical eyes, iniquitous, but, surely, not unexpected. The Church took action, claiming to assert its freedom and independence. Convocation quickly condemned the book which had been allowed by the judges. It looked like

---

[110] *The Times*, 10 February, 1864, p. 9.
[111] *WR*, October, 1870, p. 468.

pique when it was carried through after the acquittal, and perhaps that consideration ought to have weighed more heavily, but it had been threatened from the beginning. However, the haste was certainly undignified. Denison's party had their plans laid, and the campaign began, appropriately in Oxford, two days after the judgment was announced. Within three days the motion for synodical condemnation was resumed in Convocation.

The purpose of the Oxford ministerial meeting was obvious — to provide the thorough party in Convocation with a national backing that would silence any supporters of the essayists. A violent assembly of clergymen was called in the Music School and passed a *Declaration* unequivocally maintaining the two tenets of biblical inspiration and eternal punishment on which everything now seemed to rest. If the lawyers could not discover these in the formularies, the average clergyman had no such doubts. Within three weeks every incumbent and curate in the kingdom had received a copy with a covering letter entreating him "for the love of God" to add his signature. The *Declaration* claimed that,

> "...the Church of England and Ireland, in common with the whole Catholic Church, maintains without reserve or qualification the inspiration and Divine authority of the whole canonical Scriptures, as not only containing, but being, the Word of God, and further teaches, in the words of our blessed Lord, that the 'punishment' of the 'cursed', equally with the life of the 'righteous', is 'everlasting' ".[112]

Of the 24,800 clergy in Britain and Ireland, nearly 11,000 signed the statement, and High Churchmen joined with Low. Shaftesbury, as a layman, could not sign, but he and his cousin, Pusey, after years of coldness and ecclesiastical distance, agreed to band together in opposing the judgment. Wilberforce also wrote to the Evangelical leader and saw the judgment healing the separation between the parties. As the *Declaration* gathered momentum, Pusey was elated: "all but the Rationalists were united". Stanley was scandalised to find his name in *The Record*, that newspaper "which notoriously violates the first principles of truth and charity every week", appealing for support.[113] The temper of the petitioners recalled the words of the Gibeonites to David, "Let seven men of his sons be delivered to us, and we will hang them up unto the LORD". Another biblical illustration was applied to the joint appearance of Pusey and Shaftesbury: "from that day Herod and

---

[112] Davidson, I, p. 317.
[113] Liddon, IV, pp. 51-2. Prothero, II, p. 162.

Pontius Pilate were friends". The unity was certainly striking, however much the real divisions were left unhealed. Simultaneously, 137,000 lay signatures were collected in five weeks, from both parties, for an address of thanks to the archbishops concerning their part in the decision.

Of course, liberal churchmen protested. Maurice made too much of the absence of the thousands of other clergy and implied that they tacitly supported the essayists. *The Times*, which saw the coalition as another sign of suppression in the Church, gave some prominence to his claim that the *Declaration* was a new test framed by an "irresponsible, self-elected Committee". "Young clergymen, poor curates, poor incumbents" interpreted signing "for the love of God" as a threat of moral force: it was a "phrase which means, as it meant for the Chartists, the threat of physical force". The *Declaration* meant nothing and could have been assented to by both Williams and Wilson (But Wilson told the *Daily News*, somewhat self-righteously, that he could not join anything which went against the Privy Council).[114]

Maurice, however, was too saintly: he could not see the demons at work in his fellows. Many who did not sign only demurred because they were unsure about its legality — did the *Declaration*, as Tait asserted, bind its signatories to statements not permitted by the formularies? — in which case the tables might be turned and the essayists' confounders confounded. But Maurice had at least one ally. Dean Hook of Chichester wrote to Wilberforce: "I am quite determined *not* to sign the *Declaration*. After the sin I committed in taking part against Hampden, without having first examined his works, prompted rather by zeal than by a spirit of justice, I vowed a vow that I would never take part in similar proceedings until I had thoroughly investigated the subject". The *Declaration* would make it appear that "*we* are the evaders of the law instead of those who by the Judgment are admitted to be, though not punishable, yet equivocators... As to an attempt to silence men by authority, you must remember that there is only one authority before which the mind of England lies prostrate, and that *The Times* is against us".[115]

Sure now of overwhelming support, Denison raised the matter of synodical condemnation in the Convocation of Canterbury on 11 February, and Wilberforce led the debate in the upper house when the gravamen was received there. Judges might define the limits of civil rights

[114] Liddon, IV, pp. 57-61.
[115] W.R.W. Stephens, *The Life and Letters of Walter Farquhar Hook*, p. 540.

(said Wilberforce), the clergy ought to hear the Church's judgment on disputed matters. To rest content with the simple power of conviction in courts of law took from the Church its power as a church to protest against false doctrines. "We do not wish to compel thought by authority; the question is simply whether clergymen, admitted to teach upon one profession, are allowed to continue to teach upon a different profession". The bench as a whole, however, was piqued by the tone of the gravamen. Thirlwall said that it was obviously meant to rebuke them severely for delaying judgment in 1861: it bore Denison's stamp, and thus showed an extraordinary degree of innocence, simplicity, and naivety, as if nothing had happened in the previous three years. While "that profound Doctor, the emperor Justinian" might have instructed his bishops and been heard gladly, Thirlwall objected to the lower house taking such an attitude.

The *Declaration* explained some of the episcopal faint-heartedness. Tait claimed that it meant that scripture was an infallible guide, in every single syllable, not only as to faith and doctrine but in physical science as well. Thirlwall held that the Judicial Committee affirmed that the Articles and formularies nowhere maintained every part of scripture to be written under the inspiration of God. The *Declaration* asserted the contrary view. The ancient Church had never seen fit to decide on the question of eternal punishment, yet this was now held to be a matter of life and death for the present Church of England. So a new restriction of the terms of communion and of entry to the ministry was being demanded. He was biting about "an argument from numbers" which coupled with Dr Pusey's authority the suffrage of the "youngest literate — or illiterate, they often mean nearly the same thing — " who had been last admitted to deacon's orders. Thirlwall had obviously changed his mind about synodical action: either he was weary of prosecution and its futility, or the importance of any such action paled in comparison with the theological issues posed by the book, "whether the denial of all supernatural agency was or was not consistent with any form of Christianity or with revealed religion". The bishops could not settle such a dispute with a mere judgment, and he rejoiced that in this case, as in the Gorham case, no authority existed in the Church which could.[116]

Wilberforce had difficulty in finding a seconder when he proposed that a committee should examine *Essays and Reviews* yet again. The primate had to ask plaintively for more speakers, and the long silences in the debate proved embarassing. Finally, he had to take action himself when

---

[116] *Chronicle of Convocation*, 1864, pp. 1528-75.

the voting resulted in a tie. Secured by Longley's casting vote, Wilberforce's motion was accepted. A committee was appointed and it went into session, taking *Essays and Reviews* with it. So for the third time this most hurried and unprepared of volumes was subjected to intense scrutiny. The procedure took some weeks and the report was not received until 21 June. But, when it came, the committee's judgment was hostile and Wilberforce delayed no longer. On that day the shades of long past Councils were summoned up. In tones not heard since Convocation proposed to discipline Hoadly so many years previously, Wilberforce proposed the long-threatened motion: that synod should solemnly condemn *Essays and Reviews* as containing teaching,

> "contrary to the doctrine received by the United Church of England and Ireland in common with the whole Catholic Church of Christ".

It was short and to the point, and there was no ambiguity. A long debate followed, but in the end Tait and Jackson, Bishop of Lincoln, were the only dissentients. Tait, who had spoken bitterly of his opponents, took the exceptional step of asking for his name to be recorded against the decision. Thirlwall was not present.[117]

The heresy had been judged at last; the Church had vindicated herself, and Pusey and others felt an immense sense of relief. The condemnation was prominently featured in the newspapers, and the religious press was generally approving. But the bishops wished for support and invited the lower house to join with them, so that the condemnation might be a solemn act by both houses. The result was one last battle over *Essays and Reviews* as Denison and his party rose to the occasion. This time they were matched by Stanley, now Dean of Westminster, and the debate raged for three days. One archdeacon member (Wingate) said that he had never witnessed such an exchange of personalities. This was partly due to Stanley's tactic of contrasting passages from *Aids to Faith* and the essays and asking which was which? If orthodoxy was revealed by the radicals, worrying admissions came from conservative writers. Stanley also attacked Denison himself whose earlier career as a preacher of extreme Eucharistic opinions had earned him episcopal rebukes: "if ever there was a case which called for synodical judgment it was his". Stanley was on better ground when reflecting the fears of moderate churchmen that, the precedent having been established, Convocation would set up an *Index* and censure all objectionable books, while those who received no

---

[117] *Ibid.*, pp. 1655-83.

censure would claim that their views were officially endorsed. Of course, he feared for the reputation of the Church of England. "This judgment will come before the world not only as futile, but as a superfetation of futility".

But the weight of feeling was on the other side. Denison's last words were a fair sample of the tone of the debate. "Of all cruel things, the cruelty of the men who wrote the book of *Essays and Reviews* is the greatest I have ever known, They have spent all their energy and intellect in the unsettling of God's truth, but have not given us, for they could not, anything in its place". His resolution, "that the Lower House thankfully accept and concur in the condemnation of the book by the Upper House", was carried by 39 votes to 19. The house refused to allow a request from Rowland Williams, put forward by his friend Harvey Goodwin, that he might be allowed to speak for himself.[118]

Convocation's action was significant as a gesture. It carried no penalty, for the Privy Council decision protected the writers in law, and it failed to halt the sales of the book. But it was a blow for *Ecclesia Anglicana* and the immutability of Christian doctrine. That held, even though Denison had to telegraph backwoods deans and archdeacons to swell his numbers on the fateful day, and met with (as he complained) "coldness, neglect, indifference, and frivolous or irrelevant objection". It was true, despite the fact that (as *The Guardian* unfeelingly pointed out) the upper house could only muster 10 of its 21 members when the condemnation was actually carried out.[119] It could even survive the criticism of Stanley and Milman who claimed that the primate had neutralised the action by not formally signing the condemnation in the presence of both houses and seeking sanction from the crown.[120] The Church had still spoken.

Convocation heard no more of *Essays and Reviews* until 1870. But in the world outside discussion did not end so abruptly. No one aware of the nature of the controversy imagined that the condemnation had finished the matter. The essayists would not accept a rebuke lightly, and they had powerful friends. Denison and others pressed for the gesture because they knew that it would be unpopular with some statesmen and theorists, as well as the "larger liberalism" at work in society, of which Newman spoke in the *Apologia*. *The Times* published letters from important persons in support of the essayists. Questions in parliament

[118] *Ibid.*, pp. 1704-78, 1783-1833.
[119] *G*, 29 June, 1864, p. 621.
[120] *Edinburgh Review*, July, 1864, pp. 268-81.

were asked about other aspects. On 15 July, 1864, Richard Monckton Milnes, Lord Houghton, Lord of Appeal in Ordinary, initiated a debate in the Lords on the wider implications of the synodical action. The result was a fascinating discussion of the relations of Church and State in which, on one side, Houghton, with the Lord Chancellor and Lord Wensleydale, expressed fears for the royal supremacy which lay behind the concept of a national Church, while, on the other, the spiritual peers led by the primate argued that to be "national" did not preclude the Church from passing a condemnation while yet upholding the supremacy.

The judiciary naturally felt aggrieved at the lack of regular procedure in the condemnation. It had not been handled in a formal manner; there was no hearing of witnesses, and the appeal of one of the condemned men to be heard was ignored. But the anti-clericalism and sarcasm of both Houghton and Westbury suggested that more than mere questions of law was involved. "My interest is for the freedom of opinion and the liberties of literature", declared Houghton — and also against a religious body which must not be allowed to discipline her majesty's subjects as it liked. Houghton had been helped in his researches by J. A. Froude, and he spoke passionately as the pupil of Thirlwall and friend of Bunsen. He proposed that the opinion of the Law Officers should be sought regarding this "perilous precedent", which he traced back to the spirit animating the Borgia popes and Charles V and the first condemnation enacted by Convocation in the sixteenth century — that of Cranmer's work on the sacrament of the altar, which was largely the Book of Common Prayer, and a suspect version of the bible which became the foundation of the present authorised version. The spiritual peers winced, but Houghton obviously saw the essays in noble company:

> "...in itself it is a matter of regret that a book of this nature should have been selected by Convocation as the commencement of an *Index Expurgatorius* of which English literature may expect to be the subject in future, unless prompt objection is taken to this process".

Houghton saw the lower house as the self-appointed censors of the Englishman's reading matter. In the past the bishops had restrained their political violence and religious zeal — why had they not protected the eminent writers from injury to their future careers? What if one of them rose to the highest position in the Church: "would not the fact of the censure hanging over them diminish their influence and prevent them from occupying that position in the state to which by their talents they are justified?" (Temple, Archbishop of Canterbury more than thirty years later, may have felt that the prophecy was vindicated by the length of time that it had taken him to reach the primacy). "It is no use arguing that these censures were not meant to inflict any injury on a man's character or prospects", said Houghton, referring to the "injustice" done to Williams and quoting a letter from him.

The Lord Chancellor's contempt (Wilberforce described it as "ribaldry") was obvious, and he did not waste time on precedents, lest that gave Convocation an importance that it did not deserve. He deeply regretted that it had been re-established and warned that any eccentricities of judgment would be checked. An attempt to give force to the sentence would incur the penalty of *praemunire*, involving the primate and his brethren appearing in sackcloth and ashes before the bar of the house to do penance for their misdemeanours (!). Westbury saw Wilberforce as the architect of the condemnation, and his offensive remarks obviously referred to his nickname of "Soapy Sam". The "*ridiculus mus*" of the synodical judgment was a "well-lubricated set of words — a sentence so oily and saponaceous that no one can grasp it. Like an eel, it slips through your fingers. It is simply nothing... it is literally no sentence at all". He repeated Houghton's warning. Though the words of the condemnation were innocent and innocuous, "they do not, probably, proceed from a spirit that is equally harmless".

The spiritual peers denied any intention to injure; "we did not condemn the men, while we condemned much that was in the book" (Wilberforce). The primate asserted the rights of Convocation and was supported by Tait and Wilberforce. Tait said that Convocation was not a debating society, and there was a growing disposition to revert to its action and authority. "Our position will be intolerable if we are told, on the one hand, that we are violating the law, and if, on the other, we cannot obtain an authoritative opinion as to what the law really is". Houghton's hot words on the desirability of the condemnation were matched by the primate:

> "I ask your lordships whether since the Reformation there has been any crisis in the English Church of so grave a character... and whether there is ever likely to occur in the next 200 or 300 years so serious a case or one calling so urgently upon Convocation, the Synod of the Church, to pronounce its opinion".

Essays and Reviews, he said, struck at the foundations of Christian belief. Longley quoted only one sentence to prove this, Powell's remark that "no testimony can reach the supernatural". "If such a doctrine is to prevail there is an end to the Gospel of our Lord Jesus Christ".[121]

Little else seems to have been discussed in the Lords that day. But with the close of the debate, and no action taken on Houghton's suggestion, the proceedings about *Essays and Reviews* were finally at an end. It was unlikely that the Law Officers could have given an opinion. As the primate said, they were unwilling to do this when asked before Convocation made its decision. But the temper of the Lords had been made plain; if they could not mete out dire penalties as Westbury described them, they resented the intrusion of any alien ecclesiastical principle, and they thought that the condemnation went against the character of the national life. Houghton had used Parliament as a theatre to air his views, and he would do so again if Convocation persisted in an *Index*.

Of the bishops, Tait took the warning to heart, as he indicated in the debate: the experience of the last fifteen to twenty years had shown, he said, that disputes between the civil and ecclesiastical powers, unless treated at the beginning with great care and caution, would lead to very serious evils. Gladstone was also sufficiently alarmed to seek an interview with Houghton the day after the debate.[122]

Essays and Reviews did not at once sink into the obscurity which writers thirty years later noted. A controversy in miniature, which prompted the fifteenth and final edition of 2,000 copies, making 24,000 in all, occurred in 1869 when Gladstone, as part of his policy to deal fairly with all the church parties, proposed to appoint Temple as Bishop of Exeter. The situation was embarrassing for Temple, but he allowed Wilson to authorise the reprinting. He wanted, wrote Wilson to Pattison, "neither to break up the book nor stop it suddenly... but to have a sufficient number reprinted... and then let it die out as it was dying before".[123] An approving glance came from Canterbury, for Tait was now the primate, but elsewhere the old protests appeared above the old signatures. Pusey exclaimed against the "horrible scandal of the editor of *Essays and Reviews* to be a Christian bishop". William Keane said that it was a sin against the Holy Ghost. J. W. Burgon warned Wilberforce that the bench would admit a dangerous man, and he thought that Temple himself was dishonourable to accept the appointment.[124] Pusey

[121] Hansard, 3rd series, CLXXVI, pp. 1563-5.
[122] *The Gladstone Diaries*, VI, p. 290.
[123] MSS Pattison 112, f. 92.
[124] D.C. Lathbury, ed., *Letters on Church and State of William Ewart Gladstone*, I, p.

was mistaken about Temple's editorial role, but it was true that he had given the book an aura of respectability, and his withdrawal from the team after the first edition would have dealt a mortal blow. Others wondered how a writer who had been condemned by Convocation six years earlier could now sit in the upper house. (Goldwin Smith later said of Temple's elevation to Canterbury, "as supreme guardian of the orthodox faith", that, "one cannot help wondering what was the mental process of transition"[125]).

The fears that an outcry would provoke a reaction in the nation were expressed again, this time by R. W. Church. He told Asa Gray, "we shall smart for all this... Mere disestablishment will be the least of the mischiefs". Pusey, despite his learning and piety, was blindly and intemperately "casting away all the lessons of a lifetime" in countenancing the violence of the zealots. But he saw that the violence was the "direct result of the extravagant measures which were taken years ago against the *Essays and Reviews*. People then got committed, in Convocation and elsewhere, to a false position against it, and now they are obliged, in consistency, to shriek at the very name of it. Temple, as you say, is certainly not in the same boat even with Stanley".[126]

The threatened clash did not materialise — perhaps because some believed that Temple had learned his lesson. Temple was eventually consecrated after the protests of the Exeter Chapter had been overcome, by Thirlwall, E. Harold Browne, now Bishop of Ely, and Philpott of Worcester, and went on to fulfil an outstanding episcopate in the West country. In February, 1870, he withdrew his essay: he could say things as Frederick Temple, he told Convocation, that he could not say as a bishop.[127] It was a judicious act, though Temple refused to make the withdrawal a condition of the bishopric, just as he had not allowed the appointment to Rugby to depend on his not writing for *Essays and Reviews*. His friends accepted his explanation: Temple stressed that no retraction or censure of the book was implied. If the circumstances reccurred, he would do the same. He believed that the volume had done its work and that a trend for the better was now in sight.

---

199. J.W. Burgon, *Protests of the Bishops against the Consecration to the See of Exeter*, and cf. his *Dr Temple's "Explanation" Examined*. W. Keane, *Protest against Dr Temple's Consecration to the Bishopric of Exeter. Letters Literary and Theological of Connop Thirlwall*, p. 312.

[125] Goldwin Smith, *Reminiscences*, p. 73.

[126] Church, p. 220.

[127] Temple Appreciation, p. 227. Temple Memoirs, I, pp. 301-4.

Photographs taken of Victorian churchmen in these years may well have shown grim expressions, furrowed brows, and the marks of battle. H. W. Baker's hymn, "Lord, Thy Word abideth", written in 1860, sought the comfort of scripture, "when the storms are o'er us, and dark clouds before us". But scripture itself was at stake, and the storm and cloud deepened. Wilberforce delivered his opening speech against the essayists, in November, 1860, from "within the encampment", and the figure was chosen deliberately. In perilous times the call was for consolidation, retrenchment: a beleagured Church must look to her defences. These were not the conditions for advance and adventure. Just as the literary controversy diverted energies from a constructive movement in theology, so the synodical and court proceedings concentrated on punishment instead of settlement. The contrast with the essayists' ideal of a liberalised church going hand in hand with a progressive nation was sometimes startling.

What were the issues in this reaction which was still effective even in the 'seventies? The first concerned the XXXIX Articles as an effective test of right belief, and this developed into a question about the ministry which professed the Articles. The second dealt with the independence of Convocation, the third with the rights of the Privy Council.

The effect of the legal suits against *Essays and Reviews* was plain : the Articles were ambiguous and unreliable as an instrument of discipline. They may have served the sixteenth century in setting an infallible bible against the pretensions of the Roman Church or the total private judgment demanded by the Anabaptists. But *Essays and Reviews* challenged the infallibility, and, since the lawyers had no other legal standards by which to test their orthodoxy, they had to acquit the writers. In a sense this was a gain; it meant that the Church of England was given room for manoeuvre in the difficult conditions of the nineteenth century — a less easy matter had her formularies included a confession like those of the Reformed churches. However, the immediate result may have seemed, paradoxically, to restrict the freedom of the ministry. An interior restraint proved to be more onerous than an external one. Previously some latitude was possible because conservatives could always threaten legal proceedings without actually instituting them, but after 1864 they wished to open windows into men's souls and inquire what they really believed. Hort commented bitterly on this, and thought that liberally-inclined men, for fear of the consequences, now professed conservative beliefs.[128]

---

[128] Hort, I, pp. 436-7. Cf. Temple Appreciation, pp. 214-5.

Despite what the radicals believed, the majority of clergymen probably welcomed this closer scrutiny. *Essays and Reviews* had focused attention on the loyalty of the ministry in a way that single offenders like Maurice, MacNaught and others, could not have done. The essayists asked for greater freedom as a natural right, but many demurred and wondered about the authority of the ministry if it was no longer safeguarded by the formularies, and then questioned the motives of the essayists for speaking as they did. In the eyes of the world the Privy Council judgment guaranteed rights which otherwise might have been suppressed. "Only the secular arm stopped a whole series of ecclesiastical prosecutions which would have made the ministry of the Church of England impossible except for fools, liars and bigots".[129] Of course, protection of liberal opinion was necessary for the health of society; but the average clergyman felt that his professional status was threatened by *Essays and Reviews* like no other book in the nineteenth century. A large part of the parish priest's work was the exposition of the catechism, and this rested on a traditional, not to say conservative, understanding of the bible. *Essays and Reviews* undermined the catechism, suggested a new attitude to faith itself, and a new sort of ministry of a far less paternalistic kind than before. Moreover, these bold ideas came from within the ministry itself. Had the essays been written by laymen, little would have been heard of them, but they seemed to be a *trahison des clercs* which must weaken the hold on one's congregation.

The synodical proceeding was thus the clergyman's judgment on his own kind. In a subjective and volatile body of men these questions were always a matter of intense self-concern; economics and social position were obviously involved, but the Tractarians had also taught them the supernatural origin of the ministry, and its other-wordly calling (which the essayists challenged), and not since 1850 had another opportunity for a bout of introspection occurred.

The spectre of an intellectual laity overtaking the clergy did not deter them. The ministry's duty was plain, as Liddon said: "when ...the Church is no longer protected against the most serious forms of error, individuals cannot but feel that their moral responsibility to God and man for appearing publicly to countenance such errors is almost indefinitely increased".[130] Far better, then, to hold back, in case opinion would supersede law. Liddon would certainly have pointed to the change

---

[129] W.R. Inge, *Outspoken Essays, The Victorian Age*, p. 204.
[130] Prothero, II, p. 169.

in the subscription act as a justification for the clergy drawing in upon themselves. It was no accident that the relaxation of the terms of subscription followed within a few months of the Privy Council decision — there was no point in demanding a strict assent to the formularies if it could not be upheld in the courts. The reprieve came from parliament and from Gladstone who took to heart Stanley's important pamphlet on the subject in 1863 and, with Jowett, Pattison and others acting as a lobby, persuaded the Commons to pass the clerical subscription bill in 1865. This substituted a more general assent to the formularies. The clergyman no longer had "to assent *ex animo* to the Book of Common Prayer, the Articles and the Ordinal, and all and every statement contained therein".

The reaction next turned from the authority of the ministry to that of the Church itself. The assertion of the rights of Convocation and opposition to the Judicial Committee both followed from the failure to convict the essayists and so uphold the ecclesiastical principle. The reaction, to begin with, was simple : it sought political alliance against the Liberal government which the radical writers supported; and that was to expected in the mood of the country following the near-success of the Church Rates bills by 1861. The Bishop of Oxford regarded the action against the essayists as the sign of a new militancy in the Church of England, which must include a fresh political conscious- ness. He coupled his speech at the High Wycombe Deanery with the beginning of an onslaught against the Church Rates measures, while his article in the *Quarterly* appeared in the "principal organ of the Tory Party" (Stanley).[131] Disraeli was present at that meeting and also spoke of the re-forging of the old alliance between the Church and the Conservative party. 1860 was the year of the rebirth of the Church party in the Commons, and he contrasted this with the attitude of the late primate (Sumner) who, anxiously perplexed by the anomalous position of the Church, counselled surrender whenever momentous questions involving her interests arose.[132] Pusey wished for political involvement: if a Conservative government wanted support, Lord Derby should be told that this depended on "his not nominating Neologians to high ecclesiastical preferment".[133] Gladstone disagreed with such a policy and contended that Wilberforce had developed a reputation with statesmen for "asking for everything and giving nothing

---

[131] R.G. Wilberforce, *op,. cit.*, III, p. 11. *Edinburgh Review*, April, 1861, p. 465.
[132] G.E. Buckle and W.F. Monypenny, *The Life of Benjamin Disraeli*, IV, p. 62.
[133] Liddon, IV, p. 93.

away".[134] But Wilberforce was more typical, and it would be years before High Churchmen of a more tender age and open mind, like R. W. Church, saw the greater wisdom in Gladstone's approach. The political hardening seemed an obvious tendency at the time.

But alliances with political parties were uncertain. Far better to employ the organ which the Church had for asserting its independence in a naughty world, Convocation. The deans, archdeacons and others in the lower house were not united, but most of them felt that the Church was at a disadvantage and they welcomed the opportunity to speak — and the *entrée* to the upper house afforded by Wilberforce. The whiff of independence was heady: the establishment of the Church congresses, where the laity could speak *their* mind, followed soon after.

Given this mood, it was perhaps inevitable that Convocation voted to censure *Essays and Reviews* and was prepared to do the same about Bishop Colenso's books. Denison lifted the rights of Convocation to the highest plane: "Synod has the promise of the HOLY GHOST".[135] He invoked a conciliar theology. Convocation was no *ad hoc* gathering of excited clergymen but a council of the Catholic Church proceeding solemnly to its appointed task of securing the faith, abjuring heresy and restoring peace within the communion. Outside the Church such views provoked either laughter or indignation, but the primate had come round to this opinion by 1864, and even Thirlwall, though he opposed the condemnation, allowed that a person might acquit as a judge that which, as a divine, he must condemn in synod.[136] If such a conversion was possible in high places the aggressive party could expect support in the lower house.

Convinced of its role, Convocation was prepared to face the penalties which its action might entail. Did the royal licence by which it met permit synodical censure of books and thus involve the crown in a purely religious matter, or did Convocation act on its own authority, only to confront the crown which protected the condemned writers? The Law Officers did not know the answer, but Sir Hugh Cairns and Mr John Rolt held that a censure was legal. When Convocation condemned Hoadly's book, no one alleged that they were disabled by statute from doing so. The primate, therefore, spoke unequivocally: "I hold that this synod has the power, and that it is its province and function, to condemn heretical

---

[134] D.C. Lathbury, *op. cit.*, II, p. 82.
[135] *Faith and Peace*, p. xi.
[136] *Chronicle of Convocation*, 1864, p. 1682.

books".[137] Wilberforce quoted the twelve judges who sat on the Whiston case in 1700. They said, "We conceive that heretical tenets and opinions may be condemned, if authorised by Royal licence". But he had to press the claim : "the authority of the Royal licence is the licence which calls Convocation together". That was the point which the Law Lords opposed: Houghton mangled his case by a slipshod reference to the Whiston judgment but he suggested correctly that the bishops in the past had been unsure about the licence, and they had restrained "incon-siderate action" in the lower house for fear of incurring *praemunire* under the statute *25 Henry VIII.*[138]

To pass from this attitude to attacking the presumption of the Judicial Committee was an easy matter. Dissatisfaction about the Committee had existed since the Gorham judgment, but the revival of Convocation heightened everything. The conciliarists asked, why should the Judicial Committee exist at all, and when it protected those who had been censured by the Church, was this not grievous? In 1851 Bishop Blomfield, in a search for some other authority, proposed that the bishops should be constituted as a final court of appeal, while Denison, Pusey and Keble had condemned the Gorham judgment as heretical. Now, in 1864, Wilberforce held that it was "evidently packed" for the purpose of reversing the decision of the Dean of Arches, "no one who ever sat on such questions having been put on it". He claimed, further, that Lord Brougham who first proposed the tribunal never imagined that it would bring such consequences; by "ecclesiastical cases" he meant wills, divorces and the like, never questions of doctrine.[139]

The *Christian Observer* proclaimed that some redress was urgently necessary. "We are suffering a grievous wrong... We are not advocating a return to Star Chambers or Courts of High Commission; but some tribunal we do seem to want in which justice may be done without enormous expense or unreasonable delay".[140] Pusey wrote a preface, "to those who love God and His Truth" to a pamphlet on the judgment, and was criticised by *The Times* for its "inflammatory" tone and for his "threatening" proposals to change the court. Both he and Keble expected great things from a "Court of Appeal Amendment Association", and Keble, in a rebuke to *The Times*, said that the judgment was "but a step in an inevitable process which will rid us of

[137] *Ibid.*, p. 1681.
[138] Hansard, 3rd series, CLXXVI, p. 1559.
[139] H.L. Farrer, *op. cit.*, II, p. 167. *Chronicle of Convocation*, April, 1864, p. 1463.
[140] *Christian Observer*, 1864, p. 240.

dogma altogether". An apathetic reaction would cause a scandal that would be felt by both friends and enemies of the Church. Keble also published a *Litany of our Lord's warnings*, to show the lay judges that Christ did not take eternal punishment as lightly as they did, while he preached at Cuddesdon on the spirit of God's most holy fear, on the same theme.[141]

Convocation itself was the setting for two full-dress debates on the wrongs of the Judicial Committee, the first initiated by Denison and his supporters within a few days of the judgment. Denison held that it had consequences full of evil for both Church and State, and he proposed that no archbishop, bishop or other spiritual person should sit on the Committee. James Fendall said that the judgment infringed the compact between Church and State. "It is of the utmost importance to the Church that steps should be taken to maintain the constitutional rights of the spirituality in deciding causes where the law Divine comes into questions" — Fendall wanted a new court. With high words about a "formidable grievance", Dr Jebb believed that the principle involved in the judgment, if accepted and acted on by the ecclesiastical courts, would undo all doctrine and discipline whatsoever. Other speakers protested against the idea that the Articles — drawn up with reference to errors and questions of a day long past — should be taken as the final authority, to the exclusion of the liturgy and other authorities.

The house appointed a committee, and this reported in June, 1864, that the Judicial Committee was "absolutely a lay court without any admixture of the spirituality", and therefore not competent to act as the highest ecclesiastical court. It contradicted the primitive church by delegating jurisdiction in ecclesiastical cases to others as well as to the spirituality, and it compromised the ancient rights and liberties of the Church of England as guaranteed by *Magna Carta* and confirmed by numerous subsequent statutes. There should be new canons and Articles if the formularies were not clear and explicit about the great doctrines. The committee considered whether the final hearing of ecclesiastical appeals should be delegated to the upper house of Convocation, sitting as a court, or to the primate, sitting as patriarch, with bishops and ecclesiastical judges as assessors. But it finally recommended only improvement of the present tribunal. The debate was resumed in both houses in 1865, and the record of the speeches covers 126 pages: it ended with the upper house laying the question on the table, and the lower

---

[141] Liddon, IV, pp. 90-1.

house, with Denison's protest being lost by only one vote, accepting that the "court is open to grave objection, and that its working is unsatisfactory".[142]

Nothing came of this agitation, which occupied churchmen between 1864 and 1866. For various reasons the Judicial Committee proved stronger than its assailants. Some churchmen realised that an altered Committee might be worse than the present one. Jowett wrote to Miss Nightingale: "...the English people don't like clerical tribunals, and the Evangelicals are beginning to be afraid of being delivered into the hands of the High Church".[143] Pusey admitted to Keble, "the Low Church would leave us on any definite plan which would put more power into the hands of the Bishops".[144] For his part, Tait made the most of the fact that the Church of England possessed an advantage, denied to the Nonconformists, of having its own representatives on the Committee. Ultimately, the Committee could never go against the good of the Church, nor could it be captured by one party in the Church.[145]

Gladstone also thought that the Committee was not as bad as the Denisonians claimed, and particularly after the revival of Convocation gave the Church a means of expressing its opinion. He told Döllinger, "no longer is the Church in the helpless condition of the Church under the Judicial Committee".[146] Convocation prevented discontent from going to extremes, and it was significant that, in contrast to the Gorham case, no one fled to Rome in 1864 because of the Privy Council's decision about *Essays and Reviews*. He therefore refused Keble's plea that Church-minded politicians should try to alter the Committee. "I even now think that a Court both wise and honest might hereafter, notwithstanding this Judgment, deal wisely as well as honestly with the questions it involves".[147] The Court, indeed, expected Convocation to do its part — being concerned only with legal interpretation it showed the need for additional action: "and it is plain that they [the judges] are disqualified by their own confession from looking to the preservation of the Christian faith — and consequently they leave that to others who must use other means".[148]

---

[142] *Chronicle of Convocation*, 1864, pp. 1684-9, and *ibid.*, 1865, pp. 1981-2005, 2020-52, 2061-2103. *G*, 22 June, 1864, pp. 597-8.

[143] Jowett MSS, f. 92, letter to Florence Nightingale, 4 December, 1864.

[144] Liddon, IV, p. 86.

[145] P.T. Marsh, *The Victorian Church in Decline*, pp. 121-2.

[146] D.C. Lathbury, *op. cit.*, II, p. 82. I, p. 170.

[147] Keble MSS, Box K, no. 90, letter of Gladstone to Keble, 13 March, 1864.

[148] S. Meacham, *Lord Bishop*, p. 251.

One thing was obviously necessary; the character of the bishops who served on the Committee should be above reproach. Gladstone did not say it but he implied that a liberal High Churchman might accomplish wonders in this direction. He had no use for the Latitudinarians, since he thought that they might betray the Church. Significantly at this time he clashed with Tait, ostensibly for a tendentious preface to a book of sermons but, in reality, for his part in siding with the lay judges. He thanked God that the primates had dissented from the judgment, in contrast to Tait's compliance. Tait had mistaken the issue; it was not about liberty exercised in matters "unconnected with religious faith or moral duties", but about the liberty taken in regard to scripture as the Word of God.[149]

Thus, there were many lessons to be drawn from the reaction. Gladstone, moving towards a cautious Catholic liberalism, pointed to the future. Yet even he found Tait a compromiser, even a trimmer, while the aggressives in Convocation were a fair guide to the feelings of the clergy generally, particularly the country parsons who were more conservative than their town brethren. Gladstone was right to stress Convocation's usefulness as a safety-valve, and the upper house admitted the fact by giving the other members their head, at the risk of seeming to be ineffective themselves. Surprisingly, anti-clericals like Houghton and Westbury did not recognise this, when they threatened reprisals from the state. The explanation lay in their fear for the cause of "freedom of opinion and the liberties of literature", as Houghton put it in the Lords debate. After more than a century that fear is still to be understood: the Church between 1860 and 1864 apparently adopted a provocative attitude, stood opposed to the liberal instincts in the national life, and employed "rusty engines of intolerance", which men thought had long been forgotten, to drive out radical teachers. Of course, the secular attitude was too simple, and the Privy Council judgment, though undoubtedly a "deliverance", and a landmark in the nineteenth-century Church, raised grave problems about discipline and authority. Yet reaction *seemed* to have won the day; the voices of Maurice and Gladstone were faint, compared with the mighty chorus against.

Was there an ultimate significance in these events, which raised *Essays and Reviews* itself to some new plane? Pattison, writing a brilliant though one-sided article in the *National Review* in 1863, thought so. He chose the subject, "Learning in the Church of England", because, he said, the

---

[149] D.C. Lathbury, *op. cit.*, II, p. 82.

treatment of the essayists had been so unscholarly. But behind Pattison's plea for academic fair-play a much larger argument took shape. He pointed to the bearing which the political movement of the day had on the decline of true learning. The present "Conservative reaction" might be, as liberals claimed, a temporary matter, but, far down in the deeper waters of society, causes fatal to freedom in religion were operating, "not in antagonism to the general movement, but — and this it is which makes them formidable — are entirely of it, and are strong by its strength". The advancing tide of civilisation brought with it a general levelling, a "tyranny of public opinion" which was the master of all government. On the present condition of the population, it must be unenlightened. The same levelling had taken place in the Church: the cathedral endowments had been broken in pieces, and in the universities, which the reforming Commission hoped to change from being places of elementary instruction to institutions of higher learning, revenues had been voted away for practical, non-academic purposes; "the public could not see the use of higher knowledge". And as practical statesmen hated "ideologists", so the practical party hated a philosophical, learned Christianity which admitted, but left behind it, the popular formulae.

Pattison did not mean to sound arrogant, but as he described the "vanity of the semi-instructed", and the "instincts of a democratic majority" which had an aversion for culture, he isolated the liberal from most of his fellow men. He continued in the same spirit:

> "That the Gospel is for the poor, the simple, and the unlettered, is construed to mean that there are no ideal elements in religion but what are accessible to them. Because the uninstructed can use the Bible for devotional reading, it is denied that the instructed can see in it a historical record of past events. In all ages the multitude of the semi-educated have resented these transcendental pretensions, whether of the philosopher or the saint. It is the old standing schism of the man of the letter and the man of the idea".

The essayists must be protected, and he ended with the gravest warning: hitherto, the tendency of the congregation to legislate doctrinally had been kept in check by the presence in the Church of men of superior attainments and more comprehensive knowledge. But if that were eroded the Church of England would be beaten down to a dead level of democratic orthodoxy, and the mistake made by Rome in the sixteenth century would be repeated.[150]

The perspective is fascinating, but what did Pattison's fastidious

---

[150] *National Review*, January, 1863, pp. 213-7.

distaste for religious democracy really suggest? There were certainly new elements at work in the reaction, as he said. The Church of England, like other bodies, had become more open to popular ferment and control, and used its institutions like Convocation and the religious press to facilitate that end. Moreover, this was the century on the move; speedy forms of transport spread the reaction more widely. Denison, quite logically, ensured that the liberals were defeated in Oxford by arranging railway excursions so that the Masters of Arts could come up in force to vote. This new importance given to rank and file opinion was necessary because Pattison's old understanding — of a church governed by scholars and gentlemen who held intellectual converse with their corresponding dignitaries in the state — had broken down, if it ever actually existed.

But Pattison's aversion to the "mob" revealed more than he would have admitted. The great strength of the reaction was the support from the laity as well as the clergy. The *plebs Christianorum* were a guide which no one should dismiss. *"Vox Populi, vox Dei"*, Pusey must have murmured at the spectacle of 137,000 lay signatures condemning *Essays and Reviews*. Why did the "babes in Christ" feel so passionately about the essayists? There was a great deal of ignorance, but in their awakening selfconsciousness there was also a protest about feelings which the radicals had too lightly passed over and rights which they too easily dismissed. The laity, perhaps, sensed in the essayists that old fateful Gnostic demarcation between the *pneumatic* men, the intellectuals, and the *sarcic* (fleshly) men, the great mass of the unlearned who — by a predestination more total than anything in Augustine or Calvin — could never attain salvation. The bishops seem to have agreed. When it came to a matter of choice, they had to support the *plebs*; for who, ultimately, had the supreme authority, the inspired scholar, or the bishop as guardian of the faith of the common people?

The controversy had one last aspect. The emotional engagement and the ruthlessness suggested a peculiarly Oxford way of doing things. As Kingsley said, "Cambridge lies in magnificent repose, and shaking lazy ears stares at her more nervous elder sister and asks what it is all about".[151] The same point was made "with great pride" by another Cambridge man, Harvey Goodwin, in the first debate, when it seemed possible that the all too obvious intentions of the thorough party might yet be thwarted. Harold Browne, also from Cambridge, spoke of his

---

[151] *Charles Kingsley: His Letters, and Memories of his Life*, II, p. 127.

university's preservation from the "danger of Romanism, and I trust also
from the danger of Rationalism, by the general prevalence amongst us of
a liberal and forbearing spirit. On the whole, for the last thirty years, we
have been free from violent party spirits and sound in the faith of the
Church".[152] All these opposed the Convocation campaign, not simply to
protect Williams and Charles Goodwin as the two Cambridge essayists,
but because, "it is a course which Oxford has delighted in pursuing — the
university which has condemned books and writers and has had one
school growing up, and then another, and has endeavoured to put them
down".[153]

The petition of the 11,000 was sent out from Oxford, and while
thirteen of the heads of houses and nine professors signed it, none of the
29 Cambridge professors did so, and only three heads of houses. The
great protest meeting after the judgment was held in the Music School,
the Christ Church chapter figured prominently in the letters of abjuration (Jelf was their proctor), and Wilberforce was, of course, the bishop
of the diocese. The same pattern occurred in the controversy as in other
clashes in nineteenth-century Oxford, and the same figures were involved. Thus, the High Churchman, William Josiah Irons, a Fellow of
Corpus, drew up a list of extracts from Hampden's writings in 1838,
published a larger version ten years later, and in 1861 collaborated with
the Evangelical A. C. McCaul in broadcasting a similar list from *Essays
and Reviews*. R. B. Kennard remarked ironically on Irons' "aptitude"
for this work.[154] But Irons' defence rested on the similarity between
neology old and new and the need for the same tactics to combat it. The
Oxford associations need, however, a separate chapter to describe them
properly.

---

[152] G.W. Kitchin, *Edward Harold Browne, A Memoir*, p. 210.
[153] *Chronicle of Convocation*, 1861, pp. 403-4.
[154] R.B. Kennard, *op. cit.*, p. 157.

CHAPTER FIVE

AFTERMATH 1864-1889

Henry Nutcombe Oxenham, writing his brilliant article in *The Rambler*, said that *Essays and Reviews* was the most important volume to emerge from Oxford since Tract 90. By 1861 it was inevitable that comparisons of this sort should be made; it seemed astonishing that Oxford which twenty years before had been aflame with High Churchism should now be outdoing Germany in radical religious opinion. So *The Rambler* and *The Record* and other journals contrasted the two movements and sought a connection between them. For the Catholic Oxenham it was a demonstration of the essential Protestantism of Englishmen: the Tractarians had attempted to revive Caroline theology, but Jowett and Temple, as the successors of Newman and Manning, simply showed the English Church reverting to type.[1]

Extreme Protestant reviewers took an opposite view. The Tractarians had replaced the authority of the bible with that of the Church: Oxford now reaped the whirlwind in new teachers who denied the bible but could not believe in the Church either. Since there were more Protestant reviewers than Catholic, this version was repeated with different variations and led to some curious theses: for instance, that Jowett was a renegade High Churchman and that Pusey held his tongue about the essays because, in fact, he supported them.[2]

But most of the comparisons missed the point. *Essays and Reviews* was not an example of Oxford perversity, nor simply a delayed reaction to the Tractarian movement (though it was that), but a reassertion of the university's traditional liberalism. That tradition reached back through the Tractarian period to the earlier Latitudinarian age which had produced Clarke, Paley, Blackburne and others, and it was now brought up to date. An age which saw a great deal of agitation for relaxation of subscription, which held that Dissenters ought to be comprehended in

---

[1] *The Rambler*, March, 1861, p. 301.

[2] Anon., *Puseyism the School of Infidelity*, p. 3. *The Record*, 11 July, 1855, saw Jowett as another Froude or Pattison, an extreme High Churchman moving from anti-rationalist "Romanism" to scepticism. Cf. A. Ollivant, *A Charge delivered to the Clergy of the Diocese of Llandaff, August, 1857*, p. 24, "If dogmatical teaching is overstrained, a spirit of scepticism is sure to arise, that will scarcely tolerate any dogmas at all".

the established Church — and the theology of which disliked the
pretensions of dogmatic or mystical religion, preferring, instead, a
simple, literal approach to scripture — was obviously nearer in spirit to
Essays and Reviews than the Catholic revival which had come in between.
Paley, for instance, could find no divine sanction for the Church of
England; the Church was merely "a scheme of instruction".[3]

Stanley and Pattison made much of these connections, as an historical
justification for the essays. They would have improved their case by
tracing an actual succession of Latitudinarian teachers at Oxford
throughout the eighteenth century and extending into the nineteenth.
Perhaps this was not possible. But two figures suggest something of the
sort — Harry Bristow Wilson, father of H. B. Wilson, and
John Eveleigh, Provost of Oriel for over thirty years. Wilson senior,
born in 1784, was an historian and antiquarian, and two books of
sermons showed some similarity to his son's ideas. In *The Sympathizing
High Priest* (1828) he upheld the national Church because it was able to
embrace all men; there must be bad as well as good in the visible Church,
and Christ's death was a sacrifice and expiation for all men. He
commemorated the death of Copleston with a sermon in 1849 which
preferred a type of universalism against the "gloomy and unscriptural"
Calvinistic scheme of Atonement; God had the power to save most of his
creation and, although some men were lost, the fact that reprobates
outnumbered the elect by four to one suggested that God had provided
for them, whether they belonged to the Church or not.[4]

Eveleigh was more important because he confirmed the claims of a
liberal leadership in Oxford before the Tractarians' arrival. Provost of
Oriel from 1781 to 1814, he was the initiator of the reformed scheme of
examination for degrees, and Copleston's sermon at his funeral was
quoted by Pattison in his *Memoirs* as evidence of Eveleigh's innovations
in this matter.[5] As his published sermons show, Eveleigh believed that
theology was progressive and, further, that man's reason, assisted by
divine grace but independent of information received from divine
authority, could arrive at a state of natural religion. Thus, he was able to
say that millions partook of redemption through Christ in equally or
different ages and degrees, notwithstanding their ignorance of him in this

   [3] R.N. Stromberg, *Religious Liberalism in Eighteenth Century England*, p. 134.
   [4] Harry Bristow Wilson, *The Sympathizing High Priest*, pp. 28, 35, 41, and cf. his
Contention for the Faith, pp. 14-15.
   [5] M. Pattison, *Memoirs*, p. 73. Cf. V.F. Storr, *The Development of English Theology in
the Nineteenth Century*, p. 94, and W. Tuckwell, *Pre-Tractarian Oxford*, pp. 1-16.

life.[6] In character Eveleigh seems to have been of the quick, sharp turn of mind of the Noetics; he prized logic and wished to maintain the liberal reputation of his college. Needless to say, he was a Whig in politics.

The old provost ushered eighteenth-century Latitudinarian theology into the nineteenth, and his pupil Copleston followed him. In the Noetics who gathered round Copleston at Oriel in the 'twenties there was an awakened scientific interest in theology and the beginnings of a new liberal churchmanship. The claim should not be pressed too hard: the Noetics were too varied to be called a school, and Copleston himself disliked enthusiasm and an unscholarly belligerence. But with Richard Whately's appointment as Principal of St. Alban Hall in 1826 the Noetics became a force in the university. In that year Whately issued his *Elements of Logic* — in which Newman assisted him to repay his intellectual debt to "Dr Copleston, the first defender of Logic in Oxford"[7] — while Whately-inspired works came from Gilbert, Hampden, Huyshe and others.

Seen through the veil of the Tractarian period, pre-1833 Oxford looked, no doubt, odd and unenlightened. The essayists, however, were right to claim a family connection and, because Tractarian publicity made memories short, to stress the importance of the earlier teachers. Nor was the connection really broken, for "Latitudinarians" kept up a continuous protest during the "Newmania". Newman himself antici- pated this: on his foreign tour in 1833 he had, he said, "fierce thoughts against the Liberals".[8] Arnold, Hampden (who, critics said, came out of Arnold's stable), Powell and others were all examples of the protest. The furor over Hampden's Bampton lectures, his *Observations on Religious Dissent* (1834), and his appointment as Regius Professor in 1836, was intended to punish him for affirming consistent Latitudinarian ideas such as the ending of religious tests.

But old and new were not the same. Dean Church made a famous distinction when he said that the pre-1833 Latitudinarian school was unattractive, "dry, cold, supercilious, critical... there was nothing inspir- ing in them, however men might respect their correct and sincere lives". They made free with the pet conventions and prejudices of Tories and High Churchmen. But the post-1845 liberals, with a far larger width in views and sympathies, were imaginative, enthusiastic, and penetrated by

---

[6] J. Eveleigh, *Sermons*, I, pp. 196, 246-7.
[7] J.H. Newman, *Letters and Diaries*, XX, p. 537.
[8] J.H. Newman, *Apologia Pro Vita Sua*, p. 42.

a sense of the reality and seriousness of religion. They were "interested in
the Tractarian innovators and, in a degree, sympathised with them as a
party of movement who had had the courage to risk and sacrifice much
for an unworldly end".[9]

To maintain the continuity which Stanley and Pattison claimed, a man
must pass from the one to the other. Whately himself could not do it,
nor could Hampden. The essayists appreciated Hampden's attempt to
find a new method in theology, away from the confident assertions of the
old verbal orthodoxy (a worship of words, rather than facts), which
knew nothing of the methods required by an age of science. Hampden
spoke in his Bamptons of the "destitution of Scripture facts for the
support of theological structure": facts and doctrines must not be
confused with one another. "The facts of Scripture remain the same
throughout all ages, under all variations of opinion among men. Not so
the theories raised upon them". "We must not suppose that the same
immutability belongs to Articles of religion which we properly ascribe to
facts alone". Jowett and Wilson assented wholeheartedly, and Powell, in
arguing for the triumph of the inductive principle and the absolute and
not simply probable certainty that it gave, echoed Hampden's claim that
by the inductive method one obtained absolute certainty in theology.[10]
Hampden, despite his criticism in his charge of 1862, saw the new
liberals' similarity to his teaching, for they believed that the "revelation made by the Bible is, in its own nature, distinct from all such
imperfections in the matter of the sacred volume" — they wished to
retain divine revelation.[11]

The essayists accepted that Hampden in his days in Oxford was a
witness to the truth; indeed, Powell was his colleague and supporter at the
time (and denounced by the *British Critic* as such) and deplored the
insolence and pettiness of the High Churchmen's attack. But Hampden
remained in the past. His theory in the Bamptons depended on scripture
as a "complete volume of inspiration": whatever was recorded in matters
pertaining to the kingdom of God was indisputably true, even if it was an
inerrancy of facts, not words. His charge did not answer Jowett's
contention that the interpretative element in the recording of the so-called
insulated facts, which historical criticism ever more elicited, must be
recognised. He remained firmly convinced, also, that the assent to divine

    [9] R.W. Church, *The Oxford Movement*, p. 338.
    [10] R.D. Hampden, *The Scholastic Philosophy considered in its relation to Christian
Theology* (1 ed.), pp. xlix, 376, 381, 385.
    [11] H. Hampden, ed., *Some Memorials of Renn Dickson Hampden*, p. 215.

truth was an act of faith in no way different from an act of reason — but
the essayists had moved a long way from such a pre-Kantian approach.
Hampden made no gesture to the Romantic feeling as they did.

Whately, appointed Archbishop of Dublin in 1831, lingered on until
the 'sixties, an anachronism in Ireland and also in Anglican theology. To
be sure, the earlier Whately, in his essay on St. Paul in 1828, had
suggested, as Jowett later did, that words like "righteousness", "grace",
"election", etc., had acquired an interpretative and technical meaning far
removed from the original; and, in any case, in scripture the same terms
did not always mean the same thing. Moreover, the teaching of the bible
was practical, not speculative.[12] But in the 'fifties he was still recom-
mending a rational, essentially eighteenth-century solution to the ills of
the Church. In a lecture on Paley in 1859, following his re-issue of the
Evidences a year earlier, and similar remarks in his charge for 1856, he
noted that "there are some persons who from various causes deprecate
this study altogether" (periodicals as far apart as the *British Critic* and
Edinburgh Review evinced this); but (he asked), had not God created
man as a rational being?[13]

Within Whately's family circle, however, there was someone who
evolved from an old Latitudinarian into a new liberal and from whom,
significantly, he seems to have become estranged. This was the Savilian
Professor, his relative by marriage and, like him, a former pupil of
Copleston and Oriel Common Room member. The quarrel between the
two men suggested the difficulties in the transition, though Whately had
good reasons for his annoyance. Powell had certainly learned from him,
for example, that the idea of an operative, creative God could not be
inferred from natural theology, which spoke only of an ordering
Intelligence, the nature and attributes of which must be approached by
other lines of argument (Whately wrote two letters on the subject to him,
after the appearance of *Tradition Unveiled*). But Whately detected an
unfriendly gesture towards himself in Powell's mounting criticism of
Paley and his advocates in *Christianity without Judaism*, the *Oxford
Essays* of 1857, and *The Order of Nature*. Powell was quite open in his
five references to Whately in *Essays and Reviews*. "What is the *real*
conclusion from the farfamed 'Historic Doubts'?" he asked — it was
much less strong than Whately believed.[14]

---

[12] V.F. Storr, *op. cit.*, p. 97.

[13] R. Whately, *Dr Paley's works, a Lecture*, p. 39, and (ed.) *William Paley's
Evidences* (n.e.), pp. 1, 18.

[14] *ER*, pp. 138-9. B. Powell, *Christianity without Judaism*, p. 74, and *The Order of
Nature*, pp. 301, 303. *Oxford Essays, 1857*, pp. 182, 184. W. Tuckwell, *op. cit.*, p. 181.

Powell's writings, which cover the period from 1826 to 1860, are a fascinating index to the new development and to his own progress to a new understanding of revelation. Fundamental "liberal" traits remained unchanged, such as the need to uphold the role of reason and free enquiry in the elucidation and defence of religion. His first work, on *The Advance of Knowledge in the Present Times* (1826), denounced the "narrow-minded counsels of those who, in a fanatical spirit, would condemn the literary and scientific pursuits of the clergy", and he resisted any increase in religious tests: nothing should be required which could not be proved by scripture, nor any standard of doctrine or orthodoxy more precise than that proposed by the early Church.[15] In the same vein he wrote an article in *Kitto's Journal of Sacred Literature* in 1849, on "Free Enquiry in Theology, the Basis of Truth and Liberality". As a scientific clergyman he believed as early as 1829 in the origin of the human race from many parents and not simply one couple. His *Natural Philosophy*, in 1834, spoke of the help afforded to religion by science. The history of science showed how man's eyes had 'been opened to the real laws and order of nature, "and in proportion they have been brought to recognise fresh proofs of design in every part". He praised Newton in terms of a physico-theology.[16]

From this angle, Powell wrote like any other intellectual clergyman of a Latitudinarian temper, of whom his brother-in-law was the best example. But Whately's philosophical and religious world-view was static: Powell, as a scientist and not merely a logician, was profoundly influenced by the discoveries in heat, light and physics generally, and he began to see that "proofs of design" might need some wider definition. Moreover, he had begun to read the biblical critics, and this acted on his already rather low view of the bible as an essentially simple, open book. In 1829, in a sermon entitled *Rational Religion Examined*, his target was the Unitarians, because they were obviously selective in their treatment of scripture. "But we must not be wise above what is written". Christian doctrine was the fruit of the study of the ages, taking the bible as a whole and accepting it in the plain literal sense, on the rational principle that the "doctrines were meant to be believed as they were revealed, and not to be explained away". Thus, "Christianity has been proved by miracle and prophecy to the satisfaction of reason", an admirable eighteenth-century sentiment.[17] However, in *Revelation and Science* (preached in 1829

[15] B. Powell, *The Advance of Knowledge in the Present Times*, p. 12.
[16] B. Powell, *Revelation and Science*, p. 13, and *Natural Philosophy*, p. 185.
[17] B. Powell, *Rational Religion Examined*, p. 58.

though not published until 1833), taking the scriptures in their plain and literal sense also meant admitting their contradictions and archaisms. Had Powell scolded the Unitarians from the standpoint of ecclesiastical tradition, he could have avoided this conclusion, but that was not his heritage. So contradictions must be faced, it must be admitted that the biblical writers used fiction and poetry as well as the record of actual fact, to teach their truths. To deny this was to misunderstand the nature of revelation.[18]

High Churchmen noticed the inconsistency, if it was such: Hugh James Rose had commended *Rational Religion Examined* as "this pleasing work", in *The State of Protestantism Described*, but by 1834 the *British Critic* held that Powell was inclined "to throw overboard not merely the *verbal* and *literal* accuracy of the scripture narrative, but its general and substantial truth in any intelligible sense".[19]

It is too much to say that a split developed in Powell's mind. To the end of his life he believed that science supported the claims of religion, and he put this in the form of an argument about the moral order suggested by the invariable laws of nature. The passage from order to mind (from nature to God) was absolutely valid, for the "order of physical causes is a dependence of ideas in reason, a series of relations existing in nature, and independent of our conception of it". "The reason pervading nature is the original, of which our reasoning is the copy". "We find in nature a sequence of phenomena, laws and causes, which we did not invent, but which agrees with a sequence of reasoning which we do invent". Feuerbach who referred everything to human subjectivity could thus be answered by a "physical" argument, the function of which was to "correct, to regulate, to confirm the internal impressions by the appeal to objective fact... A Supreme Mind in nature is the conviction of improved knowledge and scientific research". But in the same article, in the *Oxford Essays* of 1857, the Savilian Professor agreed with J. S. Mill that the inference of volition in nature had been urged from too close an application of the analogy of the human constitution. In fact, the more we considered the narrow limits of such philosophical reasoning, the more "must we acknowledge how inadequate are the mere results of science, whether physical or metaphysical, really to support those sublime inferences which involve a moral personality". These inferences

---

[18] B. Powell, *Revelation and Science*, p. 14.

[19] H.J. Rose, *The State of Protestantism in Germany Described*, p. xxiv. *The British Critic*, April, 1834, p. 415.

for the majority were derived from their knowledge of the bible — a bible which, however, he had already thrown open to the critics.[20]

The qualifications became more marked. In *Revelation and Science* Powell drew a line between the laws and structure of the material universe, which reason could investigate, and spiritual truth, which was the province of revelation — but by 1855 he began to stress seriously the confines of traditional natural theology: it could not provide proper spiritual satisfaction, and the arguments identifying the First Cause with God were specious and, moreover, unsuccessful. The analogy of an invisible Intelligence was only a "meagre skeleton needing to be filled out with those higher intimations derived from moral and spiritual sources which are, in their essential nature, alien from physical considerations". Science was not a challenge to faith, not because faith was opposed to it, but because "our theology has no concern with chronology, astronomy, or cosmogony... its objects belong to another order of things".[21] By 1860 he was saying that Christianity must be viewed apart from any connection with physical things. Though he was hardly as sophisticated in his biblical method, the former Noetic had now obviously arrived at a position similar to Jowett: the moral personality was something other than the world of fact, and truth was not dependent on history. Above all, he saw no point in "proving" Christianity: the labours of Paley and Whately were entirely mistaken.

The alliance of logic, common-sense, poetry and subjectivity, though unlikely, worked so long as the new liberals did not feel that they had to protest consciously about something. But their movement had been born in reaction, and recent experience taught them to be aggressive. Oxenham and others who saw a link between tracts and essays were right to this extent: some of the neology of 1860 was simply the counterpart of extreme claims made between 1833-45. High Churchmen had asserted the all-sufficiency of dogma, the independence of the Church, and the Catholic nature of *Ecclesia Anglicana*. The seven, in relegating these to the past, proposed some opposite truths and made common cause with forces which the Tractarians considered as enemies. An antipathy, natural or not, to Tractarian principles seemed to be part of the background to the new Oxford school.

Protestant papers which saw an interior connection between the two movements, a common intellectual fallacy so that one proceeded causally

---

[20] *Oxford Essays, 1857*, pp. 185, 203.
[21] B. Powell, *Revelation and Science*, pp. 11-12, and *The Unity of Worlds*, p. 311.

from the other, were on less sure ground. Pattison was the only essayist
with a Tractarian history, and, in some ways, he made the least direct
counter-assertions of all. If there are similarities between these opposed
convictions, it was because they were both new, both products of the
age, whatever their antecedents, both aware of the *"Zeitgeist"*.

Powell, again, provides an interesting example of this development, as
one who resisted the Tractarians from the beginning and yet, in a curious
manner, saw by 1860 that his distrust of external evidences could be
compared with theirs. Perhaps he already understood that a subtle
relationship was at work when he wrote *Tradition Unveiled* in 1839. "The
spirit of .the age" had, he said, called forth — and judged — the
Tractarian answer, and he realised that he represented an alternative
answer. That was why his opposition to the Newmanites was immediate
and continuous, from his support of Hampden in 1834 onwards.

In *Tradition Unveiled* the argument is simple: if the bible is to be
supplemented in the new age of criticism, where does religious authority
lie? Powell had learned from Hampden's Bamptons, and his own reading
in the foreign scholars, that the ordinary dogmatic statements of the
Church could not be found in the actual words of the New Testament,
"nor even so implied as to be deducible from the text in an obvious and
unquestioned manner". He accepted that "just and valuable considerations" had been built by tradition on scripture, but Newman had given
tradition an equal authority ("the divinity of the traditionary religion").
Powell blustered: that was utterly at variance with the spirit of
Protestantism, unscriptural and pernicious, and it made religion depend
on the indulgence of mere feeling. Newman had said in his article on
Plato in the *British Critic* that "an intellectual and reasonable religion is a
thing which nullifies itself", but Powell pressed the claims of private
judgment. "The alternative thus can only be between rational evidence
and an absolute infallibility"; Christianity stood secure in the multiplicity of its evidences adapted to every grade of intellect and capacity.
But he knew what Newman intended, and he had an uncanny instinct for
choosing his best and most characteristic phrases. Newman spoke of the
age being "all light; therefore the Church is bound to be — we will not
say dark, for that is an ill-omened, forbidding word, — but we will say
deep, impenetrable, occult in her views and character... we are now
assailed by science, and we must protect ourselves by mystery... mystery
fits in with this age exactly; it suits it; it is just what the age wants".
Powell protested against such superstition which led to rationalism: it
enveloped in haziness the spiritual horizon, so that the votary was unable

to distinguish between earth and heaven, and, then, finding metaphors elevated into mysteries, he might interpret it as reducing mysteries into metaphors. But the real reply came in one line: "how any point of science comes into collision with the peculiar system of church authority I fail to see".[22] That may have been simply the confidence of a clerical scientist, but, in 1860, such a statement would certainly have meant that faith found its security in a spiritual world untouched by science, and this was just as subjective as anything for which Powell earlier castigated Newman. In *The Order of Nature* he held that "mystery and parable are *more* truly congenial to the nature of faith than fact and history, which are rather subjects of reason and knowledge, far below the aspirations of the spiritual mind".[23]

The appeal to faith grew as his reference to an external order in the universe weakened. In regard to Paley the later Powell seemed to have reversed the position which he occupied in *Tradition Unveiled* when he had "...*assumed* the correctness of the view of the external evidence of Christianity, as laid down by the most approved writers; as Paley and others". He then charged the Newmanites with views which later appeared like his own:

> "Will the advocates of tradition contend that these views are *altogether faulty* in principle? Will they reject, as fallacious and presumptuous, the idea of demanding miracles as the *indispensable* credentials of inspiration? Shall we be told that these statements of evidence are merely of a nature addressed to popular apprehension; and that, to insist on them as the necessary proofs of our faith, only shows that we have not fathomed the depths of the subject? Or, allowing the existence of those difficulties in establishing their credibility which have appeared so insurmountable to sceptics, will it be considered better to avoid discussing them, and thus to discard such arguments as altogether of no force, and, in fact, concede everything to the unbelievers?"[24]

In *Essays and Reviews*, finally, he used the Tractarians as witnesses to his own view of Christianity. Newman, agreeing with Paulus and Rosenmüller, held that the Christian miracles could only be evidential at the time that they were wrought, and the *British Critic* had scorned any suggestion that "*evidence* to the Word of God were a thing to be tolerated by a Christian". This claim drew a comment from Maurice. "Extremes meet: He [Powell] may have arrived by a strange route at the

---

[22] B. Powell, *Tradition Unveiled*, pp. 15, 18, 44, 64.
[23] B. Powell, *The Order of Nature*, p. 428.
[24] B. Powell, *Tradition Unveiled*, p. 41.

very result at which so many devout Romanists arrive: faith and reason may have been as real opposites in his mind as in theirs..."[25] Powell went no further: though they both rejected the eighteenth century's externalisation of faith, there was no hope that the two sides would agree about what constituted the "peculiar system of church authority".

Jowett could, of course, be compared with Newman as another illustration of the relationship between the movements. Both Hort and Pattison suggested this, Hort in terms of a theological similarity between the two, Pattison from the point of view of the odium that they excited. Newman had certainly spoken of the "shadow of Liberalism" which had hung over his previous career, while Jowett was the most consciously liberal of all the essayists. Jowett's hold over young men evoked memories of Newman, though it was never so widely acknowledged or ever in danger of becoming a cult; and if their intellectual capacities were very different, they were emotionally akin in their strength of feeling and gifts of intuition. Hort thought that the likeness was so strong that it must have an intellectual expression. In his first letter on *Essays and Reviews* he saw Jowett as "completely leavened with J. H. Newman", and coupled this with a remark on Jowett's "blindness to a providential ordering of the accidents of history".[26]

What Hort probably meant by this may be gathered from a comment made by Mozley after reading Newman's *Essay on the Development of Christian Doctrine*. "What he does", held Mozley, "is to assert the old ultra-liberal theory of Christianity, and to join the Church of Rome".[27]

To some extent their positions were analogous. Newman and Jowett saw that "ideas" were one thing, history another. They regarded the idea as the original germ of truth, a creative understanding of reality, which lay beneath scripture. Newman saw the evidence of its existence in the convergence of the various revelatory fragments in the bible. "Ideas must be given through something", wrote Jowett. "Those of religion find their natural expression in the words of Scripture". That suggested an historical approach, as Newman and Jowett affirmed: ideas must be clothed, and their vesting in words and doctrines must be studied not dogmatically and scholastically, as if it were only a matter of logic, but historically. Both were very much opposed to mere logic, to a merely logical theology. Both, however, spoke of a "logic" which enabled one to

---

[25] *ER*, pp. 117, 119. F.D. Maurice, *The Mote and the Beam. A Clergyman's Lessons from the Present Panic*, p. 14. Wilson linked Powell with Newman in *WR*, July, 1859, p. 246.

[26] Hort, I, p. 417.

[27] J.B. Mozley, *The Theory of Development*, p. 226.

see how the idea became translated into expressions and formulae. For Newman there was a "logical sequence" in the way that, for example, our (implicit) feeling of the liabilities of our nature regenerate became the (explicit) doctrine of purgatory, though it was not a logical connection that would satisfy the schoolmen. Jowett distinguished between the "logical form and the logical sequence of thought", which was a difference in scripture itself between "the superficial connexion of words and the real connexion of thoughts. Otherwise injustice is done to the argument of the sacred writer, who may be thought to violate logical rules, of which he is unconscious".[28] In these broad aspects there were resemblances in their argument, though Newman was less tied to scripture and the essayist was always more critical of orthodoxy.

But Hort, Mozley and others were wrong: Newman, too, might be blind to a "providential ordering of the accidents of history", and Jowett saw the facts of history as subservient to its purpose: history was an educational process; but he believed in progress, whereas Newman saw only darkness, ignorance, rebellion against God. The one was full of hope for the age, the other had no faith in modern man. That inevitably affected their understanding of the development of doctrine. For Newman the idea had a strong objective reference; Jowett's idea was subjective. Newman saw the Church as God's remedy for man's sin, and doctrine, therefore, was no accidental matter. The idea possessed its own momentum, development was intended, and the astonishing fertility of theology in the early Church reflected the dynamism inherent in the process. He said in 1858, "Every Catholic holds that the Christian dogmas were in the Church from the time of the Apostles; that they were in their substance what they are now; that they existed before the formulas were publicly adopted, in which, as time went on, they were defined and recorded".[29] He agreed that language might be inadequate, but the later verbal expression carried out the intention of the original truth.

Jowett, however, sought an earlier age, even before language itself; formulas, verses, even words themselves, presented barriers which must be broken down. "When we pass from the study of each verse to survey the whole at a greater distance, the form of thought is again seen to be unimportant in comparison of the truth which is contained in it", he wrote. "The same remark may be extended to the opposition, not only of

---

[28] *ER*, pp. 337, 399, 400, 404. Cf. O. Chadwick, *From Bossuet to Newman*, p. 157.
[29] J.H. Newman, *Tracts Theological and Ecclesiastical*, p. 287.

words, but of ideas, which is found in the Scriptures generally, and almost seems to be inherent in human language itself". Jowett, too, had entered into the Latitudinarian inheritance, which Newman knew perfectly well, of a notion of progressive theology which ended as a theory of progressive revelation. But, while he accepted the potentiality for expansion of intellectual ideas, religious ideas must be eternal and changeless; the role of historical study was to strip away the layers of interpretation and meaning which had accumulated. Consequently, he made little of the creativity of the primitive Church. Newman would say that the presence of developed doctrine suggested an original infallible authority; but for Jowett it only urged the necessity of separating "the history of a doctrine from its truth", "clearing away that part which is verbal only".[30]

Pattison's parallel, which appeared in the *National Review* in 1863, was one made by a friend of both Newman and Jowett who was more emotionally committed than Hort. He meant it as an attack on popular religion which had dismissed the two because they offended the general taste. The rich genius of Newman (he wrote) had clothed the aridness of this religion with patristic and catholic interpretations, but his attempt was condemned not as "popish" but "mystical", while the doctrine of reserve in communicating religious truth excited more rude clamour. Nor was it the "crudities, blunders and hasty opinions" of *Essays and Reviews* which stirred indignation but the transcendental treatment of religion from within. "Newman's constant effort was to 'realise' the doctrines of the Church; it was his favourite word at one time. Jowett is ever idealising the language of Scripture. To the common understanding both alike are felt to be not only passing beyond its ken, but to be taking truth away with them into some region in which it cannot follow".[31] Pattison meant that both rejected a commonplace or merely sensible religion, they wished to elevate the truth and churchmen along with it. They had turned their backs on the eighteenth century.

The comparison was an interesting one, of religion treated from within, of a "realising" and "idealising" of doctrine and bible. But, as became apparent when the article was taken as a whole, Pattison's theory was only meant to serve his own ends. Anyone who offended public opinion was a martyr to the cause of free enquiry and scholarly research, and it did not matter if the martyrs were bitterly divided amongst themselves. Admittedly, Newman and Jowett took scripture and dogma

---

[30] *ER*, p. 401. Epistles (2 ed.), II, p. 570.
[31] *National Review*, January, 1863, p. 216.

a stage beyond the form in which they were left by writers and compilers, but there the comparison ended. Pattison had a point in referring to Newman's teaching on reserve in communicating religious truth. Jowett thought that too many doctrines were pushed constantly into the public eye and debated when they should have been left alone. But perhaps this was no more than a liberal's fastidious distaste for doctrinal enthusiasm. Jowett's idealisation of the bible was for the subjective mind of the individual, Newman wished to serve the Church.

Perhaps the best judgment on all such notions which placed tracts and essays side by side came from Newman himself. He knew that the new radicalism was traced to his paternity and that it was not enough to claim that his Anglican career had little bearing on what he now taught and believed. In 1863, therefore, he discussed the differences between *Essays and Reviews* and himself in a paper on the inspiration of the bible. It might be said (and Newman was aware of this) that while he had argued convincingly enough in the essay on development, that the idea which lay beneath scripture was inspired, he was ambiguous about the inspiration of its actual evidences on the page of scripture. He had emphasised the importance of subsequent intellectual growth in understanding the bible. But so had the essayists: when Jowett said that the reformers (for instance) had "thrown an intensity of light upon the pages of scripture", Newman knew what he meant, even if he saw the connection between bible and creed very differently. The question of the inspiration of the original writers must be affected by this historical perspective, but inspiration was a vexed issue by the 1850's when Genesis was challenged by geology, and the *Vestiges of Creation* (praised, of course, by Powell) troubled many minds. What more than the essayists did the Catholic Newman mean when he wrote to Pusey in 1858, having read Buckland and others, that "little was determined about the Inspiration of Scripture, except in matters of faith and morals"[32] — was the bible, therefore, mistaken in matters of physical and scientific fact?

In his paper of 1863 he took these aspects to heart. The ambiguity, he suggested, was in the Church itself which had not defined inspiration. He agreed that the attempted reconciliation of scripture and science was mistaken: the truth of the bible was of a sort that could not collide with either history or science. But the experience of Christians throughout the ages could not be put on one side: they found that the bible was inspired in its entirety insofar as it related to salvation (and here, indeed, it was

---

[32] Liddon, IV, p. 78.

proper to talk of infallibility). Thus, Newman moved beyond his position in the essay on development, to connect the inspiration belonging to the idea with the religious content or aspect of the passages which were dictated by it. The inspiration, however, lay in the minds of the sacred authors, not in the actual text.

Newman was careful here to avoid Jowett's distinction between religious and non-religious passages, which his statement might imply: the charism was present in the whole bible as a book of religious truth. Moreover, the inspiration must derive from a supernatural source, whereas Jowett denied that evangelists and apostles had any inward gift, "or were subject to any power external to them different from that of preaching or teaching which they daily exercised; nor do they anywhere lead us to suppose that they were free from error or infirmity".[33]

Newman, however, did not publish his paper, and by the time that he had finalised his thoughts on inspiration, in an article in *The Nineteenth Century*, for February, 1884, he and Jowett had moved so far apart that no one could dream of a connection. But the obvious contrast between the two men was always present: it was there in all essentials when Newman in the *British Critic* in the 'thirties spoke of the Church's function as protector and guardian of scripture; the bible must always be confirmed by the Church — one more reason why the Evangelicals came to distrust him. And what was Jowett's essay but an elaborate attempt to separate bible and Church? In his letters about *Essays and Reviews* Newman claimed that the Catholic Church had never been committed to plenary inspiration for this reason, while Protestantism, lacking a true sense of the Church, had come to depend on it (and so the essayists were the true Protestants).[34]

Not only Newman's past history needed defending, but also the movement which he had once led. Had he not become a Catholic, would he have emerged as a rationalist? The Protestant writers who implied this meant that present-day Tractarianism was infected with the same errors as the essayists. There were two ways of answering this charge, and one was to claim that Newman — despite all appearances to the contrary — had not been a true, consistent High Churchman and Tractarian. His background had been different from Keble, Pusey, and the others who had remained within the English Church; and here not only his former

---

[33] *ER*, p. 345. Cf. J.T. Burtchaell, *Catholic Theories of Biblical Inspiration since 1810*, pp. 71-4. *The Nineteenth Century*, February, 1884, pp. 185-199.

[34] J.H. Newman, *Letters and Diaries*, XIX, p. 488.

discipleship of Whately was meant but also his Evangelical upbringing. One could then read volumes into Newman's strong abjuration of the Evangelical appeal to the heart alone in Tract 73 (1835), entitled *On the Introduction of Rationalistic Principles into Religion*, which spoke of the atmosphere of subjectivity in which liberalism was fostered. Newman criticised the peculiar piety which directed attention to the heart itself, not to anything external to us, whether creed, actions, or ritual. "I do not hesitate to assert that this doctrine is based upon error, that it is really a specious form of trusting man rather than God, that it is in its nature Rationalistic, and that it tends to Socinianism. How the individual supporters of it will act as time goes on is another matter — the good will be separated from the bad, but the school, as such, will pass through Sabellianism to that 'God-denying apostasy', to use the ancient phrase, to which in the beginning of its career it professed to be especially opposed". Liddon, when quoting it, saw it as a prediction of the career of several essayists: it was certainly true of Newman's brother Francis, whom Powell and Williams so liked.[35]

Gladstone, who was spokesman for this aspect of the High Church defence, thought that the touchstone was Newman's attitude to Butler. He distrusted Newman for the same reason that he admonished Jowett — that, coming out of the Evangelical school, he had taken that school's principle of private judgment to extremes. Butler could have been an antidote, but, since 1845, Gladstone had believed Newman to be "thoroughly unsound" as a Butlerian ("there is an infinity to be said upon the relation of Newman and Butler"), and he put the essays down to that "cruel" deposition of Butler in Oxford which was "perhaps the worst determinate result of that great anti-Newman reaction" that brought in liberalism in religion.[36]

Newman, perhaps, admitted part of the charge when Butler and *Essays and Reviews* appeared together as the subject of a letter which he wrote in 1861. He saw the seven as representatives of a new Deism, but Butler had stopped the earlier variety "only by lowering by many pegs the pretensions of Christianity". "Without wishing to speak disrespect-fully of a writer to whom I owe so much, as many others do, still it does seem as if the practical effect of his work was to make faith a mere *practical certainty* — i.e., a taking certain statements of doctrine, not as

---

[35] *Tracts for the Times*, No. 73, p. 53. Liddon, IV, p. 3.
[36] D.C. Lathbury ed., *Letters on Church and State of William Ewart Gladstone*, I, p. 406.

true, but as safest to act upon".[37] That was exactly Pattison's complaint about Butler in *Essays and Reviews*, of course.

Pusey, however, would have none of this. Newman, Anglican or Catholic, would always have remained on the side of truth. The origin of *Essays and Reviews* had nothing to do with Tractarianism or the differing qualities of its leaders. The second way of vindicating the movement of 1833-45 was by an appeal to history, and Pusey made it in a letter to Keble in 1861. Only extremists, he said (meaning Pattison), who neglected the traditional Catholicism of *Ecclesia Anglicana* had gone wrong, while liberalism, out of its Arnoldian-Latitudinarian background, had been promoted by university politics. The true heir of Newman was a remodelled Tractarianism. The letter is worth quoting in full for its intrinsic interest and for Pusey's vehemence. He asked Keble to remonstrate with the Bishop of Lincoln, lest he become the Tractarians' slanderer on the bench:

"In last week's *Guardian* there is an extract from a Bishop's Charge (if my eyes did not deceive me, and I scarcely believed them), the Bishop of Lincoln's speaking (as Bishop Trower does) as if unbelief were the reaction from the Tractarian teaching. We know how false this is. Any one of real observation knows that it is absurd. Still, it is a very palatable doctrine to all but ourselves and the unbelievers, who would not like their parentage. For it throws all the blame off everyone else, upon us as scapegoats. *We* know well enough with what anxiety we watched every fresh importation from Rugby; and how, year after year, we warned Heads and others as to the one-sidedness of their attacks; that they were letting in Rationalism at the back gate, while they were trying to drive us out. They seemed, by their acts, indifferent as to unbelief, while they were struggling to exterminate us. Heads of Houses eliminated Tractarians from tutorships and carelessly let in Rationalisers.

"As for Cambridge, a great proportion of its intellectual men were Rationalists before the Tracts began. Tractarianism could have held unbelief in check. The Heads and Bishops broke it, and, as J. H. N. foresaw so long before, Rationalism spread, as the dam was withdrawn.

"Then, too, poor F[rancis] Newman and Froude gave us the history of their unbelief, with which Tractarianism has nothing to do. What Jowett rebels against is not Tractarianism but mystery; he wrote even more against the Evangelicalism in which he was brought up than against us. B. Powell was a Rationalist of old, before the Tracts. Wilson, an old opponent and heretic in his Bampton Lectures of 1851. Temple an Arnoldite. Pattison alone, whose Essay is the most moderate, is a renegade Romaniser of the Ward School.

---

[37] J.H. Newman, *Letters and Diaries*, XIX, p. 480.

"Then there has been that continual stream, of London infidelity, the *Westminster Review*, the Scotch, the *Edinburgh* (which is older than we are), Chapman's Quarterly Series, the translators of German infidelity, etc".[38]

Had the letter been published, the critics and their episcopal supporters, would have been silenced at last. Pusey also shows that there was no need to postulate any deeper relationship between liberals and Catholics — they were simply opposed parties in the university, as Latitudinarians and High Churchmen had been in the eighteenth century.

Pusey's tone in this letter of October, 1861, contains a warning. The liberal movement began in earnest after 1845 and drew its strength from a reversal of university politics. But fashions changed. By 1860 the Tractarians' heirs had recovered and were determined that the victors should be vanquished.

Eventually, this last factor was more important for the failure of *Essays and Reviews* and radical hopes in Oxford than anything else. That "reservoir of posthumous spites" was still being tapped by the remaining Tractarians even in the 'sixties. The "blue book" of 1852, and Pattison's "Oxford Studies" of 1855, received a mauling which showed stiffening opposition to liberal ideas in the university committees. The revised examination statute, passed in 1864, was only a shadow of what Pattison had proposed, though *The Times* held it to be a victory for the party of radical change. If there was a period of consistent liberal influence, it was the decade after 1845, and the Commission of 1850 was its monument. The liberals were too confident that time was with them — the mood of the century could not be altered. That fatal remark of Bunsen's in 1849, "there is no hurry", which referred to a proposed critical edition of the New Testament, with introduction and commentary, was typical; but Arnold died, and so did Hare, and the volumes remained unwritten.[39] The decline of their influence on the Hebdomadal Council was still masked in 1858 when Dean Liddell took the chair; but within two years "the liberal tide seemed to be running out".[40]

The euphoria over the essays did not last long. A story circulated, after the British Association meeting in Oxford in 1860, that a distinguished Frenchman had asked a student to name the two great intellectual

---

[38] Pusey MSS, letter to Keble, 23 October, 1861.

[39] F. Bunsen, *A Memoir of Baron Bunsen*, II, p. 237.

[40] W.R. Ward, *Victorian Oxford*, p. 217.

influences in the university; he was told, "Jowett and J. S. Mill", but it seemed a quaint opinion.[41] Students read Mill eagerly, but they could not help being affected by their elders' disapproval of Jowett. And, then, grey hairs began to show: the Stanleyites were no longer young men after 1860, and Pattison repelled rather than attracted undergraduates. Stanley's appointment as Dean of Westminster in 1862 was a setback. Pusey told Keble, "Stanley's absence will give us peace", and Jowett warned, "you will be thought to have withdrawn from the Liberal cause at Oxford".[42] Liddell tried to dissuade him, while Ewald said that his departure would only leave "more scope for the powers of evil", i.e., university reaction.[43] But Tait, realising that the liberal position in Oxford was becoming more difficult, supported the move for the sake of Stanley's personal happiness, and he went. By 1865 Jowett felt that there was something "strange" in the atmosphere of the university:[44] theological rigidity had proved stronger than the liberal government patronage which had given them the act of 1854.

The High Church victory was marked by a number of fundamental appointments in the years after *Essays and Reviews*. W.W. Shirley succeeded to Stanley's chair, to Pusey's great satisfaction, and William Stubbs followed Goldwin Smith in the Regius Professorship of Modern History in 1867. Mansel secured the Church History chair in the same year — though Jowett had hoped for a liberal candidate — and it later went to William Bright; Liddon was appointed Dean Ireland Professor in 1870.

The final irony occurred when the honours school of theology, earlier the darling of the Stanleyites, was admitted, at last, in 1869, but now as the handmaid of orthodox theology. Pusey astutely proposed a curriculum devoted to carefully guarded biblical studies and the Fathers, but not to the comparative and historical approach, undertaken by scholars owing no particular allegiance to the Church, which Jowett wanted. Jowett was pointedly ignored when the new Theological Studies Board met, though, as Regius Professor of Greek, he might have expected to serve on it. Oxford never gave Jowett a D.D., the gesture was made instead by a Dutch university. When the parliamentary commission politely inquired about the state of theology in Oxford in 1872, a witness

[41] J. McCosh, *The Supernatural in Relation to the Natural*, p. 359.

[42] Pusey MSS, letter to Keble, 4 February, 1862. Prothero, II, p. 143.

[43] H.L. Thompson, *Henry George Liddell, A Memoir*, p. 189. *The Autobiography and Diary of Samuel Davidson*, p. 89.

[44] Jowett MSS, f. 102, letter to Florence Nightingale, February, 1865.

told them, "no theology of any sort is much read in Oxford". Jowett,
who spent a good deal of time before the commission, implied that this
was what might be expected. Certainly, there was too little study of
German, rather than too much.[45]

Observers noticed the change in feeling in the university. Acland said
in 1865 that Oxford was a "queer place", the older men liberal and
reasonable, but the younger tutors sometimes violently obstructive; and
by 1869 Goldwin Smith dismissed as a delusion the idea that young
Oxford was a liberal body.[46] Perhaps that was the price that the
Stanleyites paid for devoting themselves to immediate aims, university
reform, the correction of obvious abuses, rather than long-term ones.
This was the opinion of E. W. Benson who thought that Cambridge
men, with their painstaking work on texts and editions, still had a task to
perform: "so has not Stanley now — nor Jowett". Though Stanley could
still preach his old message, there was nothing more in his line of thought
to emerge, and only Temple had a theological contribution to make.
That was in 1865.[47] But Temple was immersed in Rugby School
business, the intellectual promise never fulfilled, and perhaps he was
already conscious of his distance from the others. Indeed, when he
returned to Oxford for a visit in 1870, he was struck by the "pervading
melancholy of the older men",[48] with whom, less than twenty years
before, he had shared such bright hopes.

The most obvious gain of these years, the final removal of religious
tests in the university in 1871, encouraged no revival, though Jowett was
active on the committee. Stanley implied that they had done with
fighting: Oxford was becoming "not the battlefield of contending
religious factions, but the neutral, the sacred ground".[49] He was
certainly more partizan in his *Letter on the State of Subscription* in 1863
which, publicised by the "go-aheads at Oxford" (Mozley's description)
and taken up by Tait in his charges and by Ebury in the Lords, led to the
Clerical Subscription Act of 1865. That was also a liberal monument, but
a long overdue one.

All this provided a sad comment on the plans which were still forming
in Jowett's mind in 1861. He told Miss Nightingale that what theological
radicalism had done for university education previously "is as nothing in

---

[45] E. Abbott and L. Campbell, eds., *Letters of Benjamin Jowett*, p. 22.
[46] W.R. Ward, *op. cit.*, pp. 210, 235.
[47] Benson MSS 1853-78, f. 1065, letter to J.B. Lightfoot, 9 January, 1865.
[48] Temple Appreciation, p. 187.
[49] Abbott, II, p. 25.

comparison with what may be done in the course of the next ten years".[50] He predicted an adoption of the Jesuits' tactics, with liberals permeating the public schools after winning the universities.

Had the Stanleyites established themselves in the university after 1860, entrenched in the larger colleges and with a band of young disciples engaged in research and publication, they might have withstood the greater onslaught outside, the synodical condemnations, the huge petitions, the heresy hunts in the press.

Party strife in Oxford itself, a hostile reception from the Church of England generally — how should the liberal react? Stanley and Temple, free of Oxford entanglements, thought that salvation lay in individual effort; there was no decline in their liberal activities after 1860. But it was obviously more difficult for the others. True, there was a design for a second *Essays and Reviews* which kept Wilson and the Oxford members buoyed up for a time, but it came to nothing. The mood in the years 1862-70 was one of resignation. The essayists became more aware of themselves as individuals, less part of some great movement. So the effects were intensely personal. The fire went out of Williams. Wilson's experience in the courts hastened on his illness. Pattison grew more bitter and taciturn. Jowett felt a marked man. This produced a counter-reaction, to have done with theology, and it was no coincidence that the essayists did little major work after 1860. They felt a distaste for the Church; their faith was shaken; their sense of isolation increased.

Williams spent the rest of his short life defending himself. There was a spark in *Persecution for the Word* (1862), and he maintained that the leaders (Hengstenberg, etc) of the German anti-rationalist movement held opinions that would have brought them into the English ecclesiastical courts.[51] His lengthy *Hints to my Counsel* showed how much the defence had drained him. By 1864 he was speaking of a book of sermons, "*Essays and Reviews* applied to the pulpit", and when this appeared he admitted the faults of the essay; he now allowed a greater value to the Old Testament.[52] Accordingly, he concentrated on the prophets whose moral witness was, he thought, so much more important than their supernatural function. Part I of his translation of the prophetic books appeared in 1866 and Part II in 1871; he was still at work on the final section when he died in 1870. Meanwhile, in March, 1868, he wrote a

---

[50] Jowett MSS, f. 164, letter to Florence Nightingale, 31 August, 1865.

[51] R. Williams, *Persecution for the Word*, p. 28.

[52] Williams, II, pp. 184, 234.

paper for the *Fortnightly Review* which would reach a wider audience; he wished to "set himself right with the public on the point" of prophecy.[53] Ewald hailed the translation as a "work quite unparalleled in English literature", but perhaps he was simply keeping faith with his old friend, or knew nothing of the prospects of English liberal theology, or of Williams' own career, by this date.[54] Williams now refused to be called a Broad Churchman: he claimed in 1868 that he taught baptismal regeneration, which contrasted oddly with his essay, and he refused to join a free Christian union, set up by the Unitarians James Martineau and J. J. Tayler, on the grounds that he was an orthodox churchman.[55]

Williams' best service to the liberal cause was posthumous. His wife published a biography in 1874 which evoked a good deal of sympathy for a misunderstood figure who had spoken valiantly, if not always wisely, for his beliefs. *Essays and Reviews* loomed as a great shadow in the book, halting the promise which Williams had displayed in the 'fifties. Bishop Thirlwall regretted his passing: "he had the *défauts* of some of his *qualités*, and the irritability which usually accompanies a very fine organisation".[56] Jowett spoke of "poor Williams" and of the warmth of his temper, which "might have been troublesome" in regard to the projected second volume of *Essays and Reviews* (but would Williams' "orthodoxy" have allowed him to take part?)[57] R. B. Kennard — as he was to do for Wilson eighteen years later — read the funeral service and preached the panegyric.

It is difficult to draw conclusions from Goodwin's career, which would have followed an erratic course even if *Essays and Reviews* had not given him a brief period of notoriety. He continued his work on Egyptology, publishing various papers and an important article in *Fraser's Magazine* in 1866. He was for a time the musical critic of *The Guardian* and succeeded John Morley as editor of the second series of the *Literary Gazette*. These were interests far removed from theology, and Goodwin ended his career in the unlikely situation of an assistant judge in the newly-created supreme court of China and Japan, residing in Shanghai and finally Yokohama. His death in 1878 was unnoticed by the remaining members of the seven.[58]

---

[53] *Contemporary Review*, April, 1870, p. 71.
[54] *Dictionary of National Biography*, XXI, p. 452.
[55] M.A. Crowther, *Church Embattled*, p. 104.
[56] C. Thirlwall, *Letters to a Friend*, p. 256.
[57] Abbott, I, p. 442.
[58] *Dictionary of National Biography*, XVIII, pp. 142-3.

H. B. Wilson wrote little of importance after 1860. John Muir published a *Brief Examination* of prevalent notions of biblical inspiration, in 1861, and, with an eye to improving the sales, asked Wilson to contribute an introduction. Wilson seems to have learned from Williams, for he held that the indwelling spirit which had caused the scriptures to be written continued in the Christian communion : "inspiration", therefore, had not ceased, and we were able to judge that the biblical writers were reporting interpretation as well as fact. The point was more positive than in the essay on the national Church, for the bible (Wilson held) contained a spiritual continuity and growth such as was found in no other book. If these were retractions, they were little noticed at the time.[59] The second work was an expansion of his court defence, issued as a tract of some 300 pages in 1864.

Wilson's remaining energies were concentrated on his book reviews and notices, which ended with an article in the *Westminster Review* for October, 1870, a survey of recent theology and philosophy. As a farewell to theology, for the writer suffered a severe stroke shortly afterwards, it showed that Wilson remained an unrepentant liberal. His facility in German was obvious, he spoke warmly of Spinoza, and there was a hit at the Moral Sciences school in Cambridge for not being aware of real philosophy, still less metaphysics, their treatment of Kant being an example of plain backwardness. He affirmed the "Protestant principle itself", as he had always done, "the principle of Reason, as opposed to the principle of Authority", which meant that the "best informed Reason of today is to be preferred as a guide, where they differ, to that which may have been the best informed Reason of past ages". And, by way of Schenkel's study of Luther at Worms (1870), he criticised the reformer for falling back from his original position onto the principle of authority, "which it was essential to the consistent progress of the Reformation to have repudiated altogether". Wilson welcomed the republication of Charles Hennell's *Inquiry Concerning the Origin of Christianity* at a time when the "clouds of a kind of mystical reaction are gathering over the ground won from superstition". He quoted that author's doubts about the resurrection. Newman's views about the life of St. Anthony, in the *Miscellanies* of 1870, were dismissed: "Nothing can be more pitiable than the perversion of a great influence to the promotion of such miserable superstitions".[60]

---

[59] J. Muir, *Brief Examination of Prevalent Notions of Biblical Inspiration*, p. lxvii and *passim*.

[60] *WR*, October, 1870, pp. 469-73.

Pattison's growing alienation was marked in his occasional articles, while his practical energies were absorbed in university reform. His essay on *Academical Organisation*, published in 1868, was judged by Gladstone and Hort, among others, to be both original and powerful. In 1863, writing in the *National Review* on "Learning in the Church of England", Pattison passed a harsh verdict on the essays controversy while it was at its height. He spoke of terrorism and a "crusade against knowledge". But he also defended his argument about religious development, against reviewers who asked why the Church of England still manifested Catholic and even medieval traits when the Reformation was supposed to have abolished them. Pattison implied that only the first reformers were faithful to the Protestant conviction that each new generation had the right to form its own conceptions and not be judged by the past, and after them there was a return to the old ways.[61]

However, in the *Westminster Review* for April, 1867, Pattison admitted that his pristine Protestantism corresponded to none of the present-day dogmatic systems of the confessional churches, which were no better than Romanism. "If we look to the improvement of men or the glorifying of God, they are failures alike; and of both, as deadly enemies to inductive enquiry, and as crushing the mental activity which they profess to foster, all who without secondary aims seek only to learn the truth of facts are unspeakably weary".[62] The weariness was evident in his other articles for the Review, in April, 1861, January, 1862, and October, 1863. Pattison was encouraged by Wilson to write more for the *Westminster*: a letter of 7 July, 1868, asked him for help with some of the theology and philosophy reviews.[63]

Most strikingly of all, Jowett remained silent. He realised that he had written the Commentary and Essay long before their time, but he retained a wistful interest in theology and disclosed his heart to Florence Nightingale. In August, 1865, he said that after his work on Plato he would give his whole mind to sermons. "I have not told this design to anyone but you, and I mean to go about it as quickly as I can, putting off the more heterodox aspect of things until I have gained (if I can) some hold. Though I regard the B. of London as a friend I don't feel certain that he would not act to silence me..." so the liberals, perhaps, felt pressure in high places. Jowett had various schemes in mind,

---

[61] *National Review*, January, 1863, pp. 187-220.

[62] *WR*, April, 1867, p. 344.

[63] MSS Pattison 112, f. 90. Cf. *The Autobiography and Diary of Samuel Davidson*, p. 101, referring to a similar request from Wilson to Davidson (1871).

a joint New Testament commentary ("at once true and practical"), tracts for the poor, a liberal magazine.[64] The letters of 1865 were full of such designs, and the great aim was the conversion of the middle-classes to a forward-looking faith.

The Regius Professor of Greek continued to buy works on theology, as the catalogue of his personal collection at Balliol shows. This includes numerous German works — three volumes of Bunsen, seven of Baur, nine of Ewald, thirteen of Lessing, 26 of Schleiermacher, as well as de Wette, Fichte, Niebuhr, Ritschl, Schelling, Strauss, Tholuck, and others. In November, 1865 he sent Miss Nightingale a copy of Strauss' *New Life of Jesus*, and a month later recommended her to read Seeley's *Ecce Homo* which he thought was "powerful".[65] But Jowett could not get pen to paper. In the long vacation of 1882 he had "thoughts on reforming the English Church"; in 1883 he wrote, "I must try to revive religion in Oxford"; and in 1892 the great life of Christ was still projected — at the age of 70 he had proposed spending two years on it.[66] Yet he was still at work on Plato. Goldwin Smith said that in translation Jowett sought a "mental refuge".[67] But Jowett himself showed where much of his impotence in Oxford lay, in the efforts of Pusey and his followers generally, particularly in relation to the Theological Studies Board, to thwart radicalism in any form. Jowett the theologian was *passé* by 1878 when W. H. Mallock wrote *The New Republic*, maliciously portraying "Dr Jenkinson", the great Broad Church divine, for whom Christianity was not dead but changed by his party in the twinkling of an eye.[68]

Stanleyite hopes were pinned on a second volume of *Essays and Reviews*. It was certainly in Jowett's mind that the first volume would have been quickly supplemented, but that was before the controversy developed. Again, there was a fatal delay, as there had been with *Essays and Reviews* itself, which might have commanded far more success in Oxford in 1855, when events were in the liberals' favour, and even in the Church as a whole. The opportunity should have been seized in 1864 or 1865, answering the synodical judgment with a defence and explanation of the positive aims professed by the writers. Jowett's letters, however, show that he was too bruised, even to consider a new preface, and there is a bitter tone in the notebook of 1867 in which he recorded his personal

[64] Jowett MSS, f. 164, letter to Florence Nightingale, 31 August, 1865.
[65] *Ibid.*, f. 167 (15 November, 1865) and f. 204 (24 December, 1865).
[66] Abbott, II, pp. 195, 242.
[67] Goldwin Smith, *Reminiscences*, p. 84.
[68] G. Faber, *Jowett, A Portrait with Background*, p. 377.

feelings.[69] By 1870 the proposal had a period flavour about it. *Essays and Reviews* had already been overtaken by the course of events, and any remaining cohesion vanished when the project came to nothing in 1871.

The second *Essays and Reviews* was entrusted to the same team, where that was possible, and on the same plan as before, with Wilson as editor once more and Jowett as his assistant. Wilson thought that the long-awaited moment had arrived when Temple withdrew his essay from the original volume, on his appointment to Exeter. It was clear that the book could never be issued again. Two days after the announcement was made in Convocation, in February, 1870, he wrote to Pattison, "Jowett and I have determined to get out another volume of *Essays and Reviews* and hope you will join us... Our object is to have a much better volume than the last". Wilson also wrote to Samuel Davidson.[70]

Jowett had been thinking of the volume in 1869, perhaps in anticipation of Temple's withdrawal, and had written some of the essay by December. In February, 1870, he canvassed Edward Caird, Lewis Campbell, and a reluctant Max-Müller. By that time Wilson was at work on his essay on the progressive spirit of Protestantism, which was intended to show the element of progress in the Reformation and the element of fixedness. Jowett was to examine in his two contributions the relation of the laws of nature to morality and the impossibility of basing religion on miracles, though he changed these to an essay on "The Life of Christ as the Centre of the Christian World". He also thought of another essay on the future position of the Church of England, discussing its present state and the possibility of a different type of establishment or even disestablishment.

The tone sounds familiar, but Jowett defended it. "Of course... the old name is likely both to command attention and bring odium", but the book would be written in a religious spirit. And its importance for liberalism was as a gesture, perhaps a fresh declaration of war. "The adversaries will probably be bitter, because they think that they have extinguished us, and will find that they have not". Jowett knew that the bishops would do nothing to aid new thought, and Temple's elevation would make no difference. The essayists would stand alone once more, and Jowett intended inserting a preface commemorating Baden Powell and Williams (to whom he was about to apply as he died) to show the continuity with the repudiated volume of ten years previously. He was

---

[69] *Ibid.*, p. 146, n. 1.
[70] MSS Pattison 112, f. 94. *The Autobiography and Diary of Samuel Davidson*, p. 100.

more circumspect when writing to Edward Caird : "the more we can avoid Hegelianism, Germanism, or direct assaults upon received opinions, the better". The caution about Hegelianism was necessary in Caird's case, but Jowett had been noticeably less reserved about Germanism and assaults on received opinion in 1860.[71]

The volume was proposed for publication on 1st January, 1871. An amended list of contents among Jowett's papers at Balliol shows its wide range: Stanley on reform of the liturgy, Wilson on the principle of Protestantism, Lewis Campbell on mistranslations and misreadings of the New Testament, Caird on the history of doctrine, Pattison on miracles, the reign of law, and the moral and historical nature of religions, Max-Müller on the Eastern religions, W. H. Fremantle on religious education, and Alexander Grant on ethics. Other subjects projected were the relation of the Church of England to other churches, the dates of the books of scripture, and the composition of the gospels. The papers bear the date 1874, so Jowett continued to hope for something.[72] No important Cambridge figure appears on the list, and the liberalism is wider. Fremantle, later Dean of Ripon, and Max-Müller came from a less radical tradition, and the Anglican and specifically theological purpose of the volume was weakened by the inclusion of Freechurchmen and Hegelians.

The flavour of the second *Essays and Reviews* can be caught in the two extant essays, by Samuel Davidson and Lewis Campbell, published separately in 1873 and 1876. Both were concerned with the forthcoming revised version of the bible and the liberal expectations about it. The event seemed to be a great omen. The authorised version had been the bastion of the conservatives and traditionalists, but a new bible, cleared of all accretions, could be the foundation of a true Christianity and a fresh start for a modern understanding of the place of the scriptures in religion. Both articles were very similar in tone to those in the first *Essays and Reviews*.

Davidson dealt with the revision of the English Old Testament. He had throughly imbibed the spirit of Jowett and Williams, and his own experience of persecution made him even less patient with traditionalism. The bible was the book of the people, and the translation of the revised version must be a national concern and not merely an ecclesiastical one.

---

[71] Abbott, I, pp. 441-3, 445. E. Abbott and L. Campbell, eds., *Letters of Benjamin Jowett*, p. 181.

[72] Jowett MSS, Box E, J. 6, varia.

The aim (he said) was an honest translation, without note or comment. "And how is it to be got?" :

"Only by machinery which the civil power can set in motion. It cannot be done thoroughly by the Church of England in its present condition. Were that Church indeed practically Christian, its bosom wide enough to embrace earnest men of different opinions on theological points, as it should be, the work might well be entrusted to its hands; but while the fetters of ancient creeds confine its freedom, and bishops are chosen for other reasons than an enlarged knowledge of the Bible, it cannot accomplish a proper revision of the English version with success.

"The work should be done outside ecclesiastical bodies, by men who feel their responsibility all the more strongly that they are servants of the State rather than of the Church or Convocation; who will not have to consult the thing called 'public religious feeling' for the extent of the revision allowable, but will respond to the scholar's vocation alone".

Davidson believed that a new translation demanded a new (liberal) interpretation, otherwise the nation would subject itself to the despotism of a book, instead of using it as an aid to rational godliness (so he commemorated Rowland Williams as well). In approaching this subject it should be acknowledged that the New Testament did not furnish an infallible hermeneutical standard. The sense that it attached to passages in the Old Testament was not necessarily correct: "the only sense is the historical and grammatical one, all besides being assumptions or accommodations". A new commentary on the bible was, therefore, required, "exemplifying the relative independence of faith on scripture; shewing the difference between the *Word of God* and the *Scriptures*, not merely in regard to form but subject matter; making it evident that the Bible is divine because it is human, and cannot be exempt from the weakness, imperfections, and inaccuracy that cleave to man in every stage of his spiritual development on earth". The new commentary would be a monument to the pioneers who had toiled to bring about this happy result.[73]

Lewis Campbell, who wrote on the revision of the English New Testament, dwelt on the doctrinal considerations which had altered the meaning of biblical texts in the period before the history of texts had become known. He admitted that the passages whose authority was thus weakened "represent the most direct Scriptural testimony, and perhaps three-fourths of the Scriptural testimony, to the Divinity of Christ and to

---

[73] S. Davidson, *On a Fresh Revision of the English Old Testament*, pp. 143, 145, 151. Cf. Wilson's similar remarks in *WR*, January, 1857, pp. 134-172.

the Athanasian doctrine of the Trinity". In a sense, the revision of the English version was more difficult than in regard to the Greek. But "to clear the Scriptures from suspicion is an important part of the work of clearing religion from suspicion". He ended exactly as Jowett would have done:

> "...in so far as the attempt succeeds, it will not leave theological questions where they are. In spite of protestations to the contrary, the removal of texts on which dogmas have been supposed to rest will produce an impression. Even if it be granted that the doctrines have an independent standing-ground, this nemesis for the misplacement of the foundation of faith is still inevitable. It will be sought, no doubt, to make up for the narrowing of the Scriptural basis by strengthening the authority of the Church, or by making appeal to the general Christian consciousness. But the authority of the Church is only another word for the assumed certainty of an opinion, and the Christian consciousness can hardly be thought to testify to anything as one of the essentials of the faith which is not expressly recognised in the teaching of Christ or of St. Paul".[74]

Their opponents probably did not read these articles and they knew nothing of a second *Essays and Reviews*; but, if they had, they would have said that the authors learned very little from the fate of the earlier book. If there was any inkling of the hopes which the liberals attached to the new translation, those in authority ensured that they were not realised. The revised version, which finally appeared in 1885, was a mainly Church production and not that "version truly national", the bible for the people, produced and guaranteed by the state alone, which Davidson wanted. (Many of Campbell's critical points about the Greek text and accuracy of translation were, of course, met). Neither Davidson nor Campbell was asked to serve on the Committee of Revisers; but the greater slight concerned Jowett, whose counterpart in Cambridge as Greek Professor (B. H. Kennedy) was invited from the beginning; Jowett seems to have felt his exclusion from the committee rather more than his disappointment over the Theological Studies Board at Oxford.

If radical hopes were finished in the universities, the prospects outside seemed no better. Stanley and Temple, to their credit, maintained a liberal witness where they could. Stanley accepted the Westminster deanery for the "enlargement of the Church of England", principally by emphasising the abbey as a national shrine and by throwing open the pulpit to all the Church parties. He continued to write voluminously, and

---

[74] *Contemporary Review*, June, 1876, p. 107, August, 1876, pp. 477, 493.

two addresses, in 1865, on "The Theology of the Nineteenth Century", and in 1877, on "The Hopes of Theology", show an interesting development in thought.

Stanley laid *Essays and Reviews* before the London clergy in 1865 as the book which exemplified the historical tendency acknowledged and used by scholars of all denominations and parties, from Catholics and the French liberal Protestant school at Strasbourg, to Pusey, Keble, Newman and most of the authors of *Aids to Faith;* and the "memorable words" of the preface expressed what all claimed with one voice. We now had a "nearer approach" to scripture, ridding ourselves of preconceived ideas of what scripture ought to be and of the layers of interpretation which intervened; the symbolic books, the *Summas* and confessions, had consequently become less important. "Is not this of itself almost equivalent to a new Reformation? ...It is this which produces a kind of unity of religious thought unknown since the sixteenth century". A greater understanding had, in turn, arisen, of the mutual connection of the different stages of history, philosophy and religion with one another; Rowland Williams' *Christianity and Hinduism* was a manual showing how these new approaches in religion could be applied. East and West, Catholic and Protestant, were much nearer to a better understanding than at any previous time; even the relations between faith and doubt had now shifted. "Is there not, or ought there not to be, a corresponding change of tone among Christian theologians?"

Two other principles of modern thought detected by Stanley were, the development of doctrine, within the bible and outside it, and the "undogmatic" approach which penetrated beneath the veil of words to their inmost spirit and meaning. Stanley referred to Temple's essay. "Once look on the course of events as the 'education of the world', and each of the great epochs, systems and races of mankind, will take its proper place..." The negative aspect of modern theology (he quoted Max-Müller's *Lectures on the Science of Language*, and he might have quoted Jowett) was in protest against that use of words which saw them as unchanging, completely explored and therefore dead. The dean warned of the dangers of reaction, with an allusion to Wilberforce and Disraeli: "a combination has been attempted between a powerful ecclesiastical and a powerful political movement, with the avowed object of driving from the Church those who are supposed to be the representatives of this new teaching". In reply to Disraeli's predictions of its failure, he gave seven reasons why the theology of the age must succeed, one being the calmness of its advocates and the alarm and vehemence of its opponents (he contrasted Jowett with Pusey).[75]

Yet the tone of the address was noticeably defensive: Stanley avoided mentioning the condemnation, passed a few months before, and the detailed charges against *Essays and Reviews*; he felt that the merits or demerits of books or parties were small beside the inevitable progress of theology, obeying the law of development, which would issue in a liberal victory. It was the broadest of answers and looked to the future when the temporary misfortunes of liberal divinity in England would then be seen in perspective.

Twelve years later the hope had receded. In his address in 1877 Stanley admitted that the victory would not come with the present generation, of whom he said that he despaired. "The day, the year, may perchance belong to the destructives, the cynics, and the partizans. But the morrow, the coming century, belongs to the catholic, comprehensive, discriminating, all-embracing Christianity, which has the promise, not, perhaps, of the present time, but of the times that are yet to be".[76]

Temple preached the Bampton lectures of 1884 on the relations between religion and science, thus returning to the theme of the sermon which lay behind his essay in 1860. He used Darwin as a way of updating the argument from design. Darwin had shown, he said, that things had not come into existence as Paley had supposed. But Paley had allowed that for a watch to produce itself was still evidence of design; Darwin implied that it produced a better copy than itself. It was more worthy of the majesty of God not to make things but to cause them to make themselves, so evolution was necessary and it also suggested the unity of creation under one designer and not many. Nor did evolution account for the introduction of life, it left room for miracle. Here Temple reiterated the point made by Powell and Goodwin. "The purpose of the revelation [in Genesis] is not to teach science at all. It is to teach great spiritual and moral lessons, and it takes the facts of nature as they appear to ordinary people".

Temple used the analogy of the growth in apprehension from childhood to manhood to illustrate the claims of the moral law, which was beyond the realm of science and could not be produced by it. The history of revelation showed "an evolution in our knowledge even of the Moral Law... the fullness of its meaning can become clearer and ever clearer as

---

[75] *Fraser's Magazine*, February, 1865, pp. 252-68.
[76] *Macmillan's Magazine*, May, 1877, pp. 1-14.

generation learns from generation". What better ground could religion ask for?[77] Temple was not really interested in resurrecting the argument from design, and Darwin's thesis was, surely, more intractable than he allowed. But he wished to rob *The Origin of Species* of some of its terrors, while courageously facing churchmen who thought that it was an infidel book. For Oxford itself he meant the Bamptons as a liberal gesture.

These were all individual answers. What of the prospects for an actual Liberal party or movement in the Church of England? Events proved that Stanley was correct. By 1870 it was obvious that a radical platform was doomed. In particular, any substance which the Broad Church notion had once possessed — the idea of an alternative party to High Churchmen and Evangelicals — was now vanishing rapidly. The average Broad Churchman lacked a sense of direction, he knew what he disliked rather than what he held. For him the essayists had distinct limitations: they belonged mainly to one university, they were too convinced, and they were extreme. When called to subscribe to one point of view, the Broad Church ranks fell into confusion, and the reaction did the rest. Despite the optimistic prospects in the 'fifties, there were fewer Broad Churchmen in the universities, and far fewer in the parishes, ten years later. W. H. E. McKnight in 1873 believed himself to be alone among the clergy of his neighbourhood as a Broad Churchman. One of his correspondents said that he was the only Broad Churchman in North Wiltshire.[78]

The eclipse of the ideal was easily traced in three articles on churchmen's allegiances which appeared between 1853 and 1874. The first of these has already been discussed — W. J. Conybeare's work on "Church Parties, Past and Present", in the *Edinburgh Review*, which gave great prominence to the Broad Church movement. It was too confident, because Conybeare himself was liberally minded; and, of course, there was the question, which Maurice raised, whether Broad Churchmanship could ever be designated as a party. The third article, by R. F. Littledale, in the *Contemporary Review* for 1874, was too critical, indeed contemptuous: Littledale was a partizan High Churchman. The second article, by E. H. Plumptre, in the *Contemporary Review* for 1868, was more significant. Plumptre was a man of moderate, new opinions, though educated at Cambridge and a disciple of Maurice and Thirlwall. But his advocacy of the Broad Churchmen lacked passion; there were

---

[77] F. Temple, *The Relations between Religion and Science*, pp. 111, 115, 181.
[78] *Recollections and Letters of the Rev. W.H.E. McKnight*, pp. 231, 235.

many qualifications and an admission of mistakes. He devoted more space to the other parties and suggested a Broad Church on the defensive: the thunder over *Essays and Reviews* could still be heard in the background.

Aggressive action by Broad Churchman, Plumptre argued, had proved to be disastrous; evidently, any change in religious life must be brought about gradually — and indeed, perhaps, only by the other parties, for Broad Churchmen as individuals might perform a great service but as a party they could do no effective work in national or ecclesiastical life. Such individual efforts were best made in the academic sphere, not simply because there they would do least harm, but because any narrow, doctrinaire school could not harness the ideals of youth. But even that had an unhappy history: "their very latitudinarianism may make them narrow; their very zeal for tolerance intolerant". These individuals could not see the good in their opponents, and this was a reflection of their negative approach in general. "They write essays, reviews, treatises, commentaries, which seem to have but the one aim of showing that the Bible is full of erroneous statements, and the date and authorship of its books uncertain". Jowett and friends had harmed the Broad Church cause, therefore: they could do nothing for the poor and ignorant; they could not lift up the soul oppressed by sin; they did not write any devotion. Plumptre implied that Broad Churchmen should not neglect those ecclesiastical and social sides of Christianity to which the other parties witnessed. It was a just criticism of the essayists' failure in this matter, but it meant that the impetus had gone out of the movement.[79] The contrast with Conybeare's hopes of fifteen years earlier was startling.

For Littledale the events which brought about the Broad Church decline followed from the shock and revulsion caused by *Essays and Reviews* and from a misplaced confidence in the party. Indeed, the position was worse than it appeared: "the truth is that the fighting strength of the advanced Broad Church school now consists of about fifteen persons", of whom only the aged Thirlwall could claim lucidity of thought and strictness of mind.[80]

Writing from an equally unsympathetic point of view, Leslie Stephen was another witness to the Broad Church's state of disarray, in *Fraser's Magazine* in 1870. The party, he said, did "serious injury not to the

---

[79] *Contemporary Review*, January, 1868, pp. 321-46.
[80] *Ibid.*, July, 1874, pp. 304-19.

Church of England or to Christianity, but to the highest interests of truth
and sincerity", by using language in an unnatural sense as a means of
concession to the interests of the Church.[81]

Who benefitted from this situation? Of course, the diagnosis, the talk
of "parties" and the numbering of heads, could be challenged. Thirlwall,
in a smart reply to Littledale in the next issue of the *Contemporary
Review*, upheld an ideal of the Church of England very different from the
picture of warring groups and graphs of allegiance. The real difference
between churchmen, he suggested, was not between "High" and "Low"
but "Broad" and "Narrow", and this cut across the usual boundaries. In
this sense, Christ himself was a Broad Churchman, while the Church of
England had always cherished such an approach. It was ludicrous,
therefore, to see signs of a decline in the lack of productive energy, or less
fighting strength, in a so-called Broad Church "party", but no one
should rejoice if Broad Churchmanship itself seemed to be dwindling
away and ceasing to have any notable representatives in the national
Church.[82]

At the age of 77 Thirlwall had lost none of his skill, and his protest was
justified. Identifications were made too easily. Littledale, for instance,
was mesmerised by figures, and produced a table in which parties were
divided up as follows: High Church, 50 per cent; Low Church, 25 per
cent; "Nondescripts", eighteen per cent; Broad Church, seven per cent.
The table looked suspect because his way of gathering statistics was so
odd : Trench's petition, in 1862, as Dean of Westminster, which protested
against Low Church and Broad Church attempts to reform the
liturgy, had been signed by 10,000 clergy, while a similar petition
presented in 1834 had only been signed by 7,000. *Hymns Ancient and
Modern* ("a High Church book"), denounced by Evangelicals in 1861,
now circulated in eight million copies, and his own *Priest's Prayer Book*,
first published in 1864, had reached its fourth edition with 9,000 copies.
The Low Church also lost by the decrease in sales of *The Record*, which
was matched by an increase, to the tune of several hundred copies per
year, in the circulation of *The Guardian*. Nor did Littledale's account
agree with the different graph put out in John F. Hurst's *History of
Rationalism* in 1867, which had High Churchmen in a less commanding
position, at 39 per cent, followed closely by Low Churchmen at 37 per

---

[81] *Fraser's Magazine*, March, 1870, p. 319.
[82] *Remains Literary and Theological of Connop Thirlwall*, III, p. 481.

cent, while the Broad Churchmen stood at 22 per cent (this included a figure of 300 "extreme Rationalists").[83]

But Littledale had grasped something, though he attempted to prove ·the point in the wrong way. A growth in High Church opinion, if not in party, was admitted by most observers by 1870, and this was something which Conybeare could not have predicted in 1853. He spoke of the "steady flow into the High Church school of the very best elements in the other two parties", and perhaps the difference between his own estimate of High Church strength and Hurst's may be accounted for by the fact that the increase was most marked after the late 'sixties. There was no diagnosis of this situation from the Broad Church side, but Low Churchmen suggested why the lead had passed to the other party. The *Christian Observer* ran articles on the Laodicean state of the Church in 1866 and was critical of the lack of leadership and initiative among Evangelicals. In 1867 J. C. Ryle spoke of "dry rot" in the Evangelical movement.[84]

For Catholic writers all was grist to the High Church mill. Their advance did not owe anything directly to the Broad Churchmen's eclipse, but it filled the vacuum in the absence of Broad Church and Low Church effort, and it did not matter if the actual percentage of convinced Catholic or Tractarian churchmen was small in the party.

Palmerston's policy of appointing men who were "safe" over *Essays and Reviews* also affected matters. Jowett always held that a sure passage to the Bench was to write a book condemning the "*Septem Contra Christum*", but Tait suggested that it had a curious result. The Shaftesbury *clique* which influenced Palmerston was "filled with the idea rather of fit opponents of the *Essays and Reviews* than with the desire of promoting their own people", and when the supply of suitable Low Churchmen ran out, men other than party Evangelicals were appointed.[85] Disraeli explained in 1863 why High Church bishops got in: the death of the Prince Consort had checked Broad Church hopes, and "it was known that no more Low Church Bishops were to be appointed. That vein had been overworked. Some of the last appointments in that way had been mean and insignificant".[86]

Another indication of the state of opinion was the successive Church congresses in the 'sixties and early 'seventies, beginning with the congress

[83] J.F. Hurst, *History of Rationalism*, p. 438.
[84] W.H.B. Proby, *Annals of the Low Church Party*, II, p. 194.
[85] Tait MSS, Diaries Miscellanea, 1828-79, f. 220.
[86] G.E. Buckle and W.F. Monypenny, *The Life of Benjamin Disraeli*, IV, p. 369.

at King's College, Cambridge, in 1861 and thereafter at various regional centres, including Bristol in 1864, when more than 2,000 attended and Pusey, Keble and Denison led a debate deploring the Privy Council judgment on *Essays and Reviews*. The congresses were not dominated by High Churchmen, but Broad Churchmen did not attend them, and the other parties had free rein. Thirlwall, significantly, was suspicious of the congresses. Thirlwall also saw, like Stanley, a deep design in the first Lambeth Conference of 1867. High Churchmen were its main supporters, and this time Evangelicals refused to attend because they saw in it another attempt by the Catholic party to become the final authority in the Church.[87]

Was the High Church triumph inevitable once *Essays and Reviews* had failed, once the Broad Church was crippled? Would another movement (Arnold's social Christianity, for instance, or a far larger intercourse between English and German theological science) have been possible if this shift in emphasis had not occurred? Not for nothing was the fourth volume of Liddon's life of Pusey entitled "the victory". But was it a disaster for the nineteenth-century Church? Wilson, ill and out of sorts, wrote sadly to Pattison in November, 1867, "I seldom hear anything of Oxford now. I am afraid that of late years the extreme Churchmen have been having it all much their own way". In another letter, three years later, he disagreed with a writer who thought that the tendency of present Church of England divinity to be in the direction of freedom.[88] Jowett, writing in 1878, said that High Churchmanship had become a very important factor in English life, and his tone was one of surprise as well as regret.[89]

The strongest statement of this kind was made by Pattison in 1863. He looked at the history of the Tractarian movement since 1833 — "the life of a generation" —and saw disturbing tendencies. Its spread and momentum had become a social phenomenon, and its significance had been concealed under the guise of a theological squabble. The school began as a movement of writers, a welcome change from the Evangelicals who professed contempt of all learned enquiry, but now made common cause with all the social elements which were against intelligence. "The Church of England is Anglicanised", which meant for Pattison that it had become a party Church. "The tone of the High Church triumph, as it swells louder and louder on the breeze, becomes more vulgar, more

[87] Prothero, II, p. 197. *Letters Literary and Theological of Connop Thirlwall*, p. 257.
[88] MSS Pattison 112, ff. 86, 98.
[89] E. Abbott and L. Campbell, eds., *Letters of Benjamin Jowett*, p. 100.

violent, more partizan... the calm tone of historical enquiry is intolerable to it. Storm and rage and commination, the borrowed note of Machale or *L'Univers*, is becoming its style". Meanwhile, the Low Church party, effete in 1833, "now merely cumbers the ground with its ruins".

The party, said Pattison, made the worst possible use of its advantage. It adopted the bad traditions of the Church of the West, "the idea of the sacred inviolability of all notions and usages once adopted by the 'church', an idea fatal to all improvements in human affairs", and which Pattison described as a "*damnosa hereditas*". It hastened "to ally itself with a party in the state, to strengthen its connexion with property, to plant its fabrics over the face of the land, to get the primary schools into its own hands; in short, to carry the visible institution everywhere". Would the movement rise to its high calling? "The party guided by the Bishop of Oxford will not be so unwise in its generation... The loss of caste which the Church will suffer by an overt breach with the intelligence of the country will be far more than made up to it by its becoming more at home with the majority, whose opinion controls the government".[90] The decision for the future of the Church of England would thus be made by a party which shunned the best and most forward-looking elements in the national life. The Church would sink into a mere Gothicism, concerned only for itself and refusing to consider the altered rôle demanded of the religious institution in a reformed and changing society.

The issues raised by Pattison are obviously very important. The final judgment on *Essays and Reviews* will depend on them, whether the controversy was more significant than most people realised, uncovering a whole movement of thought and action which was otherwise undisclosed, whether, indeed, the book itself was more momentous than its authors understood — a battle for the soul of English Christianity.

How far did Pattison's theory and his view of the "Anglicanisation" of the national life, correspond with the facts? Was there any other explanation for the "reversion" to High Churchmanship?

In the first place, despite the tradition of thought about the national Church, the Stanleyites surely built too much on it; they idealised, or Germanised, it, exchanging a Utopian model for the reality of the English Church. Pattison's preoccupation with an intellectual ministry, a priestly elite engaged in pure research — or Wilson's professional class equivalent to J. P. 's and M. P. 's — took little account of life outside

---

[90] *National Review*, January, 1863, pp. 187-220.

the academic cloister, though both had good reason for alarm at an increasing non-graduate ministry. But there were various reasons why the average churchman became more "catholic" minded after 1860. Whether the essays had appeared or not, Broad Churchmanship would need to contend with a new brand of men who wished to be *bishops*, despite Pattison's sneers about active higher clergymen with their myriad committees and schemes of one sort or another, with Tractarianism of the second generation permeating the parishes, and with an ecclesiological revival which transformed the physical appearance of the churches. However, in a strange and (of course) quite undesigned way, *Essays and Reviews* confirmed this trend. It was exactly those qualities of the Church's beauty, mystery and historical uniqueness, for which the new churchman was seeking, which were missing in the book. After their Christology, the essayists' ecclesiology was always their weakest point.

Secondly, there was Maurice. Maurice, too, was concerned about the "social principles" of Christianity, and every bit as committed as the Arnoldites to the realisation of the kingdom of God in man's life and the need of the Church to equip itself for this. Yet Maurice's view of the seven was unfavourable. He did not think that great things depended on *Essays and Reviews*. The Oxford men, according to him, lacked a true interest in theology. If that sounds odd, it was explained by what Maurice understood "theology" to be, a blessing to mankind because factual, historical, based on the Divine Son uplifting all who sought him, reconciling culture, concerned for social alleviation. Men to be theologians must be prophets, mediators, who exemplified the scriptures in their personal lives. Compared with that the Oxford teachers were dry, abstract and unnecessarily sceptical. In 1830 he had felt that they were ready to tolerate all opinions in theology, "only because people could know nothing about it, and because other studies were much better pursued without reference to it". In 1871 he felt no nearer to them. "They have acquired a new name. They are called Broad Churchmen now, and delight to be called so. But their breadth seems to me to be narrowness. They include all kinds of opinions. But what message have they for the people who do not live on opinions?" [91] Maurice thought that it was "hopeless" to try and extract any "theology or humanity" (a significant coupling) from *Essays and Reviews*. [92]

For Maurice, evidently, therefore, the book could never have fulfilled

---

[91] Maurice, I, pp. 183-4.
[92] *Ibid.*, II, p. 384.

the hopes of its authors, whatever the situation. This also suggests that, however much he deplored the sound and fury, Maurice thought that the popular reaction was right. Party politics, sheer muddle, obscurantism, all played their part in the repudiation, and many other ventures apart from *Essays and Reviews* were damaged by them, but the reasons, finally, were sound theological ones, based on the fitness, or otherwise, of the essayists' teaching. Something instinctive told the churchman that the book lacked body as a Christian work; it denied too much and affirmed too little. In that case, if the Low Churchmen really were as effete as Pattison claimed, the High Churchmen were bound to emerge the stronger, for the Tractarian concern with the Church was always, at bottom, as Newman said, a doctrinal matter. On the same "principle of dogma", the essayists were found wanting.

Both Maurice and Mansel explored the essayists' background to suggest some reasons for their deficiencies, and both suggested that they lay in the Oxford tradition itself. Maurice, first, criticised Conybeare and Stanley for describing Hare as a Broad Churchman. Hare, he said, was not influenced by Whately. He was educated at a different university and was most indebted to Coleridge, "whom Dr Whately probably regards with feelings not far removed from contempt".[93] Maurice's distinction was between a liberalism nourished on philosophy and poetry and one devoted to logic and political economy, or between Cambridge Platonism and Oxford Aristotelianism. "We start from exactly opposite points; we, naturally, from that which is above us and speaks to us; they, naturally, from that which is within them and which *seeks* for some object above itself". He meant this originally to apply to the difference between English and German ways of approaching theology, but it did just as well as a description of liberalism in Cambridge and Oxford, particularly when the latter took so readily to German thought. Yet should not the truth "look down upon us if we would look up to it... Truth must be a person seeking us, if we are to seek him".[94]

But why should Aristotelianism lead to German "neology"? Mansel, in an article in the *North British Review* in 1851, was clearly worried about current trends in Oxford. He accepted that, after Locke, logic had been neglected in the eighteenth century until revived by Copleston, Whately and others, and he praised the revival. But now it was cultivated with much ill-regulated energy, due to the baleful influence of Kant. If

---

[93] J.C. Hare, *The Victory of Faith*, pp. xviii-xix.
[94] Maurice, I, p. 468.

the critical philosophy had not limited the understanding to the field of experience, the metaphysician would not have felt that either he must resign his position or assume the existence of a faculty of reason *directly* cognitive, independent of the laws of finite thinking. Mansel protested against the abuse of the term "Logic" which had occurred. Thought and being had become one and the same: "the reasoning process is a continual creation of the universe, and Logic, the science of pure thinking, is at the same time a revelation of the whole mystery of existence".[95] The reference in Temple's biography to the young logic lecturer at Balliol making havoc of the manuals of Whately and Aldrich now becomes significant.[96] The older teachers not only lacked a proper understanding of scholastic logic, they also knew nothing of the new developments. Thus, Temple's reading of Kant and Hegel bore fruit. And Jowett's copy of Hegel's *Logik*, with its heavily annotated pages (the copy which he shared with Temple in their joint translation), is a clear witness of his own interest in the new metaphysic.

Both old logicians and new started at the same point, with Aristotle, so developments in Oxford itself were indicated by new approaches in the understanding of the master. This was pointed out by Edwin Hatch, the later radical Broad Churchman, while still an undergraduate. In an article in the same review in 1858, on a study of the *Nicomachean Ethics* by Alexander Grant, a friend of Jowett and one of the projected essayists, Hatch said that the "changes in the interpretation of Aristotle are the key to the inner workings of the Oxford mind".[97] Wilson, reviewing the book for the *Westminster*, agreed: for half a century the *Ethics* had been the textbook for the greatest honours and had exerted much influence theologically on the tone of the higher order of men at Oxford — an influence distinctly adverse to Calvinism or Lutheranism.[98] It could not have happened in Cambridge in the same way: the liberal scholar who began with logic and then passed to German thought, succumbing to what Mansel called the "inversion" (or perversion) of the science, must belong to Oxford. All this might have remained a quibble between academics, had not the new metaphysic brought with it problems about revelation, the scriptures, and the nature of Christian history. It could still have been contained if its devotees had a sense of

---

[95] H.L. Mansel, *Letters, Lectures and Reviews*, pp. 39-76.
[96] Temple Memoirs, I, p. 88.
[97] *North British Review*, November, 1858, pp. 367-95.
[98] *WR*, January, 1858, p. 245.

the mystery and wonder of the Church Catholic, instead of being heirs of a sceptical tradition. It might also have been countered in a stable university which lacked warring parties and dramatic swings of fashion. But Jowett admitted the dire results of the continuous history of controversy in Oxford: it was notorious, and "we have always been in a state of unrest since I have been in Oxford". The tendency of one party, perhaps of all the parties, was to exclude the other party as much as possible. "A certain amount of sceptical tendency has been a necessary reaction from this state of affairs".[99]

The essayists were not, of course, silent in their own defence. Most of them spoke of bigotry, ill-will and ignorance in explaining the failure of their book. Pattison openly rejected Maurice's biblical humanism and made a virtue out of academicism. "It is the old standing schism of the man of the letter and the man of the idea".[100] But Jowett had rather more to say. Given the opportunity, radicalism could have been theologically creative. He was unable to prove this: he could only suggest that men should look at the life and work of the liberal theologian, and pass their verdict accordingly. Maurice would surely have appreciated the claim, for he recognised the moral sincerity of the essayists, even if he suspected their teachings.

Jowett's own career is an exemplification of this defence of *Essays and Reviews*, and it is worth studying. Its virtues were many: the drawbacks were also large. Though he wrote nothing specifically religious after *Essays and Reviews*, his theological interests were revealed to friends and pupils, in sermons, collected in editions in 1895, 1899, and 1901, his correspondence, and his great life's work, the commentary on Plato. The Christianising of Plato may be out of fashion now, but Jowett, like Schleiermacher before him, had no such reservations, and he also thought that Plato was a master of the spiritual understanding. Jowett the preacher appeared annually at Westminster, soon after Stanley was appointed dean, from 1866 to 1893, and various pulpits were open to him in Oxford and elsewhere. Wilson in 1870 recorded an event in his farmworking parish : "the great *Master* was here and preached for me a few Sundays ago, to the great admiration of '*Agricola*' ".[101]

The principal theme in Jowett's thought was man's search for truth and goodness, beyond all systems whether of religion or science — in his version of Plato's words, "the power and faculty of loving the truth and

---

[99] E. Abbott and L. Campbell, eds., *Letters of Benjamin Jowett*, pp. 33-4.
[100] *National Review*, January, 1863, p. 216.
[101] MSS Pattison 112, f. 97.

doing all things for the sake of the truth". "Let us not be too much the servants of the hour, falling under the dominion of this or that theory", he appealed to students when referring to Darwinism in a sermon (*Feeling after God*) in 1877.[102] Even the historical criticism which examined all systems had its dangers. "Even if we knew the manner of the composition of the Old and New Testament, and were sure of every reading and every date and fact, we should be no nearer the true form of religion".[103] That was to Mrs Humphrey Ward, and to Miss Nightingale he wrote that free thought and German theology, despite their zeal for criticism and truth, had never found a substitute for that which they were displacing. "They have never got hold of the heart of the world". The second *Essays and Reviews* must show a greater social interest. "Our principles are not worth much if they are not intended to elevate life, and are only a matter of academical discussion".[104]

"A Church which is liberal may also be indifferent", Jowett admitted. "Having attained the form of truth, it may have lost the power of it. It may be sunk in rationalism and indifferentism, and never lift a hand for the improvement of mankind" — no less convinced than Pattison of the need for victory, he was also aware of the dangers.[105] Truth, thus, was the prerogative of no one party or age — nor of one religion. In a passage in the third edition of the *Republic*, representing the last phase of his thought, Jowett spoke of two ideals which "never appeared above the horizon in Greek thought" but "float before the minds of men in our own day". These were the future of the human race in this world and the future of the individual in another. But there was a third, the Divine man, the Saviour in whom divine and human were indissolubly united. "Neither is this divine form of goodness wholly inseparable from the ideal of the Christian Church... or at variance with those other images of good which Plato sets before us".[106]

Jowett could only ascribe this eternal destiny of man to the existence of "God", and its clearest expression was the immortality of the soul. To deny immortality "takes the heart out of human life", and he always sought to expand his view in the first edition of the *Republic* that "...we cannot suppose that the moral government of God of which we see the

---

[102] B. Jowett, *Sermons on Faith and Doctrine*, pp. 6, 20.

[103] Abbott, II, p. 445.

[104] Jowett MSS, f. 80, letter to Florence Nightingale, September, 1864.

[105] B. Jowett, *Sermons Biographical and Miscellaneous*, p. 296.

[106] B. Jowett, *The Dialogues of Plato, translated into English with Analyses and Introductions* (3 ed), *Republic*, p. ccxxxi.

beginnings in the world and in ourselves will cease when we pass out of life".[107] Jowett's last thoughts, in the third edition of 1892, led to five new paragraphs on the subject.

Jowett would not define matters more clearly than that. There was an irreducible aspect in religion, he wrote in the Commentary. "We can feel but we cannot analyse it... It is a mystery which we do not need to fathom".[108] Jowett never satisfactorily explained what he meant by "mystery", but no description of his thought is complete without it. He criticised divines who left it out of account and who ended in a "verbal Christianity".[109] And, since the intellectuals and "wise" const- antly made mistakes about the mystery in religion, they must be contrasted with those who accepted it and understood it on its own terms — the poor, the uneducated, those who walked by the light of intuition. Jowett's references to the "poor" need to be noticed. He told Frederic Harrison, when speaking of *Essays and Reviews*, that any religious movement must be concerned with the poor and uneducated, and that this "constructive side" was left out of sight in the book.[110] In the essay the poor were commended for reading the bible unconsciously; like "those who are educated in a higher sense", they were not affected by the difficulties raised by criticism.[111] In the Commentary the poor answered the charges of Westcott and others that Jowett's careless approach to language was a "prelude to philosophical scepticism". "It is the peculiar nature of our religious ideas that we are able to apply them, and to receive comfort from them, without being able to analyse or explain them. All the metaphysical and logical explanations in the world will not rob the poor, the sick, or the dying of the truths of the Gospel".[112] The truths of religion were simple. "Reason, and reflec- tion, and education, and the experience of age, and the forms of manly sense, are not the links which bind us to the communion of the body of Christ ... it is with the weak, the poor, the babes in Christ, — not with the strong-minded, the resolute, the consistent, — that we shall sit down in the kingdom of heaven".[113]

This was the note which his old pupils caught as they gathered each year in the abbey with their wives, children and friends to hear the high

---

[107] B. Jowett, *The Dialogues of Plato* (1 ed), II, p. 180.
[108] Epistles (2 ed.), II, p. 248.
[109] *Ibid.*, II, p. 539.
[110] E. Abbott and L. Campbell, eds., *Letters of Benjamin Jowett*, p. 16.
[111] *ER*, pp. 417-8.
[112] Epistles (2 ed), II, pp. 108-9.
[113] *Ibid.*, II, p. 249.

clear voice speaking as Plato and Origen might have done. It was impossible not to be moved, and the emotion was heightened by the knowledge that the Church in general had ceased to listen to Jowett, despite the fact that, as Hort said, the Commentary met the "real *ultimate* difficulties better than anything I know",[114] or, as Walter Bagehot claimed, Jowett had proved, in several cases by a chance expression, that he had "exhausted impending controversies years before they arrived, and had perceived more or less the conclusion at which the disputants would arrive long before the public issue was joined".[115]

Yet if Jowett had been allowed to change the course of English theology, he would also have bequeathed problems that he himself was unable to solve. On the question of history he remained true to his earliest convictions. He praised the Greeks for attaching no importance to the question whether religion was an historical fact. "We have been too much inclined to identify the historical with the moral", he wrote in the *Plato*. "The facts of an ancient or religious history are amongst the most important of all facts; but they are frequently uncertain, and we only learn the true lesson which is to be gathered from them when we place ourselves above them".[116]

Was God personal or not? The first edition of *The Statesman*, in the introduction, spoke of the dangers of both personal and impersonal views of God, but the "philosopher or theologian who could realize to mankind that a person is a law, that the higher rule has no exception, that goodness, like knowledge, is also power, would breathe a new religious life into the world".[117] That remained unchanged in the third edition. Christ lived this law, but he was not the being whose equality with God could be described in credal language. Preaching in 1882 Jowett asked, "Is it not more intelligible to us and more instructive to think of him as one with God, because Christ and God are one with righteousness and truth?" "Christ does not so much assume to be God as he naturally loses himself in God".[118] Jowett's Christ moved further away from his historical accidents. "It is not with the very words of Christ, but with the best form of Christianity... that we are concerned today. There is an ideal which... may be conveniently spoken of as the life of Christ".[119] Jowett spoke of the "sense that we know as much as

[114] Hort, I, p. 448.
[115] *Works and Life of Walter Bagehot*, VIII, p. 75.
[116] B. Jowett, *The Dialogues of Plato* (1 ed), III, pp. xxxvii-iii. Cf. Abbott, II, p. 306.
[117] B. Jowett, *The Dialogues of Plato* (1 ed), IV, p. 442.
[118] *Oxford University Herald*, 28 October, 1882.
[119] Abbott, II, p. 445.

Christ did, or might know, if we had given ourselves for men 'learning by suffering' ".[120]

What did Jowett actually know of the poor? His biographers said that he was distressed at the brutishness of working men, while William Thomson in *Aids to Faith* described faces "eloquent in wretchedness" in "black London alleys teeming with ignorance, improvidence and vice", for whom Jowett's exemplarist doctrine of the Atonement meant nothing.[121] There was some point in that. His portrait of Christ was too indistinct: Maurice, like Plumptre, could not find the "divine and the human side" brought together in it, and the need for forgiveness was stronger than Jowett could ever imagine. He wrote to Florence Nightingale on Easter Day, 1865, "I don't suppose that we either have or could by any possibility have sufficient evidence of the resurrection to justify us in resting religion upon anything of the sort. I sometimes think that the death and not the resurrection of Christ is the really strengthening and consoling fact — that human nature could have risen to that does show that it is divine".[122] The "extraordinary intensity" of the belief in immortality in the first ages of Christianity was not the "result of the resurrection of Christ... the origin of the belief is rather to be sought in the mind than in the faith in any external fact, such as the resurrection of Christ".[123] Both statements repay close study.

It may be unfair to suggest that Jowett's later thoughts on theology were a paradigm for his colleagues. But he was given no real chance to develop after 1860, and the historical relativism, the lack of a clear dogmatic basis, and the idealisation of Christ himself, were all strikingly present in *Essays and Reviews* as a whole. This was also true of the later Temple and Stanley, and of Hatch, the solitary Broad Churchman of the same type active in the 'eighties. Perhaps Maurice, therefore, was right: *Essays and Reviews* might have achieved little, even if the reaction had not been so strong. But Pattison ought not to be forgotten. *Essays and Reviews* was a bad book, but did a far better cause depend on it?

There were many other reasons why the volume failed to win support, and most of these have been described already. *Essays and Reviews* appeared at the worst psychological moment: a feeling of crisis and frustration had built up to explosive point by the late 'fifties. There was no proper preparation for a radical movement, by means of a liberal

---

[120] *Ibid.*, II, p. 311.
[121] *Ibid.*, II, p. 224. *Aids to Faith*, p. 354.
[122] Jowett MSS, f. 127, letter to Florence Nightingale, 16 April, 1865.
[123] Abbott, II, p. 241.

Church periodical or school of literature. The seven were too isolated;
again and again, the absence of any proper connections in Cambridge
told against them. Above all, they made the worst possible choice in the
form of their book. Seen in the light of the achievement of his
Commentary, Jowett's essay and its companions seemed perversely
intended to destroy all that he had built up. They paid the price for
writing in a style that sometimes suggested the unbelief of a clever young
littérateur. These factors together produced the most violent controversy
in the Victorian Church.

Did the reaction end everything? It was possible to take the gloomiest
view, like Pattison. Cambridge men saw Oxford impatience matched by
an answering intolerance, and the fair field of theology in ruins. Hort and
Westcott feared for some years that new thought had been stifled
altogether, and Thirlwall agreed with Stanley who said that, as a result of
the controversy, books which had been previously allowed to pass
without prosecution were now assailed as incompatible with the doctrines of the Church.[124] J. S. Howson, in the Cambridge Hulsean
lectures of 1862, complained of the indiscriminate lumping together of
"Broad Churchmen", and of references to "German" theology, "as if
there was not in Germany a greater multiplicity of theological varieties
than among ourselves".[125] In Germany itself liberal writers saw an
ominous change: August Knobel, professor at Giessen, spoke of the
hostile attacks of the "men of darkness", and felt that the situation had
become worse in England than in Germany, while Ewald, commenting
on the court cases against Williams and Wilson, said that there could be
no desire for real knowledge in England, and no true appreciation of the
deeper evils in the national life.[126]

The scant treatment given to the period from 1860 to 1885 in
John Tulloch's *Movements of Religious Thought in Britain during the
Nineteenth Century* suggested that the time of theological adventurous-
ness belonged earlier: consolidation, or even a retrogression, set in after
that. It was also Tulloch who claimed, on good authority (presumably
the later Jowett, whom he knew well), that *Essays and Reviews* had no
revolutionary intentions.[127] But Jowett in 1860 would have disputed

---

[124] J.C. Thirlwall, jnr., *Connop Thirlwall, Historian and Theologian*, p. 231. Cf. Temple
Appreciation, pp. 214-5.
[125] J.S. Howson, *Five Lectures on the Character of St. Paul*, pp. xi, xii.
[126] *The Autobiography and Diary of Samuel Davidson*, p. 89.
[127] J. Tulloch, *Movements of Religious Thought in Britain during the Nineteenth Century*,
p. 46.

that: the whole aim of the reaction was to suppress the revolution proposed in the book. Support for this view came from Otto Pfleiderer, who wrote a history of German Protestant thought in the nineteenth century, in 1890, and was obviously astonished at the small headway made by liberal theology in England. True, *Essays and Reviews* was second only to *Das Leben Jesu*, but only in the furor which it caused.[128] That was not a happy analogy: *Das Leben Jesu* was universally reprobated, and its actual influence on the mass of Christians was small.

Again, the eclipse of the Broad Church had to be explained. Vernon F. Storr, in his classic treatment of the epoch before 1860, gave great prominence to the movement, and to *Essays and Reviews*, for emancipating religious opinion. But Storr realised that the latitude allowed by 1890 had little of the radicalism of the Oxford Germanists, and it was not, strictly speaking, "Broad Church" either.[129] The luminaries of this free thought, Sanday, Cheyne and others, were able to work more easily, but the Latitudinarian continuity had been broken, a casualty in the fierceness of the conflict, and Broad Churchmanship came to be known by another name. A. M. Fairbairn wrote a sad eulogy of Jowett in 1897 as a theological giant who, forty years before, had led a renaissance and had then been overtaken by events. His Commentary, better than Baur's *Paulus*, and more creative and constructive than Lightfoot, represented only the first fruits of his labours — "though alas, the first fruits were destined to be also the last!". "One may almost venture the prophecy that if he had not turned from theology to classics he would have done here the work for which England was waiting; and which, by supplying it with a basis at once Biblical and reasonable, might have saved the Broad Church from the extinction which he lived to see overtake it".[130] Fairbairn overstated his case, but he was accurate enough in describing Jowett as the "*last* Broad Churchman of the old school".

Another and more significant witness came from Edwin Hatch who best appreciated the attempt of the earlier radicals. He wrote of the outlook for liberal theology in the commemorative volume of 1887 entitled *The Reign of Queen Victoria: A Survey of Fifty Years of Progress*. Hatch believed that the inner history of the Church of England in the period justified the endeavours of the three great parties in their fight to exist. He acknowledged that the largest and most important place was occupied by the High Church movement, and noticed the

---

[128] O. Pfleiderer, *The Development of Theology in Germany since Kant*, p. 387.

[129] V.F. Storr, *op. cit.*, p. 381.

[130] *Contemporary Review*, March, 1897, pp. 342-65.

Evangelicals briefly. "Liberalism is still attacked, but it has secured its place, and twenty years of comparative immunity from the violence which once assailed it have given it an opportunity of changing its attitude. From having been critical and pugnacious, it is becoming constructive and sympathetic; and in the accurate study of Biblical exegesis and Church history it is finding a basis for distinguishing itself, no longer as the negation of the ecclesiasticism of the middle ages, but rather as the assertion of the simpler faith with which, in ages of mental doubt and social pressure not unlike the present, the first preachers of Christianity 'overcame the world' ".[131]

But Hatch's proof of the change in atmosphere was not as strong as he believed: Archbishop Howley had refused to allow Arnold to preach at Edward Stanley's consecration in Lambeth Palace chapel in 1837, but forty years later Arnold's successor and admirer (Tait) presided in the same chapel as archbishop. Jowett, however, thought that Tait would not hesitate to gag him if necessary. In any case, Hatch was clearly referring to his own labours, and he had to fight against great opposition in Oxford itself. Further, it seemed as if the virtues of the previous radicals, their pugnacity and daring, were the things that he now condemned.

An alternative explanation was possible, one which saw the reaction of 1860-64 as a catalyst. The sheer volume of the controversy was held to be its real significance. In this spate of literature, though most of it was critical, pent-up feelings were at last released. For this reason, *Essays and Reviews* was a watershed, a suitable point at which to begin or end the church histories of the period. After *Essays and Reviews* the Church of England was different : at least, that was the perspective by the last years of the century. A stone had been cast through a window to let in fresh air, and a slow process of adjustment could begin. Without the crisis it would not have been possible, and the revised version of the bible (1885) and *Lux Mundi* (1889) would probably have been delayed, or another outlet must needs have been found — such as the heterodox books of Bishop Colenso. Some argued that the process was more true to the cautious native genius of English religious thought than the rash, impetuous change proposed by the essayists. It was certainly slow: Denison only in extreme old age admitted that he would no longer be willing to sign the denunciation of *Essays and Reviews*.[132]

---

[131] T.H. Ward, ed., *The Reign of Queen Victoria: A Survey of Fifty Years of Progress*, pp. 364-76.
[132] G.K.A. Bell, *Randall Davidson*, p. 109.

Perhaps the change would have come about despite the upheaval: the tide of liberalism moving in Victorian life was gradual, but not even the most bigoted churchman, in the end, could have resisted it. That was the standpoint of W. E. H. Lecky in his *Democracy and Liberty*, in 1896, when he saw the importance of *Essays and Reviews* in the round and not as something narrowly ecclesiastical: the writers were coupled with Renan, Buckle, Colenso and Darwin in making possible the great enlargement of the range of permissible religious opinions. "The effect of this work in making the religious questions which it discussed familiar to the great body of educated men was probably by far the most important of its consequences".[133] Merz, in his history of European ideas, agreed: *Essays and Reviews* contributed to the great unification in the intellectual world in which from 1860 onwards converged many different and frequently distant lines of reasoning and research.[134] And A. W. Benn, in his *History of English Rationalism in the Nineteenth Century*, though he saw the publication as the "most important single event in the history of the Church of England in the last two hundred years, and certainly the most important in the history of English rationalism during the nineteenth century", claimed no novelty for the opinions of the authors nor any high intellectual distinction for the manner in which these were expressed: the essayists were unconscious agents in a movement far larger than they realised.[135] This, then, was the ultimate purpose of the great sales.

The relationship which *Essays and Reviews* bore to these later developments was best shown in *Lux Mundi* in 1889. *Lux Mundi* confirmed the High Church triumph and showed the confidence and theological creativity of the young men of the party. But it affirmed that "theology must take a new development". Over the preface glanced, perhaps, the shadow of the essayists' introduction, expressing hope, and there was thankfulness that past controversies had seen the scholastic side defeated. There were some interesting omissions: no essay on the evidences was included, and Charles Gore, the editor, said nothing about everlasting punishment.[136] J. R. Illingworth's statement on miracles might have come from Powell: for the large mass of the people, "it is not so easy to believe Christianity on account of miracles, as miracles on account of Christianity. For now, as ever, the real burden of the proof

---

[133] W.E.H. Lecky, *Democracy and Liberty*, p. 343.
[134] J.T. Merz, *A History of European Thought in the Nineteenth Century*, IV, p. 515.
[135] A.W. Benn, *The History of English Rationalism in the Nineteenth Century*, II, p. 114.
[136] But see *Lux Mundi*, p. 309.

of Christianity is to be sought in our present experience".[137] These
writers did not have to protest about an "abominable system of
terrorism", and this much they owed to *Essays and Reviews*. Gore
himself was a pupil of Jowett and kept a portrait of the Master in his
study. "When I feel I am stressing an argument too far I look at Jowett
and he pulls me up".[138] The influence was no more direct than that, and,
as R. W. Macan said, from *Essays and Reviews* to *Lux Mundi* was a
far cry, "but the latter is descended, collaterally perhaps, from the
former".[139]

There is an obvious difference in background between the two books:
Lux Mundi is not querulous, it is also rather less exciting to read, it
replaces the sense of urgency and discovery with careful judgment. But
revelation was its main theme also. The acceptance of evolution led
Henry Scott Holland to deny the totally radical nature of sin, and
presumably he felt, like Jowett, that sin could not be eternal (thus there
could be no everlasting punishment) if more understanding was still to be
revealed to man. Both he and Illingworth enlarged the frontiers of
natural theology, though not to the extent of suggesting that it was
practically self-sufficient or antagonistic to the wisdom of the Church, as
the earlier writers had done. Scott Holland came nearest to Jowett in
speaking of faith in the widest possible terms as a divine substratum in
man, the very core of each man's being, its seat lying behind the region of
knowledge itself. But the source of faith was most certainly elsewhere
and not in man himself, and there was an implicit rebuttal of
Schleiermacher. "You can no more shut up faith to the compartment of
feeling than reason to the compartment of the intellect".[140]

Illingworth was strong in playing down the problem of knowledge,
and overcame the supposed chasm between special and general revelation by affirming divine immanence and the Word in history. So all
great teachers of whatever kind were vehicles of revelation, and the
history of the pre-Christian religions was like that of pre-Christian
philosophy, a preparation for the Gospel.

"But secular civilisation is, as we have seen, in the Christian view, nothing
less than the providential correlative and counterpart of the Incarnation.
For the Word did not desert the rest of His creation to become Incarnate.
Natural religion, and natural morality, and the natural play of intellect have

---

[137] *Ibid.*, p. 208.
[138] G.L. Prestige, *The Life of Charles Gore*, p. 38.
[139] R.W. Macan, *Religious Changes in Oxford during the last 50 Years*, p. 26.
[140] *Lux Mundi*, p. 67.

their function in the Christian as they had in the pre-Christian ages; and are still kindled by the light that lighteth every man coming into the world. And hence it is that secular thought has so often corrected and counteracted the evil of a Christianity grown professional, and false, and foul".[141]

More than this cannot be said. The writers of *Lux Mundi* were unrepentant High Churchmen on such subjects as the independence and uniqueness of the Church and her freedom from political alliances; they rejected the Wilsonian theory of an equivalence of Church and State. All that they said positively was a reassertion of a broader Catholicism that was sometimes muted in the struggle for the faith thirty years before. There was no looking back to the essays, and the only quotation from the old radical group was from a sermon of Pattison's and that was typically negative. Pattison himself had no love for the young Catholic liberals and saw no connection; the honey from the new Hegelian school was going into the Tory hive, he growled on an earlier occasion.[142]

The most interesting comment on *Lux Mundi*, and the theological climate which it reflected, came from Jowett, who seized on that issue which was so central to *Essays and Reviews* and which, he held, the Catholic essayists avoided. He wrote to a correspondent in May, 1890: "The point on which the High Church party tend to give way is Scripture, and especially the Old Testament. They feel that as the Bible is seen more and more to be like other books, the greater the need of the Church, an aspect of the question which is not wholly displeasing to them. I have read a considerable portion of *Lux Mundi*, but am a good deal disappointed in it. It has a more friendly and Christian tone than High Church theology used to have, but it is the same old haze or maze — no nearer approach of religion either to morality or to historical truth. I am convinced that the High Church party might do something much better for the world, and that without shaking the foundation of their own faith".[143]

In the same year, 1889, theological liberalism suffered a reverse in another way in the sudden death of Edwin Hatch at the age of 55. Hatch raised hopes and propounded theories which had been silent for a generation, and he suggested that a radical Broad Churchmanship might have changed the face of Victorian theology, if given the chance. Observers in Oxford in the 'eighties recalled *Essays and Reviews* and

---

[141] *Ibid.*, p. 212.
[142] M. Pattison, *Memoirs*, p. 167.
[143] Abbott, II, pp. 376-7.

compared Hatch with Jowett, or saw in him the man whom Jowett might
have become, though Hatch was by far the better scholar and more
meticulous researcher. His solitary witness was a matter for surprise or
indignation, but what did he actually owe to the pioneers? Hatch was *sui
generis*; he was not a pupil of the Stanleyites, and he left Oxford shortly
before *Essays and Reviews* appeared. But he caught the prevailing mood
of liberalism while an undergraduate, and his absence from the university
cushioned him from the shock of the reaction which blighted other
incipient radical careers. When he returned in 1867 he took up his
previous interests and became strongly attached to Jowett, though this
did him little good and probably delayed the full flowering of his thought
until his Bamptons of 1880 on *The Organization of the Early Christian
Churches*.

His letters and diaries show that Hatch, as an impressionable student,
had not made up his mind about churchmanship, but he felt drawn to the
future essayists for their personal as well as intellectual qualities, while
traditional teachings were already alien to him. His diary for 16 April,
1854, records: "I was struck in reading portions of Locke today to find
how several of his great notions correspond with those which I had
reasoned out for myself, e.g., that ideas come to us by sensation and
reflection". On 22 April he "read Hegel all the way and enjoyed it", and
a few days later there is a reference to Hegel's philosophy of history. His
fondness for Hegel led him to send an article to the *Quarterly Review* on
the philosopher. He frightened Tait, who ordained him, by ending a
sermon at the bishop's examination with the words, "and so the
anthropomorphism of the book of Genesis expires in the anthropopathy
of Isaiah". A. S. Farrar told Tait that the young Hatch was quite
correct, and he replied, "Yes, but look at the conceit of the man in saying
it!" That was in December, 1858, and, also at Fulham, he "came back
part of the way with Dr Stanley — talked about Hegel, Jeune, etc". On
14 February, 1859, he returned from London with Jowett, an anticipation of those many "glorious talks" which he enjoyed with him in later
years. Back in Oxford he mentions a "long walk with Jowett"; again, he
"dined with Dr Stanley at Christ Church... had a pleasant talk on
Inspiration". Hatch attended lectures in that term by Jowett, Max-
Müller, and Stanley. "Heard Pusey on Joel (insufferably dry)". In the
summer he was at a garden party at Fulham and met Jowett and
Stanley.[144]

---

[144] MS. Life of Edwin Hatch, I, pp. 47, 78, 87, 90, 98-9.

Between 1859 and 1867, Hatch was in Canada as a schoolmaster and university teacher, and began to suffer for his "broad ideas". He wished to return to England, but not as the incumbent of a parish, for "I want above all other things... to be quite free to think out my own thoughts, and not only so, but to state them unreservedly. It is becoming harder every day for a clergyman to do this: for although the law allows us great latitude, there is a very strong and growing party which has for its object to crush everyone who thinks as I do... It is only just to myself to seek an opportunity of expressing ideas which I believe that no one but myself holds". He thought that Oxford would be freer, and he came back in the summer of 1866 to seek the advice of Tait and Jowett. "The man who can be of most use to me, next to the Bishop, is Mr Jowett". He left, finally, for England in January, 1867, determined to secure a post in Oxford. He found Jowett "just the same kind, almost affectionate friend as ever". On 15 February he had "a glorious evening with Mr Jowett... you know that there is no one whose friendship I value more, and there is no one who is more disposed to do all he can to help me. It was just one of those evenings in which I revel : every thought a new one, and never a word spoken at random". Hatch wrote to his wife on 14 March, "on Sunday I had a glorious long evening with Mr Jowett, who wants me to stay in Oxford permanently". Jowett urged him to write for the *Saturday Review*.[145]

Years later, on his death bed, Tait regretted that he had been unable to help "poor Hatch", and Hatch had financial worries to the end of his life. But he found a place in Oxford, as Vice-Principal of St. Mary's Hall, and supplemented his salary with other duties, notably the Secretaryship of the Boards of Faculties and Studies, and, in 1878, as University Reader in Ecclesiastical History. Ill-health dogged his later years, yet he was able to say, "how I thank God for my disappointments. They have been so good for me... I might have been a different man but for them".[146]

One who appreciated Hatch's nobility of spirit was Jowett, who now became his best friend, the godfather of his son, and a frequent visitor to the family home in North Oxford. There are many references in the diaries to dining with Jowett (sometimes weekly during term), Pattison, and other older liberals. An interesting note occurs on 12 April, 1880, "dined at Max-Müller's, to meet Renan".[147] Jowett wrote encouraging letters, "I hope that you will not lose sight of your great object, and that

[145] *Ibid.*, I, p. 79, II, pp. 85, 102, 104.
[146] *Ibid.*, IV, pp. 71-2.
[147] Diary of Edwin Hatch, 12 April, 1880.

you will not give up any position which you hold in Oxford". Hatch proposed a convalescent holiday in Switzerland with him.[148]

The character of Hatch's liberalism is found in his Bamptons, his study of *The Growth of Church Institutions*, and the posthumous *Influence of Greek Ideas and Usages upon the Christian Church*, given as the Hibbert lectures in 1888. Hatch, according to A. S. Farrar, had returned to England "full of, not the Hegelian philosophy, but the Hegelian method... the historic method was to permeate every branch of learning".[149] The impact was plain as his successive works developed his ideas, and nothing could be exempt from it. Opinions (he wrote) were the result of the forces of the present and the past, and in the same way that the scientist studied the stages in the development of a group of phenomena, the conditions of their existence and the law of their succession, so "it is the task of the theologian... to find out in the first place the conditions under which each group of thoughts exists in a particular stratum, in the second place its relations to the groups that precede and follow it".[150]

Applied to ecclesiastical history, this approach suggested that the internal organisation, government and administration of the early Church were borrowed from pagan precedents, in particular the guilds of the ancient world. Thus, Christ did not break the continuity of the historical process: he did not transmit to his disciples any specific type of Church order, and the Church came into being when forces in society acted on already existing institutions and elements. The Church was human society itself, and church order had differed from age to age. There could be no fixity of government or doctrine, though Hatch did not deny that religious progress, like all genuine progress, was under the guidance of the Spirit.

In their final form Hatch's theories were similar to the teachings of Harnack and the Ritschlian school: Christianity was essentially a religion of moral values based on the example of Jesus himself. Its historical evolution in the Greek world meant that the relatively primitive or unsophisticated Semitic concepts were elevated into a complex, metaphysical system, later accepted as dogma, while its organisation in the Roman world demanded a hierarchical structure. The pristine form was, however, a "religion of stern moral practice and of

---

[148] MS. Eng. Lett., e. 86, f. 4.
[149] MS. Life of Edwin Hatch, III, p. 41.
[150] *Contemporary Review*, June, 1889, p. 867.

strict moral discipline, of the simple love of God and the unelaborated faith in Jesus Christ".[151]

Hatch's employment of the comparative method was most crucial in regard to the primitive ministry. By placing early Christian writings on a level with others he implied that the use of terms like *diakonos, episkopos* was similar. The presbyters, the true model of the ministry, belonged to the Jewish churches, the bishops (*episkopoi*) to the Greeks, though Hatch did not make the earlier rationalistic mistake as to the original identity of bishops and presbyters: they were equivalent in rank, but the bishops did not evolve out of the earlier presbyterate. Harnack accepted this, and it led to his theory of the charismatic and official ministries.[152]

These views — the desire to find, scientifically, the unseen currents of thought and the Spirit moving in history — provoked great opposition. Hatch was defeated in his first application for the Bamptons but, urged on by Jowett, tried again. In 1880 he was successful, and Pattison went to hear the lectures on *The Organization of the Early Christian Churches*. The Rector arrived at his friend's home one winter's day and told Mrs Hatch: "I seldom go to a University sermon, as you know, but so many people were talking about these lectures, that I was anxious to hear what he had to say... Well, I was prepared for power, I was prepared for eloquence, but I was not prepared for what I *did* hear... it is the finest thing that we have heard from that University pulpit for years. There has been nothing like it in Oxford since the days of Newman!" Then Pattison added, "but he has done for himself now — no promotion for him — don't look for it — don't expect it; he will never have it".[153] Hort said that "Anglican prejudice and excessive theory" barred the way to acceptance of these ideas, while Mrs Hatch thought that personal antagonism in Oxford was the real reason.[154] Farrar believed that the fault lay in confusion over Hatch's use of epigraphy: Hatch's history of Church terms and names did not affect the question of things and offices or disprove the divine origin and providential growth of the Christian ministry. As Hampden did not touch Church dogmas but analysed the historic origin, derived from the middle ages, of the language in which they were expressed, so Hatch did not assault the Christian institutions but sought their historical antecedents.[155] But Hampden defended

---

[151] E. Hatch, *The Organization of the Early Christian Churches*, p. 192.
[152] N.F. Josaitis, *Edwin Hatch and Early Church Order*, pp. 67 f., 90.
[153] MS. Life of Edwin Hatch, III, p. 38.
[154] Hort, II, p. 358.
[155] MS. Life of Edwin Hatch, III, p. 43.

himself in his second edition with an explanatory preface, while Hatch could never be persuaded to do this.

The real cause, however, was deeper. Hatch's greatest opponents were High Churchmen for much the same reasons that they had fought against the essayists. In a less developed form Jowett and the others held the same point of view as to the natural ordering of early Christianity, and Jowett's desire was always to return to that truth enunciated by Christ which had been overlaid by centuries of evolution and interpretation. Hatch did not follow F. C. Baur's theory that the Pauline teaching was a virtual corruption of Jesus's gospel, but he believed that the "true communion of Christian men — the 'communion of saints' upon which all Churches are built — is not the common performance of external acts, but a communion of soul with soul and of the *soul* with Christ",[156] and such sentiments might have come straight from Wilson or Jowett. Hence, he attacked the Tractarian approach which referred all questions to the standard of the patristic age. Liddon, Gore and their party saw spectres once laid to rest now rising again with all the trappings of foreign scholarship, and they made a quick reply.

Gore, in *The Church and the Ministry*, made the issue a Christological one. Hatch had suggested, like the essayists, that Christ and the Church were not a radical new introduction in the normal religious evolution of man, but its product. So truth was relative. Gore, despite his acceptance of evolutionary notions, held that the starting point for the Christian scholar must be theology, not history, and revelation in Christ was given once for all. The truth in Christ was absolute. "It is of the essence of the New Testament revelation that, as given in Christ and proclaimed by His apostles, it is, as far as this world is concerned, in its substance, final and adequate for all ages. It is this because of its essential nature. If Christ is 'the Word made flesh', the 'Son of God made Son of man', then finality essentially belongs to this disclosure of Godhead and this exhibition of manhood". Further, a "once for all delivered faith and grace associates itself naturally with a once for all instituted society and a once for all established ministry". The manifestation of Christ was a supernatural event, so also the Church that he established was of the same character, for a "supernatural cause suggests supernatural effects".[157]

The High Churchmen did not doubt that grave practical consequences followed from Hatch's point of view. If his article on "From Metaphysics

---

[156] E. Hatch, *The Influence of Greek Ideas and Usages upon the Christian Church*, p. 114.
[157] *Lux Mundi*, p. xxxix. C. Gore, *The Ministry of the Christian Church*, p. 8.

to History"[158] was allowed, then the approach to Christian doctrine shifted from an essentialist to a phenomenological position. When he wrote on "A Free Anglican Church", in *Macmillan's Magazine* in October, 1868, he implicitly opposed ideas of disestablishment and obviously preferred to think of the Church as a national, comprehensive body. His experience of the Church in Canada suggested the pitfalls of too easy an independency.[159] His Bamptons would certainly have undermined the insistence, in the Lambeth Quadrilateral, on the threefold ministry of bishop, priest and deacon, as put forward by the Lambeth Conference of 1888.

Such basic theological differences blocked Hatch's career, and he never received in Oxford the recognition that he deserved. Among other things he hoped for the Dean Ireland chair when Liddon resigned it in 1882. Liddon had long wanted to vacate the chair ("but so long as Dr Pusey was with us I could not allow myself to entertain the question; it distressed him so much"[160]), but sent a noncommittal reply to Hatch, and the post went to another High Churchman. Hatch knew that he was alone. "We have had in Oxford the great misfortune of having no one in high position — round whom young men could rally — who was at once liberal, religious, and sympathetic. Liberalism in religion has been identified with destructive criticism". Oxford still did not believe that a man had the right to doubt the Virgin Birth and Resurrection, and support Colenso, and still retain his orders; and anti-clericals as well as clergymen accepted this.[161] However, he did not waver in his convictions. "Ignorant people in England may carp away as much as they like: my views will be accepted as the standard authority in time to come". And at the end he thought that the atmosphere was changing. "It isn't as it used to be. I am working with the stream, not against it as formerly".[162] The last lecture that he gave was full to overflowing, and another room had to be obtained.

Hatch's death was a tragedy. Hort mourned its effect on scholarship. "We are all grieving over Hatch's loss. So much remained for him to do, that no one else can do as well".[163] Harnack, who translated the Bamptons into German, spoke of a "glorious man". "I loved and respected Hatch. I saw in his activity the future of Church historical

[158] *Contemporary Review*, June, 1889, p. 868 f.
[159] *Macmillan's Magazine*, October, 1868, pp. 449-460.
[160] MS. Life of Edwin Hatch, III, pp. 56-7.
[161] H.D.A. Major, *The Life and Letters of William Boyd Carpenter*, p. 156.
[162] MS. Life of Edwin Hatch, IV, p. 71.
[163] Hort, II, p. 408.

studies in England... I have never found a church historian whose judgment I so much trusted as his, and never have I met with a fellow worker whose ways of looking at things harmonized so much with my own... he was a great writer".[164] The blow to liberal studies was severe. Otto Pfleiderer, the historian of nineteenth-century German theology, said that the High Churchism and obscurantism of Newman and Pusey had met their match: with Hatch at work Oxford could never be the same again.[165] The vision of thirty years before, that English writers would contribute to the new theology launched in Germany, hovered again, only to fade. Harnack, thinking of Hatch, had even written that "there no longer exists any distinction between German and English theological science. The exchange is now so brisk that scientific theologians of all Evangelical lands form already one concilium".

The earlier days were evidently in the preacher's mind at the funeral service. Jackson, Rector of Exeter College, said that "his was the same spirit as that of our great living divine, and commentator on St. Paul, the acknowledged leader of theological learning in England", though only a prejudiced admirer could have spoken of Jowett in this way.[166] Jowett himself wrote at least part of the obituary in *The Times* and enlarged on the loss to Hatch's friends, to the university, and to religious thought. "No Englishman of the present generation has ever given a greater promise of becoming a distinguished theologian".[167] But Liddon put the opposing side's point of view. After hearing Hatch preach in 1885 he would have given anything for his "style of composition", yet he now wrote that the death "removes from our midst a striking mind of great sublety and vigour, steadily directed to the work of destroying all Catholic belief whatever in the Church and the sacraments, and — it must be added — in a great deal besides".[168]

While that spirit reigned Hatch obtained no preferment. Had he not died from overwork, however, High Churchmen might have lost some of their dominance in Oxford, and *Essays and Reviews* would not have been the dusty volume, or mere curiosity, that it appeared by the end of the century. It is certainly unjust that Hatch should have been so neglected; historians of the period took it to mean that he was unimportant, when the truth was that the High Churchmen's long memories could never allow him to be appreciated for himself.

---

[164] N. F. Josaitis, *op. cit.*, pp. 15-6.
[165] O. Pfleiderer, *op. cit.*, p. 401.
[166] S.C. Hatch, ed., *Memorials of Edwin Hatch*, p. xvii.
[167] *Ibid.*, p. xviii.
[168] MSS *Lux Mundi*, ff. 18-19, letter of Liddon to D.C. Lathbury, 24 November, 1889.

CHAPTER SIX

THE WIDER IMPLICATIONS

There are two faces to *Essays and Reviews*. One is the standard image of the most controversial religious book of the Victorian era, which adopted the obvious causes of biblical criticism, evolutionary science and clerical liberation, and suffered obviously for doing so. But there is another level of scholarship, a deeper range of interests, a background shared with authors and concerns far wider than the narrow ecclesiastical questions for which the volume was condemned by Convocation and the Church lawyers.

Stanley proposed such a view at the time: he judged *Essays and Reviews* ecumenically, as part of a movement found in Germany, France and America, but also manifested in Russia with Khomiakov, and in Catholicism with Acton, Döllinger and the young Count Torlonia: "we know that genius, freedom and knowledge have a uniting tendency". "The tendency of Christian consciousness (as the Germans would say) moves towards the same result".[1] The seven belonged to a fellowship of scholars which must bring in a better world — Döllinger said as much — banishing doubt and ignorance like the humanists of an earlier age.

Stanley was right in his approach, though wrong in his details. The world victory of theological liberalism never happened, and the actual outcome of *Essays and Reviews* itself was meagre, although the reaction could also be given a wider significance: Stanley said that the synodical judgment was the exact counterpart of Pius IX's *Syllabus of Errors*, and both arose from the same fear of a new Renaissance and Reformation. To speak of another face to *Essays and Reviews* is justified if its writers, even superficially and confusedly, grasped ideas and looked to horizons undreamed of in the monuments of the old divinity produced at the same time, such as the Bamptons of Rawlinson on the bible, Mozley on miracles, and Liddon on Christology (Mansel's Bamptons are in a rather different category). Again, revolutions are not always made with solid critical works, and *Essays and Reviews* now needs to be revalued more

---

[1] *Edinburgh Review*, July, 1864, pp. 302-7. *Fraser's Magazine*, February, 1865, pp. 252-68.

than (for instance) *Lux Mundi*, however carefully composed and well written — a model of its kind — that volume was.

The essayists' treatment of Bishop Butler provides an introduction to this discussion. Most of the essays contained critical references to *The Analogy of Religion* and its author. Paley suffered alongside him, and Pattison spoke for all when he said that Paley had "unfortunately dedicated his powers to a factitious thesis". Pattison, who devoted most space to the subject, showed that there were two reasons for this change in feeling. Churchmen, first, placed too much confidence in Butler for allegedly routing the Deists. But Butler could not answer present-day objections to religion. Moreover, he was an unsure guide: he did not disguise the fact that the evidence for revelation "is no stronger than it is". Pattison, like Martineau and others, spoke of the unambitious nature of the *Analogy* and of Butler's judicial wariness. "He does not doubt himself, but he sees, what others do not see, the difficulty of proving religion to others", and a reference to Pitt's view followed, that the *Analogy* was a dangerous book; "it raises more doubts than it solves". Churchmen ought to resort to the neglected Warburton, whose proof, little short of a mathematical certainty, did not higgle over degrees of probability. Butler's merit lay not in an irrefragable proof but in showing the nature of the proof and in daring to admit that it was less than certain. In that sense he *was* relevant, "to own that a man may be fully convinced of the truth of a matter and upon the strongest reasons, and yet not be able to answer all the difficulties which may be raised upon it".

Secondly, and more importantly, Butler was to be criticised for his cold, withdrawn view of faith, and here the essayists were joined with Maurice, Hort and their colleagues. His theology showed how little he cared for subjective matters. Butler appealed to the common reason of man, but (said Pattison) his teaching forfeited depth to gain in comprehensiveness. It could not afford to embarrass itself with the attempt to prove what all might not be required to believe. Accordingly, there could be no mysteries in Christianity. To make the proof of revelation universal, religion had been resolved into the moral government of God by rewards and punishments, especially the latter. This anthropomorphic conception of God as the "governor of the universe", "excludes on principle not only all that is poetical in life, but all that is sublime in religious speculation". The *Analogy* was depressing for the soul to read, and he quoted Tholuck: "we weary of a long journey on foot, especially through deep sand".

Pattison held that Butler's preoccupation with morals as the proper study of man and his only business denoted a period of spiritual debasement and poverty, denying scientific theology, keeping the transcendental objects of faith in the background, and restricting our faculties to the regulation of conduct. Its effect was to make human nature the centre around which all things revolved, and this was produced "not by exalting the visible, but by materializing the invisible". In short, this was a utilitarian theology, condemning all employment of mental power which did not bring in fruit. "His term of comparison, the 'constitution and course of *nature*', is not what we should understand by that term; not what science can disclose to us of the laws of the *cosmos*, but a narrow observation of what men do in ordinary life". Altogether one missed in Butler not only distinct philosophical conceptions but a scientific use of terms. Whewell had spoken of Butler's "indirect modes of expression", but the case was worse than he imagined: Butler did not think in one form and write in another, out of condescension to his readers: he thought in the same language in which he and those around him spoke, and it was unfitted for religion. Hort's remarks in the *Cambridge Essays* of 1856 completed the argument: "Butler's writings are stoic to the core in the true and ancient sense of the word".[2]

In an otherwise impartial essay, the time and heat spent on Butler was noticeable. The Pattisonian line came out in the other radicals. Paley was no advance on Butler; Powell thought that the two might actually be set off against each other. Paley was now "entirely disused" in Oxford, and Butler's resources, so much less formal, technical and positive, offered wider and more philosophical views of the evidences. Yet Butler also did not supply altogether that "comprehensive discussion which is adapted to the peculiar tone and character of thought and the existing state of knowledge in our own times". Dr Williams held that biblical criticism was not Butler's strong point; he foresaw the possibility that every prophecy in the Old Testament might have its elucidation in contemporaneous history, but resisted it as an unwelcome idea. Jowett put his own position squarely: "from the fact that Paley or Butler were regarded in their generation as supplying a triumphant answer to the enemies of Scripture, we cannot argue that their answer will be satisfactory to those who inquire into such subjects in our own". The reason for

---

[2] *ER*, pp. 286-97. On Maurice's qualifications concerning Butler and Paley cf. *What is Revelation?*, pp. 172-3, 451-3.

this was obvious, though Jowett, as always, made it too sweeping: "criticism has far more power than it formerly had".[3]

Many factors explained the rejection of Butler. Of course, the essayists used him for their own purposes — there was more mystery in the *Analogy* than Pattison allowed — and especially when the traditionalists magnified him. Mansel trumpeted his excellencies in 1858 because he knew that he was unpopular in young Oxford, and Whately, as an old Latitudinarian, used Butler to express his displeasure at the new Latitudinarians. The *National Review*, on the one hand, said, in 1859, that to question him had become "little short of the sin against the Holy Ghost"; on the other hand, the *Christian Remembrancer*, also in 1859, — quoting Mansel — held that a "sound religious philosophy will flourish or fade in the University according as the works of Bishop Butler are studied or neglected".[4] The *Remembrancer* said that the whispers against Butler had begun 25 years before, and the *Quarterly Review* mourned a simultaneous change of feeling about Butler's companion; "'poor Paley', as we have lived to see him called".[5] After *Essays and Reviews* there were various attempts to update Butler, notably John Napier's defence of his view of miracles, in 1863. Butler's continued importance had already been suggested by Hugh James Rose in 1826: he was so much more reliable than the foreign rationalists.[6] Jowett in a letter to Florence Nightingale in 1865 put the opposing opinion of the go-aheads: "When I was an undergraduate, we were fed upon Butler and Aristotle's Ethics, and almost all teaching leant to support of doctrines of authority".[7] That was the main factor: authority was challenged, or sought in a different manner, and its classical exponent was dethroned. Jowett was early a critic; he and Stanley, in their anonymous *Suggestions for an Improvement of the Examination Statute*, in 1848, proposed substituting the *Analogy* with Adam Smith and Ricardo. When Butler finally disappeared from the statute in 1864, Gladstone held that Pattison was also "the cause of the expulsion".[8] Provost Hawkins reported an Oxford tutor as saying in 1858, "Bishop Butler! Bishop Butler was a fool".[9] It was not surprising that *Essays and Reviews*, when recasting

---

[3] *ER*, pp. 65, 104, 419.
[4] *National Review*, January, 1859, p. 214. *Christian Remembrancer*, April, 1859, p. 352.
[5] *Quarterly Review*, July, 1858, p. 159.
[6] H.J. Rose, *The State of Protestantism in Germany Described*, p. 111.
[7] Jowett MSS, f. 164, letter to Florence Nightingale, 31 August, 1865.
[8] *Autobiography of Montagu Burrows*, p. 201.
[9] W.R. Ward, *Victorian Oxford*, p. 389.

theology, should so so hostile to Butler, and this attitude was a guide to the spirit of the work as a whole.

In any case, it was not as if Butler had written in an unambiguous situation: part of his work was to answer the challenges to traditional divinity which had already arisen, and of these the essayists were well aware. Jowett in the same letter of 1865 mentioned Bacon, Locke and Mill as the writers who had shown the impossibility of returning to the old doctrines of authority. Mozley, retailing common room gossip in 1855, reported Jowett as dining with Gladstone and being disgusted to find him opposed to the University Commission and all its religious ideas, "and talking against Locke and for Butler".[10] Powell, in one of his books, mentioned a similar list beginning with Bacon, and said of Hume's essay on necessary causation and his theory of a simple, unvariable, "or, as J. S. Mill puts it, an unconditional sequence of events", that it was of a "magnitude commensurate with Locke's demolition of innate ideas, and like it marks an epoch in the history of philosophy".[11] That was a philosophical commonplace, but such scepticism was a powerful element in the historical background of the essayists.

The rehabilitation of Locke in Pattison's work has been discussed previously, and it was the counterpart of his attack on Butler. The radicals as a whole echoed Locke when he held that if the evidence for revelation depended on probable proofs, "our assent can reach no higher than an assurance or diffidence, arising from the more or less apparent probability of the proofs" — a statement which also recalled Lord Herbert of Cherbury : "All tradition and history ... possesses for us only probability, since it depends on the authority of the narrator".[12] So they emphasised the force given by Butler to probability, though they understood it negatively, as when Wilson remarked on "how great [an] extent the history of the origin itself of Christianity rests ultimately upon *probable* evidence".[13] In their attitude to language Jowett and Wilson suggested similarities to Locke's section, "Of the imperfection of words" in the *Essay Concerning Human Understanding*, and there was a good deal of Locke's "plain historical method" elsewhere in *Essays and Reviews*. In *The Reasonableness of Christianity* Locke believed that we were unjust to the scriptures when we searched

---

[10] *Letters of the Rev. J.B. Mozley*, p. 158.
[11] *Oxford Essays, 1857*, p. 174.
[12] G.E. Lessing, *Theological Writings*, Introduction by H. Chadwick, p. 33.
[13] *ER*, p. 202.

for abstruse principles: the obvious sense was the true one and was "therefore generally, and in necessary points, to be understood in the plain direct meaning of the words and phrases".[14] That might have come out of Jowett, whose open bible, so clear and unambiguous, also recalled Clarke or Toland with their view of scripture as containing a few essentials resting on natural theology. After Locke there was Hume: Powell held that the argument against miracles, on the grounds of experience, was philosophically as strong as ever but it now cohered with the scientific world view. And when Hume drove a wedge between sensory experience as wholly objective and faith as subjective, that had a modern flavour which the seven recognised.

Their opponents naturally made much of the writers' obligations to such malignant thinkers, and they were right to see some significance in the essayists' deference to Locke. Locke was a symbol, though not a mentor to be slavishly followed. Jowett emphasised this when giving his own version of his preference for Locke in the *Parmenides*. "Without ideas philosophy is impossible. There is no philosophy of experience; 'it is the idea of experience rather than experience itself with which the mind is filled'. Locke's system is indeed based on experience, but with him experience includes reflection as well as sense". That was in the same breath as a remark on Hume which also showed Jowett's independence of mind. However much he respected him, Hume's philosophy was "nothing more than the analysis of the word 'cause' into uniform sequence".[15] The importance of these thinkers, and particularly of Locke, was as pioneers who questioned the old confident philosophy on which traditional Christianity had been based and to which present-day defenders of orthodoxy wished to return. They had left a legacy of scepticism which some of the essayists found valuable.

As an alternative to Butler a fresh series of answers had also been proposed by S. T. Coleridge and the Maurician school which followed him, and the essayists wrote in the light of their criticism of the *Analogy*. What the Oxford radicals derived directly from Coleridge is, however, difficult to assess. They repeated the generalities of the *Aids to Reflection* and *Confessions of an Inquiring Spirit* about man's religious nature and the superiority of religious experience over a mere evidential theology. When Williams was prosecuted for saying that the bible was the expression of devout reason, the Coleridgeans rushed to his defence : they

---

[14] J. Locke, *The Reasonableness of Christianity*, p. 25, and *An Essay Concerning Human Understanding*, pp. 299-306.

[15] Abbott, II, p. 411.

knew what he meant though the statement itself came from Bunsen. Kant's practical reason had become in Coleridge a means of inward knowledge about God himself, and the scriptures, when read "devoutly" or "inwardly", were its true expression. The essayists certainly saw a demarcation between outer and inner approaches to scripture, without using Coleridge's, as Maurice's, technical distinction between understanding and reason.

In two other ways a knowledge of Coleridge was implied. According to Coleridge, the moral sense was a factor latent in every man; it sprang to life, became aware of itself, when stimulated into reflection. Reading Wilson's Bamptons suggested that he drew on the theory and held that the Church's duty, above all else, was to awaken such moral sense in the individual man.[16] Secondly, Wilson's "ideology" drew on Coleridge's belief that a subject could be defined by its "idea", "that which is given by the knowledge of its ultimate aim", and this could be considered without necessarily referring to the historical or practical realisation of the idea.[17] But Wilson applied this in a reductionist manner to the bible, idealising persons and facts in a way which went beyond anything sanctioned by Coleridge. This, perhaps, suggested the extent of Coleridgean colouring in *Essays and Reviews*. The references to the sage of Highgate were obligatory: so Powell spoke of his suspicion of the evidences, Pattison of his dismissal of the evidence-makers, and Wilson of his innovations in the understanding of Church and State, and, in particular, the theories of usufruct and nationalty. Jowett emphasised his importance as a pioneer of biblical criticism. But all this was *en passant*: the essential Coleridge was lost in the essayists' hectic pursuit of a new theology. For them Coleridge did not go far enough, and Powell, indeed, criticised him in *The Spirit of the Inductive Philosophy* for identifying the First Cause with God as older thinkers had done.[18] Powell's concept of faith, however indistinct, could not be understood apart from Coleridge; it depended on the inherently and objectively given reality of conscience as much as anything in Coleridge. But always there lurked a reference to Locke — and, unless understanding (human) and reason (divine) were properly distinguished, the logic of the understanding would be imposed on the conscience and the reason.

---

[16] H.B. Wilson, *The Communion of Saints*, pp. 217-8.

[17] *ER*, pp. 200-3.

[18] B. Powell, *The Spirit of the Inductive Philosophy*, p. 162. Cf. *Oxford Essays, 1857*, p. 180.

Maurice seized on these differences to show the contrast with the positive Platonism of Cambridge. The age had exalted the understanding above its place, and he criticised the esteem in which Locke was held and the dominion of empiricism and logic. "What Aristotle was to the German in the sixteenth, John Locke is to the Englishman in the nineteenth century. His dogmas have become part of our habitual faith; they are accepted without study as a tradition".[19] Hort thought that Locke (with Zwingli) was the real originator of Wilson's Bampton lectures; the "Germanizing", so much criticised, merely lay on the surface.[20] Coleridge himself had anticipated these verdicts. He had read the Cambridge Platonists as well as the German Romantics and early Idealists, and that emancipated him not only from the Deists but also from the tradition of English empiricism, from a deterministic universe, and from the necessitarianism of Hartley and the "mechanico-corpuscular" theology of Locke; so, unlike Jowett or Pattison, Coleridge actually spoke of the "misgrowth since 1688" with its celebration of "Mr Locke's reputation".[21] (That qualification is obviously more true of Jowett or Pattison than of Temple and, perhaps, Williams. Temple had some claim to be on the side of the Coleridgeans against Locke; he spoke for a less assertive, more reflective theology which was not totally absent from *Essays and Reviews*).

Another figure who interposed between the essayists and Butler was Thomas Arnold. The great educationist had cleared a passage for all the radicals who followed him, in his views about reform of the Church and the modernising of the university, in his acceptance of a moderate biblical criticism and first-hand knowledge of Niebuhr, Herder and others. Stanley spoke of his "idea" of the early Church in his commentary on I and II Corinthians. Wilson saw him as a precursor when evolving his own theories of the Church — Arnold had said, among other things, that the ministry was given only a *legal*, not supernatural, qualification by the bishops[22] — and Powell might have quoted Arnold on the evidences : "the main point [is] not the truth of Christianity *per se*, as a theorem to be proved, but the wisdom of our abiding by it, and whether there is anything else for it but the life of beast or devil". The evidential arguments no longer served as they had done in the eighteenth century. "It is what we call the *Time-Spirit* which is

---

[19] F.D. Maurice, *Theological Essays*, pp. 464-6.
[20] Hort, I, p. 210.
[21] S.T. Coleridge, *On the Constitution of Church and State*, p. xi.
[22] T. Arnold, *Principles of Church Reform*, Miscellaneous works, p. 329.

sapping the proof from miracles, — it is the '*Zeitgeist*' itself".[23] Williams held that Coleridge "threw secular prognostication altogether out of the idea of prophecy", and added that "Dr Arnold, and his truest followers, bear, not always consistently, on the same side".[24]

Perhaps Williams' qualification was significant, for who were Arnold's "truest followers"? Pusey and his supporters maintained that *Essays and Reviews* was an Arnoldian book, and, taken in its broadest sense, the seven would not have denied that. But, though his practical proposals could be given easy labels, Arnold's actual intellectual legacy was more difficult to trace. Arnold died early, before the promise was fulfilled; would an older Arnold have accepted the negativisms and hesitancies of *Essays and Reviews* as his own? If the Broad Church was capable of being divided into moderate and extreme wings, Arnold would have been found in the former with Hare, Maurice and the Cambridge thinkers. In a fundamental respect, that of the analogy between individual and race in the education of mankind, he parted company with the Oxford school.[25] Jowett criticised Arnold's theory of the Church. "Its fault is not simply, I think, that it is too concrete, but that it does not acknowledge the true *concreteness* of the Church as it is. When it gets out of the Ideal, it is not merely impracticable, but a falsehood". Arnold, like Bunsen, was mistaken in thinking that any "true external form" of the Church could correspond to that true reality of the Church which was "spiritual". What needed to be changed was not the system but the moral tone of the English Church. He judged Arnold's outward form in two lines from Hegel:

> "Was ist wirklich, das ist vernünftig:
> Was ist vernünftig, das ist wirklich".
> (The real is the rational, the rational is the real).[26]

Forsaking these earlier thinkers, what other choices could the essayists make? On the theological Left, more radical than they were themselves, were intuitionists and Unitarians; scepticism was represented by Mill; and a third choice was the embryonic school of English Idealism. The essayists were sympathetic to each, and yet asked for something more.

Of the radicals, Francis W. Newman was mentioned by both Powell and Williams. The latter allowed that Newman, in his book on Hebrew

[23] A.P. Stanley, *Life and Correspondence of Thomas Arnold*, I, p. 252.
[24] *ER*, p. 66.
[25] See below, p. 288.
[26] Abbott, I, pp. 150-1, 154.

monarchy, was "historically consistent in his expositions", but failed in
the "*Ideal* element; else he would see that the typical ideas (of patience
or of glory) in the Old Testament, find their culminating fulfilment in the
New". Powell linked Newman with John Sterling, Theodore Parker
and Emerson among those who evinced a "deep-seated and devout belief
in the Divine perfections", yet held that the acceptance of theistic
principles "in their highest spiritual purity", was utterly at variance with
all conception of suspensions of the laws of nature, or with the idea of
any kind of external manifestation addressed to the senses, as over-ruling
the higher and more worthy convictions of moral sense and religious
intuition — which explained Powell's own position, of course. Powell
pressed the right of an appeal superior to that of all miracles, to our own
moral tribunal, to the principle that "the human mind is competent to sit
in moral and spiritual judgment on a professed revelation", even if that
meant, as in Newman's case, a rejection of all miracles. He agreed with
Newman that "if miracles are made the sole criterion, then amid the
various difficulties attending the scrutiny of evidence, and the detection
of imposture, an advantage is clearly given to the shrewd sceptic over the
simple-minded and well-disposed disciple, utterly fatal to the purity of
faith".[27]

A. S. Farrar, indeed, thought that little separated the essayists from
the author of *The Soul* and *Phases of Faith*, and he did not mean this
entirely critically: the essayists reached out to someone who was on the
fringe of the Church and showed how much could be said in common;
like him they questioned the extent and manner of revelation and
searched for the eternal element in scripture and Church teaching which
could be separated from the temporary elements now under pressure
from intellectual evolution and speculation. But they were different from
Newman in loyally holding that God had revealed his will to men, and in
being conservative of revelation, desiring to surrender a part in order to
save the remainder.[28]

However, no one could pretend that Newman was a major thinker; the
essayists were better compared with a figure who dominated the
intellectual scene. J. S. Mill did not influence them in any direct
manner, but he provided a comment on the subjectivism championed in
their book. Mill certainly read *Essays and Reviews*; when, some years

---

[27] *ER*, pp. 67n., 114, 122-3.
[28] A.S. Farrar, *Critical History of Free Thought*, p. 492.

later, he wanted to refer to it, he found that he had lent his copy to someone who did not return it.[29]

Taine reported in the *Revue des Deux Mondes* of his experience in meeting a young Englishman of genius at the British Association meeting in Oxford in 1860 who, when catechised on the philosophy of his country, named Jowett and Mill as the original thinkers of England.[30] It did not need a genius to see *some* similarities. His essay on *Liberty*, read alongside Wilson's essay on the national Church, breathed the same spirit, at least in Wilson's section on the need to free the intellectual class of the ministry from restraints which hampered the work of moral regeneration, and in the call to the Church to release the moral energies in the national life, instead of being concerned about its own prerogatives. Like many of their contemporaries, the essayists were indebted to Mill for his philosophical justification of the science of induction. Powell referred to the *Logic* in *The Spirit of the Inductive Philosophy*, while emphasising that experience was more than a mere collection of facts such as sense and observation furnished, and that in the analogical process, "a large assumption is necessarily implied beyond and independent of any accumulation of facts".[31] Jowett's remarks on doctrinal language recalled Mill's teaching that words altered their character in the process of time, becoming, not enriched, but mere ghosts of their old self, losing both range and character — an outstanding example being the term "catholic". Among other references to Mill, Pattison, in his article on "Learning in the Church of England", in the *National Review* for January, 1863, lifted an idea from *Representative Government* when warning of a majority in the Church which became supreme and "has no longer need of the arms of reason".[32]

For his part, Mill was sympathetic : he had the essayists in mind when he declared in his inaugural address at St. Andrews in 1867, "I hold entirely with those clergymen who elect to remain in the national Church, so long as they are able to accept its Articles and confessions in any sense or with any interpretation consistent with common honesty, whether it be the generally received interpretation or not". If they deserted the Church the national provision for religious teaching and worship would

[29] *The Later Letters of John Stuart Mill*, IV, p. 1673.
[30] J. McCosh, *The Supernatural in Relation to the Natural*, p. 359.
[31] B. Powell, *The Spirit of the Inductive Philosophy*, p. 6.
[32] *National Review*, January, 1863, p. 218.

be left to those who took only the narrowest view of the formularies. It would be an evil hour if such reformers were cast out.[33]

But Utilitarianism as such could not have been very attractive to the essayists' mind: it was too sober, too earth-bound; it cut too easily through the paradoxes and complexities which Jowett thought were the stuff of human reality. Logic in Mill and Jowett led to very different results. The gulf between them was shown in Mill's readiness to entertain a restated argument from design, in his study of *Theism* in 1874. Of course, it was hedged about with qualifications; nonetheless, "sight, being a fact not precedent but subsequent to the putting together of the organic structure of the eye, can only be connected with the production of that structure in the character of a final, not an efficient cause; that is, it is not sight itself but an antecedent idea of it that must be the efficient cause. But this at once marks the origin as proceeding from an intelligent will".[34]

For the essayists, however, such language lacked a "religious" tone, as its eighteenth-century precursors did. Mill considered, on purely object-ive, rational grounds that the argument from design might be looked at again; no personal interest was specially engaged, and the result only reached the lower levels of probability. Like the other arguments in *Theism*, it suggested the existence of a Demiurge, lacking infinite power, wisdom, justice and the like — for Jowett and the others the God of the Old Testament and of popular misconceptions which they wished to avoid. Powell, as the clerical scientist who talked most about an intelligence behind the moral order of the universe, was yet at the furthest remove from Mill because, ultimately, "Christianity, as a real religion, must be viewed apart from connexion with physical things". Was this an example of that "intuitive philosophy" which Mill so chastised at various points in his career?

Perhaps in the Idealist school, as represented in T. H. Green, may be seen the real point of the essayists' references to Locke. Like Hume Locke had clarified the processes of thinking and thus the way was made open for Kant — though (as Green said), "they only half realised what they were professing", and a "mistaken materialism" had resulted in the nineteenth century from this confusion.[35] Green was only beginning his career when *Essays and Reviews* was published, but his philosophy may suggest the background to the further development of the essayists'

[33] Abbott, I, p. 294 n. 3.
[34] J.S. Mill, *Theism*, pp. 30, 32.
[35] *Works of Thomas Hill Green*, III, pp. lxxxii-iii.

thought, had their book been successful. Certainly, Hegelianism at Balliol filled out the meagre skeleton of Jowett's theology, and the personal connection between the two men was close. (Yet Jowett's hatred of all systems continued; he eventually discouraged Green from teaching at Balliol and even spoke harshly of his own German gods in this connection. "He intoxicates himself and others with Kant and does not see that these dead German philosophies cannot be revived and end in nothing"; again there was a reference to Locke — Green would do well to "recognise his greatness" [36]). Green helped Stanley in 1861 in drawing up the *Statements on Christian Doctrine and Practice* from Jowett's works, which was intended to stop the mouths of his accusers, and he rejoiced at Jowett's election as Master in 1870. Like Jowett he read Baur's *Paulus* which suggested that Christian theology was virtually the creation of St. Paul, and he, too, preferred the fourth gospel, with its idealisation of Christ, to the more "historic" tone of the synoptics.

A fine passage in Green's address on *Faith* in 1877, as expounded by R. L. Nettleship, suggests the higher intentions of the essayists' acceptance of historical criticism, though Green's teaching was obviously more sophisticated than Jowett's view of Christianity as a body of universal truths. Faith was "absolutely independent of anything that can be called historical evidence. It is a certain disposition of man's mind or character, consisting in the consciousness of his potential unity with God, and issuing in the effort to realise this unity in his life". Any attempt to derive or account for faith from antecedent efforts was necessarily fallacious; "it is because his consciousness is already faith that the events are accepted and interpreted by him as evidences of faith". As the seven did he thus criticised the view that the spiritual life "depended" on past events; the result of such an effort was dogmatic theology, a phase of the human mind which had lost its hold on the original religious experience of the founders of Christianity.

Could the essayists have gone on to affirm Green's concept of faith? "Faith and knowledge, rightly understood, cannot come into conflict, for both alike have their source in reason and self-consciousness. The impulse to knowledge is due to the consciousness, however dim, of a reality 'one, complete and absolute' which the self potentially is... The known world, then, is never actually what it is in possibility, and if by 'nature' we understand the known world, we must say that nature and the knowledge of nature never satisfies the demand for complete reality

---

[36] Jowett MSS, Box F, letter to J.A. Symonds, December, 1880, Cf. Abbott, II, p. 199.

which reason makes and cannot help making, This inextinguishable and unfulfilled demand is faith".[37] The language was Idealist, but some of the aspirations would be familiar from the pages of *Essays and Reviews*.

Green can only suggest what might have been; there were no radical Broad Churchmen in the 'eighties, except Hatch, to take up his themes; his immanentism was, however, put to good use (though in a way of which Jowett and Pattison disapproved) in *Lux Mundi* by his pupils Charles Gore and J. R. Illingworth. Green's temper was also, of course, quite different; the polemics and acerbity of a generation before were missing. He was also different in being "no despiser of ordinances". "We cannot afford to individualise ourselves in respect of outward symbols. We do wrong to ourselves and to them if we allow any intellectual vexation at the mode in which they may be presented to us to prevent us from their due use".[38] Such caution was certainly absent from *Essays and Reviews* — perhaps because it was a transitional work. Had Idealism been stronger, more native at the time, the writers could have anchored themselves firmly. As it was, they were not sure, in rejecting the old theologies, what they should turn to instead.

But if English landmarks on their horizon were not clear, others were. Already in 1846, in his sermons on the Apostolic Age, Stanley had contrasted Butler and Paley with new superior divines from Germany — with Bunsen, Rothe, Schelling and others. In his lecture on "The Theology of the Nineteenth Century", in 1865, he quoted from Torlonia, the Roman Catholic scholar, speaking a year before *Essays and Reviews* appeared: "Without the knowledge of German theological speculation and research, England *must* know it — no deep study of Christian doctrine may be achieved".[39] In *Essays and Reviews* the contrast was accepted completely; as Williams said, there was in Germany a "pathway streaming with light" for the theologian, while darkness reigned elsewhere. Bunsen, as his chosen subject, was meant to recommend the rest, for he was well known to the English, moving in the highest circles and, with his astonishing output and creativity, "touching anew everything that he produces".[40]

Another candidate who might have been equally suitable for Williams' eulogy was Richard Rothe, leader of the "School of Conciliation" in Germany. Arnold had long given his blessing to Rothe's "first position,

---

[37] *Works of Thomas Hill Green*, III, pp. xcvii-xcix.
[38] *Ibid.*, pp. cv-cvi.
[39] *Fraser's Magazine*, February, 1865, p. 253.
[40] *ER*, pp. 66-7.

that the state and not the Church is the perfect form under which
Christianity is to be developed", while J. R. Seeley's *Ecce Homo* in 1865
echoed his teaching that the Church was destined to dissolve into the
state as the latter realised its moral potential.[41] Rothe met Erskine of
Linlathen; Stanley made a detour in one of his German journeys to see
him; Jowett thought Rothe an "excellent man"; Pattison attended his
lectures and, like Williams, mentioned him in his various writings.[42]
Wilson's Bamptons repeated Rothe's argument that while science and
philosophy had moved into the modern period, the Church, which had
once shared a common language with them, still clung to the expressions
and symbols of the past, which had now passed out of the experience of
ordinary men. "If these warnings are necessary for the theologians of the
country in which they were written, much more so are they for those of
our own; for, while our theology has been isolated and stationary, our
science has been ecumenical and progressive".[43] Rothe was not mentioned in *Essays and Reviews*, but Edward Garbett felt his presence as
"one who had advanced speculation for the assistance it gave to religious
feeling", and Wilson's work showed some similarities.[44]

More than anything which they owed to the eighteenth century, or to
Coleridge, Arnold and others, the essayists' "Germanism" is the most
important element in their book. It needs to be analysed carefully.
Readers who kept abreast of translations, in T. and T. Clark's Cabinet
series and Foreign Theological Library, which had published a number
of important works since 1846, found little that was fresh; those who
knew the philosophical histories of Lewes and Morell, which described
German intellectual development since the eighteenth century in great
detail, or Cousin's studies of Kant, might have wished for clearer
references. Nor were the essayists mere parrots, as Hengstenberg — who
saw the German influence everywhere in their work — claimed.[45] Jowett
said that clearly in his Commentary. After noting Kant, Schleiermacher,
Fichte, Daub, Schelling and Hegel (the latter more sympathetically), in
their theories about the Atonement, Jowett remarked that "Englishmen,
especially, feel a national dislike at the 'things which accompany
salvation' being perplexed with philosophical theories". And, though

[41] A.P. Stanley, *op. cit.*, II, pp. 92-3. J.R. Seeley, *Ecce Homo*, c. 9.
[42] F. Lichtenberger, *History of German Theology in the 19th Century*, p. 186. Prothero, I,
p. 258. M. Pattison, *Memoirs*, p. 301.
[43] H.B. Wilson, *op. cit.*, p. 53 n.
[44] E. Garbett, *The Bible and Its Critics*, pp. 89, 99, 155. Cf. *Aids to Faith*, p. 163 n.
[45] *G*, 26 March, 1862, p. 303.

Hegel and Schelling had been made to look absurd in uncouth English translations, "yet it may be doubted whether this philosophy can ever have much connexion with the Christian life. It seems to reflect at too great a distance what ought to be very near us. It is metaphysical, not practical; it creates an atmosphere in which it is difficult to breathe; it is useful as supplying a light or law by which to arrange the world, rather than as a principle of action or warmth".[46]

With that qualification their "Germanism" is explained. They would have used French or American thought if it had illuminated their position — Wilson launched his essay on the basis of some lectures at Geneva which, he believed, raised issues "of wide Christian concern, and especially to ourselves". But the Germans had advanced further along the course on which the Stanleyites held that all religious systems, of whatever country or origin, had embarked, and they provided useful illustrations and, perhaps, warnings. The influence is present in a much more broad and pervasive sense than the occasional allusion or citation, and it is certainly more radical than at first sight. Conservatives like Hengstenberg or Kliefoth were not mentioned, except disparagingly, and Bunsen, who was so prominent, was less important than the writers who lay behind these general assumptions, like Lessing, Strauss, and, above all, Kant and the thinkers who followed him.

The extent of the impress of this thought on *Essays and Reviews* can only be shown by using the essayists' writings in general, but it should make much in their book clear. Stanley's high claims for his friends can be vindicated; they were too deferential — "the capital of learning is in the hands of Germans" wrote Pattison[47] — and they could hardly make English theology ecumenical simply by making it so continental; but when placed side by side with native divinity, *Essays and Reviews* was truly revolutionary.

Lessing appeared early in Jowett's intellectual biography; and not long before his death the Master quoted the "remarkable" saying which he used in the essay: "the Christian religion had been tried for eighteen centuries, the religion of Christ remained to be tried".[48] The "Counter-Propositions" of the *Wolfenbüttel Fragments* lay beneath Jowett's essay, as others, and one line had particular echoes: "The religion is not true because the evangelists and apostles taught it, but they taught it because

---

[46] Epistles (2 ed.), II, p. 585.
[47] WR, April, 1857, p. 332.
[48] Abbott, II, p. 362. ER, p. 362.

it is true".[49] Lessing's importance for the nineteenth century was noticed by the *Prospective Review* in 1854, in speaking of the "wonder and delight, the awful sense of intellectual space" kindled by the essay on the "Education of the Human Race".[50] That conviction three years earlier caused F. W. Robertson to re-translate the work (an English version in 1806 was before its time), which he prefaced with suitable evolutionary lines from Tennyson and the argument that the doctrine of everlasting punishment must give way to the nobler idea of man's growth in moral education.[51] It was entirely appropriate, therefore, that Temple's essay celebrated some of Lessing's ideas and was evidently written with Robertson's work in mind.

Temple followed Lessing's theme of the three ages of man and of man's life as an analogy of the growth of the human race from childhood to maturity. "The human heart refuses to believe in a universe without purpose", said Temple. "The human race, no less than the individual, was educated for a purpose", said Lessing. Both saw revelation as education, "what education is to the individual man, revelation is to the human race" (Lessing), and close similarities were found in their interpretation of the first stage in the process. The Jews were for Lessing the "future teachers of the human race"; Temple spoke of the "Jewish nation, selected among all as the depository of what may be termed, in a pre-eminent sense, religious truth" (Temple wrote less stylishly than Lessing). The education of the Jews was one "adapted to the age of children, an education by rewards and punishments addressed to the senses" (Lessing): Temple said that the Jews represented the childhood of the race and were taught by discipline, as was suitable for a child. For both the Jews' schooling was in the understanding of the oneness of God, "the idea of the One" (Lessing), "the unity and spirituality of God" (Temple), and the post-exilic period looked to a coming deterioration which was in turn succeeded by a higher stage — "Christ came!"

Other similarities were less close, and Christ for Temple was more than Lessing's preacher of immortality. But his concentration on the liberated study of scripture was illuminated by Lessing's concluding section in which he held that in the final stage the bible would give way to a higher knowledge. Temple, believing that the final age had arrived, did not say

---

[49] G.E. Lessing, *op. cit.*, p. 18.
[50] *Prospective Review*, X, 1854, pp. 407, 409.
[51] G.E. Lessing, *The Education of the Human Race*, translator's preface. Cf. S.A. Brooke, *Life and Letters of Frederick W. Robertson*, I, pp. 330-2.

that the bible was superseded, but his only interest was its "immediate" critical study, and he cut short his remarks.[52]

Other members of the team saw revelation in terms of stages of education. Williams spoke of the "law of growth, traceable throughout the Bible, as in the world": history showed God to have trained mankind and to have educated men and nations. Goodwin held that the plan of providence for mankind was a progressive one. "God made use of imperfectly informed men to lay the foundations of that higher know-ledge for which the human race was destined", and the Mosaic cos-mogony was a human utterance, "which it has pleased Providence to use in a special way for the education of mankind". Jowett, speaking of the "education of the world", postulated a connection between the develop-ment of thought in scripture and the "increasing purpose which through the ages ran". "Such a growth or development may be regarded as a kind of progress from childhood to manhood". But, the "anticipation of truth which came from without to the childhood or youth of the human race is [now] witnessed to within; the revelation of God is not lost but renewed in the heart and understanding of the man". The continuous growth of revelation was part of a larger whole extending over the whole earth and reaching to another world.[53]

Lessing stood for the historical outlook. The essayists thus affirmed the first and abiding principle of their book — the proper study of the past and its relation to the present. The choice of Lessing also suggested a particular understanding of the historical question. What did the eight-eenth-century thinker mean by progress? Here Thirlwall's criticism of Temple's essay was worth noting. Thirlwall's charges, throughout his long episcopate, were the witness of a learned liberalism that did not lose its critical spirit in the face of sudden enthusiasms. Thirlwall felt that Temple had abandoned that position by taking over Lessing's analogy between the development of the race and the development of the individual.[54] Lessing saw progress as the "March of Mind", a concep-tion that was largely mechanical and utilitarian and altogether too abstract. The older Liberal Anglicans, Arnold, Hare, Milman, and Thirlwall himself, contended for a view of history which took the concrete reality of the individual man seriously, and so made a real philosophy of history, and a scientific approach to the subject,

---

[52] G.E. Lessing, *Theological Writings*, pp. 82-98. *ER*, p. 1-49.

[53] *ER*, pp. 52, 77, 250, 253, 387, 388-9. For similar views on progress as education cf. B. Jowett, *The Dialogues of Plato* (1 ed), II, p. 177.

[54] D. Forbes, *The Liberal Anglican Idea of History*, p. 6f.

possible. From their point of view there was no real analogy in this respect between the individual and the whole race: the human race was not one, nor was the unity of history actual — it was teleological, it existed in hope, as the individual in his cycle of growth from childhood to maturity overcame the contradictions within himself caused by sin, and so made "progress" possible. They were prepared to extend the analogy to the life of nations but not to the entire race itself — a position also held by Ewald.[55]

In contrast to this, Temple said, "man cannot be considered as an individual. He is, in reality, only man by virtue of his being a member of the human race... we are to look for that progress which is essential to a spiritual being subject to the lapse of time, not only in the individual, but also quite as much in the race taken as a whole". The power by which the present gathered into itself the results of the past, "transforms the human race into a colossal man, whose life reaches from the creation to the day of judgment".[56] This lack of concrete historical reference allowed the essayist to multiply his analogies — thus, he suggested a new category, the Church also developed from childhood to maturity, and its growth was also the "development of the human race" — but at a cost, for they seemed highly forced and artificial.

Temple did not use Lessing uncritically, and he also owed something to Comte and to the *Homme Moyen*, the "mean man", of Quételet and Buckle, who was the statistical product of moral as well as natural regularity, and denoted the average or collective mind rather than the individual. He did not see progress simply on sensationalist psychological lines, as the mind being filled by the machinery of the association of ideas, and he was too aware of sin to mistake material advance for spiritual growth. But a view of history on so vast a scale obviously had dangers. Thirlwall warned about them, Robertson provided an example. One must allow, said Robertson, the "inevitable necessity" that the mind must pass through phases of ignorance, doubt and even error, before it could be capable of receiving pure truth.[57]

If progress was so inexorable, if one stage followed another, how could certainty be found? Lessing's gift of historical consciousness was ambiguous; a gap yawned between contingent historical facts and the "necessary truths of reason". He himself believed that if facts were to be the ground of faith, they must be of the repeatable variety, witnessing to

---

[55] *Göttingische Gelehrte Anzeigen*, 24 July, 1861, p. 1161.
[56] *ER*, pp. 2-3.
[57] G.E. Lessing, *The Education of the Human Race*, translator's preface, p. xiii.

the persistent and essential life of the universe and humanity. The real could teach us only insofar as it had an ideal kernel, redeeming it from the character of solitary phenomena.[58] The theory of progressive education was obviously a way of crossing the "ugly wide ditch", whether or not Lessing himself intended it, and the essayists accordingly presented history as a schooling in truths which yet had no final dependence on history. Temple suggested that man in his maturity at last realised what as a child he had grasped intuitively, the ageless verities enshrined in the life of Christ and the early Church, "perfect simplicity, the singleness of heart, the openness, the child-like earnestness". All the essayists spoke of conscience, intuition and feeling in the sense that these escaped the straitjacket of the merely historical. Thirlwall said that this was no answer, and others recalled Coleridge's criticism of Lessing for teaching that the "most unquestioned and unquestionable historic evidence is in no degree a substitute for the evidence of my own senses"[59] — so the scholar might be as historically radical as he liked; truth did not need the security of such studies and, indeed, he might be embarrassed if eye-witnesses claimed a specific historical vindication of it. It is doubtful if the essayists saw the point of Coleridge's argument, even if they were aware of it. They accepted the definition of the debate laid down by Lessing, and they readily took to the tradition which followed him, to Kant ("the historical can serve for illustration, not demonstration"), Fichte ("only the metaphysical can save, never the historical")[60] — and David Friedrich Strauss.

Strauss in *Essays and Reviews* present a problem. The essayists were sensitive in case a real connection was detected, for he would do their cause no good, and Christology was not their main concern. Powell and Williams both disliked Strauss's scepticism and hard-heartedness.[61] But all the conservatives from F. C. Cook downwards said that he was there, and Bishop Hampden spoke of "their great text book, *Leben Jesu*".[62]

The two books were obviously similar in the notoriety that they achieved. Strauss had accepted Lessing's challenge and wielded all the weapons of historical criticism. For those whose task it was to write on

---

[58] *Prospective Review*, X, 1854, pp. 409, 421-2.
[59] G.E. Lessing, *Theological Writings*, Introduction by H. Chadwick, p. 32.
[60] *Ibid.*, p. 32.
[61] B. Powell, *The Order of Nature*, pp. 335-52. *Edinburgh Review*, 1847, p. 415.
[62] H. Hampden, ed., *Some Memorials of Renn Dickson Hampden*, p. 212. Cf. *British and Foreign Evangelical Review*, 1861, pp. 407-30, "The Oxford Essayists — Their Relation to Christianity and to Strauss and Baur".

current difficulties about the bible, he provided a quick way out. "If the mythical view be once admitted, the innumerable and never otherwise to be harmonised discrepancies and chronological contradictions in the gospel histories disappear, as it were, at one stroke".[63] The escape was too easy, it would also have deprived the essayists of a livelihood as biblical critics. Yet if one admitted a large element of the ideal in scripture, as Jowett, Williams and Wilson did, how were his conclusions to be avoided? Strauss stigmatised all Kantians (the name did just as well for the essayists) who lacked the courage of their convictions. They saw that long before the existence of the biblical records the disposition towards a moral religion was latent in the human mind, though its first manifestations were directed to the worship of the deity and, on this account, gave occasion to the "pretended revelations". Kant admitted that the sense that he gave to the sacred books had not always existed in the intention of the authors but (Strauss implied, and most of the essayists would surely have agreed) he saw nothing incongruous in this if, in fact, the moral sense had preceded everything else. The moral thoughts were, therefore, the fundamental object of the history, though Kant had failed to show the relation between the Ideal and the symbolic representation suggested by it and how it was that the one came to be expressed by the other.[64]

The difficulties of remaining in a half-way position were personified in Wilson. He sounded a proper note of caution. "An example of the critical ideology carried to excess is that of Strauss, which resolves into an ideal the whole of the historical and doctrinal person of Jesus". But he wished to show that the XXXIX Articles permitted a non-historical interpretation of scriptural "facts", and thus made complete the freedom of the Anglican clergyman in the nineteenth century, and so he added: "...it by no means follows, because Strauss has substituted a mere shadow for the Jesus of the Evangelists, and has frequently descended into a minute captiousness in details, that there are not traits in the scriptural person of Jesus, which are better explained by referring them to an ideal rather than an historical origin". Wilson shunned any mention of "myth", but his principle of ideology was obviously meant to cover Strauss's term.

The historical parts of the bible (he wrote) had a value which consisted rather in the significance of the ideas which they awakened than in the

---

[63] D.F. Strauss, *The Life of Jesus*, pp. 56-7.
[64] *Ibid.*, pp. 51-2.

scenes themselves which they depicted. "And as Churchmen, or as Christians, we may vary as to this value in particulars — that is, as to the extent of the verbal accuracy of a history, or of its spiritual significance... these varieties will be determined partly by the peculiarities of men's mental constitution, partly by the nature of their education, circumstances and special studies". The ideal method could be applied both to giving an account of the origin of parts of scripture, and also in the explanation of scripture, and he claimed that this principle was derived from the bible itself. "...it would be wrong to lay down, that whenever the New Testament writers refer to Old Testament histories, they imply of necessity that the historic truth was the first to them. For their purposes it was often wholly in the background, and the history, valuable only in its spiritual application. The same may take place with ourselves, and history and tradition be employed emblematically, without, on that account, being regarded as untrue. We do not apply the term 'untrue' to parable, fable, or proverb, although their words correspond with ideas, not with material facts; as little should we do so, when narratives have been the spontaneous product of true ideas, and are capable of reproducing them".

The origin of Christianity might rest only on probable evidence, but the ideologian possessed a method which relieved him of many difficulties. "For relations which may repose on doubtful grounds as matter of history and, as history, be incapable of being ascertained or verified, may yet be equally suggestive of true ideas with facts absolutely certain". The spiritual significance of the Transfiguration, Christ's healings, and the feeding of the 5,000 was the same, though we applied to them a non-factual basis. The same was also true of Christ's descent as son of David and of the circumstances of his nativity. Wilson was plainly referring to Strauss, who had found a mythical explanation for all these events and, in particular, for the Annunciation: but (said the essayist), "the incarnification of the Divine Immanuel remains, although the angelic appearances which herald it in the narratives of the Evangelists may be of ideal origin according to the conceptions of former days". The story of Adam and Eve was an example of the form in which tradition would throw itself spontaneously, but the great moral truth which it represented, of the brotherhood of all human beings, of their community in suffering, frailty, even in moral "corruption", remained. The writer proposed similar emblematic interpretations of the Eucharist, baptism, the Church's hierarchical government, and eschatological expectations of Christ's second coming.

This was Strauss without tears — but also without the creativity and insight which made *Das Leben Jesu* so outstanding. Wilson's vague eternal truths distilled from the gospel histories might seem less offensive than Strauss's mythical categories, but his Christ was more shadowy. The conclusions were the same: "The ideologian may sometimes be thought sceptical, and be sceptical or doubtful, as to the historical value of related facts; but the historical value is not always to him the most important; frequently it is quite secondary. And, consequently, discrepancies in narratives, scientific difficulties, defects in evidence, do not disturb him...".[65]

There was one other possible allusion to Strauss, on the last page of Jowett's essay. Its appeal to the modern interpreter to witness to the truth, no matter what the cost, recalled Strauss's final paragraphs on the "relations of the critical and speculative theology to the Church" and the dilemma of the thinker who must either elevate the people to his ideas, or adapt himself to the conceptions of the community, or — to avoid betraying himself — to leave the ministry.[66]

Whatever their reservations about Strauss, allegiance to Kant was a far easier matter. His critical philosophy confirmed the native scepticism which held that religious and moral convictions were not innate but acquired, and doubted any reality other than the *a priori* structure of human knowledge and experience. Their opponents saw Kant in the essayists' preoccupation with the question of knowledge and their consequent difficulties about divine revelation. Wilson expressed these difficulties in clear Kantian terms in the *Oxford Essays* of 1857. "The question is not, whether we will believe on God's word, but what is his word? how far has he spoken? what has he said?" How did man "know" about God?[67]

There were few direct references to Kant in *Essays and Reviews*, but some allusions were obvious, and that was to be expected since Jowett had read the two *Critiques* (and catechised Stanley on his knowledge of them) as a young man, so had Temple; and Pattison thought that Kant's critical approach was already foreshadowed in the problems which beset English divinity following Locke and Hume.[68] His teaching had definite advantages over Butler. The distinction between the pure and practical

---

[65] *ER*, pp. 199-204.
[66] *Ibid.*, pp. 431-3 cf. with D.F. Strauss, *op. cit.*, pp. 781-4.
[67] *Oxford Essays, 1857*, p. 120.
[68] Abbott, I, p. 90. *ER*, p. 257. Cf. Temple Memoirs, I, p. 78 n: "To Kant he [Temple] was faithful to the end of his life, often basing a sermon on him".

reason meant that they could use the former to admit rigorous examination of scripture, early Christian history, and doctrine, and thus be thoroughly up to date, while the practical reason allowed one to postulate in a quite new way the existence of God, the immortality of the soul, the freedom of the will and so forth, on the basis of the mind's own ability to perceive these realities. Kant's emphasis on the categorical imperative, on the voice within, was highly attractive to these moralistic, didactic writers, and cohered so well with the outlook of their age. Whatever the objections about traditional religion, the honest doubters still believed in conscience and duty, and that provided a valuable apologetic weapon.

Nor did Kant deny the need for faith. To be sure, to equate moral consciousness with faith removed it out of the sphere of theology, and it also meant that faith could not inform knowledge in the way which older divines taught. "I had to do away with knowledge in order to make room for faith", said Kant. There was clearly danger in that, and Powell reflected it faithfully: "Matters of clear and positive fact, investigated on critical grounds and supported by exact evidence, are properly matters of knowledge, not of faith", and he preserved Kant's ambiguity, "It is rather in points of less definite character that any exercise of faith can take place".[69]

The Kantian division of reality, the separation between the phenomenal realm and the moral sense, ran through *Essays and Reviews*, from the opening sentence to Jowett's study of scripture at the end. Mansel expostulated in vain, but it was pointless to argue that knowledge of God would not have become a problem had they challenged the division in the first place. The essayists accepted that the world of Newtonian science ruled by necessary causal laws was one thing, the supersensuous world of the free moral agent and of God was another. Kant did not discover this for them, but he stated it with a force and persuasion that they found difficult to resist.

However, they thought that the division could be put to positive use. It meant, first, that any one-sided view of reality, whether that of agnostics or of conservative divines, could be rejected. Powell and Wilson used this aspect of Kant in the service of religion against the Comtists. Despite his popularity in Oxford in the 'fifties, they did not think highly of Auguste Comte's positivism. Powell said that the scientific era had not superseded the metaphysical, nor could induction cover everything. He criticised

---

[69] *ER*, p. 128.

Comte in *The Order of Nature* for not merely placing theology apart from science but for rejecting and disowning theology altogether. "Now, with the strictest acknowledgement of the positive principle in *philosophy*, it does not at all follow that other orders of conceptions do not exist *beyond the region of science*, beyond the analysis and deductions of reason, or the dominion of the positive system, in fact, such are the whole range of moral and aesthetic sentiments, — all matters of taste, of feeling, and of imagination; — and such must be all those higher ideas of spiritual and invisible things which are the proper objects, not of knowledge, but of faith, and which, from their nature, can never enter into the range of philosophical investigation, and can consequently be in no hostility to the strictest positivism in *science*". In opposition to such "grovelling utilitarianism", Kant had given the "most enlarged view of the entire subject".[70] In the *Oxford Essays* of 1857 Powell praised Kant ("that great metaphysician") for drawing, "with a clear and masterly hand the important distinction between strict philosophical reasoning and that kind of moral persuasion which prevails among mankind at large, and suffices for all practical purposes". Kant was not inconsistent, therefore, as Cousin (for instance) had suggested, in seeking conviction for the ideas of the existence of God etc., in the ground of man's moral nature.[71]

Wilson, for his part, saw Comte's drawbacks in his disciple G. H. Lewes, as he said in the *Westminster Review*: "Positivism is the only resting place, as we are told, against scepticism. Positivists must not be too sure of that; questions will recur respecting the observing subject, to reopen all the controversies which they think will shortly be closed for ever". Lewes "must not imagine that philosophy is dead — that there are none to do battle for metaphysics — that all thinking persons have given up as utterly hopeless the endeavour to penetrate some way into Ontology". The Kantian method, "which, however defective it confesses itself to be, however merely relative, after all, its conclusions are, is the only method available with any prospect of result". Indeed, Kant allowed one to go beyond him : "in the perceptions and conceptions the understanding possesses nothing original. But in every judgment, besides these perceptions and conceptions, there is an original element underived from without — the form of the judgment. Hence the 'transcendental clue'".[72] Jowett read Lewes' *History of Philosophy* : he thought it a poor

---

[70] B. Powell, *The Order of Nature*, pp. 195, 197-8.
[71] *Oxford Essays, 1857*, pp. 175-7.
[72] *WR*, January, 1858, pp. 247-9.

296 THE WIDER IMPLICATIONS

thing to have studied all philosophies and to end in adopting that of Comte.[73]

Secondly, Kant's division opened up a new avenue of theological exploration. Opponents held that it was a plain dualism: religion and the external world had become independent of each other, and God's presence in the latter could be described only in immanentist terms. Powell, Temple and Jowett believed that it gave the means for a new unity, which they expressed in different ways. Powell preferred a cosmo- or physico-theology; Temple and Jowett found the division overcome in the concept of God as lawgiver; Jowett also spoke of opposites being brought together, theoretically, in a type of Hegelian metaphysic, and, practically, in the daily experience of believing men. None of the solutions escaped the conservatives' criticisms, but each attempted to take theology into a new world of philosophy, and each rejected the very different employment of Kantianism seen in Mansel.

Powell dismissed Comtism because it split man from nature and failed to give any sense of a divine reality which held them together. The Enlightenment view of a patterned causality — the laws put there by "God" were the explanation for nature's coherence and order — was supplemented by a notion of the life within nature. He spoke of the "sacredness of nature", and of an ultimate unity of principle and universal intelligence, and finally of a "cosmo-theology". He quoted Bunsen on von Humboldt: "The world and the universe itself is a *kosmos*, — a divine whole of life and intellect, — namely by its all-pervading *eternal laws*. Law is the supreme rule of the universe; and that law is wisdom, is intellect, is reason, whether viewed in the formation of planetary systems or in the organisation of the worm". Von Humboldt's *Kosmos* (from which he quoted in *The Order of Nature*) was a "great and masterly work".[74] Other illustrations came from Oken's *Elements of Physico-Philosophy* and, more significantly, from Hans Christian Oersted, the Danish scientist and philosopher of religion. Oersted was a friend of Fichte. Schelling and Schleiermacher, and that gave an extra dimension to his own discovery of electro-magnetism. As the laws of light, electricity, galvanism and magnetism were universal, so were the essential principles of morality; God was to be found in the eternity of law itself and not in arbitrarily setting aside the invariable laws of the physical world. His infinite wisdom was able to guide everything without

---

[73] Abbott, I, pp. 130, 261, II, p. 187.
[74] B. Powell, *The Order of Nature*, p. 167, and *The Spirit of the Inductive Philosophy*, pp. 112-3.

requiring any casual alteration. "The principle of action and the order in existence are not... two distinct objects, but one living, constantly creating and regulating totality of Reason, an eternal living Reason which is God". He denied the Fall, and preferred a theory of the development of the human race from lower to higher on the analogy of the development of the individual man. Oersted entitled his book *The Soul in Nature*, and it was translated into English in 1852.[75]

Powell, who worked in a similar scientific field, found the metaphysics congenial: *The Soul in Nature*, with its vision of a physico-theology, "in almost every point" sanctioned and corroborated his own views in *The Unity of Worlds*, he said.[76] When Oersted held that the "laws of Nature are the thoughts of Nature; and these are the thoughts of God", Powell agreed, and added some remarks on the "conception of order, arrangement and uniformity throughout nature". "This, however inadequately comprehended by our science, is again the evidence of supreme mind, and the universality of order in time and space, the manifestation of the universality and eternity of that supreme mind".[77]

Temple, as a logician, probably had a clearer grasp of the division than Powell, and he was also more aware of the possibility of an agnostic or even anti-Christian science. He drew a total distinction in the opening paragraph of *Essays and Reviews* between a "world of mere phenomena, where all events are bound to one another by a rigid law of cause and effect" ("a supposition possible to the logical understanding") and a "world of spirits which cannot be a mere machine," and which evolved in obedience to a law of its own. As a solution the essay offered little, but he returned to the subject in his Bampton lectures more than twenty years later. The problem was still a Kantian one; Temple said that man's faculties seemed to be hopelessly at variance with each other, the scientific imposing on us one belief, the spiritual another. Kant himself provided no way forward in teaching that man's character was in itself free, "but his separate acts are what that free choice becomes when translated into a series of phenomena, and are bound each to the preceding by the law of unvariable sequence". "It is plain at once that this does not satisfy our consciousness". We *must* reconcile the "mechan-

---

[75] H.C. Oersted, *The Soul in Nature*, pp. 77, 88, 183.

[76] B. Powell, *The Order of Nature*, p. 201.

[77] B. Powell. *The Spirit of the Inductive Philosophy*, p. 112. The term "physico-theology" was not, of course, Powell's own, and his use of it was limited by his belief that only phenomena can be really known; cf. his references to Kant's criticism of the term in the *Oxford Essays* of 1857.

ical firmness of an unbroken law of uniformity in nature with the voice
within", which was free. "In spite of all attempts to explain it away, the
fact that we think ourselves free and hold ourselves responsible remains,
and remains unaffected".

Temple proposed two tentative answers. "The fixity of a large part of
our nature — nay, of all but the whole of it — is a moral and spiritual
necessity", because man was as yet incomplete: in his struggle towards
perfection he needed something constant or permanent in his nature by
which each step was made good. So law in the external world and order
in the moral world were analogous. His other solution was to hold that if
miracle, though exceedingly rare, was possible, and if freedom of the
human will, though limited, could affect conduct, then a unity was
possible; a spiritual purpose could be seen if the two worlds were taken
together — and much in science remained only approximately known in
any case. On his argument there could be no real conflict between science
and religion. "The strictly spiritual in all religion cannot be got out of
phenomena at all". The unity that he found was, of course, an interior
one, and religion ceased to make claims on the external order.
Conscience spoke of a knowledge not derived from phenomena but one
which was a knowledge of ourselves as we were in ourselves, and without
this sense of identity there could be no moral law. The moral law itself
was not simply the command of God but his nature. "He does not make
that law. He is that law. Almighty God and the moral law are different
aspects of what is in itself one and the same". Thus, "external evidences
of revealed religion must have a high place, but cannot have the highest.
A revealed religion must depend for its permanent hold on our obedience
and our duty on its fastening upon our spiritual nature, and if it cannot
do that no evidence can maintain it in its place".[78]

Jowett quoted Kant directly in the Commentary. "There are two
things of which it may be said, that the more we think of them, the more
they fill the soul with awe and wonder — The starry heaven above and
the moral law within". He translated a lengthy section from the *Critique
of Pure Reason*, and then took Kant a stage further:

> "'There are two witnesses', we may add in a later strain of reflection, 'of
> the being of God; the order of nature in the world, and the progress of the
> mind of man. He is not the order of nature, nor the progress of the mind,
> nor both together; but that which is above and beyond them; of which they,
> even if conceived in a single instant, are but the external sign, the highest

---

[78] F. Temple, *The Relations between Religion and Science*, pp. 12, 41, 59, 60, 62, 75, 90.

evidences of God which we can conceive, but not God Himself. The first to the ancient world seemed to be the work of chance, of the personal operation of one or many Divine beings. We know it to be the result of laws endless in their complexity, and yet not the less admirable for their simplicity also. The second has been regarded, even in our own day, as a series of errors capriciously invented by the ingenuity of individual men. We know it to have a law of its own, a continuous order which cannot be inverted; not to be confounded with, yet not wholly separate from, the law of nature and the will of God' ".[79]

The passage was obviously important for Jowett, for he believed that it answered the problem of a divided reality which the philosopher raised. Like Temple he found Kant's solution, of a transcendental freedom, out of time and space, independent of the laws of cause and effect, unsatisfactory. Instead, we should "return to fact and nature". Nature was not empty or merely material. Jowett may, or may not, have drawn on Fichte and Schelling, but he used language reminiscent of them in speaking of the relationship of the will of God and the laws of nature. Certainly the old conceptions of nature which conflicted with the modern scientific view must be abandoned. He spoke of "past and present striving together in our minds": "the modes of thought which we have derived from Scripture and from antiquity are at variance with the language of science... But there is no resting place until we admit freely that the laws of nature and the will of the God of nature are absolutely identical".[80]

If this was the case, then one could use extreme language to emphasise Kant's dualism, to stress the uniformity of nature, and thus to bring home to the reader the implications of the "notion of law". "It seems as if nature came so close to us as to leave no room for the motion of our will". "Wonderful as the human will is, nature, or the God of nature, will not allow us to interfere with the structure of the world in which it is placed":

> "...so wavering and indefinite a sense as our own internal consciousness cannot be brought as a witness against facts of outward experience. These remain as they are, whether we admit them or not. Still, we cannot deny that there are two ways in which the world within and the world without may be considered. We may set a great gulf between them; so that it is impossible to pass from one to the other, opposing God to man, mind and matter, soul and body. We may speak of mind as the correlation of matter, and describe

---

[79] Epistles (1 ed), II, p. 414.
[80] *Ibid.*, (1 ed.), II, p. 413, omitted in second edition.

the soul after the analogy of the body. Morality and religion often seem to require that we retain such distinctions, even in opposition to experience. Or we may regard these pairs of opposites as passing into one another; the opposition of the will of God, and the free agency of man, being lost in the idea of a communion of the Creator with His creatures; that of the soul and body in a higher conception of nature; that of necessity and freedom in the notion of law, which seems to partake of both".[81]

Perhaps the reader might be encouraged to accept such a "higher conception of nature" if he saw the law of God as behind not only the evolution of nature itself but also of religion as a human activity. Jowett was not particularly novel in suggesting this, for Hare had faithfully reported Sterling, as the latter reflected Schelling: "all beliefs have followed each other, in the history of the world, according to a fixed law, and are connected by the same with all the circumstances of each generation; and in obedience to this law they emerge, unfold themselves, pass away, or are transmuted into other modes of faith".[82] Temple also said, in *Essays and Reviews*, that man, as a spiritual as well as material creature, "must be subject to the laws of the spiritual as well as to those of the material world...".[83] Jowett went on to ask, "why should it be thought a thing incredible that God should give law and order to the spiritual no less than the natural creation? That the same strata of stages should be observable in the religions no less than the languages of mankind, as in the structure of the earth?"[84]

If divine law controlled all, what was the place of the human will? Jowett — in a section on Predestination and free will — replied that it was only theology which bothered about the demarcation between divine grace and human action. That was partly because theologians paid too much attention to words. But language was "unequal to the subtlety of nature". We now knew that "no innovation in the use of words or in forms of thought can make any impression on solid facts". "When, instead of reading our own hearts, we seek, in accordance with a preconceived theory, to determine the proportions of the divine and human — to distinguish grace and virtue, the word of God and man — we know not where we are, the difficulty becomes insuperable, we have involved ourselves in artifical meshes, and are bound hand and foot."

---

[81] *Ibid.*, (1 ed.), II, pp. 503-5, omitted in second edition.
[82] J. Sterling, *Essays and Tales*, I, p. 281.
[83] *ER*, p. 2.
[84] Epistles (1 ed.), II, pp. 411-12.

"But when we look by the light of conscience and Scripture on the facts of human nature, the difficulty of itself disappears. No one doubts that he is capable of choosing between good and evil, and that in making this choice he may be supported, if he will, by a power more than earthly. The movement of that Divine power is not independent of the movement of his own will, but coincident and identical with it. Grace and virtue, conscience and the Spirit of God, are not different from each other, but in harmony. If no man can do what is right without the aid of the Spirit, then every one who does what is right has the aid of the Spirit".[85]

In this way, Jowett cut the Gordian knot of a whole series of philosophical and theological questions.

Beyond Kant the German background to *Essays and Reviews* is less distinct. Wilson had spoken of the "transcendental clue" to the evolution of the critical philosophy, which anticipated the later Idealism. Jowett recognised the preoccupation of Daub, Fichte and Schelling with the cognising activity of the mind, in organising the chaotic data of sense. He met the "old twaddler" (his affectionate description of Schelling) several times and thought that the *Verhältniss der bildenden Kunst zur Natur*, which he read in 1849, showed a mind " 'sensitive to every breath' of beauty, and combining with this the highest metaphysical power". Two years earlier he had become "transcendentalised" after reading the *Systems der Naturphilosophie* : it convinced him that the "spiritual world is so much like the ideal one that it is impossible to stir a step in theology without them...".[86] Interest in Schelling would not have been surprising (Fichte — a favourite with the Prince Consort — appeared more abstract, less the Christian): Coleridge had spoken of a genial coincidence between the *Philosophy of Nature* and his own ideas, and Maurice urged Hare to translate the philosopher who had laid the "axe to the root of that Rationalism of which Straussianism and all the kindred notions of our time are the flower".[87] The *Philosophy of Art* appeared in an English translation in 1845. But Wordsworth, reported by Caroline Fox, long before warned of the perils: "Kant, Schelling, Fichte: Fichte, Schelling, Kant; all this is dreary work and does not denote progress".[88] Jowett himself admitted that the new metaphysics was rather a "necessity than a great good": as he said in the Commentary it viewed man as a "microcosm, and we do not feel quite certain whether the whole system is

---

[85] *Ibid.*, (2 ed), II, pp. 618, 620.
[86] Abbott, I, pp. 98, 160, 162.
[87] Maurice, I, p. 289.
[88] C. Fox, *Memories of old Friends*, p. 196.

not the mind itself turned inside out, and magnified in enormous proportions".[89]

The search for unity which the essayists as a whole exemplified was a familiar Idealist theme, and, like Fichte, Schelling and Hegel, they also regarded their own epoch as that new age in which the human spirit had become conscious of the significance of its historical activity and the direction of the whole time process. There were other traits which their opponents detected. Mansel, for one, thought that they had capitulated to a philosophy of the Absolute. Powell, Jowett and Goodwin (why should the latter spend so much time on demolishing Genesis?) demurred about the idea of creation and of a First Cause; was that because there could not be a first moment in time if the Absolute was always and spontaneously manifesting itself?

In two of his books the Savilian Professor touched on these philosophical implications. In *The Order of Nature* he referred to Fichte (Works, volume five) for the difficulty which modern metaphysicians felt about the creation of matter out of nothing, for it was "inconsistent with the philosophy of the absolute".[90] In *The Philosophy of Creation* Powell looked obliquely at those who found it impossible to conceive of eternal matter, "because (it is alleged) it must be self-existent and the like. But, without entering upon them, it will suffice to observe, that all such reasonings are of very different degrees of force to different minds, and, perhaps, have little effect upon the generality". Of course, matter was not divine, "but the organic world is, and always has been, emphatically *one*: modelled on one plan, and amid all diversity exhibiting one common feature of a grand *recondite and comprehensive unity of design*; or as Oersted has expressed it, 'The animals and plants of former periods are all different emanations from the same great thought' ". The term "creation", especially as respecting new species, was adopted by geologists as a mere term of convenience, and Powell thought that it was better understood as a perpetual process. "The idea of a *beginning* or of *creation*, in the sense of the original operation of the Divine volition to constitute nature and matter, is beyond the province of physical *philosophy*, and can only belong to that of *faith*, and find expression in the language of *inspiration*"[91] — again, Powell's division between truths of knowledge and truths of faith was complete. In *Essays and Reviews* he agreed with Mansel that a philosophy of the Absolute must end by

---

[89] Epistles (2 ed.), II, p. 585.
[90] B. Powell, *The Order of Nature*, p. 256 n. 1.
[91] B. Powell, *The Philosophy of Creation*, pp. 445, 448, 480.

denying all active operation of God in this world whatever, as inconsistent with unchangeable infinite perfection; but he did not say in what sense he opposed this or whether, indeed, he tacitly accepted it.[92]

Two other thinkers in the post-Kantian tradition provide more light. The great difficulty of the new metaphysics was to reconcile its view of reality with the factual and historical world presented in the bible and affirmed by orthodox belief. Fichte and Schelling had both emphasised the disingenuousness of Christian language, while Bunsen embraced New Testament terms "with more than orthodox warmth" (Williams), and was thus able to interpret Christology in a "philosophical sense".[93] It was obviously necessary to go on to a philosophy of meaning which held that opposites could be held together and that the linguistic question led, in fact, to a deeper understanding of religion.

Hegel has little obvious relevance in *Essays and Reviews*, being mentioned only by Williams, who had read the *Philosophy of History*, and referred to Bunsen, in his belief in the Eternal Thought manifesting itself, as the "countryman of Hegel" (though he failed to add that Bunsen himself was suspicious of Hegel).[94] Pattison passed Hegelianism in review in his study of the present state of German theology, in 1857, and Powell, in *The Philosophy of Creation*, described as a "remarkable work" Oken's *Elements of Physico-Philosophy*, which classified the whole creation under Hegelian categories.[95] But Hegel played a role in some of the authors' Germanism; they accepted Darwin more easily because of the philosophical evolutionism mediated by Hegel and others.

Jowett, in particular, introduced what he called an "adapted Hegelianism" into English intellectual life, a work carried through by his friends T. H. Green and Edward Caird, and he said that in the 'forties the German teacher had been the greatest influence on his thinking. Jowett's eclectic mind was incapable of one-sidedness, indeed had a horror of it, and he readily took to the new dialectic. He commented in pencil on one of the pages of the German edition of the *Logik*, which he bought in 1845 and which he partly translated with Temple, "the object of philosophy [is] not to oppose two things accidentally but to learn the nature of necessary opposition — to show that oppositions exist, but in unity". There were many similar remarks in the volume. His early essay on Christ, written in 1846, saw traditional Christology sublimated and

[92] *ER*, p. 114.
[93] *Ibid.*, p. 80.
[94] *Ibid.*, p. 60.
[95] B. Powell, *The Philosophy of Creation*, p. 436.

held in solution by an application of the Hegelian method. That was it: Hegel had "given him a method". He wrote in 1885, "though not an Hegelian, I think that I have gained more from Hegel than from any other philosopher", and the influence was personal, for Jowett had met Erdmann, Hegel's purest interpreter, at Dresden, and learned from him.[96] Some of Jowett's opposition to Paley derived from his preference for Hegel, for he felt that there must be something wrong with a writer who expressed himself so clearly: Paley gave the reader a fallacious advantage in making him think that he understood more than he had. But thought must surely be more complex, more intricate in its shades of meaning.[97]

Jowett's Hegelianism sat oddly in the pages of the Commentary; as a first attempt at interpreting St. Paul by another, very different, thinker it failed, and Jowett was never given a second chance, for the essay of 1860 left the question of Hegel and scripture on one side, perhaps intending to revive it later. But the Commentary does show how it affected his thought, and there are faint echoes in the essay.

Thus Hegel's doctrine of *Widerspruchlehre* (described by Jowett's critics as "the identity of contradiction") loomed in Jowett's claim that the objects of thought, considered in their most abstract point of view, contained both a positive and negative element: "everything is and is not; is in itself, and is not in relation to other things". St. Paul spoke of Christ reconciling God and man; Jowett thought that the opposition between "God and man, mind and matter, soul and body" could be overcome by our regarding "these pairs of opposites as passing into one another", a process which seemed to embody the Hegelian theory of "Moments", in which the *Seyn* and the *Nichts* interacted to form the *Daseyn*. Application of the method was suggested in other fields. The religious mind still considered the bewilderments and entanglements of traditional divinity a proof of the unsearchableness of the Divine nature. But if problems like the origin of evil and the freedom of the will could be resolved, then some simple and consistent expression might make even the Divine scientifically comprehensible, as Hegel claimed. Certainly, scripture yielded up its secrets. "Historical and topographical inquiries" were useless to the student of the New Testament, and a "geographical idea of all the countries of the earth... is quite different from that, shall we say, spiritual notion of place which occurs in the Epistles". Moreover,

[96] Abbott, I, pp. 117, 120, 261, II, p. 250.
[97] Epistles (1 ed), I, p. 109, (2 ed.), I, p. 204.

an "inversion of modes of thought" had taken place between our age and St. Paul's, "so that what is with us the effect, is with the Apostle the cause, or conversely". But a logic which allowed cause and effect to pass into each other and form substance by their union also offered an explanation of this. Even the "mixed modes of time and place" in the bible were now clear to the modern commentator.[98] It seemed as if the ancient writings and habits of thought had been waiting for Hegel.

Busts of Kant, Fichte, Schelling and Hegel, were all presented to his college during Jowett's Mastership, and he welcomed them, for Kant and Hegel (at least) "have been more read in Balliol College than probably anywhere else in England".[99] In 1885, or soon after, a likeness of Schleiermacher was also set up in the library, the gift of Lord Arthur Russell, or someone else who had divined the Master's philosophical tastes. The bust is a terracotta version of one executed by Christian Rauch in 1829 which so affected Heinrich Steffens with dread, because the beloved teacher seemed to be present "and about to open the firm closed lips for some striking utterance".[100] Schleiermacher's place in this company of Kantians, Idealists and metaphysicians indicates his stature for the essayists. They reflected some general traits of a theology of feeling; they thought that he was unjustly neglected; some felt that the *Critical Essay on St. Luke's Gospel* had never been given the importance that it deserved.

Jowett possessed all the collected works of Schleiermacher as well as a further edition of the *Glaubenslehre*, so that, as a prolific author, if no more, he dominated his personal library. It was noticed in Oxford in the 'forties that Jowett was reading Schleiermacher: the fruits of that were the references to the *Glaubenslehre* in the Commentary, and the hypothesis, derived from the *St. Luke*, in the essay, which held that the synoptic gospels were three forms of one tradition, rather than three independent witnesses of Christ's life.[101] Wilson's use of Schleiermacher, in his Bamptons, has already been described, as has Pattison's recognition of his posthumous importance in Germany, and Williams' obligatory mention of him in the list of divines whom he had read. Powell and Temple also had some knowledge. Powell drew on the *St. Luke*, in *The Order of Nature*, for Schleiermacher's "elaborate theory" of the origin of

---

[98] *Ibid.*, (1 ed.), II, pp. 39-40, 488, (2 ed.), II, pp. 115, 599. Cf. criticism in *Quarterly Review*, December, 1855, pp. 153-60.

[99] Abbott, II, pp. 249-50.

[100] H. Steffens, *Was ich erlebte*, V, p. 143.

[101] Abbott, I, p. 211. Epistles (2 ed.), II, p. 583. *ER*, pp. 370-1.

the gospels, and on R. C. Trench's book on Christ's miracles for his
claim in the essay on the evidences that the Jewish belief in miracles was
(*pace* Schleiermacher) relative to the apprehensions of their age.[102] He
also realised the stimulus behind Sterling's theology, when chiding him
for his gloomy views about science, in *The Spirit of the Inductive
Philosophy*. Sterling ought to have trusted in his own principles, to
"transfer the belief in a Deity altogether from the domain of *reason*, to
place it in that of *feeling* : to ground it on the sole consciousness of the
internal emotion, or the intuitive impressions of individual experience"
— and to this philosophical argument "*offers no disparagement*, although it does not reach up to it".[103] Temple's memoirs contain no
mention of Schleiermacher, but he wrote to Robert Scott in 1857, "our
theology has been cast in the scholastic mode, i.e., all based on Logic. We
are in need of and we are being gradually forced into a theology based on
psychology. The transition, I fear, will not be without much pain; but
nothing can prevent it".[104]

Archbishop Whately thought that their book held religion to be
altogether a matter of feeling,[105] but that was too sweeping. Their
perspective was, however, that of the *Reden* than the *Glaubenslehre*,
indicating an interest in religion rather than Christocentric faith, and
they shifted the basis of belief — and so made Christianity less open to
objection — from the critically assailed scriptures and credal formulae to
the actual facts of religious experience. Wilson's Bamptons proposed
beginning with man as he actually was and finding the ground of religion
there. Temple spoke of "instincts of doubt, and reverence, and awe"
which were messages from the depths of man's being,[106] both correcting
the rigidities of traditional divinity and the rudely utilitarian approach of
rationalists who did not recognise the "religious understanding" and the
need for its cultivation. The conclusion was plain in *Essays and Reviews* :
the old distinction between natural and supernatural was unreal, for the
whole area of moral and spiritual experience was the "natural". The
Christian faith should be seen from the standpoint of religion as a whole,
and thus the distinction between general and special revelation also
disappeared. According to Jowett, Christianity was not different in kind
from the other religions but was their fulfilment. It was wrong, therefore,

---

[102] B. Powell, *The Order of Nature*, p. 480. *ER*, p. 116.
[103] B. Powell, *The Spirit of the Inductive Philosophy*, pp. 149-50.
[104] Temple Memoirs, II, p. 517. Temple Appreciation, p. 109.
[105] R. Whately, *Danger from Within*, p. 23.
[106] *ER*, p. 19.

to insist on dogmatic definitions of the truth or, indeed, on any merely external account of religion.[107] The best defence of Christianity was an internal one, and Powell proposed that it must resign all claim on "physical things" — science, history, though not on morality.[108]

These similarities to a school of religious experience were no deeper than might be expected in a book so concerned with protest and demolition as *Essays and Reviews*. The philosophy of Idealism had taught them a universe alive with meaning in which a new man emerged, as part of its spiritual evolution, but to build a distinctive humanism on this being with a "longing and taste for the Infinite" demanded more talents than they had. They would have appreciated Schleiermacher's search for unity, but they understood feeling more as a psychological category than a mystical participation in the world. As thinkers weaned on Aristotle they needed to advance to Schleiermacher's vision of a restored Platonism, of Christianity returning to its ancient basic philosophy after long centuries of neglect — though Jowett certainly made this transition.

Williams, at least, recognised that new models of liturgy were required which diminished the present discrepancy between "our feelings and our logical necessities".[109] A theology must be capable of being prayed, it must be in accord with man's religious instinct, and if there was a conflict, then the theology and not the instinct must be judged. Perhaps this was also the motive in Jowett's teaching that the lead of the bible (understood as the "book for the heart") must be followed "in subjecting the purely supernatural and spiritual" (by which he meant ecclesiastical) "view of human things to the laws of experience".[110]

Jowett's one reference to Schleiermacher in the essay concerned only the negative aspect of his work: he spoke of the difficulties in reconciling the discrepancies in the infancy narrative, as pointed out by Schleiermacher in the *Critical Essay on St. Luke's Gospel*.[111] The lack of feeling for the Church suggested how far Jowett was from Schleiermacher, and in the essayists as a whole there was little sense of Christian continuity and of the dynamic manner in which faith was transmitted in the community's experience. However, Cook, Mansel and other critics saw Schleiermacher in the book, a faint but perceptible

[107] Epistles (1 ed.), II, pp. 380-421.
[108] *ER*, p. 128.
[109] *Ibid.*, p. 91.
[110] Epistles (2 ed.), II, p. 434.
[111] *ER*, p. 351.

shadow falling across its pages, and that confirms the impression that he was better known in England than has been sometimes imagined,[112] though no-one suggested that he might have corrected their views, for the essayists themselves did not see Schleiermacher in that light.

From these references it should be obvious that the essayists used the German teachers for their own purposes. Jowett quoted Kant to support his argument against too minute a concentration on logical forms and on mere words in a manner that had little to do with Kantian philosophy directly. It is, therefore, not difficult to reconcile these references with his warnings about Kant which appear elsewhere in his writings. Powell's knowledge of Kant and the thinkers who followed him was second-hand, derived from translations. Nonetheless, the nineteenth-century march to progress opened up a thrilling vista for theology, and "Kantianism" seemed to take full advantage of it. It was at this point that the significance of Locke could be seen, as T. H. Green had suggested. Locke as a pioneer had presented a challenge to that lazy taking on trust of traditional religious arguments which contemporary English divines still offered — those blind guides who, to quote Powell, betrayed "an almost entire unconsciousness of the advance of opinion around them".[113]

Whether some creative genius in English theology, such as a new Coleridge, had he existed, could have drawn the essayists away from their attachment to foreign thinkers is a debateable matter. (It was always the question posed by the early death of Arnold). Maurice was never considered because, though he was aware of the essayists' motivations, his own answer to the age was so singular, and so distinctive, that Jowett, for one, never understood him ("he is always misty and confused"), to the undoubted impoverishment of them both. In these ways the "Germanism" of *Essays and Reviews* was qualified and conditioned.

If *Essays and Reviews* has two faces, there are also two sides to its failure. The first has already been suggested — the English Church in general refused to be converted to the models, whether German, French, American, or simply radical English, proposed by the seven. The second aspect is more obvious today — the fact that many of the causes to which *Essays and Reviews* nailed its flag were lost ones. Their brightest ornaments like the scholars of the extreme Tübingen school, and the

---

[112] Cf. the author's article, "Schleiermacher in Britain", in *Scottish Journal of Theology*, 1980, pp. 417-52.
[113] *ER*, pp. 130-1.

"physico-theologians", von Humboldt, Oersted and others, are examples of a nineteenth-century theology which has worn badly. Wilson's new national Church would have fared no better than Bunsen's or Rothe's when faced by the twentieth-century totalitarian state and its demand that the "religious interest" be subservient to the national ideology. Much present-day theology has thus by-passed *Essays and Reviews* and works like it (Bishop Colenso's book on the Pentateuch, published in 1862, was another example), or long ago assimilated their concerns.

But something more can be said. Among contemporary issues in theology hermeneutics remains an important field of study. This concentration on the problem of interpretation today is the outcome of the movement known as 'biblical theology' and of developments in Christian philosophy, and is related to similar studies in other disciplines (literature, linguistics, sociology, etc) which have hermeneutical interests, but also looks back to the old liberal attempt to translate belief and doctrine in terms of its own time. The sympathy for the early pioneers is important. It has shown again, for instance, how significant Schleiermacher was in his own day, for he was, in addition to everything else, a "hermeneutical revolutionary".[114] This was understood even in England. E. N. Goadby, writing in the *Westminster Review* in July, 1861, described Schleiermacher as "the inaugurator of a newer era in hermeneutics".[115] It may also help to resurrect *Essays and Reviews*. If the seven were at all accurate in reflecting the tendencies in the new religious thought of their age, they should display some awareness of the problem of hermeneutics.

In this perspective Jowett's choice of subject and title has some interesting implications. The purpose of Jowett's disquisition on past methods of interpretation was to show the ambivalence between scripture and faith in action, however much the orthodox protested. Meanings had *always*, of necessity, been added to the text — the bible had ever to be interpreted, Jowett said — and conservative scholars were being merely dishonest or naive in denying this. Because of their refusal to acknowledge the problem, interpretation had now become confused with original meaning. But "no other science of Hermeneutics is possible but an inductive one, that is to say, one based on the language and

---

[114] Cf. R.R. Niebuhr, *Schleiermacher on Christ and Religion*, pp. 42, 79, *Journal for Theology and the Church*, 1970, No. 7, "Schleiermacher as Contemporary", and *Scottish Journal of Theology*, 1968, pp. 268-82.

[115] *WR*, July, 1861, p. 35.

thoughts and narrations of the sacred writers" — and nothing else.[116] But Jowett's further remarks suggested another theme: beyond mere "hermeneutics", as an old commentator understood it, beyond the interpretation of the words on the page, was the question of the relationship between writer and reader: both were men of faith, both were united in obedience to the "truth". What kind of relationship was it, what kind of truth?

No more profound change occurred in nineteenth-century theology than the adoption of a secular hermeneutic, the admission that as *literature* the bible is no different from any other book and must be subject to the same principles of examination. It was at the heart of *Essays and Reviews*. Hitherto, the bible had been interpreted in a sacred manner, though it employed the same language and tools as a secular book. In all other writings man was the subject, but in the holy scriptures he was the object of God's word and, therefore, they could not be expounded with reference to the common rule of hermeneutics. But now men asked, if the bible had been written like any other book, why should it be exempt from the usual literary and textual procedures? Wilberforce's argument in the *Quarterly Review* was crude and unfair but he guessed rightly that a revolution had occurred, and the seven had answered as no traditionalist would: "Holy Scripture is like any other good book... This, then, is the great principle of their Hermeneutics".[117]

The great precursors who had anticipated the mood of the century proposed the change long before. Toland had said, "nor is there any different rule to be followed in the Interpretation of Scripture from what is common to all other Books". Lessing added, "read the Bible just as you read Livy".[118] There was, indeed, a lengthy preparation for the essayists. Coleridge thought that scripture should be treated like other literature, and that was its best defence. "The Bible and Christianity are their own sufficient evidence".[119] Bishop Marsh, as ever a pioneer, had written in the early part of the century, in his *Lectures on Criticism*, "the Bible must be examined by the same laws of criticism which are applied to other writings of antiquity", and again, "the words of Scripture must still be interpreted by the same rules which apply to the words of merely human authors".[120]

---

[116] *ER*, p. 378.

[117] *Quarterly Review*, January, 1861, p. 258. Cf. *G*, 19 June, 1861, pp. 581-3, and *Aids to Faith*, p. 140, for similar recognition of the issue.

[118] G.E. Lessing, *Theological Writings*. Introduction by H. Chadwick, p. 20.

[119] S.T. Coleridge, *Confessions of an Inquiring Spirit*, p. 21.

[120] H.G. Marsh, *Lectures on the Criticism and Interpretation of the Bible*, pp. 264, 319.

Nearer home to the Oxford tradition, R. D. Hampden, in the second edition of his Bampton lectures, held that "we must study the Sacred Records as we study Nature. The method of Induction is to be used here, as there".[121] Thomas Arnold, acting to some extent on Coleridge's distinction between reason and understanding — the former judged divine things, the latter only human — allowed critical interpretation of the bible as of other literature. "The understanding has its proper work to do with respect to the Bible, because the Bible consists of human writings and contains a human history". That meant that the Old Testament could not be a perfect revelation but a group of documents clearly showing that the "revelation made to the early patriarchs consisted of some particular point only", and the patriarchs in a great many others may have been no better informed than the heathen around them: the use of the normal human understanding elicited this.[122] John Sterling, asked if Neander was a neologian, replied, "why, just as every German is one — that is, submitting the Bible to the same rules of criticism as are applied to other ancient records", which, he implied, was true for himself as well.[123] That was in 1842. In 1846, announcing the new liberal era, Stanley told his Oxford congregation, in his sermons on the Apostolic age, that scripture records must be read like other written records.[124]

Samuel Davidson, in his much criticised second volume of Horne's Bible Introduction in 1856, also held that the bible was to be explained "on the same principles as other books", and he rejected Chalmers' notion that scriptural hermeneutics was merely a work of pure grammatical analysis. "History and philosophy are consistent elements of a true and broad philology, such as is capable of explaining the language of an author", said Davidson.[125] Davidson's wider definitions pointed the way ahead: talk of the propriety of using literary and grammatical tools on the bible, as on other texts, seemed unremarkable — indeed, Chalmers used it as a way of warding off deeper, more unwelcome investigations; but to stress the personal interest of the reader gave the tools a sharper edge. The bible was no longer unique as a text, while the

---

[121] R.D. Hampden, *The Scholastic Philosophy considered in its relation to Christian Theology* (2 ed.), p. xlix.

[122] T. Arnold, *Miscellaneous Works*, pp. 149, 269.

[123] C. Fox, *op. cit.*, p. 149.

[124] A.P. Stanley, *Sermons on the Apostolic Age*, p. 4.

[125] T.H. Horne, ed., *An Introduction to the Critical Study and Knowledge of the Holy Scriptures*, II, pp. 207-10.

reader's interior needs placed it on a level with other literature which attracted him.

Much of this heresy was, however, lost to view — in Davidson it was submerged in a volume 1100 pages long — and only with the English translation of Schleiermacher's *Brief Outline of the Study of Theology* in 1850 did it become the cornerstone of a theological system. The redefinition of the place of the bible followed naturally from Schleiermacher's premise that religion began in the individual's subjective awareness. Schleiermacher did not make scripture simply part of general literature and experience, but he was not concerned to uphold the traditional belief that the bible had been written in a manner different from other books. Numbers 117-148 of the 338 theses in the *Brief Outline* were devoted to hermeneutics, and Schleiermacher stated, "the Special Hermeneutics of the New Testament can consist only of more precise determinations of the general rules [of hermeneutics] made with reference to the peculiar circumstances of the Canon". Again, "the New Testament Critic is both bound to follow the same rules, and entitled to make use of the same means, as are applicable elsewhere".[126]

Ten years later a howl of rage went up when Jowett rendered such Teutonic utterances into plain English and gave a statement as clear as anything in Toland or Lessing: in the "externals of interpretation, that is to say, the meaning of words, the connexion of sentences, the settlement of the text, the evidence of facts, the same rules apply to the Old and New Testaments as to other books". "*Interpret the Scripture like any other book...* The first step is to know the meaning, and this can only be done in the same careful and impartial way that we ascertain the meaning of Sophocles or of Plato".[127] In one way or another all the seven shared this conviction: Williams praised Bunsen for saying much the same thing, and Wilson's ideological principle depended on his statement, in the *Oxford Essays* of 1857, that the inferences from the evangelists' writings must be drawn according to the ordinary rules of interpretation. Pattison spoke similarly in the *Westminster Review* in 1857.[128]

That the essayists were ahead of their time was shown in the treatment of hermeneutics in *Lux Mundi*. Gore and his colleagues found the guarantee of scripture's reliability in the preservation of Christ himself and the witness to him from basic error: the priority of the bible was, therefore, re-established, though the Church's role as interpreter was

---

[126] F.D.E. Schleiermacher, *Brief Outline of the Study of Theology*, pp. 137, 143.
[127] *ER*, pp. 337, 377.
[128] *Oxford Essays, 1857*, p. 118. *WR*, April, 1857, pp. 337-8.

stressed, as Jowett said; he believed that *Lux Mundi* was more dated than *Essays and Reviews* in that respect. Gore did not actually say that the Church made up scripture's deficiencies, now that it was seen like any other book, nor did he try to separate words and meanings, as Jowett had done, but he felt that the alleged difficulties of understanding the bible in a critical age were exaggerated. The fact that holy scripture contained truth capable of expansion (such as the *kenosis* theory, newly emphasised in *Lux Mundi* out of its basis in Philippians 2) implied that the early Christians and ourselves were closer in thought than had been suggested, and this was because the same Christ illuminated all.

Gore admitted much; spiritual illumination, even in the highest degree, did not lift men out of the natural conditions of knowledge which belonged to their time; there was no miraculous communication of facts (he said) which would make the recorder independent of the ordinary processes of historical tradition. The Old Testament showed how God had produced an ideal, which was realised in the New, but the "absolute coincidence of idea and fact is vital in the realization, not in the preparation for it", and this allowed that much in the Old Testament was "dramatic" (i.e., characters, real or imaginary, were the vehicles for an ideal presentation), while the earliest narrative consisted of "myth or allegorical picture, which is the earliest mode in which the mind of man apprehended truth". Churchmen must see the difference between the New Testament as simply "some old manuscripts" and "an antecedent state of conception and expectation" which made us believe the facts contained in the documents and which was kept alive by the work of the Spirit in the Church. "Belief in the Holy Scriptures as inspired requires to be held in context by the belief in the general action of the Holy Spirit upon the Christian society and the individual soul. It is, we may perhaps say, becoming more and more difficult to believe in the Bible without believing in the Church".[129]

Thus, the Spirit, energising the Church, brought past and present generations of Christians together. But Gore did not conceive of a radical cultural and intellectual difference between the biblical authors and modern man which the essayists so eagerly anticipated, and it was a serious weakness in his theory that the Old Testament contained a lower level of inspiration, so that far more critical work could be allowed on it than on the New. The essayists also held this but, then, they were not so

---

[129] *Lux Mundi*, pp. 338, 354.

committed to upholding the unity of the bible and a consistent principle
of exegesis.

Having welcomed the change from a sacred to a secular hermeneutic,
the essayists had to deal with the results of their revolution. Jowett
affirmed piously, "when interpreted like any other book, by the same
rules of evidence and the same canons of criticism, the Bible will still
remain unlike any other book; its beauty will be freshly seen... it will
create a new interest and make for itself a new kind of authority by the
life which is in it".[130] He meant by this, first, that scripture was a
transparent medium for moral and universal truth. Already in 1848
Jowett spoke of his hope that the "meaning of Scripture, like that of any
other book, might by this time have become fixed, and raised above the
fancies of sects or individuals".[131] The truth, however, was clothed in
language that was sometimes foreign or alien. Jowett did not really
understand the literary importance of ambiguity, and he suggested in the
Commentary that the change in outlook required us not to attach too
much importance to the apostle's precise terms. Further, the change in
the meaning of words was already occurring in the New Testament itself
as it, too, obeyed the law of growth: so St. Paul spoke of "law", "spirit",
"death", etc., in various ways that earlier, classical Greek could not have
allowed. "These ambiguities are not an occasion of any real or great
uncertainty in the Apostle's meaning... but his double use of words
requires that we should interpret his Epistles in a large and liberal spirit".
The "observation of this phenomenon, instead of inflicting an injury, is
really of great benefit in the interpretation of Scripture; for it fixes our
thoughts on the general meaning, and withdraws them from remote and
uncertain conclusions based on an over-minute analysis of the letter of
the text".[132]

In *Essays and Reviews* Jowett went further: he saw the degeneracy and
decay of the Greek language by the first century A.D., as a preparation
for the gospel. Here was the "beginning of another state of man, in which
language and mythology and philosophy were no longer to exert the
same constraining power... A religion which was to be universal required
the divisions of languages, as of nations, to be in some degree broken
down". In reading scripture there was a "danger of making words mean
too much" — the interpreter must have real logical power, which meant
not the logical form but the logical sequence of thought, not the

---

[130] *ER*, p. 375.
[131] Abbott, I, p. 175.
[132] Epistles (2 ed.), I, pp. 125, 135.

superficial connexion of words but the real connexion of thoughts. The real kernel or meaning of St. Paul's language lay within. "When we pass from the study of each verse to survey the whole at a greater distance, the form of thought is again seen to be unimportant in comparison of the truth which is contained in it. The same remark may be extended to the opposition, not only of words, but of ideas, which is found in the Scriptures generally, and almost seems to be inherent in human language itself". He admitted the metaphysical difficulty of trying to arrange the words of the past in some relation to our own minds, particularly because there were differing modes of thought within the bible itself. But "Christian truth is not dependent on the fixedness of modes of thought... Though we had no words for mind, matter, soul, body and the like, Christianity would remain the same". Then followed a reference to the poor, "who understand such distinctions very imperfectly", and to "those nations of the earth, who have no precisely corresponding division of ideas". Yet all these could understand scripture, if it was presented properly to them, for it has a "sort of kindred, as Plato would say, with religious truth everywhere in the world". Christ's words especially were of the "most universal import. They do not relate to the circumstances of the time, but to the common life of all mankind".[133]

A parallel and far more suggestive approach was also implied in the essay. Jowett had spoken of the "life in scripture". This was generated by the experience which had inspired the writer but which might also be known to the modern reader. Here Jowett was joined by Temple and Williams, whose tastes, usually, were rather different, in an early attempt to "de-mythologise" doctrine. Experience lay behind the traditional formulae — what life-situation in the modern world could correspond to it? In the Commentary of 1855 Jowett argued that the ideas of sacrifice, of resurrection, and of the Last Things, all needed to be "spiritualised" if they were to mean anything to contemporary man,[134] in the essay of 1860 that "the Christian scheme of redemption has been staked on two figurative expressions of St. Paul to which there is no parallel in any other part of Scripture". Beneath the veil of language about the Atonement, something of great human significance could be grasped, without any need to talk of "penalty" or "punishment". Atonement, as we now saw, meant moral and spiritual sacrifice, not pouring out of

---

[133] *ER*, pp. 390, 399, 401, 402-3, 413.
[134] Epistles (1 ed.), II, pp. 477, 480, 481.

blood but doing the will of God, and Jesus's death as a martyr to the truth was the perfect symbol for it.[135]

Such proposals were not popular. People said that Jowett preferred modern ways of thinking to St. Paul's way. Temple replied, in a letter to Jowett in 1856: "what we want... is to point out that, in saying our Metaphysic is different from St. Paul's, we do not say that our Theology is therefore better than his, but that we are compelled to state the same fundamental truths in another form. Whether our Metaphysic is better than his is simply beside the question".[136]

Williams wrote at some length on interpreting the meaning behind the original doctrines, on the ground that the feelings and emotions evoked by these concrete conceptions were a sure guide to what the authors themselves intended. "Why may not justification by faith have meant the peace of mind, or sense of Divine approval, which comes of trust in a righteous God, rather than a fiction of merit by transfer?" he asked. The impetus came from the Chevalier Bunsen, but the elaboration was Williams' own:

"Regeneration is a correspondent giving of insight, or an awakening of forces of the soul. By Resurrection he would mean a spiritual quickening. Salvation would be our deliverance, not from the life-giving God, but from evil and darkness, which are His finite opposites. Propitiation would be the recovery of that peace, which cannot be while sin divides us from the Searcher of hearts. The eternal is what belongs to God, as Spirit, therefore the negation of things finite and unspiritual, whether world, or letter, or rite of blood. The hateful fires of the vale of Hinnom (Gehenna) are hardly in the strict letter imitated by the God who has pronounced them cursed, but may serve as images of distracted remorse. Heaven is not a place, so much as fulfilment of the love of God. The kingdom of God is no more Romish sacerdotalism than Jewish royalty, but the realization of the Divine Will in our thoughts and lives".

Williams applied such "purely spiritual" meanings to the Trinity, Christology, and the doctrine of original sin as well. "The fall of Adam represents with him [Bunsen] ideally the circumscription of our spirits in limits of flesh and time, and practically the selfish nature with which we fall from the likeness of God, which should be fulfilled in man".[137]

In this manner the three essayists suggested a unity of shared experience between past and present. It was only a step to explore the

---

[135] *ER*, p. 361.
[136] Jowett MSS, Box E, package δ.
[137] *ER*, pp. 81-2, 88.

nature of the unity: perhaps the bible was unlike any other book because a degree of mental sympathy could be achieved between the reader and the writer who had witnessed the divine event? Traditionalist divines said no less, of course: in his *Hermeneutical Manual* in 1858 Patrick Fairbairn argued that the "interpreter must endeavour to attain to a sympathy in thought and feeling with the sacred writer".[138] Jowett, however, wrote two pages on the act of interpretation which proposed something more. It required (he said) an effort of thought and imagination, the "sense of a poet as well as a critic — demanding, much more than learning, a degree of original power and intensity of mind". The unity would not be possible if anything else (he meant past exegesis) intruded, thus the "true use of interpretation is to get rid of interpretation and leave us alone in company with the author". Again, the interpreter's task was "to place himself as nearly as possible in the position of the sacred writer". This was no easy matter, to call up the inner and outer life of the contemporaries of our Saviour, and it was even more difficult in regard to the words of Christ himself. To enter into their meaning one must not mar their simplicity. "The interpreter needs nothing short of 'fashioning' in himself the image of the mind of Christ. He has to be born again into a new spiritual or intellectual world, from which the thoughts of this world are shut out".

> "The office of the interpreter is not to add another, but to recover the original one; the meaning, that is, of the words as they struck on the ears or flashed before the eyes of those who first heard and read them. He has to transfer himself to another age; to imagine that he is a disciple of Christ or Paul; to disengage himself from all that follows. The history of Christendom is nothing to him; but only the scene at Galilee or Jerusalem, the handful of believers who gathered themselves together at Ephesus, or Corinth, or Rome... The greater part of his learning is a knowledge of the text itself; he has no delight in the voluminous literature which has overgrown it. He has no theory of interpretation; a few rules guarding against common errors are enough for him. His object is to read Scripture like any other book, with a real interest and not merely a conventional one. He wants to be able to open his eyes and see or imagine things as they truly are".[139]

What Jowett meant here may be compared with Schleiermacher's hermeneutics when the latter asked the question, how did nineteenth -century man bridge the gap between the text and himself, between the

---

[138] P. Fairbairn, *Hermeneutical Manual*, p. 63.
[139] *ER*, pp. 338, 380, 384.

writer's experience and his own? Schleiermacher held that interpretation was a talent or art, going beyond philology. Jowett, too, faced the problem of encountering the bible in an age grown tired of traditional ways of expounding it. Schleiermacher had spoken of his method as an "intensive" one, opposed to the "extensive" approach of traditional exegesis.[140] Jowett also, without learning anything from Schleiermacher directly, said that the interpreter must possess an "intensity" of mind, and he decried the "externals of interpretation".

Thus, Jowett opened up a new vista in hermeneutics. He saw clearly the need for a profound subjective involvement of the reader with the author, a new means of interplay between the two, a new sort of penetration to the heart of the text. Interpretation was an effort of thought and imagination, demanding much more than mere learning.

Jowett could have gone on if he had wished to; he spoke of the interpreter as poet, wanting to be "able to open his eyes and see or imagine things as they truly are", of being born into a new spiritual or intellectual world. But he said nothing further, and the fertile ideas, as so often in his work, were thrown out and never taken up. The reason for this lay in his limited understanding of what an "historical" approach to the text demanded. After all, Jowett mentioned F. C. Baur in his correspondence far more than Schleiermacher. He thought that Baur's *Christentum* was the "best critical attempt to write the early history of Christianity", and his commentaries on St. Paul's epistles showed a "remarkable combination of philological and metaphysical power". He seems to have accepted the *Christus-partei* theory which so contrasted the minds of Jesus and Paul.[141] So, too, other essayists — Pattison saw Baur as the foremost mind in German theology, because he exhibited the absolute scientific nature of the historical method, at the bar of which everything must be judged and from which there was no appeal.[142] Wilson admitted the most negative aspects of the method (as well as Baur's late second-century dating for St. John's Gospel): judged historically nothing could be final or certain.[143]

The pressure of this historical awareness, coming on the earlier interest in Locke, placed critical questions so much in the forefront of their thought that some of the essayists did not allow much attention to anything else. Jowett could not forbear to ask repeated questions of

---

[140] F.D.E. Schleiermacher, *op. cit.*, pp. viii-x, 27, 31.
[141] Abbott, I, pp. 142, 163, 166.
[142] *WR*, January, 1857, p. 336.
[143] *Oxford Essays, 1857*, pp. 117-120.

scripture: he was never satisfied to take on trust its assumptions of authenticity, and not simply because extravagant claims made on its behalf provoked his reaction.

This approach to interpretation produced one last contrast between Jowett and Maurice. Maurice, too, was concerned with tracing the unity that existed between writer and reader. He conceded that the issue was important in a critical age. In his *St. John* he held that it did not need "any effort of the imagination to realize the state of mind of an ordinary Jew as he walked through the city of David", for the interpreter had only to "realize the state of mind of the ordinary citizen of London walking in our streets".[144] Jowett, taught to look at the text without *a priori* considerations, thought that this was "mystical". The critic had to work inductively on what was actually presented to him, the literary records, and these were best analysed by understanding the circumstances of the time in which they were written, their literary parallels, and so forth. There was all the difference in the world between this sober critical approach of transferring oneself to the circumstances of a past age and Maurice's spiritual elevation of the interpreter's mind to the level of the writer. For one thing, people today were so various, how much more those of the past — Jowett lacked Maurice's sense of the unity of mankind. That was why he disliked Wilson's article in the *Westminster Review* in 1857 which confused Maurice's technique with his own.[145]

Again, the legacy of the historical method made Jowett more aware than Maurice of the problems in interpretation, more aware of the apparent inconsistencies in scripture — and thus also more conscious in his anticipation of twentieth-century theological interests. Jowett was at his most modern in his discussion of the complexities and different levels in the New Testament, and his work stands comparison with present-day studies which suggest that the early Christianity reflected in the New Testament was less unified and homogeneous than was previously believed. Jowett's discussion is often illuminating, and his insights suggest that he realised the nature of the problem. But it also meant that Jowett never advanced, like Schleiermacher, to a fully developed hermeneutics of the imagination or intuition as a means of reconciling these differences, and he did not explore his own evocative picture of the interpreter as poet, as a seer who opened up the realities beyond the word lying upon the page.

---

[144] F.D. Maurice, *The Gospel of St. John*, p. 74.
[145] Abbott, I, p. 262. Cf. *WR*, October, 1857, pp. 537-8.

Jowett's solution to this complexity of the biblical witness, by separating out the moral from the historically conditioned element, leads to another example of his failure to develop his ideas, his belief that the degeneracy of language was a creative as well as a destructive principle. He pointed out that a great movement like the Reformation could give birth to a new religious terminology. There were obvious implications in this for a deeper study of hermeneutics, but Jowett turned aside to consider the "metaphysical difficulties" which changing language and thought forms provided for interpretation, and his reply was, "Christian truth is not dependent on the fixedness of modes of thought".[146] Jowett did not evaluate the bible's enigmatic strangeness, only its simple meaning: as was said of another great liberal theologian, he saw in scripture only his own reflection, as at the bottom of a deep well.

But, perhaps, no study which gives such prominence to Jowett should end too negatively. Had *Essays and Reviews* not blighted his theological career, he might have written a constructive work on scripture in the following ten years. This would have amplified his casual remarks and qualified his judgments which, in 1860, were essentially provisional.

---

[146] *ER*, p. 402.

BIBLIOGRAPHY

MANUSCRIPT SOURCES

Balliol College, Oxford. Jowett MSS. — Letters to Florence Nightingale.
— Drafts, Box 'D'.
— Letters to A. P. Stanley, Box 'E'.
Bodleian Library, Oxford — MS. Eng. Lett.
— MSS. Pattison.
Christ Church, Oxford — Phillimore Papers.
Literary Estate of Miss Ethel Hatch — Diaries of Edwin Hatch.
— MS. Life of Edwin Hatch.
Imperial College, London — Huxley Collection.
Keble College, Oxford — Keble MSS., Box 'K'.
Lambeth Palace Library, London — Longley MSS.
— Tait MSS.
Pusey House, Oxford — Pusey MSS., Correspondence with John Keble.
— Journal of W. K. Hamilton.
— MSS. 'Lux Mundi'.
Trinity College, Cambridge — E. W. Benson MSS.

PRINTED SOURCES — BOOKS AND PAMPHLETS

Place of publication London, unless otherwise stated.

Abbott, E. and Campbell, L. *Life and Letters of Benjamin Jowett*, 1897.
Abbott, E. and Campbell, L., eds., *Letters of Benjamin Jowett*, 1899.
Aids to Faith, 1861.
Arnold, T. *Sermons*, 1832.
—— *Miscellaneous Works*, 1845.
Bagehot, W. (ed. by Mrs Russell Barrington), *Life and Works*, 1915.
Battiscombe, G. *John Keble, A Study in Limitations*, 1963.
Bell, G.K.A. *Randall Davidson* (3 ed.), 1952.
Benn, A.W. *The History of English Rationalism in the Nineteenth Century*, 1906.
Bernard, H.H. (ed. by I. Bernard), *Cambridge Free Thoughts and Letters on Bibliolatry*, 1862.
Bernard, T.D. *The Progress of Doctrine in the New Testament*, n.d.
Boyle, G.D. *The Recollections of the Very Rev. G.D. Boyle*, 1895.
Brock, W. *Infidelity in High Places*, 1864.
Brodrick, G.C. and Fremantle, W.H. *Collection of the Judgments of the Judicial Commitee of the Privy Council in Ecclesiastical Cases relating to Doctrine and Discipline*, 1865.
Brooke, S.A. *Life and Letters of Frederick W. Robertson*, 1866.
Browning, R. *Dramatis Personae*, 1889.
Buckle, G.E. and Monypenny, W.F. *The Life of Benjamin Disraeli, Earl of Beaconsfield* (4 ed.), 1916.

Bunsen, C.C.J. von. *The Constitution of the Church of the Future*, 1847.
Bunsen, F. *A Memoir of Baron Bunsen*, 1868.
Burgon, J.W. *Inspiration and Interpretation*, Oxford, 1861
—— *Dr Temple's "Explanation" Examined*, 1870.
—— *Protests of the Bishops against the Consecration to the See of Exeter*, 1870.
Burrows, M. *Autobiography of Montagu Burrows*, 1908.
Burtchaell, J.T. *Catholic Theories of Biblical Inspiration since 1810*, 1969.
Carlyle, A. ed., *Thomas Carlyle: New Letters*, 1904.
Chadwick, Owen. *From Bossuet to Newman*, Cambridge, 1957.
Christianisme au quatrième siècle, Le : Séances Historiques données à Genève en Mars 1858, par Gasparin, Bungener et de Pressensé, Geneva, 1858.
Chronicle of Convocation, 1859 onwards.
Church, M.C. *Life and Letters of Dean Church* (2 ed.), 1897.
Church, R.W. *The Oxford Movement. Twelve Years 1833-1845* (3 ed.), 1891.
Clarke, C.P.S. *The Oxford Movement and After*, 1932.
Coleridge, S.T. *Confessions of an Inquiring Spirit*, 1840.
—— (ed. by J. Barrell), *On the Constitution of Church and State*, 1972.
Conybeare, W.J. *Essays Ecclesiastical and Social*, 1855.
Conybeare, W.J. *Perversion, or, The Causes and Consequences of Infidelity, A Tale for the Times*, 1856.
Cook, E.T. *The Life of John Ruskin*, 1911.
Cottrell, C.H. *Religious Movements of Germany in the Nineteenth Century*, 1849.
Cox, G.V. *Recollections of Oxford* (2 ed.), 1870.
Cripps, H.W. *A Practical Treatise on the Laws relating to the Church and the Clergy* (4 ed.), 1863.
Crowther, M.A. *Church Embattled*, Newton Abbot, 1970.
Darwin, C. *The Origin of Species* (n.e.), 1894.
Davidson, R.T. and Benham, W. *Life of Archibald Campbell Tait, Archbishop of Canterbury*, 1891.
Davidson, S. *Sacred Hermeneutics, Developed and Applied*, Edinburgh, 1843.
—— *Facts, Statements and Explanations connected with the publication of the 10th edition of Horne's Introduction*, 1857.
—— *On a Fresh Revision of the English Old Testament*, 1873.
—— *The Autobiography and Diary of Samuel Davidson*, Edinburgh, 1899.
Davies, J. Ll. and Garden, F. *The Death of Christ*. Tracts for Priests and People XIII, 1861.
Denison, G.A. *A Letter from George Anthony Denison to Edward Bouverie Pusey*, 1864.
—— *Supplement to Notes of my Life*, 1893.
Dictionary of National Biography.
Dorner, I.A. *History of Protestant Theology, particularly in Germany*, Edinburgh, 1871.
Drummond, J. *The Life and Letters of James Martineau*, 1902.
Eliot, G. (ed. by G.S. Haight), *The George Eliot Letters*, 1954.
Ellicott, C.J. *Historical Lectures on the Life of our Lord Jesus Christ*, 1861.
Essays and Reviews (8 ed.), 1861.
Eveleigh, J. *Sermons*, Oxford, 1792.
Faber, G. *Jowett, A Portrait with Background*, 1957.
Fairbairn, P. *Hermeneutical Manual*, Edinburgh, 1858.
Faith and Peace, Being answers to some of the "Essays and Reviews", 1862.
Farrar, A.S. *Critical History of Free Thought*, 1862.
Farrer, H.L. *Life of Robert Gray, Bishop of Cape Town*, 1876.
Fendall, J. *The Authority of Scripture*, 1861.
Forbes, D. *The Liberal Anglican Idea of History*, Cambridge, 1952.
Fox, A. *Dean Inge*, 1960.
Fox, C. (ed. by H.N. Pym), *Memories of old Friends*, 1882.

Froude, J.A. *Thomas Carlyle: A History of his Life in London 1834 — 1881*, 1885.
Garbett, E. *The Bible and its Critics*, 1861.
Girdlestone, C. *Negative Theology an argument for Liturgical Revision*, 1861.
Gladstone, W.E. (ed. by H.C.G. Matthew), *The Gladstone Diaries*, vols. V and VI, Oxford, 1978.
Gore, C. *The Ministry of the Christian Church*, 1888.
—— *The Incarnation of the Son of God*, 1891.
Goulburn, E.M. *The Life of John William Burgon*, 1892.
Green, T.H. (ed. by R.L. Nettleship), *Works of Thomas Hill Green*, 1889.
Grote, Mrs *The Personal Life of George Grote* (2 ed.), 1873.
Hamilton, W.K. *Charge of the Bishop of Salisbury, 1861*, 1861.
Hampden, H. ed., *Some Memorials of Renn Dickson Hampden*, 1871.
Hampden, R.D. *The Scholastic Philosophy considered in its relation to Christian Theology* (1 ed.), 1833, (2 ed.) 1837.
Hansard, 3rd series, 1864.
Hare, J.C. (ed. by E.H. Plumptre), *The Victory of Faith* (3 ed.), 1874.
Hatch, E. *The Organization of the Early Christian Churches*, 1881.
—— *Progress in Theology*, Edinburgh, 1885.
—— *The Growth of Church Institutions*, 1887.
—— *The Influence of Greek Ideas and Usages upon the Christian Church*, 1890.
Hatch, S.C. ed., *Memorials of Edwin Hatch*, 1890.
Hawkins, E. *A Dissertation upon the Use and Importance of Unauthoritative Tradition*, Oxford, 1819.
Hennell, S. *Essay on the Sceptical Tendency of Butler's Theology*, 1859.
—— *Thoughts in aid of Faith*, 1860.
Hinchliff, P. *The One-sided Reciprocity*, 1966.
Hinds, S. *The Three Temples*, Oxford, 1836.
Horne, T.H., ed., *An Introduction to the Critical Study and Knowledge of the Holy Scriptures* (10 ed.), 1856.
Hort, A.F. *Life and Letters of Fenton John Anthony Hort*, 1896.
Houghton, W.E., ed., *Wellesley Index to Victorian Periodicals*, 1979.
Howson, J.S. *Five Lectures on the Character of St. Paul*, 1864.
Hurst, J.F. *History of Rationalism*, 1867.
Inge, W.R. *Outspoken Essays, The Victorian Age*, 1919.
Iremonger, F.A. *William Temple, Archbishop of Canterbury, His Life and Letters*, 1948.
Jackson, T. *Aids to Truth and Charity*, 1862.
Johnston, J.O. *Life and Letters of Henry Parry Liddon*, 1904.
Josaitis, N.F. *Edwin Hatch and Early Church Order*, Louvain, 1971.
Jowett, B. *The Epistles of St. Paul to the Thessalonians, Galatians, and Romans* (1 ed.), 1855, (2 ed.), 1859.
—— *The Dialogues of Plato, translated into English with Analyses and Introductions* (1 ed.), 1871, (3 ed.), 1892.
—— *Sermons Biographical and Miscellaneous*, 1899.
—— *Sermons on Faith and Doctrine*, 1901.
Kennard, R.B. "*Essays and Reviews*", *Their Origin, History, General Characteristics and Significance*, 1863.
—— *The late Professor Powell and Dr Thirlwall on the Supernatural*, 1864.
—— *In Memory of Henry Bristow Wilson*, 1888.
Kingsley, C. *The Gospel of the Pentateuch*, 1863.
—— *His Letters, and Memories of his Life, edited by his wife*, 1885.
Kirk Smith, H. *William Thomson, Archbishop of York, His Life and Times*, 1958.
Kitchin, G.W. *Edward Harold Browne, A Memoir*, 1895.
Knickerbocker, F.W. *Free Minds. John Morley and his Friends.* Cambridge, Mass., 1943.

Knight, W. *Memoir of the Rev. H. Venn*, 1880.
Lathbury, D.C. ed., *Letters on Church and State of William Ewart Gladstone*, 1910.
Lecky, W.E.H. *Democrary and Liberty*, 1896.
—— *History of the rise and influence of the spirit of Rationalism in Europe* (3 ed.), 1904.
Lessing, G.E. *The Education of the Human Race*, 1858.
—— (ed. by H. Chadwick), *Theological Writings*, 1956.
Lichtenberger, F. *History of German Theology in the 19th Century*, Edinburgh, 1889.
Liddon, H.P. *The Divinity of our Lord and Saviour Jesus Christ*, 1867.
—— (with Johnston, J.O. and Wilson, R.J.), *Life of Edward Bouverie Pusey*, vols. I — III (4 ed.), 1894, vol. IV, 1897.
Lock, W. *John Keble, A Biography*, 1893.
Locke, J. (ed. by I.T. Ramsey) *The Reasonableness of Christianity*, 1958.
—— (ed. by A.D. Woozley), *An Essay Concerning Human Understanding*, 1964.
Longley, C.T. *A Pastoral Letter addressed to the Clergy and Laity of his Diocese by Charles Thomas, Archbishop of Canterbury*, 1864.
Ludlow, J.M. *A Dialogue on Doubt. The Sermon of the Bishop of Oxford on Revelation.* Tracts for Priests and People VI, 1861.
Lux Mundi, 1889.
Macan, R.W. *Religious Changes in Oxford during the last 50 years*, Oxford, 1907.
McCosh, J. *The Supernatural in Relation to the Natural*, 1862.
Mackay, R.W. *The Tübingen School and its Antecedents*, 1863.
McKnight, W.H.E. *Recollections and Letters of the Rev. W.H.E. McKnight*, 1907.
Major, H.D.A. *The Life and Letters of William Boyd Carpenter*, 1925.
Mallet, C.E. *A History of the University of Oxford*, 1924.
Manning, H.E. *The Crown in Council on the "Essays and Reviews"*, 1864.
—— *The Convocation and the Crown in Council*, 1864.
Mansel, H.L. *The Limits of Religious Thought* (2 ed.), 1858.
—— *Metaphysics, or, The Philosophy of Consciousness, Phenomenal and Real* (2 ed.), Edinburgh, 1866.
—— (ed. by H.W. Chandler), *Letters, Lectures and Reviews*, 1873.
Marsh, H.G. *Lectures on the Criticism and Interpretation of the Bible*, Cambridge, 1828.
Marsh, P.T. *The Victorian Church in Decline*, 1969.
Maurice, F.D. *Theological Essays*, 1853.
—— *The Gospel of St. John*, 1857.
—— *What is Revelation?*, 1859.
—— *The Mote and the Beam. A Clergyman's Lessons from the Present Panic.* Tracts for Priests and People II, 1861.
Maurice, J.F. *The Life of Frederick Denison Maurice*, 1884.
Max-Müller, F. *My Autobiography*, 1901.
—— *The Life and Letters of Friedrich Max-Müller, edited by his wife*, 1902.
Meacham, S. *Lord Bishop*, 1972.
Merz, J.T. *A History of European Thought in the Nineteenth Century*, Edinburgh, 1893-1904.
Mill, J.S. *Theism*, 1874.
Moberly, G. *Sermons on the Beatitudes*, Oxford, 1860.
Morley, J. *The Life of William Ewart Gladstone*, 1903.
Mozley, J.B. *Eight Lectures on Miracles*, 1865.
—— *The Theory of Development*, 1878.
—— *Letters of the Rev. J.B. Mozley, edited by his sister*, 1885.
Muir, J. *Brief Examination of Prevalent Notions of Biblical Inspiration*, 1861.
Nash, T.A. *The Life of Richard, Lord Westbury*, 1888.
Newman, J.H. *Tracts Theological and Ecclesiastical*, 1874.
—— (ed. by C.S. Dessain), *Letters and Diaries*, 1961 onwards.

—— (ed. by M.J. Svaglic), *Apologia Pro Vita Sua*, Oxford, 1967.
Niebuhr, R.R. *Schleiermacher on Christ and Religion*, 1968.
Oersted, H.C. *The Soul in Nature*, 1852.
Ollivant, A. *A Charge delivered to the Clergy of the Diocese of Llandaff, August*, 1857.
—— *A Charge delivered to the Clergy of the Diocese of Llandaff, 1860*, 1860.
Overton, J.H. and Wordsworth, E. *Christopher Wordsworth, Bishop of Lincoln*, 1888.
Oxford Essays, 1855, 1856, 1857.
Paley, W. (ed. by R. Whately), *William Paley's Evidences* (n.e.), 1861.
Pattison, M. *Memoirs*, 1885.
—— *Sermons*, 1885.
Pearson, G. *The Dangers of Abrogating the Religious Tests and Subscriptions*, Cambridge, 1834.
Peel, A. *These Hundred Years*, 1931.
Pfleiderer, O. *The Development of Theology in Germany since Kant* (2 ed.), 1893.
Phillips, E. *The Church and the Ecclesiastical Commissioners*, 1864.
Powell, B. *The Advance of Knowledge in the Present Times*, 1826.
—— *Rational Religion Examined*, 1829.
—— *Revelation and Science*, 1833.
—— *Natural Philosophy, An Historical view of the Progress of the Physical and Mathematical Sciences*, 1834.
—— *Remarks on a Letter from the Rev. H.A. Woodgate to Viscount Melbourne*, 1836.
—— *Tradition Unveiled*, 1839.
—— *State Education considered with reference to prevalent misconceptions on religious grounds*, 1840.
—— *The State Church*, Oxford, 1850.
—— *Essays on the Spirit of the Inductive Philosophy, The Unity of Worlds, and The Philosophy of Creation*, 1855.
—— *The Order of Nature*, 1859.
—— *Christianity without Judaism* (2 ed.), 1866.
Pressensé, E. de. *Contemporary Portraits*, 1880.
Prest, J.M. *Robert Scott and Benjamin Jowett*. Supplement to the Balliol College Record, Oxford, 1966.
Prestige, G.L. *The Life of Charles Gore*, 1935.
Proby, W.H.B. *Annals of the Low Church Party*, 1888.
Prothero, R.E. *The Life and Correspondence of Arthur Penrhyn Stanley*, 1893.
Pusey, E.B. *Remarks on the Prospective and Past Benefits of Cathedral Institutions in the Promotion of Sound Religious Knowledge and of Clerical Education* (2 ed.), 1833.
—— *All Faith the Gift of God*, 1855.
—— *Real Faith Entire*, 1855.
—— *Daniel the Prophet*, 1864.
Rawlinson, G. *The Historical Evidences of the Truth of the Scripture Records*, 1859.
Replies to "Essays and Reviews", Oxford, 1862.
Report and Evidence upon the Recommendations of her Majesty's Commissioners for Inquiring into the State of the University of Oxford, Oxford, 1853.
Robertson, F.W. *Analysis of Mr Tennyson's "In Memoriam"*, 1851.
Rose, H.J. *The State of Protestantism in Germany Described* (2 ed.), 1829.
Rothe, R. *Die Anfänge der Christlichen Kirche*, Berlin, 1837.
Royal Society, Proceedings of, XI, 1862.
Ruskin, J. *Sesame and Lilies*, Library Edition of Works, vol. 18, 1903.
Sanders, C.R. *Coleridge and the Broad Church Movement*, Durham, North Carolina, 1942.
Sandford, E.G. ed. *Memoirs of Archbishop Temple, by seven friends*, 1906.
Sandford, E.G. ed. *Frederick Temple, An Appreciation*, 1907.
Schaff, P. *Germany, Its Universities, Theology and Religion*, Edinburgh, 1857.

Schleiermacher, F.D.E. *Brief Outline of the Study of Theology*, Edinburgh, 1850.
Shaen, M.J. *Memorials of Two Sisters*, 1908.
Sidgwick, A. and E. *Henry Sidgwick, A Memoir*, 1906.
Smith, Goldwin. *Reminiscences*, New York, 1910.
Stanley, A.P. *Sermons on the Apostolic* Age, 1847.
—— *The Epistles of St. Paul to the Corinthians*, 1855.
—— *Life and Correspondence of Thomas Arnold* (8 ed.), 1858.
—— *A Letter on the State of Subscription in the Church of England and in the University of Oxford*, 1863.
—— *Essays chiefly on questions of Church and State*, 1884.
Steffens, H. *Was ich erlebte*, Breslau, 1840-1844.
Stephen, Fitzjames. *Defence of the Rev. Rowland Williams*, 1862.
Stephen, L. *Studies of a Biographer*, 1898.
Stephens, W.R.W. *The Life and Letters of Walter Farquhar Hook* (6 ed.), 1881.
Sterling, J. *Essays and Tales, collected and edited with a memoir of his life by J.C. Hare*, 1848.
Storr, V.F. *The Development of English Theology in the Nineteenth Century*, 1913.
Strauss, D.F. *The Life of Jesus* (4 ed.), 1898.
Stromberg, R.N. *Religious Liberalism in Eighteenth Century England*, 1954.
Sumner, C. *A Charge delivered to the Diocese of Winchester, 1862*, 1862.
Tait, A.C. *A Charge delivered in December 1862 to the Clergy of the Diocese of London*, 1862.
Temple, F. *The Present Relations of Science to Religion*, 1860.
—— *Sermons preached in Rugby School Chapel, 2nd series*, 1871.
—— *The Relations between Religion and Science*, 1884.
Thirlwall, C. *Charge delivered to the Diocese of St. David's, 1857*, 1857.
—— *Charge delivered to the Diocese of St. David's, 1860*, 1860.
Thirlwall, C. (ed. by J.J. Perowne), *Remains Literary and Theological of Connop Thirlwall*, 1878.
—— (ed. by J.J. Perowne and L. Stokes), *Letters Literary and Theological of Connop Thirlwall*, 1881.
—— (ed. by A.P. Stanley), *Letters to a Friend*, 1882.
Thirlwall, J.C. jnr. *Connop Thirlwall, Historian and Theologian*, 1936.
Thompson, H.L. *Henry George Liddell, A Memoir*, 1899.
Thomson, W. *A Pastoral Letter to the Clergy and Laity of the Province of York*, 1864.
Tuckwell, W. *Reminiscences of Oxford*, 1900.
—— *Pre-Tractarian Oxford*, 1909.
Tuell, A.K. *John Sterling, a Representative Victorian*, New York, 1941.
Tulloch, J. *Theological Tendencies of the Age*, Edinburgh, 1855.
—— *Movements of Religious Thought in Britain during the Nineteenth Century*, 1885.
Utterton, J. *Charge to the Archdeaconry of Surrey 1860*, 1860.
Venn, H. *The Life and a selection from the Letters of Rev. H. Venn*, 1834.
Voigt, J.A. *Mittheilungen über das Unterrichtswesen Englands und Schottlands*, Halle, 1857.
W[ard], W.G. *A few words in support of No. 90 of the Tracts for the Times, partly with reference to Mr Wilson's letter*, Oxford, 1841.
Waldegrave, S. *Charge delivered to the Diocese of Carlisle, October 1861*, 1861.
Wallace, E. *Goldwin Smith, Victorian Liberal*, Toronto, 1957.
Ward, T.H. ed. *The Reign of Queen Victoria: A Survey of Fifty Years of Progress*, 1887.
Ward, W.R. *Victorian Oxford*, 1965.
Watson, R.A. and E.S. *George Gilfillan, Letters and Journals, with Memoir*, 1892.
Westcott, A. *Life and Letters of Brooke Foss Westcott*, 1903.
Westcott, B.F. *Introduction to the Study of the Gospels*, 1860.
Whately, R. *Dr Paley's Works, A Lecture*, 1859.

—— *Danger from Within. Charge of the Archbishop of Dublin*, 1861.

Wilberforce, R.G. *Life of the Rt. Rev. Samuel Wilberforce* (2 ed.), 1883.

Wilberforce, S. *Charge to the Diocese of Oxford, November 1860*, 1860.

Wild, G. *A Brief Defence of "Essays and Reviews"*, 1861.

Willey, B. *More Nineteenth Century Studies*, 1956.

Williams, R. *Rational Godliness after the Mind of Christ and the Written Voices of His Church*, 1855.

—— *A Dialogue of the Knowledge of the Supreme Lord, in which are compared the claims of Christianity and Hinduism*, Cambridge, 1856.

—— *Lampeter Theology Exemplified in extracts from the Vice-Principal's Lectures, Letters and Sermons*, 1856.

—— *Persecution for the Word*, 1862.

—— *The Life and Letters of Rowland Williams, edited by his wife*, 1874.

Wilson, Harry B. *The Sympathizing High Priest*, 1828.

—— *Contention for the Faith*, 1849.

Wilson, Henry B. *The Independence of particular Churches*, 1843.

—— *The Communion of Saints*, 1851.

—— *Three Sermons composed for the opening of a new organ at St. Chrysostom's Church, Everton*, 1861.

—— *A Speech delivered before the Judicial Committee of Her Majesty's most honourable Privy Council*, 1863.

Wiseman, N. *Pastoral Letter of H.E. Cardinal Wiseman on Trinity Sunday 1864*, 1864.

Woodgate, H.A. *"Essays and Reviews" Considered*, 1861.

Anonymous

Anselm Scriptural and Catholic, 1861.

Dr Davidson: his heresies, contradictions and plagiarisms, by two graduates, 1857.

"Essays and Reviews" Anticipated. Extracts from a work published in the year 1825 and attributed to the Lord Bishop of St. David's, 1861.

Puseyism the School of Infidelity, or, Broad Church the Offspring of High Church, 1865.

Statements on Christian Doctrine and Practice extracted from the published writings of the Rev. Benjamin Jowett, Oxford, 1861.

The Suppression of Doubt is not Faith, by a Layman, 1861.

INDEX OF NAMES AND PERSONS

INDEX OF SUBJECTS

103f., 107f., 116, 132, 136, 140, 142, 156f., 178, 180-3, 193, 211, 213f.

Patristic theology, 56, 102, 120, 149
Pelagianism, 126, 154
Pentateuch, 5, 61, 92, 118, 133, 309
II Peter, Epistle of, 61, 185
Platonism, 9, 251, 278, 307
Popular Education Commission, 39f., 91, 100
Positivism, 9f., 91, 100, 294f.
Presbyterians, 91
Private Judgment, 38, 43, 56, 95, 110, 113, 140, 150, 152, 202, 221, 228, 280
Privy Council Judicial Committee, ix, 126, 144, 158, 182, 187-192, 195, 202f., 206-8
Prophecy, 9, 26, 33, 61f., 81, 102, 126, 132, 144, 159, 185, 233, 273
Propitiation, 185, 187, 316
Protestant, 35, 68, 107, 144, 213, 221, 227, 238f., 242, 259
Providence, 59, 75, 103, 127, 223
Punishment, Everlasting, 4, 53, 68f., 121, 144, 153f., 188, 193, 195, 261f., 287

Quakers, 4, 157

"Recordites", 3, 146
Reformation, 21f., 55, 57, 68, 79, 90, 120, 199, 235f., 238, 271, 320
Renaissance, 22, 57, 68, 79, 271
Resurrection, 4, 18, 31, 96f., 119, 144, 151, 235, 257, 269, 315f.
Revelation, 16, 25f., 31f., 54, 59-61, 63f., 74, 77, 82, 92f., 99, 113, 120, 124, 139, 141, 175, 216, 218, 220, 225, 262, 272, 280, 287f., 293
Revised version of bible, 239-41, 260
Roman Catholicism, 44, 113, 141, 144, 153, 158, 165, 210
Royal Society, 44f.

Sacrifice, 47, 315. See also Atonement.

Salvation, 89, 110, 135, 166, 214, 226
Science, 44f., 61, 64f., 68, 99f., 108, 113, 116, 131f., 155, 161, 216, 218f., 226, 243, 253, 294, 297, 306
Scripture, 3f., 14, 16, 19f., 26, 31, 36f., 56f., 59f., 71, 80f., 92, 110, 115, 120, 128, 140, 148-50, 181, 185, 216, 218f., 223f., 239-42, 309f. See also Inspiration.
Socialism, 72
Socinianism, 30, 228
Spirit, 18, 27, 54, 59, 82, 109, 150, 181, 205, 266, 301, 313
"Stanleyites", 11f., 23f., 28, 34f., 38, 231f., 249, 264, 286
State, Doctrine of, 69, 71f., 88, 91, 98, 100, 158, 192, 198, 207, 209, 211, 277, 285
Subscription, 7, 36, 43, 49, 71, 90, 101, 115, 136f., 143, 204, 213, 218
Supernatural, 18, 60, 70, 81, 84, 88, 91, 99, 113, 119, 126, 159, 195, 203, 227, 233, 268, 306f.

Toleration, 55, 57, 89, 97, 138
Toleration, Act, 122
Tractarians, 12, 17, 23f., 26, 28, 33, 35, 37f., 40, 42, 45, 64, 70f., 76f., 90, 98, 101, 123, 155, 203, 213, 215, 220-3, 227-9, 248f., 251, 268
Transfiguration, 292
Trinity, 144, 151, 241, 316
Tübingen School, 7, 22f., 308

Utilitarianism, 282
Unitarians, 29, 73, 89, 140, 145, 183, 218f., 234, 279
University Reform, 10, 23-5, 33, 35f., 39, 43, 46, 210, 231f., 275
Usufruct, 72, 277

Virgin Birth, 61, 96, 269

Whigs, 5, 9, 215